Secret Sources

This book has been designed in a Victory Format. Smaller type and margins produce fewer pages which permit a vital saving of paper and labor in the manufacture of a War-time book.

WYTHE WILLIAMS AND WILLIAM VAN NARVIG

Secret Sources

THE STORY BEHIND SOME FAMOUS SCOOPS

ZIFF-DAVIS PUBLISHING COMPANY · CHICAGO · NEW YORK

For several years Wythe Williams had most of us guessing. By "us" I mean those whose occupation it is to deal with the news. Of course for years Wythe had been one of the ace reporters of the European scene. When he earned that reputation he got his stuff with the formidable machinery of the foreign service of the New York Times, *of the Northcliffe Press and the United Press at his back. After he returned from Europe, he had apparently nothing but the resources of* Greenwich Time, *a single small though soon widely read suburban newspaper. From his desk in Greenwich, Connecticut, Wythe proceeded to pull one news rabbit after another out of his hat. He had us, as I say, not only guessing but more than slightly skeptical. How could one man, we asked, dig up information not available to the great American wire services, to say nothing of the great newspapers who had their own news gathering machinery in addition? So some of us looked on the beats that Wythe was scoring with raised eyebrows. But, by jingo, history began to vindicate and corroborate him. Here is one instance:*

Some weeks before the outbreak of the war, Wythe was on the air with me as guest speaker. More or less with the idea of pulling his leg I said to him: "Wythe, you're playing the role of pundit and prophet these days, how about giving us a prophecy?" (I should add that this was completely ad lib.)

Wythe jumped at the bait. "Go ahead, Lowell," he retorted on the spur of the moment, "I'll take a chance and do my best." So I asked him the question that was in everybody's mind: "If war is coming, when will it break out?" Without hesitating, Wythe replied, naming a certain week in September, 1939. He missed the exact date of Hitler's invasion of Poland by only three days.

So I am particularly glad that he has written this book because, for one thing, on one of its pages he explains exactly how he came to make that prophecy and how he happened to hit it with such apparently uncanny precision. But he also reveals how and why he was able to get so much other news and tell it in America, news which was absolutely closed to the excellent reporters on the spot in Europe.

In more recent years, I got to know Wythe better when he founded and became first President of the Overseas Press Club. As this organization became more and more important, we came into closer association, and I found out what makes Wythe Williams go.

As you will find out from this book, there is nothing magical or metaphysical about the machinery he built up for getting news from censorlocked Europe while sitting at a desk in Greenwich, Conn. To my notion, his story is all the more fascinating for that.

LOWELL THOMAS

PREFACE

TIME IS EVERLASTING. In the endless spaces of the Universe, the count of months, years, even centuries, is lost. The light of a star may be reaching us years after its extinction.

To us human beings, however, who are confined to the small celestial sphere called the Earth, the span of life is short. It is especially short in these days of global war when lives are at their cheapest and the flower of youth is being relentlessly cut down. To us, time has grown precious. The emotions of hours are crowded into minutes. The events of yesterday acquire a completely different aspect in the light of the happenings of today.

When we wrote this book in the early months of 1942, it was to bring home to American readers the full depth of sinister forces that had arrayed themselves against the life, liberty and pursuit of happiness of the common man. The average American mind was confused on the real significance of events, and even fearful to some extent. We believed that by revealing certain secrets that had come to our knowledge through a stroke of good fortune, we might be able to contribute to the dispersion of some of this confusion.

While the publication of this volume experienced numerous delays for reasons beyond our control, time kept marching on. Events clouded in obscurity became clarified. A much greater part of the American people today understands the issues than did one year ago. Some of the then secret machinations have become public property. To this extent, certain parts of this book have become dated and of more or less historic interest.

However, the war is still far from won. The hard road to victory will involve greater sacrifices of human and material values than our country ever has known. The comparative lateness of our all-out effort will cost us much. The price America has to pay for her unpreparedness is heavy. It will grow still heavier with every step we take toward the final victorious goal. As the cost increases, some may grow faint of heart, may wish to stop at the halfway mark, may feel impelled to ask, why all this sacrifice? It is to counteract this question in some measure, to tell what would have happened if America had shrunk back from the sacrifice, that this book is seeing the light of day.

The question will be asked, how was it possible for our informants to get access to all the secret information? Actually, they did not have to dig for it, because they lived through most of it. In a sense, they belonged. They could move freely in places where secret schemes were concocted. They were unsuspected. They told what they saw, or what they had obtained from other trustworthy eyewitnesses.

The very nature of their revelations demands that their actual names and positions remain undisclosed for the time being. Germany and the conquered territories of Europe are ruled by a terror which is the most ruthless in the history of mankind. Heinrich Himmler and his notorious Gestapo hold the power of life and death. To be found opposed to Nazi designs, or even suspected of such opposition, means the end. It would be a crime on our part to provide even the least clue upon which the Gestapo might pounce. Moreover, information useful to American authorities continues to flow through these same channels. The sources of this information must be protected.

Perhaps the most difficult task in compiling this book was to present the facts so as to eliminate all clues pointing to the actual sources. It entailed a considerable amount of juggling by the authors. The various reports had to be edited most carefully. On occasions the dates and places had to be shifted. Trimmings had to be shorn or substituted. Some passages had to be rewritten time and again, to bury any loose ends. Some reports had to be omitted in their entirety, as they would have unmistakably pointed at their source. But all the salient facts were scrupulously preserved.

In presenting this book we are confident that the Gestapo will search in vain.

THE AUTHORS.

New York, April 1943.

Secret Sources

PROLOGUE

I

I<small>T WAS</small> P<small>ARIS</small>, in July, 1915. Not the grim Paris of Georges Clemenceau—the Old Tiger—but still the rather gay and exhilarating Paris of Viviani and Briand where the champagne flowed and beautiful women from all nations kept trysts with their choice heroes of a stagnant war. The Kaiser's armies were rushing headlong into Russia and the Western Front was practically asleep. As correspondent for the New York *Times*, accredited to the French Army, I had considerable difficulty in gathering news stories and getting them through an obstinate censor. Any interruption of the daily routine was welcome.

One interruption came in the form of an officer of the Imperial Russian Army who sauntered into my office and asked if he might look through files of the New York papers. He introduced himself as Captain van Narvig. He did not meet my conception of a Russian officer. He was a young man of six-feet-three, clean-shaven, nonchalant, and with little use for the Russian national drink—vodka. He professed instead an utterly non-Russian leaning toward Scotch and soda. He was in Paris en route to New York, to join the Russian Military Purchasing Commission.

We made our way to a nearby *bistro* for a drink—several drinks, as it developed. I learned that van Narvig was not really Russian. He was born in Leningrad when it was still St. Petersburg. His mother was English and his father a German. He had received his education in various parts of the globe, traveling with his parents, and spoke a dozen or so languages. He was actually a citizen of Finland, and after graduating from a Russian university, had entered the army with the rank of Lieutenant.

A decoration he wore aroused my curiosity. He confessed that he had received it for doing something or other over Austrian artillery positions in Galicia, flying a rickety Farman pusher plane. A bit of enemy shrapnel ripped one of his plane's wings, causing him to crack up behind his own lines, but he was still able to tell his divisional command what it should not do.

5

We had quite a chat. He disclosed an intimate knowledge of world affairs and was able to analyze them with a lack of bias that only a trained observer, or one who had lived in many countries and was lacking in nationalist or political roots, could possess. He revealed to me the desperate shortage of modern machine tools in Russia and predicted that the war would develop into a production race, with eventual victory going to the side with the best tooling facilities.

The next day he departed for New York. In our conversation I had obtained enough information to provide an interesting cable for my paper on his mission in the United States. I returned to my daily routine of watching for a news beat and shortly forgot all about van Narvig.

II

NEW YORK, four months later. I had returned home for a brief visit, to report to the late Adolph Ochs, publisher of The New York *Times*, on aspects of the war that I could not cable or write about. One wintry afternoon I strolled into the lobby of the old Waldorf-Astoria. A tall man, unfamiliar in civilian clothes, strode up to me and said, "The world isn't much of a place after all." It was van Narvig.

We steered a straight course for the bar. This time we became really acquainted. Van Narvig was disgusted with the Russian Purchasing Commission, to which he was still attached, and complained bitterly of the graft and indolence that marked its operations. "The amount of money they get away with each month," he said, "would equip a Russian division."

He was fed up. He had been looking into American production methods, he said, and was about to return to Russia, where he hoped to wangle a substantial subsidy from his government with which to build an automobile factory in Moscow.

He was bubbling over with theories of a coming revolution in the science of war. The horse and foot soldier, he contended, soon would be obsolete. He believed that armies would move on wheels and their striking power would be immeasurably increased by their mobility. Even though such theories were being vaguely discussed at the time, van Narvig appeared well ahead of the field.

We plunged into the war situation in general. Perhaps the numerous Scotch and sodas had something to do with it, but presently we formed a two-man peace conference. With the aid of a pocket map we carved up the world and in quick order settled all the vast international problems created by the war. At one point van Narvig indicated a spot in the Pacific—the Caroline and Marshall Islands.

"The Japanese have occupied all those German island groups," he said. "I'll bet you a bottle they will be allowed to keep them. And one day the United States will be very, very sorry."

III

Wɪᴛʜɪɴ ᴀ ᴡᴇᴇᴋ van Narvig sailed for Russia. We had agreed to write each other from time to time. For more than two years he kept his promise, as I did mine. Thus I learned that he had obtained the government subsidy and built his automobile plant. Then came the Russian revolution and the factory was taken from him. The next time I heard from him, he was on the staff of General Carl Gustav Mannerheim in Finland.

The last letter read almost like a valedictory: "Well, this brush with the Reds is over. It was only the beginning of a long and bloody struggle which is bound to reshape Russia, one way or the other. Tremendous social forces have been set on the loose. Unless they are dammed and deflected into the proper channels, they may well throw the whole civilized world into chaos. I intend to make my way to South Russia, to join the Volunteer Army of my friend, General Kornilov. No telling what will happen. Perhaps you had better drink a toast to my memory."

After that, the silence of death.

As the years roll by and take their toll, man is only too prone to let the past slip into oblivion. During the first few years I thought frequently of van Narvig, whom I believed to be one of the countless casualties of the great Russian upheaval. Gradually he faded into memory. Eventually he was completely forgotten, and never did I dream that, after the lapse of two decades, we would meet again in the shadow of a world tragedy more vast than the one which brought about our first acquaintance; that we would become partners in a great adventure; that we would establish secret sources of information at the very core of the Nazi empire; that we would be helpful to the United States authorities in our country's greatest struggle.

CHAPTER 1

In my mail one June day in 1939 I came upon a mystifying letter:

"I understand that you have acquired the habit of taking cracks at the Mystic of Berchtesgaden. Beware! The fellow can bite, and right in this country, too. However, if you wear a bulletproof vest and are interested in some real lowdown on your favorite subject, it is available. We met in an epoch which we called Armageddon. If you remember me, we might meet again."

This communication was signed, "William van Narvig, Lieutenant Colonel, K.G."

It made no sense to me. I could recall no one by that name. Judging by the typical slang which the writer used, I took him for a native American. The K.G. after the signature only added to the mystery. I knew of no Knight of the Garter who might address such a letter to me.

At the time I was editor of a daily newspaper, *Greenwich* (Connecticut) *Time*. For more than a year I had been receiving a trickle of exclusive information from Europe. This came through connections established during my many years as a foreign correspondent and also from some European refugees still able, by means of underground channels, to communicate with friends and relatives in Nazi territory. Occasional news scoops, such as the story of the horsewhipping of Dr. Joseph Goebbels by the husband of a woman to whom the Reich Propaganda Minister was paying undue attention, had been widely reprinted and quoted. They brought me a considerable amount of what is known as crank mail, along with some offers of information that at times proved valuable. At first I was inclined to place the van Narvig letter in this classification.

However, its reference to a past meeting intrigued me. I answered it in a noncommittal way, inviting the writer to meet me in New York at the Lotos Club.

When I stood face to face with him a few days later, I recognized him at once. Also, I knew what the K.G. stood for. It meant Knight of the Order of St. George—the Imperial Russian decoration which he had worn that day in Paris, twenty-four years ago.

I exclaimed, "My God! Do the dead return to life?"

He smiled. "The world really isn't much of a place after all —or is it?"

His hair had grayed and there was a slight bulging at the waistline, but otherwise he looked the same. I was thinking back. "As I remember, you returned to the wars. You stopped writing."

"One does not write from Bolshevik prison camps," he said.

"How come?" I asked.

He shrugged and said, "War."

"How long in prison camp?"

"Six months."

"They released you?"

"Prisoners weren't released in those days," said van Narvig. "They were shot. I disliked the prospect. I scrammed."

His use of slang struck a discordant note. When we were at the bar and van Narvig had ordered Scotch and soda, I asked where he had been keeping himself.

"Hither and yon," he said. "Chicago, Detroit, fifteen years

9

in Brooklyn." Then, to my amazement, he asked, "You think the Brooklyn Dodgers will win the pennant?"

For a few moments I did not know what to say. Finally I managed, "You look like the van Narvig I used to know, but you certainly don't act like him. American slang, baseball— what's come over you?"

He raised his glass with a deliberate gesture and drank. Then he said, "I believe in doing things the complete way. In being granted United States citizenship the oath of allegiance is just a symbol. It's what you do after that which really counts. If you preserve your European mentality, you're still no American. I made up my mind to become an American in every way that I knew."

I pondered this. "Isn't that rather tame after your past adventures?"

He shrugged again. "It all depends on what you call adventure." After a brief pause, "Besides, there's the family. Responsibilities. Men do settle down."

I felt somewhat disappointed. But his next words made me sit up. "I'm not quite so sedentary as I sound," he said. "I'm just back from my first trip abroad in many years. Made a 10,000-mile journey through Russia and Siberia. Wanted to know what it looks like, after all these years. On my return trip, I paid a visit at Berchtesgaden."

"Berchtesgaden!" I almost upset the glass.

My curiosity was not immediately satisfied. Instead, van Narvig explained that he had a friend high in Soviet circles whom he had helped escape "liquidation" during the Russian Civil War. This man had made it possible for him to travel throughout the Soviet Union, from the Arctic to the Crimea, from Leningrad to Central Asia and Siberia. He had talked to the plain people, had seen many things that remain hidden from the ordinary observer. He said he had gathered a wealth of material and was anxious to get it published.

All this interested me but slightly. It was the word Berchtesgaden that was important. I asked for details.

It developed that van Narvig had visited a relative who was among Hitler's associates at the time of the abortive Munich putsch in 1923. When Hitler rose to power, this man, who was getting on in years, was given a position at the Berghof* that required little hard work. As a member of the Fuehrer's household staff, this relative lived in the nearby mountain resort of Berchtesgaden. Van Narvig had stayed with him several weeks, remaining inconspicuous but at the same time keeping his eyes and ears open. The sum of his observations was that another war impended.

To me this information was not exactly startling. I had lived in various parts of Europe as a foreign correspondent for more than a quarter of a century. I returned to my native land in 1936 convinced that a second world war was inevitable. Information from friends in Europe only strengthened this belief. Anyone conversant with European affairs knew that the war of 1914–18 had really settled nothing. To add to the chaotic conditions in Europe, Asia was in turmoil.

Since 1936, when Hitler sent his armies into the then de-militarized Rhineland, he had been having things his own way by mere bluff. It was obvious that a point had to come at which the democratic nations must call a halt and be ready to fight it out if necessary, unless they were willing to sign their own death warrants. This point appeared perilously near in the summer of 1939. Hitler had managed to keep himself in power by virtue of his successful policy of German aggrandizement. If the democracies called his bluff, it would mean fight or retreat—and the one great weakness of even the most successful dictator is that he cannot afford to retreat.

The late nineteen-thirties had brought forth a new element in the analysis of news—the radio commentator. It was a role that appealed to me and for which I felt that my background fitted me. I had long been considering a venture into that field, but I felt that instead of depending exclusively on established

*Hitler's mountain roost in the Bavarian Alps.

news services, I would prefer to enlarge my personal contacts which had produced so many exclusive stories for *Greenwich Time*. The prohibitive cost of establishing a private news service, however, held me back. It occurred to me that in van Narvig I might have found a partial answer to this problem.

Before we parted that night I asked him to send me the notes and manuscripts on his recent tour of the Soviet Union and his visit in Germany. This he did. Analysis of this material convinced me that here was a man who, although never trained as a journalist, had a talent for gaining access to sources of information, a keen sense of news values and a broad knowledge of world events. I checked his stories as thoroughly as possible and found no flaws in them, but many of his conclusions were so packed with dynamite that they could not be used in print or on the air in those days when our country was so painstakingly neutral.

I explained all this to van Narvig when he visited me later at my home in Greenwich.

"I've been told this before," he said. "Seems as though I've blown a lot of my time and money."

I went on to acquaint him with my ideas for a radio news program and outlined the manner in which I might be able to use such information as he was able to procure—not then, perhaps, but later. I was prepared to make a deal with him— a gamble on the future.

"Let me sum up the conclusions on which we both agree," I said. "Right now Hitler is only playing for time. He will send his armies into Poland as soon as the harvest is gathered, probably early in September before the rains come. The Poles, of course, won't have a chance. Last year England sold the Czechs down the river but she can't do that with the Poles. She has guaranteed Poland's territorial integrity. Whether it was a wise gesture or not, the last shred of British prestige would vanish if she were to abandon Poland to Hitler. Great Britain is bound to go to war and France must go with her. You know what that means—a second world war."

Van Narvig blew smoke from his cigar, regarding me speculatively. "Not just a world war," he then said. "A world revolution."

Before I had a chance to comment, he went on, "Hitler and the Jap nationalists have conjured up forces that are mightier than their originators. Even if either of the two wanted to halt them, they could not do it. Japism, if I may call it by that name, is the same Nazism adjusted to the Asiatic mentality. These forces could not stop short of producing a world revolution."

"They must be stopped from without," I said.

"Who is going to do the stopping?" van Narvig asked. "Not France, by any chance? She will be ground to pulp. Time will tell if I am right. And when France falls, who is left? England! She'll have to fight for her empire. She could not possibly do it alone."

"And she'll drag us in again," I remarked.

"If past history is any criterion she'll try to drag everyone in, but that's not the point." He puffed at his cigar. "Here's how I look at it. Hitler could not crack the British Empire all by himself and he knows it. He'll have to team up with Japan. That will fit in only too well with Jap dreams of Asiatic hegemony, for the Japs could attain their own objective only at the expense of the British Empire. They're bound to reach for Singapore. To do this, they must first secure their rear by taking the Philippines. That's how we'll get into the war—not because England will try to drag us in."

I remembered how, many years ago in the old Waldorf-Astoria bar, we decided the peace. Here we were deciding another war.

I was infected with his arguments. "How about Russia?" I asked.

"I wonder," was all he said.

"Communist Russia and Nazi Germany are two ideologically opposed poles. Russia is bound to come in on the Allied side," I pointed out.

"Don't fool yourself," van Narvig said. "Stalin is about as much a Communist as you or I. He's engaged in building a new

Russian empire. He's a second edition of Peter the Great—for Russia, first and last."

"Just what do you mean by that?" I asked.

He smiled. "Stalin will stay out so long as he can." He paused, then said, "Then, finally, with Russia in, the whole world will go up in flames. Whichever side wins, a wholly new world order is bound to rise from the ashes. And there you are—a world revolution!"

Abruptly changing the subject, he asked, "Where do I fit in?"

I explained that while I was getting a sporadic flow of information from Europe, I needed a great deal more in order to have a sustained interest in a program depending on scoops for its appeal. I suggested that he go to Europe and travel from one Democratic capital to another, gathering information and sending me regular reports. He demolished this idea at once.

"As I understand it you now rely largely on your connections in France and England to supply you with exclusive information," he said. "But when war comes, they will be unable to urnish you with sufficient material for a very simple reason that has nothing to do with their intentions, or their ability to secure the information, or even with the censors. This war is not being planned by France or England. The master plotter is Hitler. The blueprint of conquest is being drawn by his hand. The aggression will be his. The world diplomacy leading to actual warfare is his. All the lines of aggression, including those from Rome and the Far East, meet in Berlin or at Berchtesgaden. In his capacity of aggressor, Hitler will hold the initiative for a number of years. Remember, it is the initiative that makes the news. To be ahead of the communiques, your contacts must be inside Germany, not in France or England."

I agreed with the soundness of this reasoning. But I knew the situation inside Germany, so far as it concerned getting out reliable information. I ridiculed the idea as something that could not be done. Why, even diplomatic pouches were carefully examined by the Gestapo before they left the country! Anxious though I was to settle on some plan that would have a chance of succeeding, I could not see one in what he proposed.

Van Narvig discarded the stub of his cigar and lighted a fresh one. "It might not be so utterly impossible as you think," he said slowly.

I brushed this aside. "Why, you couldn't recruit newspapermen. They would be the last ones to obtain real inside news. Even if they did, and smuggled it past the censors, the information would go to their papers."

"Quite right," he agreed. "I did not have newspapermen in mind. The contacts that we would need must be at the very source of things—in Berchtesgaden, at Karin Hall*, in the Reich Chancellery, even in the Gestapo organization. In short, at the very core of Nazism and the Hitler government. I fraternized with some people over there. I know of one or two who are close to the heart of things but who have good reason to hate the present regime. There is a chance—a slim one, to be sure—that something might be done."

"Your relative?" I suggested.

He shook his head. "No. He'd die for his Fuehrer. And anyway, he's much too old for this sort of thing. I'm thinking of others."

When van Narvig left for his Brooklyn home that night, he had agreed to make another trip to Germany to try to establish the necessary contacts. Neither of us had enough cash on hand to finance such a venture, so it became necessary to raise the traveling expenses. This took longer than we had anticipated, particularly since we preferred not to disclose the purpose to which the money was to be put.

Our undertaking and its objectives had to be kept strictly to ourselves. Even van Narvig's closest friends did not know where he was going. He dropped hints about oil properties in Texas to shake off anyone who might be unduly interested. We were quite aware of the efficiency of the Gestapo agents, even in the United States.

Van Narvig left late in July, 1939. He had planned to return

*Hermann Goering's private estate.

within two months. Ten days later I received a cablegram sent from Hamburg.

"Decided to go to Moscow," it said. "Reason later."

I admit that at this point my confidence in van Narvig was shaken. But two weeks later, on August 24th, came the official announcement that Hitler and Stalin had signed their pact of nonaggression, friendship and mutual consultation. I understood then what must have taken my partner to Russia.

Then I received a hurry call from the Hobby-Lobby radio program to fill in one night for one of the guest performers who had failed to arrive. My friend Lowell Thomas was also pinch-hitting, as master of ceremonies. I had no time to prepare a script. As a result the entire dialogue between Lowell and myself was extemporaneous—questions and answers on world affairs. It seemed natural that Lowell would mention my repeated warnings in the *Greenwich Time* of the imminence of the "next war." He did just that, first informing the radio listeners of the many predictions I had made that had proved to be true.

As I remember, Lowell said, "And now, Wythe, would you be willing to stick your neck out and give us the starting date of the new war?"

I answered promptly, for it was not a question that required much thought on my part. Van Narvig and I had discussed the subject thoroughly prior to his departure.

"I'll take a chance, Lowell," I said. "I believe another world war will start during the first week in September."

In Philadelphia, James MacFadden—the head of the radio division of a large advertising agency—was listening to the program. He told me later how he had drawn a circle in red pencil around each of the first seven days of September. On September 1, in the early morning hours, Hitler's armored units crossed the border into Poland. The war was on.

Some months later, MacFadden called me to Philadelphia to discuss a radio contract. He acknowledged my greeting at our first meeting with a gruff, "You're the guy who guessed right."

I insisted that I had not been guessing. In quick order we

arrived at an agreement on the terms of the proposed contract. Then began a period during which I worked hard to master the technique of radio news commenting.

All that I learned came from Mac. He went over my scripts with a sharp eye and a relentless pencil. We tilted frequently, but as a managing editor he was equal to the best I had encountered in a long newspaper career.

CHAPTER 2

By that time I was receiving fairly regular communications from Germany. The first word from van Narvig had come as the Germans were pounding at the gates of Warsaw. It had been air-mailed from Helsinki, the Finnish capital, shortly after the announcement of the Russo-German pact. Since it outlined the structure which van Narvig then proceeded to build, I quote from it now:

Dear Wythe:

Sorry I gave you a jolt and kept you in suspense all these weeks. It couldn't be helped. On debarkation in Hamburg I ran into a chap I had met at Berchtesgaden. I gave him the spiel they all fall for. In one way these Nazis are naïve. You tell them you're becoming converted to their ideas and they spread out their arms. At first he was cagey, but gradually I learned what he was doing—namely, directing civil defense work in and around Hamburg. Camouflage and all that sort of thing.

The two of us had quite an evening, talking world politics. This of course includes Russia. This chap originally came from the Baltic provinces. He became quite loquacious on the subject of Russia, insisting that Stalin had been merely toying with the French and British military missions now in Moscow and that he was actually preparing to make a deal with Hitler. That, he explained, was why Litvinov* was

*Maxim Litvinov, now Soviet Ambassador to the United States, who was Soviet Commissar for Foreign Affairs until shortly before the signing of the Russo-German pact. Litvinov campaigned strenuously before the League of Nations for a system of collective security against aggressor nations which was aimed directly at Germany. His campaign failed and its failure was followed by Soviet efforts to negotiate separate non-aggression pacts with European nations. Before such a pact could be negotiated with Germany, it was necessary for Litvinov to be replaced by someone less outspoken in opposition to the Nazi Reich. Litvinov remained in retirement until Germany violated her pact with the Soviet, when he returned to the political arena in his present post at Washington.

shelved and why Ribbentrop [Joachim von Ribbentrop, Reich Foreign Minister] was going to fly to Moscow, perhaps within a week, to sign what may well amount to a Russo-German alliance.

To me it seemed imperative to learn the Russian side of all this and I decided to go to Moscow, if possible before Ribbentrop arrived there. After cabling you I booked passage on the earliest plane for Helsinki. There I had a tussle with the Russian consul. He conceded that my permit was okay, but insisted that he must communicate with Moscow before issuing a visa. I knew how long that would take. I adopted an air of mystery and asked him to telephone Z———ov* in Leningrad. He was sufficiently impressed to do what I asked and the next morning, on word from Z———ov, I was in Leningrad.

I lunched with Z———ov and he wanted to know what the big rush was all about. I could have told him that I had urgent business with my brother-in-law, but he's pretty sharp. So I said frankly that I wanted to visit Moscow because Ribbentrop would be there.

That got him. In fact, he called me a few Russian names and demanded to know how I knew about it. I assured him that my information had come from no Russian source. It appeared that no more than perhaps fifty people in Russia knew about it and Z———ov was one of them.

Even then, we had quite a tilt over it. Suspecting my motives, he insisted that I remain in Leningrad until the scheduled confab was over. He said, in fact, that it was none of my business, and what was my game, anyhow? I protested I had no game whatsoever, my only motive being to write a book at some future date. He reminded me of having once before allowed me to snoop around Russia. It had been an exception, and why should he repeat the favor just because at one time I had kept him from being a target for a few bullets? I promised not to write the book for at least one year. He said, make it two years. And so off I went to Moscow.

When you pass through the north Kremlin gate and walk across Red Square you come upon a gray stone building with a large basement which houses a restaurant. At one time it was called Martyanich. Today it has an utterly unpronounceable name—for Americans—so I'll skip it. Down there you can get a fairly good meal, with vodka, especially if you have dollar bills. If you are in the company of Kremlin officials the meal is even better at half the price—in Russian roubles.

*Z———ov, whose full name cannot be told, was an influential Soviet official whom van Narvig had once saved from death. Although van Narvig had once fought against the Bolsheviks, both in Finland under Mannerheim and in South Russia, he had long since made his peace with the Soviets and had been aided by Z———ov in obtaining permission in 1938 to make an extensive tour of Russia.

Needless to say, I preferred the company of certain Kremlin officials who accepted me as a friend of Z———ov.

Z———ov had cautioned me not to be conspicuous, especially not before the Ribbentrop story had broken officially. I waited six days. On the morning of the seventh, Ribbentrop's private plane—*Grenzmark* —and a huge Junkers transport, carrying the Reich Foreign Minister and thirty-two assistants, descended on the Moscow airdrome. I stood right by the Kremlin gate when Ribbentrop was driven through in a Cadillac car carrying the swastika flag. A British colonel—member of the military mission that had spent weeks in Moscow—stood beside me muttering, "Those blasted Germans!" The sun was beating down unmercifully and I tried to console him with the well-known remark about mad dogs and Englishmen. He gave me a wry smile and offered a cigarette, after which we parted.

While Stalin and Molotov* entertained their guests at a sumptuous state banquet I was in the subterranean restaurant on Red Square, trying to glean some information from the multitude of rumors that were flying about. Luckily, one of my Kremlin acquaintances was a member of the official interpreters staff who had been present during the Stalin-Ribbentrop conversations earlier in the day. We remained together until three in the morning.

For the complete picture, I must go back to what I elicited, during my week of patient waiting, about the Russo-British negotiations which preceded the arrival of Ribbentrop. Here is the crux of the whole situation. Stalin is against engaging in a major war—with Germany or any other country. He has some excellent spies and for the present at least he wants no encounter with the German *Wehrmact*. He needs time, especially considering the events of two years ago when he was in danger of losing his power and perhaps even his neck. What he desires in particular is the prestige of an empire builder among the Russian people. He looks toward the acquisition of new territories, preferably by the bloodless conquest system used successfully by Hitler. Most definitely he does not want any weakening of Russian military strength at this time.

The particular territories on which he has cast his eyes are Bessarabia, an eastern strip of Poland inhabited chiefly by Russians, the land to both sides of the Pripet Marshes and the salient linking Poland and Latvia; also the Baltic republics of Latvia and Estonia and certain strategic parts of Finland. He desires all these not only for prestige but also military reasons. He believes that unless these territories are in Russian hands the Red Army will not stand a chance against Germany.

*Vyacheslav Molotov, Soviet Commissar for Foreign Affairs.

As always, Russian strategy is based on the defensive. Modern war depends entirely on industrial production. The Red Army staff demands that battle lines be kept far from industrial centers. In the south, Rumania is dangerously close to the great shipping center of Odessa, so Stalin wants to move the border back to the Prut River by taking over Bessarabia. In the center, the Polish border is too close to the industrial area around Kiev. In the north, the great Leningrad industrial district is within twenty-five miles of the Finnish frontier and only twice that distance from the border of Estonia.

And so, when the British and French three months ago invited Russia to enter a peace bloc with them, Stalin replied that this in fact would constitute a military alliance against Germany that would inevitably lead to war. In that event, Stalin held, Russia would find herself the most vulnerable of the three nations and the whole force of Nazi fury would be directed against her. England was protected by the sea and Hitler had no real navy. France had her Maginot Line. According to Stalin, unless essential territories were turned over to Russia, the proposal could not be considered. He agreed to receive the Allied military missions, but even before they arrived he started dickering with Hitler. The result was Ribbentrop's presence in Moscow. *

My interpreter friend was present at the only conference between Ribbentrop and Stalin. The text of the pact as officially released is the actual one—with no secret clauses. But there was an oral understanding—a new departure in diplomacy, which is possible only between dictators. A large map of eastern Europe was on the table. Stalin took a red pencil and drew a line around the territories in which the influence of Russia must predominate. Ribbentrop studied the map for several minutes, then said that the Reich could assume no obligation with regard to Rumania, since that nation was guaranteed by Great Britain and France and entirely outside the sphere of German influence. The expression, sphere of influence, was used throughout the conversation.

Ribbentrop noted with satisfaction that Stalin had no designs on Finland's independence. He promised that the Reich Government

*The official Soviet explanation of Stalin's failure to conclude a pact with England and France was that both countries had sent emissaries to Moscow who were not empowered to reach an agreement and that the proposals of the Allied military mission, according to Molotov, while guaranteeing aid to the Soviet Union in case of attack, were "so hedged about with clauses and peradventures as to suggest that in case of need their aid would prove fictitious, leaving the Soviet Union without effective assistance." The Soviet Union's need of guarantees was so urgent in order to turn the war from Russia that an agreement was then negotiated with Germany. The Allied military mission was in Russia seventy-five days. The agreement with Ribbentrop was concluded in less than three hours.

would not interfere in any frontier readjustments between Russia and Finland that Stalin had in mind. He agreed to respect Russian wishes with regard to Eastern Poland, so long as Moscow did not interfere with regard to the Polish territory west of the line drawn by Stalin. He added that the Reich would be forced to undertake certain measures against Poland which probably corresponded with those that the Soviet Government had in mind against the same "disturbing element." After these mutual measures had been carried out, a delineation of frontiers could be undertaken to safeguard the vital interests of both principals. Until then the Reich Government undertook to abide by the oral understanding. Ribbentrop likewise conceded that Latvia and Estonia belonged in the Russian sphere of influence.

Stalin withdrew for a short consultation with his aides. When they returned, Molotov declared that the German proposals were acceptable. They shook hands. The pact of non-aggression and mutual consultation was signed by Molotov and Ribbentrop. The entire procedure, including the discussions, required just two hours and twenty minutes.

The next morning I saw a long column of tanks and artillery moving through the streets of Moscow. At luncheon I asked my friend if he had any idea in which direction the troops were proceeding. In a westerly, he replied laconically. I understood perfectly. Stalin was already mobilizing his forces along the eastern frontier of Poland and Hitler had not yet struck. The picture was clear—Finis Polonia!

Before departing from Moscow I had another experience that we might put down for the future. I was having lunch with a Red Army general. His name does not enter. I asked his personal opinion on the sudden turn of international events.

He stated positively, "Don't imagine for a moment that Russia and Germany have become real friends overnight. What we did was enter a marriage of convenience. We struck the best possible bargain. After the way the British and French brushed us aside at Munich last year, can you blame us? We have never trusted the British and I doubt if we ever will. That does not mean that we are going to trust the Germans. I do not know how our government feels about this pact, but we of the Red Army are convinced that sooner or later we shall have to fight it out with the Germans. We pray that it shall be later. We must strengthen ourselves immensely and that is precisely what we intend to do in the coming years."

I am sending this from Helsinki, my first stop after leaving Russia. Hitler's armies will strike in a day or two, so I am getting this off by airmail, hoping it slips through before the censorship clamps down.

England and France will declare war on Hitler—they must. You will probably hear all sorts of high-sounding stories of French and British help for the Poles. Don't be fooled by them. No help will come. The Poles are doomed, whether they know it or not. I give them three weeks at the most.*

I'm leaving for Berchtesgaden in the morning. I can't give you any forwarding address. Don't write or cable until you hear from me again. Exactly when, or from where, I don't know just now. Surely, I won't be able to send anything of consequence from Germany. You'll just have to wait.

Yours as ever,
BILL.

By the time van Narvig's report reached me, the Polish campaign was practically over. The war between England and France on one side and Germany on the other entered a simmering stage. Aside from the war at sea, which saw the sinkings of the *Courageous* and the *Royal Oak*, the only news of action concerned occasional German flights over Allied territory and the dropping of leaflets over Germany by the Allies.

Ignorant of disaster ahead, England carried on under the old slogan of business as usual. The French sat in the underground forts of their Maginot Line, occasionally hearing Nazi loudspeakers mounted on the opposite shore of the Rhine tell them that the war was senseless. No one knew what Hitler was doing, and no one cared, which was worse. The accepted opinion was that Hitler could not last long, that the Allied blockade would starve Germany, and that the German people would throw Hitler out. It was the period of the "phony war" and the American people were as weary of the dull, meaningless news from abroad as was the rest of the world.

CHAPTER 3

THE WEEKS WENT BY, dragging into months, with no word of any sort from van Narvig. I was beginning to feel uneasy, fearing that he might have been arrested, when one

*Poland was defeated by Hitler's panzer divisions in eighteen days.

day in December the postman delivered a thick envelope post-marked Rio de Janeiro. It was from van Narvig. Evidently he had found some way of sending the report to Brazil by a plane of the Italian-operated Lati line to South America, where it was mailed to my Greenwich address. No censor had caught so much as a glimpse of the letter.

At this point let me explain that van Narvig, while he still retains traces of an accent when speaking English, writes our language extremely well. Having spent years in many different countries and speaking many tongues, he accustoms himself as readily to the idiom of the other languages, as does a child living in a foreign land.

I hardly knew what to expect as I ripped open the envelope. What I found left me speechless, considering the possibilities it presented. Here is what he wrote:

Dear Wythe:

How're tricks in your orchard? I understand that, with the phony war, you in the United States read daily reports that Hitler is practically through and does not know which way to turn. Don't believe one word of it. From what I've seen here, a military avalanche is in the making and I only wish that someone could open Allied eyes to the true state of affairs. I hear that in France the correspondents of American newspapers are being conducted through the Maginot Line and shown how abundantly the soldiers there are provided with food and wines and how they are entertained with vaudeville, radio shows and all sorts of games. I wish to God that the French would run short on wines and actors, and overstock with tanks, guns and planes. But what's the use hoping against hope?

American correspondents in Berlin are even worse off in securing real military news than their confreres on the other side of the line. Not that German officials don't pretend to be very accommodating. Foreign pressmen here receive ration cards under the classification of "heavy workers." All their questions are being readily answered. The only trouble is that these answers are doctored, if not outright untruths. No person in Germany today is so watched over by the Gestapo as a foreign correspondent. His only official contacts are with the Foreign Office and the Ministry of Propaganda. He is kept from all the places where real news is in the making. You did well not to accept a job over here.

Turning to my personal experiences, I arrived in Berchtesgaden the day after England and France had declared war. Ran into some trouble on the way. Was detained two days in Sassnitz, coming from Stockholm via Trelleborg. War restrictions were in force and the examination even stricter than before, but I managed to slip through.

Eugen, my relative, was astonished to see me, inasmuch as I had previously advised him from Hamburg that I was changing my plans and proceeding to Finland and Russia where we both have relatives. I explained that the change had resulted from a serious involvement in which my brother-in-law found himself, and I went to see him through. I had prepared plausible evidence with which to back up my story and it registered.

As I told you back home, Eugen, though a confidential member of the Berghof household staff, does not actually reside there. He has a little house of his own in the outskirts of Berchtesgaden. Like almost everyone here, he uses a bicycle. I volunteered to assist him with his work. With Hitler away for quite a spell, Eugen had to catch up with some work that he could not do while daily secret sessions were taking place. He found himself short-handed. This was rather a stroke of luck. During my previous visit here I had set foot in the Berghof only twice. This time I could roam about almost freely.

I found Berchtesgaden rather depopulated. For the first time since Hitler had ensconced himself on top of the Obersalzburg, virtually his entire retinue was absent from the place at once. General Alfred Jodl, chief of Hitler's personal staff, who, I believe, could match his power with that of Goering and Himmler, had taken the entire staff to the Fuehrer's headquarters at the front. Also with Hitler were his chief adjutant, Colonel Schmundt, his army aide, Major Engel, his air aide, Major von Below, his navy aide, Captain von Puttkammer, and his chief bodyguard, Julius Schaub. Two of Hitler's secretaries, Frau Daranowsky and Frau Wolfe, were in Berlin awaiting orders, while a third, Frau Schroeder, was at headquarters. With the top members of the staff had gone the black-uniformed *Schutzstaffel* men and the Gestapo agents who ordinarily would have been swarming about the place.

What surprised me most of all was that Fräulein Evi Braun—as the household staff calls her, in deference to the Fuehrer's wishes—had also left the Berghof. Eugen, who holds Evi in very high esteem, confided to me that she had removed both herself and her personal belongings to her own house in Munich. There had been, it seemed, something of a rift. Eugen deplored this deeply, fearing the possible effects upon his Fuehrer.

Many potentates have had their affairs of the heart, but certainly there was none stranger than the relations between Adolf Hitler, the all-powerful, and Evi Braun, the blond, bourgeois girl. Intimates of the two claim they are married. I spoke with two persons who asserted they stood outside the chapel doors when the ceremony took place. But it is the Fuehrer's desire that she never be referred to as Frau Hitler. I never met anyone who had any evidence that Evi had ever shared Hitler's bedchamber.

According to Eugen, whose devotion to his Fuehrer cannot be questioned, Evi exerts a unique influence over Hitler. Eugen maintains that despite the marriage—if there actually was one—Hitler and Evi are nothing more to each other than good friends. He also insisted that despite the platonic nature of their relationship, Hitler cannot live without Evi. There have been times when the two were separated for months. But whenever Hitler is on the verge of a breakdown, he calls for Evi, and she goes back to him. Under her care and with her companionship Hitler finds peace and relaxation, recovering with amazing rapidity.

Certain members of the Nazi hierachy—among them Himmler, Goebbels and even Goering—are jealous of Evi's influence. They are said to dread the possibility that Hitler might have an official offspring and heir—a situation that could lead to all sorts of unwanted complications. I was told—by Eugen in this case—that high interests of state rather than Hitler's personal wishes, demanded that his marriage to Evi never be made public. It is also known that the other ranking Nazis have on frequent occasions brought beautiful women—dancers, actresses and others—to Hitler's attention. There are even a few salacious stories making the rounds but, to be frank, I haven't been able to track any one of them down beyond the doubtful evidence of second-hand hearsay—someone told someone else. Up to the outbreak of the war, Evi Braun held undisputed—if interrupted—sway over the Fuehrer. Now Evi was gone, and Eugen afraid that she might not come back.

I've rather drifted from our subject. Back in Greenwich I told you of two people whom I had in mind. My hunch wasn't so bad. One of the two is Gottlieb. He is a Gestapo man—that is, he is in the Gestapo, but not of it. Many of the Berghof staff are Gestapo agents whose duty it is to spy on those close to Hitler—also on each other—and report to Gestapo Chief Himmler. It's part of the system. Gottlieb is one of these men.

Gottlieb comes from a well-to-do Bavarian family. His people lost everything in the post-war inflation and his father committed suicide. Like many of his generation, Gottlieb became embittered by the tragedy about him and in 1929 he joined the Hitler movement. He was eventually taken into the Gestapo and promoted until he became one of the staff of Reinhardt Heydrich*, then chief of the Berlin Gestapo. Believing in the Nazi movement as a means of unifying the German people, he accepted the necessity of a Secret State Police to defend the movement from secret enemies and executed his duties, not as an ardent enthusiast, but as a disciplined soldier.

He held to this viewpoint until one day he was assigned to the task of unearthing evidence against a group of so-called Communist conspirators. This he accomplished so successfully that all the members of the organization were arrested and put to death. It was not until later, and entirely by chance, that he learned that among these Gestapo victims had been his married sister, whom he had believed to be at her home in Vienna. He also discovered that the "evidence" which he had so carefully unearthed had been just as carefully planted by other Gestapo agents. The plotters were not Communists, but merely a group that was organizing a route by which intellectual enemies of the Hitler dictatorship might be aided in escaping into Austria, then still under the regime of Dollfuss.†

Gottlieb was certain that Heydrich knew his sister was among those executed and had chosen this diabolical means of bringing her to death because it amused his sadistic mentality. But it would have been suicidal for Gottlieb to have exhibited anger or rancor, for this would have indicated that he placed his sister above his Fuehrer. Inwardly, however, Gottlieb vowed that one day he would find a means of revenge. Because he found it hard to conceal his hatred of Heydrich he sought and obtained a transfer to Berchtesgaden.

Gottlieb's trouble—if I may call it that—is that he thinks too much—for Nazi standards. He had studied for two years in the United States. That was before his father's death. The memories of his American days are reasserting themselves and he wonders how much better off his country would be if German society had modeled itself along the lines he saw in the United States. He and I have discovered much common ground. I know he's our man.

At this point van Narvig's letter stopped abruptly. I could not understand what had happened to the rest of the report. It did

*Reinhardt Heydrich was perhaps the most hated man in the Gestapo. He became Himmler's right hand man and was the Gestapo executioner, whom Europe's oppressed peoples called, "Der Henker"—The Hangman. He died on June 4, 1942, of an assassin's bullet fired at him as he walked the streets of Prague.

†Engelbert Dollfuss was Chancellor of Austria from 1932 until his assassination on July 25, 1934, in an abortive Nazi putsch which failed in its attempt to install Anton Rintelen, Austrian Nazi leader, in the chancellery.

not occur to me that van Narvig might have split it up as a precaution. I examined the envelope in which the letter had arrived but found no evidence that it had been tampered with.

I waited impatiently for a number of days. Then another envelope arrived, this time postmarked, Buenos Aires. It contained the second part of van Narvig's report. With it came a brief note explaining that he had thought it prudent to split the report in two and send the parts by different persons. The account was a continuation from the point where the first part had broken off so abruptly.

There is a second party—Clara. Clara's position is such that she has access to virtually all of the documents that are executed by Hitler—I should have said rather, their copies—or that pass through the executive and secretarial offices at the Berghof. She has been at the place almost continuously since 1932. She, too, has good reason to hate the ruling Nazis.

In 1934, Clara fell in love. The man was an aide to Captain Roehm* and she saw him frequently at the Berghof. They were married in May of that year, secretly—you know the sort of person Roehm was. Hardly a month later, the Roehm faction was purged by Hitler and Clara's husband was among those killed. Despite her intense grief, the poor girl was unable even to attend her husband's funeral. Any hint of intimacy between her and a member of Roehm's staff might have meant her undoing.

Presently Clara knew she was to have a baby. As she dared not reveal the identity of the father, she obtained a leave of absence and went to Switzerland where her child was born. Her only means of existence, however, lay in her position at Berchtesgaden and she returned, leaving her baby in the care of a Swiss peasant family to whom she transmitted funds for his keep.

It was this financial angle that brought me into the picture. Because of the new currency restrictions, it became increasingly difficult for Clara to send money abroad. One day she approached me and asked if I could help her by assigning a dollar exchange in Switzerland against her paying me in German marks. This was a comparatively simple arrangement because of my letter of credit on a Swiss bank and I could use marks for my expenses in Germany. But I was unwilling to

*Ernst Roehm, head of the S.A., or Storm Troops, was purged with the principal members of his following during the blood bath on the night of June 30, 1934. There is a wealth of evidence to prove that Roehm and many of his associates were homosexuals.

engage in any illegal transaction and asked her to explain, which she did after considerable hedging. It was through her assistance that I arranged to go to Switzerland for a few days.

Clara and I have become good friends. She has suffered greatly here and if it could possibly be arranged, she would like to get out. We understand each other perfectly and so long as she must remain here, I am certain that she will do things for us. I have yet another disciple in mind and Clara has hinted that she may be able to find us a fourth.

Now to some of my travels here. Eugen had to go to Pilsen—the Skoda Munitions Works, to be specific—in connection with some production records that were wanted here. I managed to tag along. From what I saw there, I cannot conceive that any sort of revolt against the Nazis could be expected from the Czechs. Not that they have turned pro-Nazi. God forbid! Their hatred of the usurpers remains, but it's the sort of hatred that turns to dish water. It will never congeal into the stuff that bloody revolutions are made of. I think the Czechs are simply too civilized for that.

I spoke to quite a few in Russian, which they prefer to the German language. Their sentiments can be expressed in three words—what's the use! The Munich betrayal rankles deep in their hearts. They invented the phrase, "What can one expect from a race of Runcimans?" For a while after Munich they still had some hope—Russia. But when Stalin signed his pact with Hitler, even that hope faded. Now they have lost all faith in the outside world. They work—for the mere purpose of existence.

At the Skoda Works—well, I've been through three wars but, honestly, I never dreamed of anything like the weapons they are producing today. I stood at the end of an assembly line and saw five-ton steel monsters coming out, one every 45 minutes. They're just the mosquitoes of the panzer divisions, but it's the mass that counts. I also saw some real collosi—72 tons of armor and machinery, carrying a rapid-fire 105 mm. cannon, two 37.5 mm. anti-tank guns, two flame throwers and a battery of machine guns. They are said to require a crew of 16 men each. But what amazed me most were the nine-inch mobile siege guns with long barrels, mounted on tractors. I never knew this could be done. I understand these were the guns that were used to blast Warsaw to bits. I just wonder if the French have the faintest idea of what they will be called upon to face. For their own sake I hope they do. But I'm afraid, very much afraid.

When we returned to Berchtesgaden after two days in Pilsen the place was in something of an uproar. Hitler had not returned—he was still visiting the scenes of his victories in Poland. Meanwhile, measures were being taken for the protection of the Berghof against possible bombings from the air. I counted twenty-eight large and medium flak* guns as they passed by on trucks. This was only the beginning of a long procession which included giant searchlights, listening devices and quantities of building material and supplies, including large cement mixers. Truckloads of construction workers completed the motorcade up the winding grade of the Obersalzburg. Hitler is taking good care of his own person—the burghers of Berchtesgaden will have to shift for themselves.

I ask myself—would Hitler take all these precautions unless he thought they might be necessary? I think not. Certainly his generals know that he will not stop with Poland, no matter what the Allies do. The Nazis want more than the place in the sun they have talked of for so long. They want the sun itself, and the moon, and the stars. They hope for nothing better than that the Allies will decline Hitler's forthcoming peace bid which, it is rumored here, he will soon make. Then they will be able to charge that the Allies are forcing Germany to go on with the war.

The general public is, of course, prohibited from listening to foreign broadcasts, but that rule evidently does not apply at the Berghof, at least in the absence of Hitler and the Gestapo. There are half a dozen radios here that bring in American stations as clearly as local programs. We listen also to the British, and their propaganda is simply a mess. For several days in a row we listened to a yarn, seconded by some American broadcasters, that Polish planes had bombed Berlin, when actually not one got across the German frontier. For a week we heard reports of a great Polish counter-offensive, then reports that the Red Army was marching to help the Poles. As for the constant British radio topic of a brewing German revolution against Hitler—forgive me, but it's laughable.

This sort of thing, apparently intended for home consumption rather than for Germany, will soon undermine Allied morale if it is continued. The Allies must be made to realize—and quickly—that this will not be an easy war to wage and that misleading the public is not the way to bolster its morale. The only way this war can be won by the Allies is with grim, relentless will power, with untold sacrifices and hardships —with steel and with blood. The age of idle prattlers, of laggards and of weaklings, is past. There is might being forged here—might and power.

I'm afraid I'm digressing—giving opinion instead of cold facts. Hitler is expected to return here soon and then perhaps the news will be more lively. Meanwhile, the mountain air is a tonic, the panorama

*German airmen's slang for Fliegerabwehrkanone—meaning, antiaircraft gun.

29

is a rare delight, especially the majestic Watzmann Mountain viewed against the southern sky. I'm relaxing.

I enclose an address in Switzerland. You may write to me there, but be careful not to so much as refer to this place. I cannot know through whose hands your letters may pass in being forwarded. Write only in generalities. We can talk more fully when I return. I hope that this will find you spry and in the best of health.

Yours as ever,
BILL.

I must admit that I did not share van Narvig's fears, especially with regard to France. I had lived for more than twenty years among the French and had come to share their national convictions. The French army that I had seen at the Marne, on the bloody Chemin des Dames at Verdun, was still invincible. While I accepted all that van Narvig said as factual, I felt certain that the famous French Deuxieme (II) Bureau* had all these facts and figures long before van Narvig got them. Despite the obvious weaknesses of the French Government during this period, I was convinced that the necessary precautions had been taken.

Meanwhile, the date was drawing near when I would have to start my radio program. Van Narvig's letters contained some excellent material. However, with regard to spot news they were too dated. I had to engage other sources. It was irksome, in a way, that these reports from my partner should be anywhere from four to six weeks in transit. I did not know that I had a surprise coming.

Two days before I went on the air with my first program a stranger entered my office. His behavior as he approached my desk, might be called self-conscious, almost embarrassed. I might say he gave me the impression of being a process server.

He inquired, "Wythe Williams?"

I acknowledged it and asked, "What can I do for you?"

For an answer he produced a package from his pocket, put it on my desk, turned and walked out.

Mystified, even somewhat offended, I reached for the enve-

*The counter-espionage service of the French War Ministry.

lope. It was unaddressed, with something bulky in it. I slit it open and instantly felt a thrill. It was another report from van Narvig—this one but eight days old. Evidently he had found a new method of transmitting his dispatches.

My partner wrote:

Dear Wythe:

Cheerio, my friend! It's good news. Our luck is holding. We're getting ahead—definitely. Meaning that our organization is growing. We've acquired two new converts, making four all told, with still a fifth in the offing.

Our Number Three listening post answers to the name of Wolfgang. The credit for enlisting him belongs to Clara. She considers him just a friend, but I've a notion that he hopes in time to become more than just that. The first time we met he exhibited something of a jealous streak—and this I do not like a bit. He does not know about Clara's child and I sincerely hope that when he finds out he doesn't suspect me as responsible. You see, I committed the indiscretion of visiting Clara's little boy twice, bringing him some toys and candy, and the Swiss couple with whom he is living acted sort of funny about it. I considered it an investment, you understand how a mother feels about such things—especially one in Clara's position.

But enough of that. Wolfgang works and lives at Fuschl Castle, near Salzburg, right across the mountains from Berchtesgaden. It is a beautiful old estate which Joachim von Ribbentrop—the modern Bismarck, quoting Hitler—filched for himself.

This is the story, as told to me. The original owner of the castle, though married and the father of a two-year-old son, had an affair with a local girl. When he learned the girl was to become a mother, he provided her with a husband from among his retinue. The latter was generally considered to be the father of the child, Wolfgang. He was killed in action during the First World War. Wolfgang's mother died a few years later. His real father took care of the boy, gave him a good education and kept him at Fuschl where he grew up with his half-brother. After the lady of the castle had passed on, her husband developed a conscience and confided the facts to his younger son. Both agreed to leave the matter as it stood.

The modern part of the story is rather obscure. From what I gather, Wolfgang's father was arrested and executed, possibly on some trumped-up charge. The estate was confiscated, whereupon Ribbentrop got hold of it by buying it for a song in his father's name. It sounds involved, but that's the way things are being done in this country. Perhaps someone was anxious to bury all the clues.

Anyway, Wolfgang contends that the Nazis did away with his father out of spite. He makes no accusations against Ribbentrop personally that he cannot prove. But he considers Fuschl the legitimate property of his half-brother who had to flee the country. He ingratiated himself with members of Ribbentrop's staff and stayed on in the hope that some day he might see the estate restored to its rightful owner. He occupies at Fuschl a position similar to that held by Clara at the Berghof.

The frequent interchange of documents between the two places brought Clara and Wolfgang together. As they became friendly, each discovered the other's true feelings toward the current masters of the Reich. Whether because of this or his personal feelings toward Clara— or perhaps both—Wolfgang may be counted in, as far as we're concerned.

The fourth member of our group was enlisted by Gottlieb, the Gestapo man. His name is Manfred. The two first met at college in the United States. Manfred was in his junior year when Gottlieb arrived as a green freshman. Their friendship is a natural. When Gottlieb had to drop his studies in America because of his father's death—as I wrote you previously—Manfred had just graduated. They returned to Germany together. Here both joined the Nazi party—it was Putzi Hanf-staengl* who brought Manfred in—and both entered the Gestapo.

What I did not know before is that it was Manfred who disclosed to his friend Gottlieb the facts of his sister's death at the hands of Gestapo executioners—I wrote you about this last time. But Manfred also has his personal grievance against the Nazis. Just what it is I don't know. He volunteered no information on this and I asked no questions. He seems to hate Heydrich and Himmler in particular, but his hatred is of the latent, calculating type that will have no active manifestations until it can express itself not just against one or two individuals, but against the entire system.

Manfred is attached to the central administration of the Secret State Police in Berlin and his duties involve considerable travel. Only

*Dr. Ernst Franz Hanfstaengl, a graduate of Harvard University and former Fifth Avenue, New York, art dealer who went to Germany and became the liaison officer to the foreign section of the Nazi Party's press department. Unofficially, he was something in the nature of "court musician" to Hitler and frequently soothed the Fuehrer's jangled nerves by playing Wagner on the piano. Putzi, as he was known, left Germany before the war broke out, after falling into Hitler's disfavor, and has been interned by the British. Early in 1943 Hanfstaengl was transferred to U.S. jurisdiction and is said to be supplying the Office of Strategic Services with various inside information.

recently he toured occupied Poland with Himmler. He has not sought advancement in the Gestapo because he does not want to be in a position that might necessitate sitting in judgment and possibly sentencing the unfortunate victims of the Nazi system to death. Consequently he seems to have escaped the many jealousies and intrigues that pervade the Gestapo organization.

I've gone into such great detail because I wanted you to have a complete picture of the people with whom we are to deal. It was my feeling that such knowledge would help you to evaluate whatever information they may send us and make it possible for us to avoid making any revelations that might expose our informants.

Well, Hitler is back home, and his return has brought out the Gestapo in full number. The Fuehrer may claim that he has earned the gratitude of the German people but he certainly does not trust them. This spying and prying about makes everyone nervous. Even Eugen is a bit upset by it and my visits to the Berghof are ended. When Clara and I discussed the case of Wolfgang we met in the local movies. The picture was terrible—an absurdity about Teutonic mythology. We sneaked out a side door, walked into the country and sat under a tree where no one could approach within a few hundred feet without being seen by us. This will convey to you an idea of the local jitters.

Hitler's Reichstag speech* on the conquest of Poland was a distinct disappointment to all who have not sold themselves heart and soul to the Nazis. They cannot understand how anyone can make a "final" peace offer, as Hitler pretended he was doing, without at least intimating the terms that he would be willing to discuss. Of course, the truth is, the Nazi bigwigs do not want peace now, unless the Allies hand Hitler everything he asks for. And even then he would add to his demands until the Allies were forced to refuse. Hitler simply wants to conquer Europe and then reorganize it according to his own ideas. As for the generals, they have an account to settle with France. They are certain they can do it in the coming year for they know that the French do not want to fight.

There was a sudden spurt of peace hope when Queen Wilhelmina and King Leopold made their joint offer to act as mediators.† I understand the opinion abroad is that Hitler was behind the offer. That seems most unlikely from here. Actually I believe they made the offer

*October 6, 1939.

†Belgium and Holland made a joint proposal to act as mediators on Nov. 7, 1939. Reich Foreign Minister von Ribbentrop notified the envoys of the two countries that Germany would make no formal reply. Britain and France offered to consider any proposal for settlement of the conflict which the sovereigns of the two countries could obtain from Hitler.

simply because they fear—and with good reason, from what I can see—that their countries may soon become the battleground of this war.

Now let me tell you about that bomb which exploded in the Buerger-bräukeller* within eighteen minutes after Hitler had left the building. All Germany was aroused. Eugen, being one of the old putsch crowd, was there. I remained in Berchtesgaden, availing myself of Eugen's absence to meet with Clara, Gottlieb and Wolfgang and discuss our future plans.

The versions of the incident issued by the Nazi Propaganda Ministry are untrue. Here is the story as compiled by Manfred through his Gestapo contacts.

Hess and Goebbels, who keep a close watch on the public pulse for Hitler, discovered somewhat to their dismay that despite the ease with which the Polish victory was won, the desire for peace without further conquests was strong among all classes, including even members of the Nazi rank and file. Hitler's failure to press for peace—which many had expected him to do—was a grave disappointment. At a conference with Goering and Himmler it was decided that some drastic step must be taken immediately to rally the people around Hitler and solidify war feeling in the masses.

Manfred was unable to tell me whether Hitler himself was acquainted with the plot, but he believes that the Fuehrer knew of it, at least in time to make the last-minute change in the program that brought him to the Buergerbräukeller one hour ahead of schedule. The explanations made later for this change in time were so feeble that they were hardly worth considering.

Hitler limited his customary long-winded oration to a brief address of barely thirty minutes. Himmler, whose men had planted the bomb and arranged the timing, signalled him that the moment had come for him to leave. Instead of lingering over their beers, the ranking members of the Nazi hierarchy scuttled from the place with all speed. Hitler had barely boarded the train at the railroad station when the bomb exploded.

The bombing had the desired effect. The tale that British agents had arranged it was generally believed. When I asked Eugen what possible objective the British could have had he descended upon me with all his wrath. But surely, I told him, the British knew that the German people would rally around the Nazis if Hitler was killed.

*Eight loyal Nazis were killed and 63 others were injured in the explosion on Nov. 8, 1939, which wrecked the beer cellar in which Hitler and his followers were celebrating the anniversary of the Munich putsch of 1923 which had been planned here.

34

They couldn't have been so stupidly crude. Eugen simply insisted that the British had done it in hopes of destroying German unity. They wanted to break Germany from within, since they lacked the power to do it from without. There could be no peace with assassins. They must be punished for their foul deed. Eugen's view was the view of all with whom I discussed the matter. Thus are things done in a dictatorship.

Our other friends here have also provided me with a few items that you may find of considerable interest. One comes from Gottlieb. He was on special duty in an anteroom when an important meeting was held at the Berghof, five days after the Soviet attack on Finland.

Among those present, beside Hitler, were Goering, Hess, Ribbentrop, Keitel* and Rosenberg†. The occasion for the meeting was an appeal by Finland for German help. Ribbentrop was bitterly attacked, especially by Goering, for having failed to consider the possibility that Finland would refuse Russia's demands and that war would result. But Ribbentrop held his ground, pointing out that the pact with Stalin made it impossible for Germany to side openly with the Finns. Goering's opposition was overruled and the appeal for help declined.

Another generally-unknown angle of the complicated relations between the Reich and the Soviet Union cropped up at the same meeting. It appears that Ribbentrop's original understanding with Stalin had been that Poland be divided along the line of the Vistula River, with the Germans occupying the main, western, part of Warsaw and the Russians the eastern suburbs of the Polish capital. Russia apparently had not expected the German advance to be so rapid. By the time the Red Army started rolling, the Germans had pushed far beyond Warsaw. Generals of both armies met at Brest-Litovsk to discuss the question of a demarcation line but were unable to reach an agreement. Von Brauchitsch‡ hurried to Hitler's headquarters where he accused Ribbentrop of acting without having consulted the army. He asserted that the Vistula line would be strategically indefensible. He insisted on a boundary along the Bug River.

This controversy resulted in a second trip to Moscow by Ribbentrop. He proposed a settlement by which Germany would accede to Russian control over Lithuania in return for the Polish territory between the

*Colonel General, now Field Marshal, Wilhelm Keitel, Chief of the Supreme Command.

†Alfred Rosenberg, unofficial foreign minister of the Nazi Party until his influence was eclipsed by the rise of von Ribbentrop.

‡Colonel General, later on Field Marshal, Walther von Brauchitsch, at that time Commander-in-Chief of the German Army.

Vistula and the Bug. This was satisfactory to the Kremlin and thus the affair was settled.

The Finnish war may develop friction not only between Berlin and Moscow but also between Hitler and Mussolini. In this connection I have just learned from Wolfgang about a meeting between Ribbentrop and Ciano* which took place at the time I was in transit between Hamburg and Moscow. While the information is somewhat dated you may find it of interest, especially since even the fact of the meeting was never officially released.

The two met at the inn, *Zum Weissen Rössl*, not far from Fuschl Castle near Salzburg. This secluded spot was probably chosen to keep the conference a state secret. Ribbentrop was on the point of leaving for Moscow to conduct the negotiations that led to the Nazi-Soviet pact.

The actual discussions took place in a secluded back room on the ground floor of the inn. Wolfgang was on guard outside when voices raised in anger carried through an open window. He heard Ciano shouting that Mussolini would never agree to any such step (apparently the proposed Soviet pact) that ran so utterly contrary to his steadfast policy and to the sentiments of the devoutly Catholic Italian people. It would mean a break between the Axis partners, he said.

Ribbentrop, cautioning Ciano against raising his voice, explained that England and France were seeking an alliance with Stalin. If they succeeded, the ensuing combination would be so strong that all Axis plans for expansion would be endangered. Germany, even with Italy by her side, could not risk a war on two fronts. Ribbentrop went on to say that the negotiations of the other side had been dragging for months because Stalin was demanding a price that France and England could not pay because of their own Polish commitment. It would be smart policy, he said, for Germany to meet Russia's demands in order to thwart the plans of the Western Powers.

Ribbentrop continued to explain that Japan's situation also required a pact with Russia. Japan was not yet ready to launch a large-scale campaign in the Far East because her production of heavy armaments was lagging. In spite of large German shipments for the past year, Japan was still deficient in machine tools. If it came to war with the Western Powers over Poland, he said, the British blockade would cut off all shipments to the Far East. In order to provide Japan with additional tooling facilities another route for shipments had to be found. That route would have to be over the Trans-Siberian Railroad.

Regarding Italy's own demands for territorial expansion, Ribben-

*Count Galeazzo Ciano, Mussolini's son-in-law, former Italian Foreign Minister, and currently Italian envoy to the Vatican.

trop pointed out that these would have to be met largely at the expense of France. Italy, he asserted, was not yet ready to fight France, but Germany was. He added that if the Reich won a decisive victory, Italian claims would be met for the asking.

Still dissatisfied, Ciano asked how long the pact with Russia would endure, to which Ribbentrop replied, and I quote as exactly as Wolfgang remembered the words, "As long as it serves our purposes—Germany's and Italy's."

So there you have it. Either Ribbentrop was lying to Ciano, or he entered his agreement with Stalin with his fingers crossed behind his back. And that's how Nazi diplomacy is being carried on.

Clara and I expect to go to Berlin in a few days. I'm to meet there someone who may do us a lot of good. To tell the truth, I'll be glad to get away from Berchtesgaden for a spell. I don't know, but ever since Hitler's return the pure mountain air seems charged with venom. Or perhaps it's just nerves.

I'm closing now. A chap is crossing by clipper who promised to deliver this letter. You'll probably have it within a week.

By the way, let me know if the Brooklyn Dodgers have got any new players. Stay healthy yourself.

Yours as ever,
BILL.

CHAPTER 4

My REGULAR BROADCASTS began in January, 1940. With my new program style, I soon acquired an interested audience. I believed that the American public read the news and understood it. Therefore I avoided so-called news analysis. Instead I tried to tell my audience of consequential events that usually did not appear in the newspapers.

In those early days I could use but little from the contents of van Narvig's reports. They arrived irregularly and frequently were delayed in transit. Moreover, I had to be extremely careful while he was still inside Germany. However, I was able to keep ahead of the news with occasional exclusive stories obtained from my old sources. As several of my forecasts proved true, my mail increased greatly and revealed an intensely curious audience, wanting to know who, and what, were my sources of information.

Not only my audience grew curious, but also my writing colleagues. One day a feature news writer visited me, intent on discovering my sources. It was impossible to dismiss him and, rather foolishly, I dropped a few hints about spies in key places. His story about me the following week was sensational. It claimed that I had a detailed organization of spies throughout Europe. I laughed it off, observing jokingly that Pinkerton would have envied me. Nonetheless, the article subsequently boomeranged at a very inopportune moment, of which more later.

Weeks passed and I was beginning to worry about van Narvig. Then, one Friday afternoon, the same man who had delivered my partner's previous message, walked into my office. Recognizing him, I said cheerily, "Hello there! Have you got anything for me?"

"I have," he replied, handing me another envelope.

"Thanks," I said, then asked, "Would you care to let me have your name?"

"I'm just the delivery man," he replied, and quickly walked out again.

I cannot say that I enjoyed all this secrecy, but I reflected that perhaps the fellow had excellent reasons for wanting to remain incognito. Surely van Narvig knew what he was doing and that satisfied me. I extracted the sheets from the envelope and plunged into reading.

Excited as I was to get another report, the news contained in it did not make me happy. I wanted to shout the dangerous facts to a sleeping and cozily-reassured American public.

Here is what my partner wrote:

Dear Wythe:

I was in Berlin. I was in the *Sportspalast*. I heard Hitler speak.* And I'm glad I did. In between his usual hysterical ranting I heard him make two significant statements which, I'm afraid, will either be laughed at or ignored in the United States. Hitler said, "I know exactly what the French and British are doing, but they know nothing of my plans."

*Speech of Jan. 30, 1940.

Let me tell you that for once this was not the customary idle Hitler boast. It is a frightful truth, one to which I can testify. Reports arrive daily at the Berghof. Clara has seen many of them on the desk of General Jodl, to whom they are referred after Hitler has gone through them. These reports reach Berchtesgaden via Italy and their contents are startlingly detailed.

They contain complete information on the strength of the Allied forces and their disposition. They give the location of new air fields and fortified positions. They report decisions made by the French Council of Ministers. More than that, they even include copies of General [Maurice] Gamelin's orders to the troops.

Not only does Hitler know what his enemies are doing now, but also what they will do under certain given conditions. Hitler is actually in a position today to dictate French army strategy because he possesses the working plans mapped by the French military, anticipating all conceivable moves by the German Supreme Command. Why, even a novice at Monte Carlo would stand more of a chance than the doomed French.

The original source of these reports is uncertain, but it is evident that they come from someone close to, or inside, official circles. I've been informed of this much, however. Shortly after a former French premier visited Mussolini on a farcical good-will mission, a number of extremely important reports reached the Berghof.

The second vital passage in Hitler's speech was this. He said, "Eighty million Germans are ready to go to the front."

Americans will laugh and call this a gross exaggeration, a pipe dream. It is more likely a nightmare. The Germans are out to conquer this time. Almost to a man, they are eager for a showdown with France and they will give all.

But I've rushed ahead of things. I'll tell you of an interesting experience. For a reason I'll explain later, Clara and I went to Berlin together. We secured a train compartment for the two of us. When the train failed to pull out on schedule and an armored train pulled up alongside of ours, we knew that something out of the ordinary was afoot. Then the compartment door was pulled open and in stepped Major Wartenburg, in charge of a *Schutzstaffel** detachment in Berchtesgaden, followed by Captain von Puttkammer, naval aide to Hitler.

It was rather a situation. Wartenburg and I had met. Eugen, in his introduction of me, had stressed my former military title and we'd had some sort of discussion.

I leaped to my feet, clicked my heels and extended the Nazi salute

*Hitler's Elite Guards—the S.S.

—you do these things here if you wish to stay in fairly good health.

The major reacted in the same manner. But suspicion lurked in his glance as it shifted between Clara and me. He said, "I had no idea that you were going to Berlin, Herr Oberstleutnant."*

Before I could think of an answer, Clara leaped into the breach, saying, "Please do not shield me, Herr Oberstleutnant." Then to the major, "The Herr Oberstleutnant was desirous to attend one of the Fuehrer's speeches."

Needless to say, this was news to me. Wartenburg, too, showed surprise. He said, "No one knew until last night that the Fuehrer was going to speak."

With a marvelous show of contrition Clara said, "It was I who advised the Herr Oberstleutnant late last night. I'm sorry if I committed an indiscretion."

Believe me, it did the trick. One could see how Wartenburg's suspicion evaporated. He said, "No harm done, Fräulein." To me, "I shall see to it that you occupy a good seat at the *Sportspalast*, Herr Oberstleutnant."

He introduced me to Captain von Puttkammer, and the two occupied the vacant seats in the compartment.

The next eight hours were a farce. We all fib at times, but I was called upon to excel in this department. I was wholeheartedly for the Fuehrer. I was getting acquainted with Nazi methods so that I could promote them on my return to the United States. The two officers were delighted. In fact, they thanked Clara for having provided the opportunity for a very interesting conversation during what otherwise would have been a dull journey.

At the *Sportspalast*, Wartenburg secured a seat for me next to himself and so I found myself projected into one of the weirdest spectacles I ever witnessed. In a way I'm glad. I understand better now what the rest of the world is facing. I observed some of that mass hypnotism of which Hitler is a master. I saw the boundless fanaticism of these Nazis. You cannot combat an evil unless you understand its inner workings.

After the event the major invited me to share with him a bottle of Hock. I could not very well refuse this courtesy, and so we spent another hour together.

So much for that. Now the reason that took me to Berlin. Her name is Linda. She is attractive. Honey-colored hair, sky-blue eyes, and a perfect figure. On the surface, she represents a type that in America

*Lieutenant Colonel. Van Narvig had held this rank in the Russian Volunteer Army.

is referred to as a dumb blonde, which is what she pretends to be. Actually she's one of the smartest girls I ever came across. Don't you smirk at my use of superlatives. I'm human.

Linda occupies a position at Karin Hall. She has access to the files. Because of her good looks and pretended stupidity in all things political she is frequently invited to the parties which Goering throws for foreign visitors. Hitler keeps aloof from all such affairs. This makes Goering, who likes good food and a jolly company, the official entertainer of the Third Reich. In her role of decoration on such occasions Linda overhears quite a deal of intimate political talk.

Linda is Clara's intimate friend. She knows about Clara's child—in fact, it was Linda who first arranged for Clara to go to Switzerland.

Clara gave me a brief outline of Linda's life story. Her father was a prominent citizen who joined the Nazis in 1933 and became involved in numerous affairs with them. As a result, they felt that he knew too much. There came a tragic denouement. The official version was that he committed suicide. Linda never believed this official version, but she had to accept it.

Among the things which Linda has already told me are two events that you may find of interest. The first refers to a party which Goering gave at Karin Hall in the early days of last November. It was after Soviet Premier Molotov made a speech on Russo-German relations before the Soviet Congress in Moscow. Linda overheard a conversation between Goering and Ribbentrop. According to her recollection it went something like this:

Goering: "I see where Molotov stressed Russia's fullest political support in our effort for peace."

Ribbentrop: "He did better than I had expected."

Goering: "You must have sold him a bill of goods."

Ribbentrop: "That's what I was sent to do."

Goering: "Does he really believe that we want peace now?"

Ribbentrop: "That was part of my bill of goods. If he does not believe in it he is shrewd enough to pretend that he does."

Goering: "What does he mean by, peaceful settlement of Russian interests in the Black Sea region?"

Ribbentrop: "Presumably Bessarabia. We gave no promise to that effect."

Goering: "What if they take Bessarabia?"

Ribbentrop: "Who can tell? They have their own minds."

Goering: "We don't have to take that—not from them!"

Ribbentrop: "People do not have to take medicine when they are ill, but they usually do."

Goering: "Just how long will this *Mummenschanz* [masquerade] last?"

Ribbentrop: "So long as it promotes our political and military aims."

The other thing Linda acquainted me with refers to a propaganda plot mapped by Goebbels when it became apparent that the British and French would not negotiate a peace after the Polish debacle.

It started with a meeting at Karin Hall of Hitler, Himmler, Goering, Goebbels, Ribbentrop and Hess. Conversation centered on Goebbels' plan to dupe the Allies into thinking that Germany was weak in armaments and that inner dissension was raging in the Nazi Party. The idea was highly applauded at that meeting, and Mussolini was already helping to put it over.

With the full approval of Hitler, Mussolini was whispering into the ears of the Chamberlain government that in all truth, he had no faith in Hitler's war machine. In fact, Mussolini was pretending to bargain with the Allies, promising to desert Hitler and throw in his lot with Britain and France. He went so far as to accept a token order to manufacture aircraft engines for England at the Fiat factories.

When pressed by the Allies, Mussolini happily told the British that there were differences between Hitler and Goering; that Hitler wanted war, that Goering wanted peace. He suggested negotiations with Goering with a view of overthrowing Hitler, and England entered upon them with Italy as a go-between.

The Nazis are jubilant at their success in the plot. While England forgets about war production in the false belief that Goering might become their cat's-paw in a peace barter, German preparations are going ahead day and night. The German nation is seriously girding for *Der Tag*.

Through Linda I also met Heinrich, who might become our sixth collaborator. He is attached to the Chancellery, although he is not a Nazi party member—not yet. Since Chancellery positions are in the nature of a career service, it is not a requirement to join the party. The way Heinrich is situated, he could furnish a great deal of useful information. Unfortunately, I did not find him very enthusiastic over the idea. He is a man of sound and mature judgment who does not take any risks. The only way I can think of to work on him is through Linda, to whom he is evidently attracted.

Unlike the others, Heinrich has no personal grievance against the regime. He does not like the Nazis because their ruthless methods repel him. But he concedes their capacity for organization and large-scale maneuvering. He has his own ideas on the subject of a commonwealth of Germanic nations but he wants to see it accomplished along liberal and democratic lines, and certainly not the Nazi way. I found him something of a problem. Nevertheless, through Linda, perhaps, we will accomplish one thing or another with him. At least let's hope.

The weather here has been exceedingly cold of late. It interferes somewhat with transportation. Rivers and canals are solidly frozen. Highways are covered with snow. As a result, the railroads are overloaded, which slows things down quite a bit. What difference, though, when production in England is so fearfully slow and French strategy is handed to the enemy?

Am leaving tonight for Berchtesgaden and shall try to reach America as soon as possible. I'm sick of this land. When I return, we can start the ball rolling. Greetings,

Yours as ever,
BILL.

CHAPTER 5

THE REPORT was a fearful one. Although I had some knowledge of the vastness of Hitler's preparations, I certainly had not suspected that he had procured such complete knowledge of Allied plans. I did not for a moment doubt the truth of van Narvig's statements. He had proved correct too many times before. When he reported Hitler's war machine as capable of overrunning Europe, I had a sinking feeling that this might indeed be the case.

The American people, however, were glibly chattering of a swashbuckling paperhanger with grandiose but empty ideas. And native fascists, guess-work commentators and isolationists were all shouting that Hitler was a bluff, that his house of cards would collapse in the first breeze. The wishful-thinking, gullible American public read and listened to millions of words describing the impotence of Hitler and the Nazis. Blatant misinformation was the order of the day.

Not a little of this misinformation was the work of refugees from the German intellectual classes who had fled to this country. Their experiences were confined to seeing the domestic brutalities of Hitler's brown-shirt gangsters. Voicing their personal convictions, they represented Hitler as a man thoroughly hated and despised by the overwhelming majority of the German people. They had never been allowed a glimpse into the tremendous organizing capacity of the Nazis, placed at the disposal of the German Army. Many made their living here by lecturing throughout the country. Out of deference to current American sentiment they preferred to paint Hitler as an overstuffed political buffoon rather than the potent menace to world democracy that he actually was.

Also, many of our military and naval men had turned to lecturing, book and magazine writing. Their ideas were largely based on the tactics of the First World War and they put their faith in the Maginot Line.

I continued to tell my audience what I believed to be the true facts. Although my opinions and reports were not popular in certain circles, they attracted attention.

Along with the vexations of fighting popular opinion, I was worried by the danger van Narvig was in. We had intended to establish only two or three persons at the most for our information supply. So far as I could judge, van Narvig had organized a neat little spy ring, filled with personal explosives. He had got himself entangled in Clara's personal affairs, and his evident enthusiasm for Linda's charms filled me with misgivings.

I decided to send him a warning. But while I was still debating the ways and means of communicating my fears to him, another report arrived. He wrote:

Dear Wythe:

I'm still here. Certain matters were brought to my attention that caused me to delay my departure.

Exciting events are really going on now and I must warn you immediately. Hitler intends to announce a plan for a United States of Europe, based on the American government, the Bill of Rights, the Constitution, Congress, etc.

Don't believe in it! It is another devilish plot by Goebbels to lull the outside world into complacency.

This is the idea behind it all. The extraordinary cold in Germany this winter has delayed Nazi preparations, and although their armaments are vast at the present, they will take no risks of a possible defeat. So once again they seek a delay; meanwhile, the governments of Europe are envisioning a peaceful settlement and Hitler's war machine grows more menacing daily.

In this scheme, Berlin would be the federal center. There would be one currency, abolition of trade barriers, unified national defense, representative government for the federation, another representative group based on population density. It is all a beautiful dream, a device to ensnare the gullible, and nothing more.

Hitler is considering the pronouncement. It's as false as the man himself.

Thanks to Linda, I got this information two days ago. We have checked, rechecked and triple checked. Clara has even seen a translation of the U.S. Constitution clipped to a map entitled the United States of Europe.

The map showed Poland, minus the parts of the former republic which have been annexed outright by Germany; the present state of Slovakia; the protectorate of Bohemia-Moravia; Austria and the Tyrol; Hungary; Rumania, minus Bessarabia; Bulgaria; Yugoslavia, with a line drawn between Serb and Croat portions of the country; Switzerland; Belgium; the Netherlands; Denmark.

On the same map, Germany was carved into five parts: East Prussia, the former Polish Corridor and Posen; Silesia, Saxony and the southern portion of Brandenburg; Pomerania, Mecklenburg, Schleswig-Holstein and the northern portion of Brandenburg; Bavaria, Wuerttemberg Baden and Thuringia; the Saar, the Rhineland and the Ruhr, extending to the North Sea coast. Berlin was encircled—probably into a federal district like our own District of Columbia. The map was entitled: "*Mitteleuropäischer Staatenbund*"—roughly meaning, the United States of Central Europe. The translation of the U.S. Constitution and a brief outline of the proposed governmental setup complete the picture.

You will know what to do with this information.

Linda came here for a week's stay with Clara. She is enthused and raring to go. The other day the weather was almost springlike and we both went skiing. We had lunch in a little wayside inn and there we talked things over. We agreed that Heinrich is really our key person and Linda undertook to handle him in her own way. We can leave the matter safely in her hands. She knows what she's doing. I also went over all the other angles with her along which she could be most helpful. It is really a piece of extraordinary luck that I came upon this girl.

We almost landed in trouble that day. It was very late and quite dark when we returned to Berchtesgaden. As we stopped in front of Clara's door, who should emerge from the shadows but Major Wartenburg. The man is a genius for popping up when least wanted.

To give him credit, he did not act inquisitive. The three of us exchanged a few pleasantries. It was his parting observation that I did not like. He said, "After America, I'm glad you find our German girls in the competitive class, Herr Oberstleutnant."

When he was gone, Linda breathed, "My God! Suppose he starts gossip?"

Fortunately, the major is a really decent sort. I made it a point to run into him the next day. I said I still owed him a bottle of Hock and he accepted my invitation. We discussed the political situation in general. Presently, however, he observed, as I hoped he would, "Frankly, I did not think a man of your age could still be a charmer of the attractive sex. But then, of course, you are an ex-soldier."

I said quickly, "Much as I'd like to live up to your estimate of me, Herr Major, Fräulein Linda and I merely had a good time skiing."

"Tut-tut!" he countered. "Between us men no explanations are needed."

I told him earnestly, "If there's anything special in your mind, I'd like to reassure you. Fräulein Linda is a most charming young woman, but I most definitely do not consider myself in her class."

He raised his glass in a toast, then said, "We all have our little joke, Herr Oberstleutnant. Your excursions with Fräulein Linda are none of my business. Her reputation is perfectly safe with me."

Linda proved her extraordinary ingenuity a few days later. Goering, Ribbentrop, Keitel and Funk* arrived at the Berghof. The supposition was natural that something important was up. Linda found a way by which to overhear most of what was being said. I cannot explain to you now how it was done, except that it is an acoustic trick with the ventilation system that she had learned at Karin Hall. This is what happened:

It appears that the Japanese have demanded of Germany a large supply of machine tools, claiming that they cannot increase production above the current level without these tools.

There was reluctance on the part of Hitler to accede to Japan's demand, mostly, he explained, because he had his doubts about the scope of Japan's expansionist aims. He considered, however, the future possibility of the United States' entry into the war against Germany.

They all agreed that Japan would be extremely helpful if that happened, and after much discussion of Japan's war aims, they decided

*Walther Funk, Reich Minister of Economics.

to send the tools immediately. I don't think this will be a loss on the part of Germany. At present she appears to have an over-supply of machinery.

Japanese-German ties are strong, much stronger indeed than is generally believed in America. Germany must have an ally in the Pacific, a strong one, and so the industrial strengthening of Japan will doubtlessly continue.

Now here are the figures on Germany's land and air power that you asked for. It has taken a considerable amount of time to obtain this material. As you no doubt realize, it is not to be had for the asking.

The German *Wehrmacht* is currently organized into 202 divisions. There are 16 panzer divisions, not 8, as is commonly believed. They vary in size, but approximately they add up to 450 tanks and other armored vehicles to each division. The present program calls for one tank in reserve for each two in action.

There are 24 divisions of motorized infantry, and these together with the panzer divisions constitute Hitler's shock troops.

The rest is merely infantry and auxiliary troops. There are no special engineer troops, a detachment of engineers being incorporated in each regiment of regulars. Neither is there a separate artillery weapon, the gun crews being incorporated into the armored and motorized divisions. The regular infantry is equipped with anti-tank guns, flame throwers and mortars.

To furnish a definite report on the air force is a rather complicated affair. To begin with, there are the combat air fleets of Goering's vaunted *Luftwaffe*, of which there are four. Each air fleet numbers 1,500 combat planes, plus 1,000 planes in reserve. The combat planes include fighters, dive bombers and level-flight bombers. Their respective ratio within each fleet varies, dependent on any given assignment. A special bomber command, independent of the combat air fleets, is being organized, but little is known about it as yet. Then there are the observation and liaison planes; each division of ground troops is supposed to have 12 of these. There are also the seaplanes of the *Kuestenseeflugkommando*,* the number of which I could not obtain.

In addition to all this, there is an enormous number of training and troop transport planes, as well as glider trains. It is difficult to obtain this information. Linda is closest to it, but she does not fully understand the technical matter involved in the reports.

The Nazis thus far do not anticipate wholesale bombings of civilians or large population centers. They feel this will not be necessary. But

*Coastal Command.

in cases of desperate resistance, there is likely to be civilian bombing as in Warsaw.

As for gas warfare, you may rest easy. They are certain not to use it. As a matter of fact, they rarely discuss it.

Several new plane factories—I haven't any exact details—have been built recently. However, full-scale operations in these are not expected to be under way for at least another month. Because of the transportation tie-up, due to the cold weather, some of the operating aircraft plants—notably the Junkers Works near Dessau—have had a partial shutdown. There was a shortage of parts. By April the total output in planes of all types is expected to reach 3,000 monthly, but at the moment it is considerably below that figure.

Linda has undertaken to furnish detailed monthly production statistics in the future.

Two days ago Hitler and his retinue, including even Eugen, went to Munich for a dedication of some sort. Manfred happened to be here and all of us, with the exception of Heinrich, met to discuss our plan of operations after my departure. Matters have been laid out well, so you need not worry. Every one of our group here knows how to take care of himself. I cannot give details now, but will tell you on my return.

Yesterday Linda made her departure. I was sorry. We two had had a great time together. But that's life.

See you soon,
BILL.

This last report reassured me of van Narvig's safe return shortly. True, he gave few personal details but surely, a man of his experience and incredible ability to slip past difficult censorship would be able to complete his mission successfully.

CHAPTER 6

EAGERLY I AWAITED van Narvig's arrival in New York—and with excellent reason. On March 2, 1940, Undersecretary of State Sumner Welles paid a mystery-shrouded visit to Adolf Hitler in Berlin. On the following March 18, Hitler and Mussolini met at the Brenner Pass—their first such meeting in many months.

48

There was no word from the State Department or the White House to give a satisfactory reason for Welles' journey to the capitals of the warring nations, and commentators as well as editorial writers were just guessing. The State Department apparently had a lack of faith in the ability of the people of the United States to understand, and continued to maintain secrecy.

I felt sure that van Narvig could solve at least part of the puzzle for me. He did. But, instead of appearing himself, as I had confidently expected, he sent another report which reached me through the same mysterious channel. My partner wrote:

Dear Wythe:

Sorry that I'm not there yet. But you know how things go. You're all ready to call it a day and pack up, and then some new development pops up and you stay on.

According to radio reports that we picked up, I understand that no inkling has been given to the American people on the aims and purposes of Sumner Welles' visit here. If he expected to find out something he must have met with disappointment, for the Nazis pulled a thick veil of secrecy over everything while Welles stayed here. From what we understand, Welles tried to sound Hitler out on the possibilities of any peace move by the President of the United States. According to insiders at this end, Welles had no chance to even reach first base. The Nazis do not want peace now, they want victory, well knowing that the peace terms which they have in mind would be unacceptable to the Allies and also would provoke intense bitterness in the United States.

It seems, however, that Welles, too, succeeded in putting up a mystifying air, for the top Nazis aren't quite sure among themselves just what the real purpose of his visit was. Their speculations on this point are rather interesting. Since Linda secured knowledge of what took place at several conferences, I can tell you what the chief men here think of the Welles' visit.

Ribbentrop is convinced that there is a secret understanding between London and Washington. He also claims that, according to his information, there is strong anti-British feeling in America and that the American people as a whole would vigorously protest any American involvement on behalf of England.

He contends, therefore, that the Welles mission was a farce and was undertaken primarily as a gesture to convince public opinion at home that the Roosevelt administration was wholeheartedly for peace.

He prides himself on the fact that no peace plan was offered by the Nazis. Such a plan, by the very nature of things here, would have involved a purely pro-German settlement. Since Ribbentrop feels that Roosevelt is definitely anti-Nazi, he claims that such a peace proposal by Berlin would have been used to inflame the American public against Germany. In this connection he stressed the fact that Germany was not sufficiently prepared to chance war with the United States.

Goering agrees with Ribbentrop, but he also believes that Welles was on an intelligence tour not only for America, but also for England and France. He reasons that, since England and France are completely in the dark over German plans, they wanted sufficient inside information to give them a definite idea as to what might be expected. Therefore, he contends, Welles was sent to try if he could not make the Nazi leaders open up and give him at least an inkling of what they had in mind. Goering also insists that Welles was sent to make certain just what was the actual status of the German-Italian military alliance and to what extent Mussolini would play ball with Hitler. Goering substantiated this claim by pointing out that Welles visited Rome and Berlin, before going to London and Paris. Goering felt satisfied, however, that none of this vital information was given out.

Rudolph Hess held that the Welles overture was in reality a political maneuver by Roosevelt to continue in office for a third term. By virtue of his position as deputy leader of the Nazi Party, and in charge of its political manipulations, Hess looks at things primarily from a party angle. He contended, in fact, that Roosevelt, while denouncing the one-party system in Germany, actually favored it in the United States. He said that it was necessary for Roosevelt to make a brilliant coup in foreign policy, since the President could not possibly expect re-election on his domestic policy. Hess says that if Welles returned with a pro-Allied peace plan, Roosevelt would be hailed as the great peace-maker. On the other hand, if Welles returned with a plan that the American people would consider unjust on the part of Germany, Roosevelt would have been able to embark on a violent war policy.

In that case, Hess said, Roosevelt would have told the public that it was vital to retain him in office, since it would be unwise to change administrations during such a crucial period. Hess seemed singularly annoyed that Roosevelt should expect round-about political aid from Germany when he was openly antagonistic to the present German regime.

Hitler apparently looks upon the entire affair as a personal feud between Roosevelt and himself. He blames Roosevelt alone for the outbreak of the war in 1939, saying that if Roosevelt had not promised

American backing to the Allies, Britain and France would have brushed over the Polish attack as they did the Austrian and Czech situations.

Hitler believes that the United States is the real menace in this war, although he would not say so openly. This official silence on the American-German situation is largely for the benefit of the American public. Hitler is sure that so long as Germany does not blatantly offend the United States, the American people will balk at a British alliance and stay out of the war long enough for Hitler to subdue the Allies.

To Hitler, the conflict will be essentially a war production race between a Nazi-dominated Europe and the United States. Therefore he wishes most of all to delay any real start of American production as long as possible. At the same time he is strengthening Japanese war industry to build up a counterweight against America for the day when United States participation in the war will become inevitable.

Incidentally, Evi Braun is back at the Berghof. Several months ago, you will remember, she packed up and left for her own home in Munich, with the full intention not to return. But intentions of others don't seem to count with Hitler. On his return from Berlin after the Welles visit, Hitler stopped at Munich and persuaded Evi to come back. Eugen is elated. He has always contended that Evi brings the Fuehrer good luck.

I learned in advance from Wolfgang, who idiotically risked detection by making a sudden dash by motorcycle from Fuschl to Berchtesgaden to tell me about it, that Ribbentrop was going to Rome to see Mussolini, and that he would first call at the Berghof to consult with Hitler. Thanks to this advance information, however foolishly it might have been brought to me, Clara was able to learn what Hitler and his foreign minister talked about. Hitler was scheduled to leave that night for Berlin and speak at the Zeughaus there on the occasion of the *Heldengedenktag*, * which is the German equivalent of our Memorial Day, and so the conference between the two lasted just a half hour.

The purpose of Ribbentrop's trip to Rome is to reassure Mussolini on the question of Germany's relationship with Russia, explain the settlement of the Finnish war and at the same time arrange for a special meeting between Hitler and Mussolini.

The Foreign Minister was given figures detailing Germany's military status, in order to strengthen the assurance to Il Duce that the Reich was capable of fighting any battles that may be necessary on the Western Front. Incidentally, on this particular occasion Hitler did not indicate any high opinion of Mussolini's army and navy.

Ribbentrop was given the additional task of seeking an audience

*March 10, 1940.

with the Pope and giving reassurances on the subject of Hitler's attitude toward the Catholic Church. Should his reception be favorable, he was also to launch the suggestion of a new Concordat.

Immediately upon his return from Rome, Ribbentrop reported to Hitler the failure of his mission to the Vatican and his success with the chief of the Italian state. The Pontiff rejected any proposals coming from Hitler that were not based upon concrete evidence of a change of policy toward the Church. Hitler apparently has little chance of deceiving the Holy See.

Mussolini, on the other hand, was impressed by the military statistics presented to him by Ribbentrop. He agreed to an early meeting with Hitler. That conference took place a few days ago* at the Brenner Pass on the German-Italian border, but actually on Italian soil.

Incidentally, you may as well forget about the scheme for a United States of Central Europe on which I wrote you in one of my preceding letters. It's all off. Goering and the generals have advised Hitler that they are ready. It's going to be all-out war.

As for the Hitler-Mussolini meeting, the Fuehrer took with him almost his entire staff—Goering, Keitel, Jodl, and of course Ribbentrop. Count Ciano accompanied his father-in-law. Among the Gestapo force taken along for the Fuehrer's protection was Gottlieb. It was of course impossible for him to overhear anything that took place in Hitler's car, but he did hear bits of conversation between members of the two delegations on the closely-guarded station platform. This, together with bits of information that he picked up on the return journey from the Italian border, enabled him to piece together a fairly cohesive story of the conference.

Evidently Mussolini had been afraid that Hitler was considering abandoning his Mediterranean partner in favor of a new Axis with Moscow, for the Fuehrer went to particular pains to reassure Il Duce on that score. The Russian orientation, he declared, was merely a *Vernunftsche*—a marriage of convenience. It would last only so long as the advantages to be derived from it made it worth while.

Hitler also explained that he had counseled the acceptance by Finland of the harsh terms of the Russian peace because he could do nothing else at the time. He had assured the Finns that Germany would lend her protection if Russia should attempt any further inroads against Finnish sovereignty.

It is a certainty that Hitler also outlined to Mussolini his plans for the campaign on the Western Front, although nothing definite could be learned of this. We do know, however, that Hitler asked Mussolini

*March 18, 1940.

to improvise an alarm in the Mediterranean area in order to occupy as large a part of the British fleet as possible. This is to be accomplished by loud saber-rattling on the part of Il Duce, together with many ostentatious preparations for war which would, however, stop just short of hostilities. Britain, Hitler feels, is certain to establish an impressive concentration of her naval forces in the Mediterranean as a warning to Mussolini to stay out. In return for this service, Il Duce was assured that any demands he made on France after her defeat would have Hitler's support.

That was all we were able to learn. Apparently the forthcoming western campaign is to be a combination of German might and Italian bluff.

My job here is completed. Our friends will carry on. My papers are being arranged and I expect to depart in a few days.

See you soon for certain,
BILL.

A few weeks before the arrival of this report, I had been discussing Hitler's probable next move. His threats had been directed against almost every one of the countries whose borders touched those of Greater Germany. After summing up the situation I said that very probably the place in greatest danger of attack by the Nazis was the one Hitler was not talking about. A careful study of the map and information from abroad indicated to me that before Hitler advanced against his enemies in the west he would have to safeguard his northern flank.

I told my radio audience: "Everyone is discussing the western front and the Balkans, but there is a spot on the map called Denmark. Advices reaching me indicate that Hitler is concentrating a considerable force along the Danish border. This should mean that Denmark will be his first objective." *

I had almost forgotten my prediction several weeks later when van Narvig, on his way back to the United States, cabled me briefly from a Scandinavian port where he was about to board ship. His message read:

"Greetings. Dolphi will make excursion to Alsen just as Otto did."

*Broadcast of February 28, 1940.

For a moment I was puzzled. Dolphi, of course, meant Hitler, for that was the nickname which Evi Braun had given him. But the reference to Otto and Alsen had me mystified. I knew of no place called Alsen in France, England or the Low Countries. I consulted a detailed map of Europe and found that Alsen was one of the smaller Danish islands. A history book disclosed that Prussian troops had taken it by storm during the war of 1864 when Prince Otto von Bismarck was Chancellor of Prussia.

Not long afterward, on April 9, 1940, Hitler took over Denmark and invaded Norway. My prediction of a few weeks earlier took on the stature of a major radio scoop.

Five days after Hitler had launched his Scandinavian venture, van Narvig sauntered into my office.

CHAPTER 7

I HAD COUNTLESS QUESTIONS to ask and van Narvig had volumes to tell me, yet we greeted each other silently, with a hand-shake. He tossed his coat over a chair and hung his hat on a peg, grinning happily. Evidently he felt pleased to be home.

"How was the trip?" I asked inanely.

"Fine," he said.

I looked him over. He was in excellent health; nothing about him suggested that he had spent some six months in what we in the United States were being told was a country on starvation rations.

"I see they still eat in Germany," I said.

"They do at Berchtesgaden," he replied.

We wasted no time in formalities. We talked about Denmark and the betrayal of Norway and I asked: "What do you think is going to happen next?"

For answer van Narvig walked to the wall and pointed his pencil at a spot on the map of Europe hanging there.

"Do you see this?" he asked.

I bent closer.

"Sedan," I said, at a loss for a moment. "What about it?"

"You remember what happened there?" he queried.

"Certainly," I replied, indignantly. After all, I had lived many years in France. "Napoleon III capitulated there to Bismarck. The fate of the Second Empire was decided on that day."

"It may also become the place where the fate of the Third Republic will be decided," van Narvig said.

"Explain," I said, as we returned to our chairs by the desk.

"It's not so simple as that," he replied. "I was able to find out what is likely to happen, but I'm not at all sure how it's going to be brought about."

He lit a cigar, then said, "People in Berchtesgaden who know a thing or two keep whispering about Sedan. It is the hinge, you know, where the Maginot Line itself ends and the so-called Maginot Extension begins. As a modern fortress, Sedan does not amount to much. The French General Staff believes that it is protected by the wild Ardennes Forest, but I've an idea this wilderness will give little in the way of actual protection."

"How do you know what the French General Staff believes?" I demanded.

"I don't," he admitted. "But Hitler does. Remember, I wrote you about reports on French military strength and strategy that reach Berchtesgaden by way of Italy? The fact is, everything the French General Staff has mapped is as well known to Hitler as his own plans."

"And just where does Sedan enter the picture?"

He raised one shoulder in an expressive gesture.

"I wish I knew," he said. "If I could tell you how the German armies will move when they strike against France, I would also know the French countermoves. Then I might be able to see just where the importance of Sedan comes in. As matters stand, all I can tell you is that the fate of the Third Republic will be decided there."

"The French Army will have something to say about that," I declared emphatically.

55

"Very little," van Narvig replied. He reached for a pad on the desk and began putting down figures.

"Look," he said. "Today Hitler has an army of 202 divisions. Sixteen are armored and another 24 are motorized. France has 110 divisions. Two are armored and five more are motorized. The French must keep at least 20 divisions, including their best mountain troops, at the Italian frontier, at least until they know definitely what Mussolini intends to do, and I don't see Il Duce telling them. On the other hand, Hitler has made his peace with Stalin, with profit for both of them, and keeps only ten of his divisions on his eastern frontier.

"Hitler has 12,000 combat planes, including first line reserves. France has less than 2,000 and many of these are old models which would be no match for Goering's fast Messerschmitts. Hitler has more than 1,600 dive bombers—or Stukas, as he calls them—while the French have virtually none. Hitler's guns outnumber those of the French three to one. What is more, his artillery is modern, while the French guns are mainly .75's of 1918 vintage. Figure it out for yourself."

"If what you say was true there would be some point to your argument," I said indignantly. "But your figures about the French Army are all wrong. The French have 4,000,000 men mobilized. That means 220 divisions."

Van Narvig flicked the ashes off his cigar.

"You can forget about the number of French troops mobilized," he observed. "Only men with weapons can fight. Right now France has only 110 equipped divisions ready for action."

"Well," I countered. "How about the Maginot Line?"

"You can forget about that, too," he said.

"What do you mean?" I demanded. "I've been in the Maginot Line myself. I know how those forts are equipped. Why, let me tell you . . . "

He interrupted me.

"I know all about that myself," he said. "I also know that no one at Berchtesgaden is doing the least bit of worrying over the

Maginot Line. Which to me means that they must have found some way of dealing with it effectively."

I refused to give in. "There's still the British Army in France," I pointed out.

"Six divisions, by a late count," van Narvig replied. "One of them is semi-armored. Much help they'll be."

"Just where did you get these figures?"

"In Berchtesgaden," he answered coolly.

We both fell silent then, while I turned over this information in my mind and considered what it might mean in terms of the future.

"Something should be done about it," I said.

"Sure," he agreed. "Only there's nothing that you and I can do. You are frightened by the outlook. So am I. In fact, I've been frightened by it for months. We planned to organize a little information service for our own purposes and here we are with important data on our hands that it just isn't healthy to know. We're not running an international spy organization that sells information to the highest bidder. We're just two plain individuals. All we can do is to give the American public all possible information on the danger the civilized world faces."

This was cold logic.

"What do you make of this British report about their recapture of Bergen and Trondheim, which never took place?" I asked presently.

Van Narvig smiled.

"In the first place," he said, "it was not really a British report. It was concocted in Berlin."

"In Berlin?" I echoed.

"Yes," he said. "It is necessary to understand how Nazi propaganda works. I got quite a glimpse of it and it is really childishly simple. It is based on mass psychology—on making people believe what they are longing to believe. In brief, it is based on the common failing of wishful thinking. Dr. Goebbels' thesis is, destroy the enemy's home morale and half your battle is won. If you can make the enemy believe that his armed forces have won important victories and then the reports prove completely unfounded, the letdown will be terrific. Once the people believe that their own government is deliberately issuing false reports of victory, you have the beginning of collapse.

"In practice," he went on, "it works like this: Goebbels has his radio stations broadcast that the British have retaken Bergen and Trondheim, although it is absolutely untrue. Listeners in England pick up the broadcasts. The British press asks the Ministry of Information if it is true. The Ministry inquires at the Admiralty. The Admiralty is still without information from the Fleet but it reasons that if the Germans admit the British victory it must be true. The next thing, British broadcasters proclaim the victories and the newspapers carry victory headlines. A few days later the Admiralty knows that its fleet never even came close to Bergen and Trondheim. But it had permitted the victory reports. It takes great pains to explain that there has been a misunderstanding. Instantly Nazi propaganda broadcasters, with Lord Haw-Haw in the lead, start dinning over the air waves that the London government is lying to its people. The English people, suffering from a letdown in their morale, begin to wonder and question their government. Perhaps the government is lying after all? And there you have it—Goebbels has scored."

I was digesting this information when suddenly I remembered something. In a brief message sent several weeks before, van Narvig had informed me he had acquired a copy of the secret code used by the German Supreme Command and the various armies in the field. Anxiously, I asked him about it.

"I have it," he replied calmly. "Circumstances will decide if and when we can use it. First we require a fairly powerful radio receiver to pick up the signals."

"We'll get one," I decided instantly.

"It's not so simple as all that," he said. "There is the matter of wave lengths. I know some of the wave lengths which the German General Staff uses for field communications, but I doubt very much if standard receivers are equipped to get them."

"Couldn't we have a special receiver built to order?" I asked.

"We could do better than that," he said. "We could build one ourselves, or we could change a good standard receiver to suit our purposes."

"Then let's do it by all means," I urged.

Here was a wonderul opportunity. If we could pick that kind of information from the air we would have one scoop after another.

Van Narvig did not quite share my enthusiasm.

"So far as I know they use standard signals converted into their various codes," he explained. "At one time I was fairly competent at reading code and I have brushed up a bit lately. But many factors are involved. First we must have the right location, and even then we cannot be sure that the signals will reach us. Our success will depend in part on atmospheric conditions."

"We're sailing into summer," I pointed out.

"True," he admitted. "But static is not the end of our difficulties. The fact that the signals reach us will be no guarantee that I'll be able to interpret them correctly. In fact, I'm positive that I could not do a fool-proof job."

"We don't need a fool-proof job," I countered. "Just so long as you pick up the general nature of the messages, we'll be able to figure out the rest."

We decided to try it and van Narvig explained that it would take him approximately two weeks to rig up the type of receiving set we would need.

It was then that he pulled a surprise. From a briefcase he extracted a white oblong envelope bearing four important-looking swastika seals. There was no address on it.

"What's this?" I asked.

"So far as I know, it's an introduction to the chief of the Gestapo in the United States," van Narvig stated calmly. He added, "I understand it's signed by Hitler himself."

"You understand?" I echoed.

"I haven't read it," he explained.

"Look here, Bill," I interrupted, "you didn't by any chance try to . . ."

"Don't worry," he broke in. "I'm playing with matches, but not with a flaming torch. This introduction is not for me. It's for a chap who entrusted it to my care and then disappeared. It is a rather long story."

I glanced at my watch and decided that it was time for lunch. He told me the story over coffee at the Lotos Club.

"When I was in Berlin on my way out of Germany," van Narvig began, "I met with Heinrich a few times. He helped me get my official traveling papers in order. He has quite a bit of influence. While I was with him, Heinrich introduced me to one Friedrich Homburg."

"Who is Homburg?"

"Officially, the duly accredited managing director of a respectable chemical firm," said van Narvig. "Actually, he is one of the best brains in the Gestapo foreign service. He was sent to the United States to report on the reliability of the principal Gestapo agents here. There's a story that some of the boys are rather keen on accumulating American dollars. Himmler doesn't think much of it as a habit, except for himself."

I whistled. Suddenly I understood. I asked, "Does this sealed envelope contain Homburg's credentials?"

"I assume so," van Narvig said. "As I told you before, I didn't see its contents."

"How did you get hold of it and what happened to Homburg?" I demanded.

"I didn't kill the fellow or steal it from him, if that's what you mean," he answered wryly. "Give me a chance to tell the story from the beginning."

"All right. Shoot," I said and settled back in my chair.

Van Narvig bit off the end of a cigar and lighted it. Then he said, "Heinrich introduced me to Homburg because we were booked to sail on the same ship. Later, when we were alone, Heinrich gave me the lowdown on the fellow. It seems that Homburg is a shrewd customer, who has been used by Himmler on numerous occasions to get evidence against important agents of the Gestapo who were conducting their little personal rackets on the side. You see, Himmler is not above indulging in an occasional bit of blackmail himself. He likes to have complete confidential records on people. Homburg furnished them."

"Chummy, aren't they?" I observed.

"Indeed," van Narvig agreed. "Anyway, certain other folks in Germany thought it would be a good idea if Homburg conducted his expert investigations in a different geographical location. Hence his special assignment to the United States."

"Did Heinrich tell you who these certain other people were?" I asked.

"Not in so many words," he said. "But from remarks he dropped I got the notion that Himmler himself might have been one of them. Perhaps Homburg was too smart for his own welfare and his removal from the scene was desirable. It was Heinrich's conviction that Homburg would never reach the United States."

"You mean he would be killed on the way?"

Van Narvig shook his head. "You people over here don't seem to give the Gestapo the credit for brains which it deserves," he said. "They're not so crude as all that. Murder in a foreign country or aboard a neutral ship could lead to unpleasant complications. There are easier and cleaner methods that are just as effective. The Gestapo has agents in Eire. They drop a hint to the British Intelligence Service that someone might be found on a certain ship traveling under the passport of a neutral country. The British are quick in following up such tips. The person in question is apprehended when the ship calls at a British inspection port and is sent to a concentration camp in Scotland or Canada. It is a safe and painless process. It has been worked many times."

"Is that what happened to Homburg?" I interrupted.

"I'm coming to that," van Narvig replied. "Heinrich asked me to keep an eye on Homburg. I was to let Heinrich know if anything unusual happened to the Gestapo man. Apparently Heinrich is keeping records of his own against a better day."

Van Narvig paused to relight his cigar and then he continued:

"I renewed my acquaintance with Homburg aboard ship. The first night out we had drinks together and played a few games of piquet. He knew of my extended stay in Berchtesgaden and, I take it, assumed that I was in high favor there. I thought it a good policy to foster his illusion.

"The next morning we were pulling into Kirkwall, British inspection port in the Orkneys. Homburg seemed nervous. When a cutter carrying inspection officials pulled up alongside he handed the envelope to me and asked me to keep it for him until the inspection was over. It never was over so far as Homburg was concerned.

"He was invited to a private interview by a pair of British officers and presently I saw him and his baggage taken ashore. I never saw him again. Meanwhile I kept the envelope."

"Let's have a look at what's in it," I suggested. "Maybe there's a whale of a story inside those seals."

He shook his head.

"I doubt it. And anyway, we couldn't use it without getting me involved. I've been thinking this matter over. An idea of my own has occurred to me in this connection."

I was eager to hear it.

"It occurred to me that perhaps Homburg had been given an additional little assignment—namely, to keep a tab on me. Perhaps Heinrich suspected something of the nature. Perhaps he even had a hand in Homburg's apprehension."

I nodded. The idea contained a measure of plausibility.

"There's something else I though of," van Narvig said. During his talks Homburg mentioned a name. It sounded like Motett. The man is supposed to be connected with the German Library of information here in New York. Perhaps the connection is a shield and Motett is part of the Gestapo outfit. By surrendering the envelope intact to Motett and relating the circumstances, I might get into his good graces and keep going from there on. It certainly can do no harm to try and find out what Germany's agents are doing in our own country."

The idea was a good one, no doubt, but risky. Now that van Narvig was safely back in the United States I certainly did not want him to run into a hornet's nest of his own making and I told him so. He seemed confident, however, of being able to take care of himself.

I was anxious to know the real conditions in Europe, outside of Germany. I was especially eager to confirm, one way or the other, persistent rumors of Hitler's intention to move toward the Balkans.

Van Narvig considered any move toward the Balkans unlikely.

"Why should Hitler waste men and equipment on the Balkan countries," he said, "when he can virtually have them for the asking if he overruns France. That is, if he can come to terms with Mussolini on the Balkan question."

"Just what do you mean by that?" I asked.

"It's like this," he said. "Any time the subject of Mussolini and the Balkans is broached at Berchtesgaden, it is instantly hushed. It is evidently a delicate subject. The two Axis partners thus far have never tried to reach an understanding on the Balkan question, so far as I know. This is probably because on this particular subject they are miles apart. Mussolini wants Greece and he may move to take her. He also covets Yugoslavia, or at least sizable parts of that country. Hitler is loath to concede anything unless he is forced to do so in order to hold Mussolini in line. He may let Il Duce have Greece if the Italian really has the courage to go after it.

"But when it comes to Yugoslavia, Hitler draws a line. He regards this as part of his granary and arsenal. Most of his copper and bauxite have come from that country and he hopes to hold on to the source. If the war runs into years he'll certainly need all he can get. On the other hand, Hitler knows Mussolini for a bluffer. He is not fooled in the least by Il Duce's bravado gestures. So long as the Italian can worry England and France, Hitler is satisfied, but the German generals certainly do not count on Mussolini and his army for much in the event of a real showdown. I don't think that Hitler will yield Yugoslavia."

"It seems to me that the Yugoslavs will have something to say about the situation," I pointed out. "The Serbs especially are a sturdy lot, intensely patriotic, and so are the Montenegrins, what there is of them. I'll bet they put up a battle."

"But what are they to fight with?" van Narvig countered. "You know what a conglomerate country it is. Ever since Yugoslavia came into being she has been raked by internal troubles. The Serbs and Croats are too evenly balanced for either one to take a decisive upper hand. What is more, both Hitler's and Mussolini's agents keep stirring up trouble among them. In addition, the Yugoslavs have been dependent on France for armaments and she hasn't got enough for her own needs. I'm afraid they are in a very bad spot. If France falls, the Balkans will be more or less of a walkover."

"What about Rumania?" I asked. "Have you any information on her army of two million men?"

Van Narvig burst out laughing. "How long has it been since you have seen the Rumanian Army?"

"Not since the First World War," I admitted.

"But you should know," he said, "that it is still the army of that epoch and knows nothing of modern warfare."

After a moment of silence he went on, "Poles were bad enough. Their system was rotten. Their national pride was misplaced. Their generals were inept. They sent swarms of horsemen armed with pikes to charge twenty-ton tanks. Though you can say this much for the Polish soldiers—they fought like lions. But the Rumanian Army—Oh my God!

"It would probably give an excellent account of itself in a Lubitsch film, but in serious warfare—! We speak of Rumania as a democracy. Why, it's the worst misnomer for the most mismanaged country in the world, bar none. King Carol is mostly concerned about his own fortunes and his lady love, Magda Lupescu. The leading politicians follow in his footsteps. Anyone who looks for position and wealth in Rumania today operates through Magda. Graft is rampant as never in the memory of man. Foreign loans go into the pockets of politicans. The peasants are taxed out of existence. The Siguranta—that is, the military police—is more poisonous than the Gestapo. Rumania's politicians are as corrupt as they are inept. They would sell out for anything.

"The army is dressed in discarded uniforms purchased from almost every country under the sun. Some regiments wear old American army uniforms without even changing the buttons. The officers parade in gaudy attire covered with decorations which they never earned. If they want anything they simply take it. Rumania has been under military law too long. The soldiers have not been paid in ages. Whatever is left of their pay after the politicians are done with it is appropriated by the officers. The average Rumanian soldier is so poor that for a five-dollar bill he's ready to do anything short of murder. He hates his officers and would like nothing better than to kill them all off. It isn't an army—it's a mob."

He lit a fresh cigar and continued.

"The Germans know all about Rumania. Their idea is to appropriate the country, reorganize it in true Nazi style and make it produce—for them. I have seen a map of Europe on a wall in Hitler's study; I wonder if King Carol knows about that map, for on it Rumania's fate is plainly marked. She is next to France on the list of conquests, and the preferred bloodless method should not prove difficult in her case. The Nazis know that the Rumanian peasant would gladly welcome almost any change. He couldn't possibly be worse off than he is today.

"There is still another consideration—a very important one from Hitler's point of view. One thing he wants to prevent is the unification of all the Slavs. That is why he is exterminating those among the Poles who resist Germanization. Rumania is not a Slav nation, only a sort of mongrel, wedged in between Russia and the South Slav bloc—the Bulgars and the Yugoslavs. Hitler's policy is to get a firm hold on this wedge. He wants to prevent Russia from moving south."

"But what will Stalin say to that?" I asked.

Van Narvig said simply, "The time to cross that bridge will be when we get to it."

CHAPTER 8

I DID not see van Narvig for several days after our talks. He had been away for seven months and had personal matters that needed attention. When we met again he had another story to tell.

He had visited the German Library of Information and had found the man, Motett. Whether Motett was an alias the man used, or what his first name was, we never did learn. We were not particularly interested at the time and Motett, as he was called by everyone in the Library, returned with other German consular officials to the Reich in July, 1941.

Motett, however, was not one of the principal Gestapo figures in this country. Under his cloak of diplomatic immunity he acted merely as a contact man through whom Gestapo agents communicated with their central headquarters in Berlin.

He voiced appreciation for the information brought by van Narvig and said that he would arrange a meeting with the proper persons who would be authorized to accept the Homburg envelope.

Evidently Motett did not want to risk his diplomatic status by making admissions to people he did not know. He took van Narvig's address and telephone number and promised to communicate with him. Van Narvig gathered that Homburg had been a person of consequence in the Gestapo organization.

Motett telephoned van Narvig that same evening, asking if he could come to the Library of Information the following morning to meet someone with whom he could talk freely. Van Narvig followed up this call and met a lean man of about forty, slightly less than six feet tall, with dark brown hair and eyes and a healthy outdoor complexion. He was introduced under the name of Reinhold Tugendwald. Later on we found out that Tugendwald was the chief Gestapo agent for the Greater New York district.

Tugendwald appeared rather self-confident, and immediately asked for the envelope. But van Narvig, with a view to reaching the top Gestapo man in the United States, hedged, and asked to see Tugendwald's credentials. At this Tugendwald balked, saying that his position was of a confidential nature and that van Narvig after all, was a total stranger to him. Van Narvig, however, made use of Heinrich's dossier. He hinted to Tugendwald that he was well aware of Homburg's mission to the United States and he would surrender the letter only to a person fully authorized to receive it, or to the *Landesgruppenleiter* who represented Bohle* in the United States.

Tugendwald was apparently impressed by this sort of talk. He admitted that he, himself, was not so important an official. He promised to get in touch with the *Landesgruppenleiter*, but this might take some time. He would telephone van Narvig when the chief was available. The matter was left there.

I disliked the situation intensely. In my opinion, van Narvig was courting danger. He, however, seemed unconcerned.

"Don't worry about it," he said. "I know how to handle these birds and can take care of myself. There might be a great story in it for us."

I knew that arguing the point with him would prove of little avail. We turned to other things. I wanted to know what chances there were of a revolution in Germany that might lead to the overthrow of Hitler.

"None," van Narvig stated flatly. Then he amended, "For the time being."

Everyone in the United States, including myself, was hoping for news of internal disorder in Germany. We all suspected that domestic tension existed. Van Narvig's experiences in Germany had somewhat dampened my hopes, but my convictions were strong.

"You have collected six people," I argued, "who will go to great risks for the eventual overthrow of Hitler. The reasons for their sentiments, most certainly, are sound. Surely there are

*Ernst Wilhelm Bohle, attached to the Ministry of Foreign Affairs in Berlin and occupying the position of Gauleiter, or provincial governor, of all German nationals in foreign countries.

67

many others throughout Germany whom the Nazis have harmed."

"There are," he agreed. "What of it?"

"Well, why couldn't they form the nucleus of a revolutionary movement. All revolutions have started that way."

"How many would you say feel that way about the Nazis?" asked van Narvig.

"Several thousand at least," I answered cautiously.

"I'll go you one better," he declared. "I'll guess there are at least one million—and so what? Who is going to approach them? Who is going to discover their hidden hatred and find out how much each is willing to sacrifice? Who will mold them into an effective organization? Who is going to outwit the Gestapo? Who is going to give all these men and women an acceptable guarantee of their safety in the event that one unguarded word reveals their plans?

"It took me the better part of six months to recruit six people willing to work in secret toward the eventual liberation of their country. At that, I did my recruiting under the protection of Berchtesgaden, so to speak. How far do you think I could have gone without that lucky connection?

"And if I had asked these six people to form an active revolutionary movement for the overthrow of Hitler and his regime, they would have thought me mad and paid no attention to me— and with perfect right."

"But there have been successful revolutions before," I contended. "Look at the Kaiser."

"Yes, there have been successful revolutions before," he replied, "where the masses were driven beyond endurance, or where the country was losing a disastrous war. So far the German masses eat fairly well. True, they have no delicacies or luxuries. But it has been so long since they have had these things that they are willing to go further without them, for they have been made to believe that Hitler is fighting to get these very things for them.

"Then, too, Hitler has given them nothing but victories. With a minimum of saber-rattling he annexed Austria and Czechoslovakia. He won the Polish and Norwegian campaigns with

German casualties so small that they are almost ridiculous, compared with the tremendous losses of the last war. If he conquers France, as he most likely will, his prestige will soar so high that no one will dream of challenging his leadership.

"There is yet another very important factor," he continued. "The popular conception that men make revolutions is contradicted by historical fact. Men can be driven to almost any extremes. But it is only when their women grow discontented and start egging them on that the grumbling men take part in real concerted action. Look at the women of Robespierre's reign of terror, at Rosa Luxemburg and at the women of the Russian Revolution.

"The German women of today are not grumbling. And so long as the women support a regime it is as strong as a rock. It was with amazement that I observed the German women of Hitler's regime. To them, their Fuehrer is an idol, the nearest thing to God. Why? I cannot understand—but there it is.

"If anyone voices the slightest criticism of Hitler before an average hausfrau, she will either spit at him or try to tear his hair out by the roots. They are ecstatic when they hear him speak. They will go through hell for him. And because of them, Hitler is safe."

Two weeks passed. It was early May, 1940. In Norway the Nazi invasion army had thrown the Allied expeditionary force back into the sea and was engaged in mopping-up operations. Only six German divisions had been engaged in the campaign.

We had no news from our friends in Germany. Except for the information that van Narvig had brought back with him, we had no definite news.

For some time van Narvig had been busy assembling a radio receiver. When I asked him how he was progressing, he merely shrugged and warned me not to entertain great hopes.

I was surprised, then, when about noon on May 8th he telephoned and asked that I come to his house. I was to broadcast that night and protested that I hadn't the time. He insisted.

When I arrived, van Narvig was on the roof, rigging up what

seemed to me to be too much of an antenna. The receiving set I found to be a rather unimpressive black steel box, the front panel of which contained all sorts of dials and control knobs—a mystery to me. The box seemed too small for the job it was intended to do and I had my doubts about its effectiveness.

In a few minutes van Narvig was ready. He smiled and said, "Now to see what we shall see."

"I hope we hear something," I remarked dubiously.

Without a word he adjusted a set of earphones and plugged the cord into a jack. He turned a knob and the dials lighted up. At least that's something, I remember thinking.

After a few minutes during which my impatience increased, he said, "I'm getting our wave lengths perfectly. Want to hear?"

To humor him I put on the earphones. I could hear the dots and dashes of what I took for Morse code but beyond that it meant nothing.

"It's all Greek to me," I said, handing back the head set.

"We'll soon know where we stand," he said and turned his attention back to the receiver. For quite a while he manipulated the controls, his face a mask.

"What are you doing?" I asked finally.

"Fishing," he answered. "It's the only way to find their wave lengths. They don't advertise them."

I was getting restless. I had a broadcast script to prepare. Time was pressing and here I was, an idle witness to what probably was just a futile experiment. I was thinking of a good excuse to leave when suddenly his expression became more intent.

"I've caught what I believe is the Nauen station," he said.

Now I settled more firmly in my chair. Something might materialize after all.

"Nothing but ordinary wireless messages," he said wryly, and continued to operate the knobs with both hands.

More time passed. I should have left, but I was intrigued. If van Narvig could catch just one item of importance it would be more than worth the loss of time. I rose and paced the floor.

"Quiet!" he whispered.

I bent over his shoulder, my eyes on the dials, as if I expected them to speak.

Van Narvig swore under his breath. "Not distinct enough," he said. He adjusted the phasing and oscillator controls on the panel before him. Suddenly he reached for a pad and started jotting down shorthand symbols.

The minutes passed. Van Narvig's pencil raced across the pad. He turned off the controls and pulled off the earphones.

"What is it?" I demanded excitedly.

He said, "How do I know? Have to decode it first."

Walking over to a steel filing cabinet, he produced a stack of sheets densely covered with the same crazy symbols that appeared on his pad.

"What are these?" I asked.

"The code," was his laconic reply.

"Man alive!" I shouted. "Why haven't you written it out?"

"All this is in German," he explained. "It takes much longer to type German than English—at least for me. Here are close to a hundred pages. After I had typed them out you'd still have to translate the whole thing into English. That may take a month. Then, after I had gone to all that work, no one would be able to use it but myself. Thanks, but I can read my own German shorthand fairly well."

"Will it take long?" I asked.

"I don't know. I'll do my best."

"Look here, Bill," I said. "I've got a broadcast on tonight. I must go back to the office to prepare a script."

He did not bother to reply, but kept to his work. Fifteen minutes passed. Twenty! My nerves were jumpy.

Presently he tossed his pencil aside. His eyes gleamed.

He said, "I think this code wasn't such a bad move after all. This looks as if we might have something really worth while."

"What have you got there?" I demanded.

"A scoop for your broadcast tonight," he grinned. "I'm not going to give you the number of the various units because that's immaterial. These are what we might call final marching orders issued by the German Supreme Command. Six army corps are moving up along the Dutch border, all the way from Papenburg in the north, to Kléve in the south. Fourteen army corps are deploying toward the Belgian border between Aix-la-Chapelle and Daun. Four army corps are ready to move into Luxembourg from the direction of Trier. Together, this comes to about forty-eight Nazi divisions on the move."

"And," I said with a sinking feeling, "that means that the big push in the west has been ordered. But when?"

Van Narvig removed his spectacles. "Well, here we must rely on assumptions. Obviously, the movements of such large bodies of troops cannot remain secret for any length of time. Surprise is the essence of successful attack. How many hours do you give them?"

"My guess is that they will start pouring into Holland and Belgium within thirty-six hours," I hazarded. "That would mean the day after tomorrow. Probably at daybreak."

"I don't think you can go wrong on that assumption," he said.

At the studio I had an argument with the station censor. He insisted, and rightly, that no such information had come over the news ticker. The station, he said, would find itself in trouble if my broadcast turned out to be a false alarm. Naturally it was impossible to reveal my source of information. At last we reached a compromise—at least I called it that.

I was permitted to say that "two German armies are deploying toward the Dutch frontier. One from the direction of Bremen toward Gröningen, and the other from the direction of Cologne toward Limburg." I added, of course, my assumption that an invasion of the Low Countries was about to begin.

That was the evening of May 8, 1940, and I was lucky that night. I had a second scoop in this broadcast—one that seemed relatively minor at the time, but which later assumed great importance, not only as it applied to Hitler's invasion of the Low Countries, but also to other coveted locales.

I had lunched at the Overseas Press Club and sat next to an official of the Dutch Ministry at Washington. He talked entertainingly about dozens of Dutch officers' uniforms being tailored in Holland and shipped across the German frontier. He wondered why.

My own assumption, given over the air that night, was that they would probably be used by parachutists, then known to be training in the Reich, who later would work with the Fifth Columnists in the Low Countries, at the outset of the drive. Later the Dutch Minister, following diplomatic custom, insisted on a retraction from the head of the broadcasting company, but the news followed my prediction too soon for a denial to be necessary. Thirty-two hours later, on May 10, 1940, the world reverberated to the official news that the invasion of Holland, Belgium and Luxembourg was on!

CHAPTER 9

THE FOLLOWING MORNING, van Narvig called at the office. He actually had up-to-the-minute information on the progress of the German invasion—news that our papers did not print until two or three days later, when it was officially announced by either the Allied or German High Command, or both.

"It's all clear now—Sedan and everything," van Narvig said.

"Get on with it," I demanded. "Explain."

"The Germans are across the King Albert Canal, advancing on Brussels and Antwerp," he told me.

"Not really across?" I exclaimed, not wanting to believe it.

"The Germans are across the King Albert Canal," he repeated. "They have also cut through Southern Holland and reached the big Rhine bridge to Dordrecht. They have separated Holland from Belgium. The Dutch army will cease to fight in another three or four days."

"That looks like the beginning of the end," I said. "With the Germans rushing for Brussels and Antwerp, what can the French and British do? Do you think they will move their own field forces into Belgium from the south and engage the Germans in Flanders?"

Van Narvig answered:

"That is exactly what General Gamelin's strategy calls for under the circumstances, but remember that Hitler knows these plans. He wants Gamelin to move into Flanders."

He pointed at the map.

"Follow this," he said. "If the Belgian army simply retreated without a fight and joined the French and British forces remaining behind the Maginot Extension to the sea, they might have a fighting chance. But they are not doing this because it would be unorthodox and not according to Gamelin's plan. Gamelin banks on the impenetrability of the terrain in the Ardennes Forest. He is wrong. Large German panzer forces are already breaking through the Ardennes Forest. Perhaps they are already through. They will hit the Maginot Extension at its weakest spot, Sedan, and break right through it."

"That means they'll flank the Allied right and force a general retreat," I exclaimed.

"That wouldn't be half bad," van Narvig replied stoically. "I'm afraid they'll do much worse. Gamelin will think that this German shock army is headed straight for Paris and he will pile up his reserves to block it. But the Germans will not drive for Paris. They will throw up a strong armored and artillery screen against the French reserves. Their main body will veer to their right, drive down the Somme River and reach the Channel Coast in the vicinity of Abbeville. This will not only invalidate the Maginot Extension, but Hitler will enclose the Allied field armies in a gigantic trap. They will have no chance of breaking out. They will surrender or die. All their field equipment will be lost."

A final study of the map clinched all argument.

On the night of May 13, I stated the following in my broadcast:

"Unless General Gamelin makes a complete change in his plans, the Allied armies are facing terrible danger. Hitler has laid an ingenious trap for them. If they withdraw from Belgium in

74

haste and take up defensive positions behind the Maginot Extension they may stand a chance of holding off the German onslaught. But if they throw all their available field strength into Belgium and offer battle on the plains of Flanders, strong German armored forces will break through the Meuse River Gap at Sedan, flank the Maginot Extension from the east and continue to the sea where they will cut off the Allied retreat. There may still be time for a withdrawal."

The station censor, of course, tried to prevent my broadcasting this information, but after stiff arguing I got it through. The following morning I learned that dozens of calls had poured into the station concerning my broadcast. The French and British missions in the United States protested in the following vein: "Such irresponsible talk, which has not the slightest foundation in fact, should be barred, etc., etc." Some went even so far as to declare that I was broadcasting Nazi propaganda. Certainly it was no great pleasure to me at this time to know these facts. My two sons were there, right in the line of fire. They had been art students for several years and had failed to heed my repeated warnings to come home.

However, the communiques confirmed in the next few days how correct our information had been.*

Now, with van Narvig glued to his receiving set, we had clear sailing. In every broadcast we gave precise information on the position of the advancing German armies. We reported the extension of the German pincers to Cambrai two days before Prime Minister Churchill admitted it officially from London.† We announced the closing of the Nazi trap at Abbeville thirty-six hours before the German communiques claimed it. We beat everyone on the Belgian capitulation. All official reports to the contrary, we stated authoritatively that a French counter-offen-

*The French Ninth Army along the Meuse River on the Sedan front was crushed by the Germans under Colonel General, now Field Marshal, Gerdt von Rundsted on May 15, 1940. A German panzer division under Lieutenant General, now Field Marshal, Erwin Rommel reached the Channel Coast at Abbeville on May 21, 1940, cutting off the Allied armies in Flanders.

†May 19, 1940.

75

sive against the German pincers from the south was impossible. German staffs kept Hitler's headquarters continually informed of the weakness of French units opposing them along the Somme, and van Narvig, whose decoding gained daily in efficiency, had no difficulty in picking these reports from the air.

At times there were gaps in our information, usually caused by atmospheric disturbances. We missed the Dunkerque evacuation entirely, which we wouldn't have revealed in any case until it had succeeded. However, aided by the information we had from Germany, we were frequently able to bridge these gaps. Occasionally we resorted to deductions, but because of the background against which we were operating, they proved correct nine times out of ten. Because of our hitting the ball squarely time and again, and getting the actual fighting news first, our radio audience increased rapidly and our mail assumed considerable proportions.

Some listeners, however, still harped on what evidently had become their obsession—namely, that I was pro-Nazi. But such accusations were contained almost exclusively in anonymous letters. Those who signed their names usually made favorable comments on the accuracy of our reports. Throughout the entire correspondence ran one insistent question—by what means was I getting my information? Obviously this could not be revealed at the time.

The accusations that I was pro-Nazi did not annoy me particularly. My friends knew of my feelings about Nazi Germany. They were also well aware that my name stood high on the Nazi blacklist of those who may not enter Germany.

Van Narvig would naturally be marked for death by the Gestapo if his part on our project became known. Our greatest satisfaction in those stormy days was that we were able to present the actual facts at almost the same time as they occurred. Our hearts were with the Allies, but the tide of war was running overwhelmingly against them. Our job was to report the truth, even when the truth spelled bad news.

A few days after the Belgian capitulation* the first evidence that our German friends were active in our behalf arrived. It consisted of two separate reports. The first came from Linda, as van Narvig had confidently expected. The second was a surprise to both of us. It was sent by Manfred, the coldly realistic Gestapo man in Berlin.

Linda's letter was in shorthand, the Roller method. Van Narvig had to restudy this ancient German system that he'd learned as secretary to Walther Rathenau.† The report was written on American dime-store note paper, supplied to Linda by van Narvig before his departure from Germany. It read:

Dear Willy:

I trust that you are safe in America, and fervently wish I could be there. I felt rather low after our parting in Berlin. I hope, also, that you have not become involved with Homburg in any way. He is a dangerous person and I was greatly disturbed when Heinrich introduced you to him. But you probably know what Homburg is and I shall not waste space about him.

Karin Hall has seen some "distinguished" visitors in the past few days—Japanese. Their arrival, led by General Count Terauchi,‡ came as a surprise to all of us. We really had no idea that German-Japanese relations had progressed so rapidly. Goering was presented with yet another decoration, this time from the Emperor Hirohito, and our Hermann is now the very good friend of General Terauchi. I hope the name is correct, these Japanese names are so difficult to transcribe.

The night the Japanese arrived Goering served a tremendous banquet in their honor. Most of the German air generals were present. General Ernst Udet, surrounded by several Japanese colonels, explained to them the organization and tactics of our air-borne troops. He drew numerous sketches that he explained and then carelessly tossed them on a near-by table. I noticed how one of the Japanese collected them and put them in an inner pocket of his tunic.

None of us here understands why the Nazi leaders reveal so much to the Japanese. We are suspicious of them. We feel that they will eventu-

*May 29, 1940.

†Walther Rathenau, German foreign minister under the post-war republic. He signed the Rapallo Treaty, re-establishing relations with Soviet Russia, and was slain by the Nazis.

‡Count Juichi Terauchi, a lieutenant general in the Japanese Army, led the invasion of the Dutch East Indies in the spring of 1942.

ally turn against Germany. But our leaders seem to have the greatest confidence in the friendship between the two countries.

General Terauchi and two of his major-generals formed a group with Goering and Lieutenant General Otto Keller, one of our air fleet commanders. Hermann had a large map of Norway spread out on a table and explained to the Japanese how our fliers had made it impossible for the British to hold their beach heads despite their strong naval support. Terauchi and his men drank in every word. Hermann's booming voice could be heard at the other end of the room when he agreed to have the Japanese guests taken to Norway by General Keller to study the campaign on the very terrain where it was fought.

I cannot explain this Japanese interest in our air operations. Only last year Udet was sent on a mission to Japan. On his return I heard him report to Goering that he was definitely disappointed with the Japanese air force. He said that the pilots were courageous and willing to learn but that they still had a long way to go. Their organization was based on the Italian model and neither Goering nor Udet think very highly of the Italian system.

I have delayed sending this letter because events in which you may be interested have intervened. The war in the west has broken out. Strange to say, it has brought a peculiar reaction on the part of our German people. The average burgher shows little enthusiasm. Even the initial reports of victory failed to rouse him from his comparative apathy. I was too young at the time of the last war to remember what was going on, but I understand there was a great deal of patriotic feeling. Today, this is absent. Perhaps the explanation is that to the people this war is not so much a realization of patriotic ambitions as a gigantic business enterprise aimed at capturing sources of raw materials and food. I get this reaction from Goering who always speaks in terms of so many mines added to our mineral resources, and so many additional industrial establishments with which to increase our production. There is nothing heroic in all this nor, for that matter, any romance. The victory bulletins meet few cheers.

Of course Goebbels is doing his best to glorify the German warrior. But he is successful only with the children and young people. Men and women of forty and over lean to the practical side and ask what we will get out of today's privations in terms of an easier life. Hardships and sacrifices are telling more on them. This particular age group went through it all before.

Several days have passed since General Terauchi and his staff returned from their tour of Norway. The party was recalled just before the attack in the west was launched, because General Keller was needed as chief of staff of the First Air Fleet which is now operating over France. The Japanese have gone to the Western Front as Goering's guests, to study the new techniques of warfare at first hand.

There is little political activity going on now, and probably there will be none until the decision in France is reached. I spent a day in Berlin where Heinrich told me that the busiest crowds at the moment, aside from the military, are those of the food section of the Ministry of Economics. Thousands of their field men are in Holland, taking inventory of the seized dairy products and potatoes there. Together with what was obtained in Denmark it is a sizable haul. Heinrich has learned that there will be increased rations shortly in eggs, butter, milk products and meat for the civilian population. That will please the burghers.

I intend to visit Clara at Berchtesgaden very soon, though I doubt if she will have anything to add, since Hitler and the entire staff are away. While I am there I shall give this to Gottlieb for transmission.

Please write soon. I shall wait to hear how you are getting along.

Affectionately,

LINDA.

The report from Manfred was written in Russian—in the pre-Bolshevik spelling as taught by the German universities. It read:

Dear Willy:

I am sure this letter from me will come as a surprise to you, for at the time you were here I was in doubt that I could be of much help. My personal situation has changed, however, and I am in a better position to witness important developments. I have some ill-wishers at Gestapo headquarters who have contrived, much to my pleasure, to have me transferred from office duty to a special protection detail for Hitler at the front.

I received my new assignment three days before the great offensive got under way and I joined Hitler's retinue at Aachen [Aix-la-Chapelle]. The headquarters soon moved to Trier, but the Fuehrer is rarely there. He rushes from place to place, frequently covering several hundred miles a day, and our detail must follow along. He seems to feel that the gigantic enterprise must have his personal supervision, and seeks to cover a tremendous amount of ground daily.

I shall not be able to give you anything in the way of strategic plans, for I'm not that close to the Supreme Command. I'm simply guarding Hitler's life, one among many. If any important information should come my way, you have my promise to send it to you, but by and large my notes will be concerned with roadside incidents and here is one of them.

It was on the day of the break-through at Sedan. The army was already deep in Belgium and there was little danger in frontier towns. The English bombers stayed on their side of the Channel. If they had known how little protection we had in the way of flak artillery, they would have blasted our supply lines to bits.

Part of Hitler's technique, you know, is to make special appearances, at various historical points, as liberator of territories that were once German. This he did in the case of Belgian frontier towns of Eupen and Malmedy, which have a large German population and belonged to the German Rhineland before 1918. On this particular day Hitler was to speak at noon, in the market square at Eupen, and welcome the town's re-entry into the Reich. For propaganda purposes a large crowd was required to greet Hitler, and the preceding day we were busy checking up on all persons to be admitted to the square. Early in the morning three companies of the Schutzstaffel entered the buildings surrounding the square to guard against potential bomb-throwers or sharpshooters.

Shortly before noon, all was in readiness for Hitler's appearance. A selected assemblage of local inhabitants was present, with many Gestapo men mixed in with them. The surrounding roof tops were occupied by S. S. men. The Burgomaster waited anxiously and a delegation of school girls in white, with bouquets of flowers, was also ready for the occasion.

At noon Hitler, in the open Benz car used for such ceremonies, drove into the square. Everyone heiled and he alighted from his car. He shook hands with the Burgomaster who carefully recited a prepared address of welcome. Hitler then expressed his joy in accepting the allegiance of this ancient German territory and proclaimed the indissoluble re-incorporation of Eupen into the Third Reich.

After Hitler's speech, a school girl of about ten was led forward by the Burgomaster. She also recited a welcome to the Fuehrer and presented him with a bouquet of flowers. Hitler patted the child on the head and asked a question. Evidently she was not prepared for this and did not know what to do. Then, without speaking, she snatched a chain with an ebony cross from around her neck and thrust it into Hitler's hand.

Hitler certainly had not expected this. He could not offend the highly religious populace of Eupen by refusing the gift, nor could he accept it, for that would call for a few words anent its significance. This would not be in accord with Nazi pagan philosophy.

But the Fuehrer was saved from his predicament by yet another unscheduled event. A motorcycle dispatch rider came tearing around a corner into the square. He leaped from the cycle and ran forward with a dispatch which he gave to General Jodl, who then passed it to Hitler.

Later on, I learned that it brought news of the piercing of the Maginot Extension at Sedan and said that German divisions were pouring across the Meuse.

A few moments later we were tearing southward along the road. Hitler wanted to reach the front to get immediate knowledge of what was going on. As a vanguard, six motorcycles were clearing the road ahead. They were followed by an army staff car, then a Gestapo automobile. Next came the armored Mercedes used by Hitler for his travels and driven by his personal chauffeur, slim Heinrich Kempka. Hitler's army aide, Major Engel, sat beside the driver, while the rear seat was occupied by Hitler and General Jodl. Another Gestapo automobile followed and the rear of the motorcade was made up of various staff cars.

Less than three hours after leaving Eupen, we crossed the border into the Grand Duchy of Luxembourg, now under German occupation. After passing through Wiltz we ran into a long line of supply trucks. Our motorcycle vanguard kept signaling the heavy army vehicles to one side of the road to let us pass, but even so our progress was slowed down. Much of the time we were hemmed in between sputtering motorcycles and roaring trucks. It was probably because of this bedlam that we were not aware of what was going on above us.

It was only when a captain of a flak crew barred the road some distance in front of us and a truck with a flak gun pulled up ready for action that we turned our glances toward the sky. I saw three large specks, undoubtedly enemy bombers, heading toward the supply column. I had no field glasses and from the distance I was unable to make out their nationality. We later learned that they were British.

Before the flak guns began their staccato bark the first stick of bombs came down. The aim was none too good. The bombs exploded in a field near the road, causing no damage. But one burst so close to the big Mercedes that the car swerved under the force of the concussion. Kempka tried to keep clear of a big munitions truck with the result that the Mercedes left the road and toppled on one side in the ditch.

Moments of confusion followed. The flak guns started spitting shrapnel but except for the gun crews no one paid the slightest attention to the bombers. Everyone rushed toward the overturned car. The door was jammed. A window was lowered from the inside and Jodl crawled out, followed by Hitler. Neither was scratched.

Hitler was pale. He looked up to the sky where the bombers, their crews unaware of the big game they had so narrowly missed, were speeding westward. I noticed the Fuehrer's right hand. It was clutching the ebony cross that he had received a few hours earlier. Then I heard him say to Jodl, "A little girl in Eupen has rendered Germany a great service."

I can add little to these facts and reality is bad enough without venturing into the abstract. Hitler has a brilliant and quick-acting mind and we all know that he is an accomplished actor. Of late he seems to have developed a mild streak of megalomania that may increase if his present military successes continue. He is acquiring a sort of Napoleonic complex. But thus far Hitler has given no consideration to religion. His public appeals to God are just part of his play acting. He has permitted Rosenberg to toy with the old Teutonic mythology as an experiment in religion which is a negation of the Christian concept of God, but he has taken great care never to endorse it.

The scene beside the overturned car made me wonder. On the surface it appears absurd, but I cannot forget the strange gleam in Hitler's eyes. His reference to the service rendered Germany by the little girl from Eupen was, of course, an expression of his megalomania. But there may be much more in it than just that. If I understand Hitler, he is quite capable of talking himself into the belief that he has been selected as God's tool on earth. If this develops into an obsession with him, then God help us all. And I include your side of the world, too.

By the time this reaches you, no doubt you will be fully informed on military developments thus far and so I will not bother with them here. I shall watch for developments of particular interest and keep you advised. In the meantime, good luck.

In warm friendship,
MANFRED.

As we had predicted, the French under General Weygand were unable to break through the German ring of steel enveloping the Allied armies trapped in the great Flanders pocket. Wishful thinkers insisted that Weygand would launch a powerful counter-offensive at any moment, but the brutal facts were inescapable, and I so stated, despite criticism. Events soon bore out my contention.

After the Flanders victory, the world was speculating on what Hitler would do next. Nazi propagandists filled the air waves with talk of an invasion of England. The world, dumbfounded by the tremendous losses in Flanders, felt that such an invasion was most probable. It was well known that England had lost practically all her available war equipment in Europe and that except for her navy and small air force, her home shores were virtually defenseless. There was even little hope that successful defensive action could be carried out by the British fleet in the narrow waters of the Channel.

Van Narvig kept insisting that the German propaganda activity was a bluff.

"When the Nazis keep quiet," he said, "that only means they are preparing to strike."

"But England has lost her means of defense," I pointed out.

Despite the truth of this, van Narvig clung to his opinion.

"I've seen enough of Hitler," he said, "to be able to follow his reasoning. He has a continental mind. He has set out to conquer Europe and so long as there remains an undefeated continental army his mind is not at ease. He has promised the German people to avenge Versailles. France symbolizes Versailles. England, on the other hand, is an island and Hitler is vague on the subject of islands. He has never been to sea and the thought of it frightens him. He will finish off France, counting on making a profitable peace with the British at the expense of the French."

"That's where Hitler will go wrong," I countered. "The British will never make peace with Germany now."

"They'd be fools if they did and would lose their empire," van Narvig agreed.

But we had no facts to indicate which way Germany would turn until June 1, 1940, when van Narvig came into my office thrilled with the clarity of the radio reception the night before and with the answers to our questions neatly decoded.

"All German armies on the western front are regrouping along the Aisne and Somme rivers," he said. "It is obviously going to be France."

"What are the chances for the French, do you suppose?" I asked.

"Place all your bets on Germany at any odds," he replied.

"I don't care to make money that way," I snapped. "Besides, I still hope the French will rise as they did in 1871."*

*Williams refers to the manner in which the French people rose to the defense of their country during the Franco-Prussian War, after the fall of the Third Empire and the approach of the enemy to the gates of Paris.

"Did it do them any good?" he asked, raising his eyebrows.

At times van Narvig could be most irritating. He was a realist who discounted all emotionalism when considering world affairs. He loved the phrase about being from Missouri, although his own stay in that state had been of very short duration.

"I know Weygand," I insisted. "He's a great general."

"That may be so," he replied, "but I can tell you this—the greatest leader in the world cannot win if he lacks the means with which to fight.

"When Hitler launched his campaign three weeks ago he had the Dutch, the Belgians, the British and the French against him. Today the Dutch and the Belgians are out of it completely. The British have managed to save a large part of their army at the price of all their war material. The French have lost one-half of their field army and about two-thirds of their equipment. Hitler's losses, except in the air, have been negligible. The answer should be obvious."

A few days later the German blitz armies broke across the Somme and headed for Paris. Before the new Nazi drive had advanced very far we received another report from overseas— our first from Wolfgang. It was written in the same old-style Russian as was used by Manfred and had been transmitted by Gottlieb, enclosed in a plain white envelope addressed with a soft lead pencil. Wolfgang wrote:

Dear Willy:

While you were still here we all were so enthusiastic over our enterprise. I hoped to be a great help. Alas, two months have passed and I haven't been able to contribute a thing. It is very galling. With Hitler at the front, the spotlight has shifted to his headquarters and we here have little information.

Linda came from Berlin to visit Clara and one day the two drove over here under some pretext. Linda told me that you are safely back in America and I am glad of it. You got out in the nick of time.

I have something to tell you which may be of consequence. Last week Ribbentrop arrived from Hitler's headquarters. A day later who should arrive in all secrecy but Ciano. In contrast to his manner at their last personal meeting—at the inn, Zum Weissen Rössl—Ciano acted this time in rather meek fashion. Apparently Hitler's victories have not failed to make their impression in Rome.

Briefly, Mussolini intends to declare war on France and England the moment the German army enters Paris. He is seeking an easy "victory" but perhaps it will not be so easy after all. Some previous interchange must have taken place recently between Rome and Berlin, for Ciano came expressly to find out what his father-in-law could expect in return for his active participation in the war. He was disappointed when Ribbentrop told him that Germany was really not in need of Italian help and could finish the job she had started by herself. Ribbentrop added that if Italy did enter the war actively, Germany would have no objections, but that Italy must drive her own bargain at the peace conference. Of course, he added, Germany would support Italian claims wherever possible. On the other hand, Ribbentrop said, if Italy prefers to preserve her present useful state of non-belligerency Germany will be generous at the peace conference but could make no specific advance commitments. This was the best that Ciano could get.

My guess is that Mussolini will declare war because he does not fully trust Hitler and wants to be present at the peace conference as an active participant in order to press his own claims.

That is all I have for the present, but I hope to have more shortly.

Your friend,
WOLFGANG.

CHAPTER 10

THE INFORMATION RECEIVED from Wolfgang was incorporated into a radio broadcast on June 7, 1940, in which I said: "A report just received by me claims that Mussolini is about to throw Italy into the fray at any moment . . . " On June 10, the actual declaration came, against both France and Great Britain. On June 14, the victorious German army entered Paris. It looked very bad for the French but I still was convinced that they would continue the war—from Africa, if Hitler's forces occupied all of continental France.

But I was wrong. In the early afternoon of June 15, van Narvig telephoned me at my home in Greenwich. His voice shook with excitement. He said,

"Hold on to your chair. Marshal Petain has just asked Generalissimo Franco of Spain to transmit to Hitler a request for an armistice."

I almost dropped the receiver. It was unbelievable. I insisted that van Narvig repeat his news. He did so, but I still found it hard to believe. The proud French would never do that, I told myself. Anything but that!

"It is impossible!" I shouted into the telephone. "France has an agreement with England not to conclude a separate peace. Why, only this morning [Premier Paul] Reynaud declared that France would fight on. Winston Churchill said the same thing."

"It doesn't matter what they said," van Narvig insisted. "I know that the two countries have an agreement. But agreement or no agreement, I just intercepted a message from the German military attaché in Madrid to Hitler's field headquarters announcing that Petain has asked for an armistice. I can't tell you any more about it because that is all I was able to get." He hung up, presumably to return to his listening post.

Here was a real scoop. It might easily turn out to be the biggest of the war. I was not on the air that night and the news was too hot to hold. I telephoned to Lowell Thomas, told him about it and said he could use it in his broadcast that evening. He refused to believe it at first but I told him he could quote me as his source and I would take the responsibility.

Two hours later I tuned in on Thomas' broadcast. He stated right off that Wythe Williams had just informed him that he had learned through channels of his own that Marshal Petain had asked Franco to transmit to Hitler a French request for an immediate armistice.

I was greatly relieved. Lowell had been a good sport, as usual. It was a tough story for him to handle, but it would have been hard to endure if the story had broken in the newspapers first.

The following morning the newspapers carried vehement official denials from Bordeaux and London that an armistice had been asked or was even contemplated. I became uneasy.

At noon van Narvig arrived at the office and I shoved the papers at him.

"I don't care how much they deny," he said. "We now have full details. Yesterday the French cabinet, on General Weygand's insistence, voted by thirteen to eleven in favor of an armistice. Paul Reynaud resigned the premiership in protest. Marshal Petain took over the office of premier, with Pierre Laval slated for the foreign ministry, and immediately asked Franco to arrange for an armistice."

I stared at him. The morning news had contained none of this. I telephoned to Washington and they knew nothing of it. They labeled the entire story a fake. I told van Narvig what Washington had said.

"Well," shrugged van Narvig, "the French cannot admit it before they have Hitler's acceptance, can they?"

That night, June 18, 1940, I went on the air and told of the defeat of France and the reorganization of the cabinet. Washington, London and Bordeaux reiterated their denials of the previous day. Madrid disclaimed all knowledge of such goings on. Even Berlin emphatically denied that there had been a request from the French for an armistice. Perhaps the unkindest cut of all came when my own station broadcast the official reports from the various capitals and denied my story completely.

But late that night, Marshal Petain broadcast to the French people. He told them that he had asked Franco to transmit to Hitler a request for an immediate cessation of hostilities—"as one soldier to another."

The following day a radio colleague, Gabriel Heatter, paid tribute to my "scoop," so I was content to believe that van Narvig and I had had the most sensational news beat of the year.

The following report was received several days later, but because it concerned information in regard to the armistice story, I should like to insert it at this point. It was the first personal contribution from Gottlieb and was written in Czech. It read:

Dear Willy:
I know the others have sent you letters reporting on developments because they all passed through my hands. Until now I was unable to come through with anything of my own. Berchtesgaden these days

is usually empty. The Fuehrer, as no doubt you know, is very busy elsewhere.

But, at last, there is something for me to write to you. I was among those detailed to meet Mussolini's train at the Brenner Pass and escort it to Munich.* There at the station was Hitler, waiting with Keitel, Jodl and Ribbentrop. Together with Mussolini came Ciano and Marshal Pietro Badoglio; also a swarm of minor officials. The meeting was called to reach an understanding on armistice terms with the French.

After elaborate greetings, the entire party left for the Fuehrerhaus. Happily, I know my way about the place and it was easy for me to find out what was going on. Also, the voices in the conference room reached such a pitch several times that if the windows had been open, the angry words of the conferees would have been heard by the entire street.

Official accounts of the conference maintain that it was conducted in "the spirit of friendship and deep understanding which are the basis of relations between the two allied countries." This, I can tell you, is a gross lie. The fact is that both Hitler and Mussolini were furious, one at the other, and nearly came to blows.

Mussolini first suggested that Germany and Italy conclude a mutual armistice with France as "behooved allies who have fought shoulder to shoulder in a common cause." Mussolini said that Italy would guarantee Germany's armistice terms, and vice versa. As it developed, it was this vice versa that Il Duce was really after. His proposed terms included the occupation by Italian troops of Tunisia, French Somaliland, Corsica and the French Mediterranean Coast, including the naval base of Toulon, and that all French warships in the Mediterranean should be interned in Italian ports.

It is apparent that Mussolini still is useful to Hitler, for the Fuehrer did not rage at these terms. He patiently explained, I am told, that he doubted very much that the French would accept terms of that nature. In fact, Hitler said, he feared that if pressed too hard the French might desperately carry the war to Africa. That situation, he said, would find Mussolini with his own fleet caught between the French and the British. He went on to say that although the terms to the French must be harsh, some shred of French honor must be preserved. If they were induced to sign an armistice which, on the face of things, saved their honor, it would later be possible to make gains step by step. After the French have been disarmed and committed, Hitler pointed out, what can they do?

*Premier Benito Mussolini visited Munich on June 20, 1940.

Hitler then insisted that a French armistice was imperative because it could then be used as a lever against the British. He contended that although Churchill was belligerently talking about total war, the British were realists, after all. If they were to continue the war alone, it would mean that they must relinquish their dominant world position and become a sort of appendage to the United States, inasmuch as they would be lost without American help on a large scale.

Hitler maintained that the United States must be kept out of the war, at least until the Axis Powers were in a proper position to talk terms to the United States. If the British were confronted with a French surrender, they would probably be induced to make a peace settlement at the expense of France. Then Mussolini could press his territorial claims and be certain of German support.

Mussolini, however, was not pleased and said so. He claimed that he could expect little from the British because his principal territorial acquisitions must come from the French, and he intended to have these acquisitions now, while he was holding the upper hand. He asked if, after all, Hitler would not insist on Alsace and Lorraine for himself?

At this Hitler grew quite angry and replied, pointedly, that Alsace and Lorraine were ancient German lands, whereas the territories which Mussolini was demanding had been colonized by the French and had, indeed, never been a part of Italy. Mussolini wanted Tunisia simply because a considerable number of Italians had emigrated there, and Somaliland because it would round out his East African Empire. These claims, Hitler shouted, could in no way be compared with Alsace and Lorraine.

It was at this time that the voices and tempers rose. At one point Hitler screamed that it was the German army which had conquered France, while the Italians had merely watched. Mussolini countered that it was the Italian threat which had held a major part of the British fleet in the Mediterranean and thus materially aided in the conquest of both Norway and France. Hitler shouted that it was the German people who had sacrificed for the sake of creating a great army, while the Italians led a comparatively easy life.

Ribbentrop, afraid of a break between the two dictators, proposed a compromise. He suggested that each country conclude a separate armistice with France. In this way each country could look out for its own best interests. The German-French armistice could be made conditional on the conclusion of an armistice between Italy and France. In this way, Mussolini would remain assured of German support.

This plan was finally adopted. Actually, as Hitler remarked to Ribbentrop after Mussolini's departure, Il Duce was anything but satisfied.

Hitler's opinion was that Mussolini had come to Munich to persuade the Germans to help him out. Of himself Mussolini would never dare to demand such terms of France.

This is all I have to tell you for the present. After Mussolini's departure, Hitler left immediately for the front in France. Before leaving he issued orders to ready the old railroad car in the Compiégne Forest where Foch received the German armistice negotiators in 1918. Evidently Hitler wants to dictate his own armistice terms at the same historical place.

One thing I should like to say. I am sorry that we have no leader in our little group. This circumstance leads each person to independent action. The result is a certain amount of confusion and the taking of unnecessary chances. For instance, Wolfgang, who is always impetuous, demanded that Clara permit him to leaf through some of the files at the Berghof. This is dangerous, and I shall speak to Clara about it. She can influence him at times.

After the conclusion of the armistice we all expect Hitler to return to the Berghof, and then you shall probably have a great deal of news from us.

Grüss Gott!
GOTTLIEB.

Unfortunately, Gottlieb's report did not reach us in time for me to broadcast Hitler's intention of dictating the armistice terms in the Forest of Compiegne. Naturally, we were anxious to be the first to announce the meeting place of the French and German delegations. It was in this connection that we made one of our greatest errors. Van Narvig had nothing definite to indicate the meeting place.

"This is the situation," he explained when we discussed the subject. "Hitler is returning from Munich. I have not the slightest idea over which route he is traveling. Neither do I know what rail lines in France could be used at the moment. I have been trying to catch signals on the wireless concerning the clearing of tracks. Since most of the telegraph wires in France are still down, such orders would be transmitted by wireless. Well, I caught part of a message some two hours ago. All I was able to get from it was that a special armored train traveling via Sedan should be rerouted to the south of Paris."

"That surely must be Hitler's train," I said. And it was, but the part of the message about rerouting the train south of Paris was what fooled us. We both felt that Hitler would stage a highly dramatic play at the armistice ceremony and we even considered the possibility of the meeting taking place at Compiegne. But Compiegne is north of Paris. The only likely place to the south we could think of was Versailles.

"And why not Versailles?" van Narvig asked. "It is where the last peace treaty was signed. Versailles is a hated symbol to Hitler. It would satisfy the Fuehrer's craving for revenge."

I agreed with him, especially as Versailles would certainly fit with the apparent destination of the train. We decided to state that the signing of the armistice would probably take place in the Palace of Versailles.

We learned too late that Hitler's train had circled all around Paris and reached Compiegne from the south because the direct northern tracks could not be used at the time.

We expected that Hitler then would return to Berchtesgaden and map his campaign against England. This, we felt sure, would bring us further important news from our friends at the Berghof. Instead, the next thing to reach us was a second report from Manfred of an entirely different nature. This is what he wrote.

Dear Willy:

I wish I were back in Berlin. I have looked at so many battlefields and traveled countless miles. When I was assigned to Hitler's special Gestapo bodyguard, I had no idea of his tremendous desire to see and hear everything. Ever since the fall of France my special detail with the Fuehrer's staff has meant a mad chase from one French town to another.

Hitler has developed another mania. This time, of all things, churches. Whenever he comes to a large town his first visit is to the local cathedral where he studies the architecture and carefully scrutinizes the altar and the crypt. He paid special attention to the cathedrals in Reims, Chartres, Verdun, Nancy, Metz and Strassbourg, devoting almost an entire day to each of them. Just what his intentions are with regard to the churches, none of us knows.

I shall not take time to give you an account of our trip to Munich, or a description of the signing of the Armistice. The American correspondent, William Shirer, broadcast the entire proceedings to America, straight from the spot. But I shall tell you something that I consider highly significant in view of later developments. That was our visit to Les Invalides, Napoleon's tomb in Paris.

Thirty-six of us went in with Hitler. First the atmosphere impressed itself on us, but presently some commenced talking. Hitler silenced them with a curt gesture. When we followed him to the railing, Hitler waved us back. Then he ordered everybody to leave, saying that he wished to remain alone. We of the Gestapo were in a spot, for we are under strict orders from Himmler never to let Hitler out of sight. However, we solved the problem. As the others left in accordance with the Fuehrer's demand, three of us, including myself, hid behind columns. From where I stood I could see Hitler plainly.

He stepped very close to Napoleon's sarcophagus and stared in silence at it for a long time. Then I saw his lips begin to move. None of us three could hear what he was saying, for we were all out of earshot. At times he would pause and seem to be listening, and then he would talk again. This continued for about thirty minutes. Then Hitler turned abruptly and walked out with measured steps, without casting a glance behind. His expression was one of supreme satisfaction.

Later that night I heard more about this, when Hitler believed himself alone with General Jodl, who, in the course of the French campaign, has become the Fuehrer's most intimate confidant. I do not run much in the way of risk by this sort of spying, for we are under orders from Himmler to report on everything that happens, including conversations with some of the Reich's highest functionaries.

Hitler told Jodl, in all seriousness, that he had communed with Napoleon's spirit. The spirit had assured the Fuehrer that he was carrying on Napoleon's mission and the spirit was most happy because such a worthy successor had undertaken the great task. According to what Hitler told Jodl, the spirit had said that England had been Europe's scourge for centuries. All Europe must be united and England must be removed, or at least incapacitated, from any participation in European affairs. Since Russia had been another to interfere with the solidarity among European nations, she must be eliminated from the affairs of western Europe and driven back into Asia. If this were not done, Russian barbarism would engulf European civilization.

The spirit had also said that the Church was another factor that had prevented the unification of Europe, or rather, the various conflicting creeds and sects had done it. The Church, in itself, was good as a pillar of the State, as conducted in the days of the Roman Empire. But there would have to be one church for all Europe and it must be placed in the service of the State. The question of the Church must be handled, however, with great discretion. He, Napoleon, had mishandled it in his lifetime, becoming embroiled with the Church of Rome before solidifying his empire. The spirit counseled that until Hitler's political task is completed he must temporize with the Vatican. Then, after he has consolidated his victories, Hitler must bring the Church of Rome under the State as the only recognized Church or, if the Vatican refuses, destroy it and erect another all-embracing Church in its stead.

While Hitler was relating this to Jodl, the general was intent and silent, nor did he express any opinion after Hitler had finished with his weird story. Jodl is becoming more and more the real brain behind the German military machine, but he keeps strictly to military matters and wants no connection with politics. Perhaps that is why Hitler trusts him more than any of the others.

Perhaps you will laugh at this whole story, but I just cannot look at it in the way of a joke. No doubt all these questions have been brewing in Hitler's mind for some time and he may have invented this story as a means of communicating his own ideas to his followers. On the other hand, a man of Hitler's peculiar mentality could easily convince himself that such a spiritual communication actually took place. Watching Hitler as I did in Les Invalides, I am rather inclined to the second theory. This is dangerous, for Hitler may start communication with God at any time that he talks himself into such a state.

When you will hear next from me I cannot say, for I have not the faintest idea of our future destinations.

In warm friendship,
MANFRED.

CHAPTER 11

WITH THE SIGNING of the armistice and cessation of hostilities our pick-up of military news became sparse. Hitler's Field Headquarters on the Western Front was abolished and its functions taken over by the staff of the army of occupation under General Stuelpnagel. With military telegraph and telephone lines largely restored to service, the use of the wireless was restricted.

Nevertheless, van Narvig spent considerable time at our listening post because we were expecting Hitler to launch an offensive against England and a clean-up action in the west. The code, now that the military had settled down, was practically useless.

About this time, van Narvig revived his connection with Motett and Tugendwald of the New York Gestapo. One day van Narvig received a telephone call from Motett, informing him that "the person in full charge of certain matters" had arrived in New York and was waiting for the Homburg letter. The next morning van Narvig called at the German Library of Information. From there he was taken across the hall to the German Consulate General where he met a man whom he recognized instantly.

Captain Fritz Wiedemann had been Adolf Hitler's company commander in the old World War days. It has been said that Wiedemann then held a very low opinion of Corporal Hitler. If this was the case, Captain Wiedemann has completely revised that opinion.

Officially, Fritz Wiedemann was German Consul General in San Francisco and subordinate to the Reich Ambassador in Washington. Actually, Wiedemann took no orders from Washington. He was the *Landesgruppenleiter* for Gauleiter Ernst Wilhelm Bohle's Auslandsgau, or Foreign Province, which, bereft of its diplomatic trimmings, simply meant the Nazi Fifth Column in the United States. Nor was this all. As we discovered later, Wiedemann was also the key man of the Gestapo organization in this country.

Van Narvig, forestalling an introduction, walked up to Wiedemann and said, "How do you do, Captain?"

Wiedemann was disconcerted for a moment, then he said, "I see that you know me."

"You have had considerable newspaper publicity," van Narvig assured him. "Who wouldn't know you?"

"I see," replied Wiedemann, shook hands with van Narvig and invited him to be seated. For a while the two discussed the news in France and Wiedemann praised the achievements of the German Army. Van Narvig observed that the path of conquest had been made relatively easy by the smooth work of fifth columnists. Wiedemann was silent at that. Eventually, however, he became voluble. He commented that a people given to social weaknesses and political rifts could not expect military victory. If the Germans had taken advantage of these conditions, it was the perfect right of a belligerent nation at war with another.

Presently Wiedemann asked, "I understand that by accident you have come in possession of an important document?"

Van Narvig assured him that he was ignorant of the contents of the envelope in question, but in view of the circumstances attending the case, he felt that it should be surrendered only to the proper person. With that, he handed it to Wiedemann, who quickly opened it and read the contents. Then, to van Narvig's complete surprise, he handed the letter back and said, "I'd like you to know what is in it."

The letter was signed, "Hitler," and began, "Dear Fritz." It merely stated that Parteigenosse* Friedrich Homburg was visiting the United States on a special mission and was to be extended all possible co-operation.

In retrieving the letter, Wiedemann remarked, "I hope that your scruples about delivering this letter to the proper person are fully satisfied."

"They are," van Narvig replied, but felt there was some ulterior motive behind Wiedemann's frankness, and soon discovered this to be the case.

"I presume that Herr Homburg entrusted you with a personal message in addition to this letter?" Wiedemann suggested.

"He did not, I'm sorry to say," replied van Narvig. "Perhaps he would have, had he suspected the situation he would soon face. As it was, he deposited the letter with me as just a precautionary measure."

Wiedemann then asked the circumstances of Homburg's removal from the ship at Kirkwall and asked, "Do you think that the British had advance information of Herr Homburg's real status?"

Van Narvig had expected the question and was ready for it.

*Party Member.

95

He had no intention of revealing the information received from Heinrich in Berlin. He merely answered, "I prefer not to formulate an opinion in this matter. All I can say is that it struck me as being rather odd that Herr Homburg should have been summoned even before the examination of other passengers got under way."

"Thank you," said Wiedemann. "That is precisely what I wanted to know."

"I should not like you to attach any special importance to my observations," van Narvig insisted. "It was merely an impression at the time of the occurrence."

"I understand," Wiedemann replied. He stood up extending his hand to van Narvig. "Would you object if Herr Tugendwald occasionally calls on you?"

This was precisely what van Narvig wanted. He assured Wiedemann that he could see no objection whatsoever.

It was about this time that van Narvig received an unsigned cablegram from Berchtesgaden. It read, "Eugen suffered a stroke and passed away. His will establishes you as chief beneficiary of his estate. This may prove satisfactory solution of your financial obligation. Consult with Klausmann on the matter."

Van Narvig was sure that Gottlieb had sent the message. I could not understand the financial reference in it.

Van Narvig explained. He had undertaken to establish in Switzerland a fund that any one of the group could draw on at any time in case he were forced to flee Germany. So far there had been nothing that he could do about it, but this estate of Eugen's might prove helpful.

"Who is Klausmann?" I wanted to know, never having heard the name mentioned before.

To my surprise van Narvig replied, "He's the chap who brought you some of my reports from Berchtesgaden."

I had intended asking about that tight-lipped, matter-of-fact individual, but in the rush of events I had completely forgotten him.

"What is his connection with all this?" I wanted to know.

"He makes frequent trips to Berchtesgaden," van Narvig told me. "Just what his actual status is I do not know. Gottlieb evidently trusts him and the fact that the reports come through proves that the trust is not misplaced. It's not our risk so much as that of the people over there."

"Can you get in touch with him?" I asked.

"I think I can," he said.

"How about pumping the man?" I suggested.

"I don't think it would take us very far. I suspect he is involved in an affair that would not please the Gestapo if it came out, and he has his own troubles to take care of," van Narvig answered.

Before we had time to get in touch with Klausmann, we received our first report from Clara, who wrote in shorthand, the same Roller method that Linda used. This time, however, van Narvig had some trouble with it. Throughout the correspondence, which lasted more than two years, transcribing Linda's messages was always easier than with Clara's. When finally deciphered, the letter read:

Dear Willy:

I hope you have not despaired of me. I have written nothing to you because as soon as you left Germany the Berghof became quite dull and uneventful. It has remained so with only two brief interruptions and it is about one of these that I write now.

Hitler came here for a two-day stay and it was immediately apparent that something unusual was about to happen. Then Wolfgang telephoned from Fuschl that Ribbentrop was on his way to the Berghof. There will be no report from Wolfgang on this, because he has given me his part of the story and I shall incorporate it in mine.

Ribbentrop was on vacation at Fuschl when Count Werner von der Schulenberg, our Ambassador to Russia, flew in.* He brought the startling news that Russia was about to move into Bessarabia. Actually, he was able to beat the march of events by just one day. The following morning came a message from our Minister in Bucharest advising that Russia had delivered an ultimatum to Rumania, and King Carol wanted to know if he would be supported by Germany and Italy. Hitler was already speeding toward Berchtesgaden and Ribbentrop

*On June 27, 1940.

came over immediately upon the Fuehrer's arrival for a personal consultation. By the ventilating system, which we worked out while you were still here, I was able to hear a good part of the conversation.

Hitler was in an ugly mood. When he heard that Moscow was demanding the northern half of Bukovina in addition to Bessarabia, he uttered some terrible diatribes aimed at Stalin. He accused the Moscow dictator of every known crime under the sun and called him a low, vile person. He said that Stalin was a mass murderer and deserved to be murdered himself. This, to give you an idea, was the mildest of his accusations.

Ribbentrop was in a quandary, however, for the pact which he had signed in Moscow contained a specific clause by which the signatories agreed to consult each other in all matters where their mutual interests were concerned. But Stalin was not consulted before the invasion of Norway, Hitler's generals contending that Russia could have no interest in Norway. Now, apparently, Stalin felt that Germany had no interest in Bessarabia, although it was orally agreed in September of last year that Russia had a sort of priority claim on Bessarabia. But it was understood then that the matter would be settled at the proper time and under the observance of orderly procedure. And now Moscow was demanding the surrender of Rumanian territories within forty-eight hours.

Hitler refused to listen to Ribbentrop's explanations and accused Stalin of taking advantage of Germany's embarrassment. He telephoned to Himmler in Berlin and ordered that all Russian spies were to be ferretted out and hanged. He insisted that Stalin must know that the larger part of the German Army in France and the Low Countries had been given extended leaves to recuperate from the strain of the Western campaign. It would be impossible to prepare any sizable section of the army for immediate action in the East in less than two weeks and Hitler insisted that Stalin must have been informed of this. Germany, he screamed, is overrun by Russian spies.

Presently, Hitler subsided and listened to Ribbentrop's cold logic. The Foreign Minister maintained that Russian occupation of Bessarabia had been a foregone conclusion and that the additional demand for a part of Bukovina meant little. After all, he argued, it was merely a small strip of land inhabited principally by Jews. He insisted that it was not reasonable to subject Germany's relations with the Soviets to a new strain. His advice was to permit the Russians to take just so much and let them know this would be the limit, so far as Germany was concerned.

Hitler retorted that Ribbentrop's explanations were far too simple.

Didn't he realize, Hitler asked, that if Russia were allowed to fortify northern Bukovina it would make her flanking of the Rumanian position in Moldavia so much easier, in the event that Stalin would later press into the Balkans? Russia would be that much closer to the Rumanian oil fields on which any future successful operations of the German armies depended. These oil properties belong largely to English capitalists and Hitler is convinced that the British were actually behind this Russian move, although Moscow would never admit it.

It was finally decided that nothing could really be done about the situation. Ribbentrop was ordered to inform Moscow that Germany would stand aside, but that the line was now drawn and must not be transgressed. Bucharest will be advised to submit to the Russian ultimatum. Germany is quite willing to consider the protection of Rumania against further Russian aggression, but not until Rumania has formally relinquished the present British guarantee of her territories.

This is the essence of the discussions. While all was quiet here, I had a chance to slip across to Switzerland and spend a week with my son. He is enthusiastic about the many fine things he hopes soon to see in America. You really shouldn't have told him so much, he is such an impressionable child. Neither should you have pampered him so much, but just the same I am grateful. I send you my most sincere regards.

CLARA.

Since Clara's report reached us only after the Russian occupation of Bessarabia, it did not contribute greatly to my broadcasts. However, it was interesting to speculate on the length of time it might require to break the Soviet-German pact.

A few days later we received the following brief report from Manfred:

Dear Willy:

This is merely to acquaint you with a development that may contain significant implications for the future. No doubt you already know that the British fleet has destroyed, or at least seriously damaged, a considerable portion of the French fleet based at Oran.

Hitler, his generals, and the entire Nazi clique, are jubilant. You may have heard Goebbels calling this an act of treachery by the British against a former ally who did his best to carry the burden of the war alone while England continued to make money in the world markets. This is just the official propaganda version.

Actually, everyone here is extremely gratified. During the discussion of the armistice terms among Hitler's generals and admirals the French fleet was a rather controversial subject. The final clause that went into the armistice draft, gave the French permission to retain their warships provided they would be completely demobilized in whatever French ports they happened to be. The reason for this was that Mussolini, reasoning that the French fleet for the most part was in the Mediterranean, demanded that the fleet be given to him. Admiral [Erich] Raeder contended that he could easily understand that French sailors, rather than turn over their ships to the Italians, whom they despise, would join the British navy. In any case, none of the Nazis saw reason for adding to the strength of either the British or the Italian navy.

Raeder declined to take over the French fleet himself, saying that he had not enough German crews to man the ships and, furthermore, if he did, it would require at least one year to familiarize the German sailors with the radically different mechanism of the French ships.

As for the British action, General Jodl expressed the feeling prevailing among the military when he said that the British have actually rendered the Germans a great service, in more ways than one. Mussolini will cease his demands for the fleet, which will be of no use to him now, and the Germans may cease to worry about a possible defection of the French ships to the British fleet. On the contrary, French sailors are now incensed against the British, and Germany is in an excellent position to exploit that feeling among the French people to Germany's own advantage.

There is nothing more to write about, this time.

In warm friendship,
MANFRED.

Shortly after this we received an excellent, informative report from Linda. She wrote:

Dear Willy:

I have quite a surprise for you this time. I am now in Paris, living at the Palace of St. Germain which has become, overnight, Goering's French headquarters. I have been here nearly two weeks. Hermann is living like a viceroy. The champagne is flowing and the larder is stocked with the best of French foods. But of that, later.

At the moment, you will be interested in a new scheme that is being plotted by Pierre Laval and Goering. Laval comes up from Vichy at frequent intervals, and he and Goering spend a great deal of time conferring in seclusion.

Goering is of the opinion that France, instead of Italy, should be the junior Axis partner. For the moment at least, his opinion has found appeal in Hitler's eyes. Hitler has allowed Goering to try out the scheme, but to be careful in what he undertakes. Laval, who entertains ambitions of becoming the French Hitler, is more enthusiastic. He is in fact convinced that Germany has already won the war and will be able to dictate European politics for a long time to come. He does not believe that England has a chance. Besides, as you probably know, he hates the British.

Laval's idea is to give territorial concessions to Germany and in exchange receive greater concessions at the expense of England and Belgium. According to the scheme being concocted by Goering and Laval, the French-speaking half of Belgium is to be given to France in exchange for Alsace and Lorraine which have actually already been returned to Germany, although nothing is mentioned of this trans-action officially for fear of possible rioting among the French people. The Flemish-speaking part of Belgium is to be combined with Holland as a new state allied with Germany and ruled by the Belgian King Leopold, although I am quite sure that Leopold has been told nothing so far and suspects nothing of the intrigue in which he is to be prominently involved. Before all this can be accomplished, however, there are certain difficulties to be overcome.

One of these is Marshal Petain and to this end Laval has ingratiated himself with the old soldier. However, Petain is still under the influence of his army men, among them General Weygand, and there seems to be quite a conflict between the former army command and Laval as to who will hold the power in Nazi France.

Petain and his generals also are convinced that Germany has won the war. But they insist on a strict army dictatorship in post-war France, while Laval is aiming for a political dictatorship on the Hitler model, with himself as chief and the army taking his orders.

Laval insists that the change-over must be quickly accomplished before the French people in general realize what is happening. And you would know what I mean if you could see them. They are still stunned from the shock of such a rapid defeat and still unaware of what has really occurred. Nevertheless, Laval will have difficulty in trying to handle the French, for among his own people he has no prestige and he must depend on the Germans to see him through.

Goering's stand in this is none too clear. He is, I know, in favor of the Laval scheme, but he has not yet committed himself definitely. He seems to delay deliberately. This is about all that I can tell you now of any political plotting under way.

I should like to tell you now what the Nazis are doing in France and how France is receiving them.

First of all Goering, as soon as he installed himself at St. Germain, instituted a series of nightly banquets—I should almost call them orgies —which are still going on. He, himself, however, after attending the dinner, leaves his guests to their own brand of libertine entertainment and retires to a large study where he confers on political developments, either with Laval or others.

In Germany Goering was careful not to reveal his great wealth and there was a certain amount of restraint to his parties. They were really considered state affairs. In Paris he has dropped all pretense. There is a sumptuousness to all these goings-on that would shock the good burghers of Germany if they knew about them. Not only Goering is indulging in these extravaganzas. I am told that it is the same at other places in Paris wherever dignitaries of our Nazi hierarchy have installed themselves. It is truly a madhouse.

Having been reared in a severe atmosphere, it is difficult for me to understand the French, but quite simple to grasp why their country fell so easily before the Germans. I do not refer to the plain people— peasants, workers, tradesmen. They act normally, as any hard-working German would under similar circumstances. Of course you can see their hatred for us, despite their surface manners. They avoid contact with the Germans as much as possible and when it becomes necessary to speak to a German, especially a soldier, they are painfully polite. They most definitely reject any idea of fraternizing.

But when one observes the real rulers of France, it is easy to see why their country collapsed. I refer to the monied people or those with so-called influence—the politicians, the industrialists, the hangers-on, the decadent intellectuals. Long before France was invaded, I am positive that the heart of France had died and was rotting under their rule. If this is any real example of democracy, then Hitler was right when he said that democracies are rotten and fat and soft and incapable of resistance. I trust, from what you have told me, that your America is different from this. If it wants to survive as a free country, it must be.

French society is bowing to Goering and Bohle, and to Otto Abetz, who is slated to head the Nazi regime in occupied France. Apparently their country means nothing to them. These formerly influential citizens are primarily concerned with the preservation of their personal fortunes and the easy way of life to which they have become accustomed. They seem to believe that by courting the conquerors they will be permitted to retain their mines and industries, their factories and landed estates, but they have no idea of how the Nazi machine operates. They are convinced that France will become a German ally and they are already preparing for the future when they hope to become the ruling class of a Nazi France. Poor fools!

Have you ever heard of Jean Luchaire? I understand he was a wealthy man before the war with considerable influence in the Paris press. His daughter Corinne, who is twenty and very attractive, had been acting in French films with some success. We had hardly been here two weeks when she became known quite openly as Otto Abetz's mistress. He has a wife and two children in Berlin, but that scarcely makes a difference. Young as she is, Corinne is quite outspoken in her ambitions. She expects to be first lady of Paris, and her salon is already a favorite meeting place for ranking members of the Nazi staff and their French friends. Frenchmen who seek favors and position under the occupation regime are bowing to Corinne and through her are introduced to the right men among the Nazis.

It is like an old court scene of the days of Marie Antoinette. Even Corinne's father has already taken advantage of his daughter's new position and has been installed by Abetz as chief editor of *Le Matin* and *Le Nouveau Temps* which he has promised to make the chief advocates of Nazi-French collaboration. In addition to this, he will retain his personal fortune, which is considerable.

Luchaire is just one of many. Among the others are Bonnet, Doriot and Deat.* The list is too long for me to give to you.

But I am sure that you, too, can see the real reasons for France's fall. German military might was only part of the tragedy.

May I also add that our influential Nazis can have almost any woman in Parisian society, provided the fortune of her husband, or her father, or her real lover, is assured.

This new society is what makes up the parties at St. Germain. They drink the choicest champagne and feast on the delicacies that the people of France are denied. French money, you know, has virtually ceased to have any purchasing power. Occupation marks, which have been issued in great volume, have become the real currency and you must have twenty French francs for one mark. And this is only the beginning. The only French securities of value are stocks and shares in French industrial enterprises. They belong to the wealthy, who change them into marks and continue to ride the merry whirl to which they were accustomed before the invasion. Of course, the time

*Georges Bonnet, French Foreign Minister at the time of the Munich surrender of Czechoslovakia; Jacques Doriot, former Communist leader and now one of the leading collaborationists; Marcel Deat, former leader of the French Neo-Socialists, a group which opposed the policies of Leon Blum, Socialist Premier. Deat now is second only to Laval in collaborationist circles and principal pro-Nazi spokesman in the Paris press.

will come when their securities will be gone and then Germans will really control French economic life. But the French are bringing it on themselves.

I shall now go on a shopping tour for silk dresses and stockings, perfumes and other feminine fancies that I have not seen for years in Germany. It is selfish, I know, but if I do not buy them someone else will. At first the army clamped down on almost everything, but as soon as the politicians from Berlin moved in the restrictions were lifted. For me it is a chance that will not come again and under the circumstances it would be rather foolish to display idealism, especially as I expect soon to be back at Karin Hall and the old routine. Meanwhile, my very best to you.

Affectionately,
LINDA.

CHAPTER 12

LINDA INCLUDED in her report the latest monthly figures on German aircraft production. These figures aroused great interest in my audience when I broadcast them and I received innumerable letters asking for the source of my figures.*

In analyzing Linda's report on Goering's dealings with Laval, it was evident to us that she had omitted, or had not known, certain information that would link the entire story together. The information sent by Linda was not much good in its present state, but before another week passed, a fresh report from Manfred arrived and this one contained all the missing links. It read:

Dear Willy:

Hitler decided to visit Paris another time and I had to go along again. In one way it was fortunate. While spending an afternoon at

*Wythe Williams' broadcast of August 5, 1940, included the following passage: "I am in possession today of an interesting report on the subject of changes in present and potential air strength of the two sides in the conflict. The figures I shall give are all for the month of June. According to the same confidential source which gave me the correct figures at the end of May, the number of newly-manufactured aircraft turned over by German plants to the air command of Hermann Goering, totaled 3,820, which is 140 planes below the record May figure. Of these, 420 were long-range bombers, 880 dive bombers, 560 pursuit planes, 740 combat planes, 290 combination combat and bombing planes (Kampfjadgflugzeuge) and 660 army transport planes. The remaining 270 planes were for auxiliary services. The disproportionately large number of newly-constructed dive bombers is highly significant, considering the impending air blitz against England."

St. Germain I had an opportunity to talk with Linda. She told me what she had written you concerning the Goering-Laval situation. She also said that the whole picture was not quite clear to her and I believe that I can clear it up for you now.

It is like this. Last year the Army conquered Poland but had to turn the situation there over to the Party, meaning the Gestapo. As you know, in many matters the two do not agree. The Army considers the Gestapo a pack of animals, and in spite of being one of their number, so do I. In Poland, the Gestapo insisted that the proximity of Russia held dangers of Communist infiltration and took measures in the conquered country with which the Army did not agree. You know well what occurred in Poland.

Now the Army has conquered France and again the Gestapo wanted to take charge. This time, however, the Army refused to yield. Goering sided with the Army and the Gestapo was told to keep out.

The difference of opinion between the Army and the Party as to the future conduct of the war is considerable. England presents a new and serious problem, since she is an island and the Army is unaccustomed to fighting against an island. With this in view, the Army wishes to consider defeated France as an ally. Therefore it wants peace with France at the expense of England's colonial possessions, and it cannot achieve this aim without French co-operation. That is why Goering is dealing with Laval.

The Party, however, meaning Hess and, incidentally, Himmler, has a political problem to solve. It contends that the only way to a complete Nazification of Europe is through the destruction of Russian Bolshevism. The Party looks upon the Army as a means to that end. Therefore, the Party wants peace with England at the expense of France.

Hitler is between the two. Of course, since he is more accessible to Party men, he favors them. While he has agreed to negotiations between Goering and Laval and encourages them in a way, he looks the other way while an attempt to cross the Reichsmarshal is made by the Party machine.

A secret pilgrimage has recently been made by Hess to Madrid, and other party leaders have gone there openly, ostensibly to cement friendship between the Nazis and the Spanish Falange leaders, notably Ramon Serrano Suner,* Spanish Minister of the Interior and brother-in-law to General Franco. Their actual purpose, however, is to reach

*Ramon Serrano Suner, later Spanish Foreign Minister, was ousted from this post by Franco on September 3, 1942.

directly the British appeasers of the Chamberlain, Viscount Halifax and Sir Samuel Hoare group.

Madrid was selected because Sir Samuel is British Ambassador to Spain. Through Baron von Stohrer, our ambassador in Madrid and a Party man, attempts are being made to sound out the British. General Franco of course will be pleased to negotiate because then both sides would look upon him benevolently. Recently, there have been rumors of undercover peace negotiations with England, which indicate why Goering is prevented from completing any agreement with Laval.

More later if I can get it.

In warm friendship,
MANFRED.

The reports from Linda and Manfred alarmed us for they revealed a trend in Nazi designs that contained serious implications. We felt the situation serious enough to publicize it widely over the air and the reactions to the stories were incredible. From London, within three days, came a full disavowal of intentions to negotiate with the Nazis. A few days later Neville Chamberlain, speaking for himself and the appeaser group formerly associated with him, and specifically mentioning Sir Samuel Hoare, issued a lengthy declaration that he and his collaborators did not dream of listening to any advances on Hitler's part. But he failed to deny that such advances had been attempted.

It did not take long for us to get the reaction of the Nazi leaders to this rebuff. It came in the form of a report from Clara that was lengthier than usual. She wrote:

Dear Willy:
After more than three months of relative quiet, Berchtesgaden has become the nerve center of continental Europe. You will notice the change in my phraseology. Before it was just Germany and her Lebensraum, now it has become Europe. Drunk with victories in France and with French champagne, the more enthusiastic Nazis are already boasting of a future that will make Berchtesgaden the nerve center of the world. The appetite grows with the meal.

They are all here again, parading their decorations. Hitler has not only created a dozen new field marshals, but also hundreds of new generals. Everyone shared in the victory spoils, even the plain people whose food ration was increased. Thousands of noncommissioned officers and even men from the ranks have been given commissions.

Hitler's promised victory has been won, but so far as I can see it has not brought peace any nearer. On the contrary. The Wehrmacht is to be still further increased in size. I heard General Jodl speak of at least sixty new divisions. Against whom?

The other day I had a chat with Colonel Wartenburg—he has been promoted like all the others. He remembers you quite well. He asked if I had heard from you and I said that you had not written. He expressed his sympathy that Eugen had to die just when the great victory, of which he had dreamed so many years, was at hand. He knows that you are the principal beneficiary in Eugen's will and wondered if you would come to claim the inheritance. I said that I had not the faintest idea. Gottlieb warned me not to mention the matter until Klausmann has arrived with your instructions.

Hitler returned here in something of a temper and has been rather irascible ever since. He apparently was pinning great hopes on an understanding with England and was confident that the British would be open to his peace overtures after the fall of France.

Manfred stopped here on his way to Berlin and told me about a struggle between the Wehrmacht and the Nazi Party. It is said to have caused considerable strife behind the scenes. The Army has apparently taken precedence over the Party now and remains in full charge in France and the Low Countries. The Gestapo must keep hands off. Goering, Keitel and von Brauchitsch have Hitler's ear, while Hess and Himmler are in something approaching disfavor. Jodl is meticulously neutral and keeps aloof from all politics, remaining devoted only to Hitler himself, who tells him everything. If something should happen to Hitler I wonder whether Jodl and not one of the others would take his place. Goering has returned from Paris, leaving Otto Abetz in full charge. It is mentioned that Pierre Laval will be invited soon to visit Berchtesgaden for a talk with Hitler.

For three days important meetings have been held at the Berghof. Present were Goering, Hess, Ribbentrop, von Brauchitsch, Halder, Keitel, Todt, Raeder, Milch and of course Jodl. The Italians were supposed to have someone here, but none of them arrived. The talk is that they are angry at having gotten so little out of the German victory in France and will attempt something of their own just to show us that they are still to be reckoned with. Probably in Africa. Jodl and Keitel are of the opinion that Mussolini's army will not get very far. As Jodl said, "Give me the Italian as an artist any time, but as an organizer and a warrior, keep him away from me."

These conferences have been going on almost constantly and you will understand that it has not always been possible for me to seclude myself downstairs safely. Others have access to the archive room, too. I took the precaution of placing some filing cabinets against the ventilator grille to prevent someone from stumbling upon the secret. Now when anyone comes in, I can always be pretending to be consulting the files and the notes I take do not seem out of place.

From the times when I was able to listen I have attempted to thread together some sort of outline of what was discussed. It is difficult for me at times to identify all the voices, so I am not quite certain in places which of the generals voiced the various views. I believe I have them identified correctly in most instances, however.

The discussions centered chiefly around plans of attack against England. The army had all sorts of vague ideas on the subject, but nothing concrete. I call them vague because they were predicated on certain factors that are still largely unavailable, such as a much stronger navy and sufficient transport shipping. I give you here the various opinions of some of those present.

Halder, Keitel and von Brauchitsch presented the problems of the army. It had undergone considerable strain, not so much from the enemy as from the driving tempo of the campaign. Almost no rest was had by the men between the Battle of Flanders and operations in Central France. The men were then given leaves and the majority have no doubt been fully rested by now. But the mechanized equipment was in need of repairs and general overhauling after the strain. In the first exultation over the victory and the expectation of a negotiated peace with England, insufficient attention was paid to renovation and repair of equipment. It would take at least eight weeks to have the various panzer units in condition for more serious fighting. There was also the question of the time of year. The actual sea crossing could be made within three to five hours, but embarkation of troops would have to take place inland in the mouths of rivers and canals. In view of these facts, one had to allow eight to ten hours for the Channel crossing. Each individual operation—and there would have to be many—had to be completed from start to finish under the cover of night. With all this considered, the army could not undertake an invasion attempt on a large scale until late in September.

Goering and Milch spoke for the air force. Including accidents, damage on the ground and deterioration under combat, the Luftwaffe had lost 3,200 military aircraft, including troop transport planes, during April, May and June. Total production had been considerably in excess of losses but more than one-third of the new output was in training planes. The fuel situation was favorable because huge supplies of oil and gasoline had been seized in France and the Low Countries. A successfu air offensive against England depended on two factors. First, the question of distance. British communications extending far inland must be destroyed. Stukas of the Junkers 88 type—90% of our dive bombers belong to this class—do not have the necessary range. The task would devolve largely on the level-flight bombers, which in turn demand fighter protection on a greater scale than ever before. The current Messerschmitts 109 and 110 do not possess the required range. The longer-range Messerschmitt 111 is still in the experimental stage.

Then there is the question of the British air force. The British had kept their fighter planes out of the French campaign except for the brief interlude at Dunkerque. They were conserving their air strength, probably in anticipation of a direct assault against England. It was one case where propaganda, which had so well publicized false German intentions, had boomeranged. Success in an invasion attempt, according to Goering and Milch, would be preconditioned on the destruction of the Royal Air Force. This in turn would depend entirely on the tactics which the British air command would adopt. If it accepted full-scale air battle to a decision, German superiority of numbers would assure success. But if the British chose to sacrifice ground installations rather than planes and kept withdrawing their air fields and fighter squadrons to the north, the short range of German fighters would destroy their effectiveness.

Admiral Raeder spoke for the Navy. An invasion of England across the Channel and the Strait of Dover would have to be undertaken without the support of large fleet units which would be too vulnerable in the narrow channel lanes. It would be largely a task for destroyers, torpedo boats and submarines. These craft would be vulnerable to enemy bombers, and unless the Luftwaffe held unchallenged control of the air over the area of operations, Raeder could not guarantee protection of the troops against enemy surface craft and the maintenance of communications that would be vital to success.

General Todt, who represented the supply services, was frank in enumerating the great difficulties his branch would face. In spite of the speed with which roads and railways to the Channel coast were being repaired and reconstructed, communications in the area were still largely disrupted. It would require at least two months to restore them for fairly satisfactory service. But, he added, there was an even more serious difficulty. For purposes of immediate availability, munitions and supplies would have to be stored within easy reach of the embarkation points—within a fifty-mile stretch of the French and Belgian coasts. He had personally inspected that territory and had found no facilities for underground storage. All such facilities were located in the Maginot

Line fortifications and this was too far from the coast to be of practical use. Surface storage facilities on that flat coastal stretch—especially munitions dumps and oil tanks—would be far too vulnerable to enemy bombs. To build the necessary underground facilities would require at least one year.

Ribbentrop repeated what he had apparently stated at a previous conference—that for the present, at least, the prospect of peace with England simply did not exist. The British had lost their French foothold but in return they had received promises of help from the United States. From a political point of view he saw only two possibilities that might force England into negotiations, since a direct invasion attempt evidently would meet with almost insurmountable difficulties at this time. Either the shipping lanes leading to England would have to be cut by a combined U-boat and aircraft blockade, which would prevent the arrival of American aid, or new allies must be won for direct assaults upon the outposts of the British Empire. Faced with the possible loss of her empire, England might come to terms. Among such possible allies, Ribbentrop named France, Spain, Japan and perhaps Russia.

Hess, speaking for the Nazi party, stated that from the viewpoint of long-established party policy he was against any military enterprise that would inevitably result in complete exhaustion not only for England but for Germany as well, and thus open the door for the barbaric Bolshevik hordes to sweep over Europe. Before Germany could think of an annihilation struggle with England she must build up a protective bulwark in the east, including occupation of Rumania and other Balkan countries, and achieve an alliance with Sweden and Finland. Or failing that, she must seek to establish a reliable regime in Russia, by diplomacy or by force. Any other policy, he insisted, would be suicidal.

Hitler, as usual, had the last word. He ordered full preparations to be rushed for an invasion of England in late September. If conditions at that time should make the attempt inadvisable, it would then be time enough to decide on a different policy. Meanwhile, the army, the navy and the air force must be made ready for the attempt.

I hope this is a fairly comprehensive report. I am not very strong on the subject of military matters and there is no one here to consult. Gottlieb is enjoying a leave of absence with his people in Oldenburg and I keep Wolfgang away for reasons of safety. Also, as I told you, I missed many of the conversations and have tried my best to piece the various items together. I think we shall soon see fresh developments and I shall do my best to keep you posted.

With warmest regards,
CLARA.

Despite Clara's modesty and her apologies, she had really done an excellent job for us. Her information disclosed to us a conflict of interests behind the scenes in Hitler's government and indicated clearly the course which events would follow. Ever since the collapse of France, opinion in the United States—even among the military—had it that an invasion of England would be a comparatively easy task. Clara's information gave a clear picture of the enormous difficulties that Hitler was facing. It also indicated that Hitler, himself, in his rage at the refusal of Great Britain to discuss peace, was determined on conquest of the British Isles. I stressed this point over and over again in my broadcasts, pointing toward September as the month in which Hitler would make his attempt.

In one broadcast, on August 20, I said, "According to information received by me, Goering and Hitler are currently at odds with regard to action to be taken against England. Hitler demands at least a serious attempt to blitz England from the air, while Goering is skeptical on the subject. Very likely Hitler's demand will prevail and we may see an air invasion of England early next month."

Events apparently were moving rapidly at Berchtesgaden and soon after receipt of Clara's latest report another came through, containing information of importance. Clara wrote:

Dear Willy:

In my last letter I told you of the recommendations to Hitler by his principal advisers with regard to measures to be taken against England. I can tell you now that he is evidently working toward adoption of virtually all of these recommendations, even those that appear to conflict with each other. I have gained the impression that in Hitler's brain is a plan for the domination of the whole world. The reason for this conclusion of mine you will find below, in the outline of Hitler's conversation with Dr. Heinrich Stahmer.

The name is probably unknown to you. As a matter of fact, none of us here ever thought that Dr. Stahmer might become a person of importance. He is an economist who spent many years carrying out research in East Asia. He is known here largely as an expert in oriental customs and languages. He has always advocated German acquisition of colonies in the Far East, for purely economic reasons. Since the colonial question had been subordinated by the Nazi regime except for propaganda purposes, Stahmer's views were never popular. He is a party veteran who joined up in the early days when Hitler's program seemed to so many of us the only solution to our national problems. He is also one of Hitler's few personal friends.

Stahmer never pressed for power and prominence and it was probably on this account that he has escaped the jealousies and intrigues of past years. Hitler is attached to Stahmer and has selected him for one of the most important missions in Germany's international relations today. Stahmer is now going to Tokyo as Hitler's personal representative to the new Japanese government of Prince Konoye and Yosuke Matsuoka.

Here is a resumé of Hitler's personal instructions to Stahmer, which I was fortunate enough to be able to hear without interruption. Hitler claims that he has offered Great Britain peace on favorable terms, guaranteeing preservation of a large part of the British Empire. The British have rejected all overtures. Churchill has sworn to destroy Hitler. Consequently the war can end in only one of two ways—the destruction of Germany, which Hitler swears will never happen, or the destruction of the British Empire. *— In 1940*

England has assured herself of American support, first in war materials and later by active participation in the war, as in 1917. England and the United States are two great naval powers whose combined fleets Germany and Italy can never hope to match. This requires an alliance with a strong naval power and the only one available is Japan. As an expansionist power, Japan is a logical partner in the effort to crush the world hegemony of the two Anglo-Saxon nations—England and the United States.

Unfortunately Japan has pursued her expansionist aims in the wrong direction. She has built up a continental empire in Manchukuo at great cost and it is not paying dividends. She has engaged in a war with China that will net her nothing. What Japan's teeming millions need is food and she cannot fill this need in China, which produces hardly enough to feed adequately her own enormous population. There is nothing for Japan in Siberia, east of Lake Baikal. One cannot obtain food from a beggar but only from a rich man.

Japan's rich man, according to Hitler, lives neither to the north nor to the west, but to the south. Indo-China, Burma, the East Indies, are the greatest exporters of rice in the world, and rice is Japan's staple food. It is also to the south—likewise in Burma, Malaya and the Indies —that Japan will find the oil, rubber and iron she needs to make up her greatest deficiencies in raw materials. Japan's problem is to build up self-sufficiency and this she will never be able to do in her fierce competition with the Chinese. On the other hand, the surplus riches of the areas to the south lie virtually undefended. They are Japan's for the asking.

These countries, Hitler pointed out, are largely British and Dutch possessions. England has committed herself to a war of annihilation against Germany and the Netherlands government-in-exile has joined in this undertaking. The most efficient counteraction is to hit the two where it will hurt the most. Japanese occupation of the East Indies would mean the end of any independent Dutch territory. The British Empire would break apart as soon as her rich Asiatic possessions were taken from her.

It is to be Stahmer's task to convince Japan that she must go to war against Britain. Stahmer must avoid creating the impression that Germany is asking favors of Japan. As a matter of fact, it will be Japan who will be asking favors if she is to prepare adequately for the enterprise.

Stahmer is to appeal to Japanese selfishness by striking an immense profit balance for Japan by means of his economic tables. He is to work independently of the German Ambassador in Tokyo, Lieutenant General Eugen Ott, although Ott will arrange Stahmer's introduction into the circles where he must do most of his work. It will be his task to convince the financial interests headed by the Mitsui organization of the value of his plan and leave it to them to bring the necessary pressure on the government through Matsuoka, who is their representative. Ott will carry on a similar campaign in Japanese army circles. Once the army faction and the vested interests are sold on the idea, Japan is as good as in the war.

What Hitler is seeking is an outright military alliance with Japan directed against both England and the United States. Stahmer is not to offer any terms. He is to dangle before the Japanese the idea of an alliance and its obvious advantages, and leave the suggestion of terms to Konoye's government. Obviously Japan could not dream of going to war against an Anglo-American alliance without active German assistance. The Japanese are realists. That Germany's war aims will benefit if Japan joins forces with her is likewise obvious. Each country is in a position to offer the other strategic advantages.

These are Hitler's own views as expressed to Dr. Stahmer, who is being sent out on a mission aimed at engulfing the entire world in disaster. I considered this information so important that I decided to rush it off without waiting for more.

With warmest regards,
CLARA.

The information was indeed important, but the subject certainly was a very delicate one. Cautious investigation among Washington officials as well as representative editors convinced me that both our government and the public would consider a Japanese war against us preposterous. The public, especially, seemed to consider Japan in the light of a comic-opera country with little or no power. Both government and public also felt that the little Jap country was too heavily engaged in the futile Chinese war to attempt so gigantic an undertaking as a war with both England and the United States. It was admitted that Hitler very likely would approve of a Japanese attack against us and England, but it was also felt that such an undertaking would prove futile. The consensus of opinion in the United States was that the Japanese would see through Hitler's scheme and refrain from committing national hara-kiri.

On September 12, 1940, I broadcast, "Hitler has sent Heinrich Stahmer as his personal envoy to Japan. What Hitler wants is an outright military alliance with the Japanese. Japan is a strong naval power and Hitler wants the Japanese navy to hold a considerable part of British sea power in the Pacific."

My warnings, however, fell on deaf ears, as they had before the Battle of France. The American public regarded Japan as a neutral country, as far as the war in Europe was concerned, and believed it would remain so. Furthermore, the United States had a trade pact with Japan, and in spite of professed great sympathy and many crocodile tears shed for "poor China," this country was selling large quantities of oil and iron scrap to Japan, so that Japan could manufacture munitions at an increasingly rapid pace. The United States and Japan were great friends, most people believed then, and anyone who said otherwise was simply talking through his hat.

During this period of alleged American-Japanese friendship, when I repeated my warning over the radio, the station censor was particularly sensitive, not wishing to offend Japan. He had felt the same way about Germany in the past. It was only after

Germany had walked over France that he agreed to permit me to call the German army formidable.

A few days after Clara's last letter, we received a report from Wolfgang which added considerably to what Clara had written us. Wolfgang wrote:

Dear Willy:

I understand that Clara has written you about Heinrich Stahmer and his mission, but I feel that I have more information to give you on the subject. I have not been able to contribute much until now, and I do feel that this is vital.

After Stahmer received his instructions from Hitler, he spent a few days with Ribbentrop at Fuschl. He called especially to obtain an introduction to General Ott which only Ribbentrop could give him. Although Ott is also the liaison man between the Supreme Command here and the Japanese army, as ambassador he is technically under Ribbentrop and the Foreign Office.

I should like to say now that all of our group, and also a great many others, are not pleased by our official friendship with the Japanese. We feel that Germany will eventually regret any alliance with these people. Especially the older ones among us still vividly remember Kaiser Wilhelm's warnings about the Yellow Peril.

However, to get on with Stahmer. Actually he is a soft-spoken genial man and I am surprised that Hitler is sending him. This is his first real diplomatic mission and it is an important one so far as the Nazis are concerned. Stahmer does not seem to be the right type for this game of power politics.

In securing information from Ribbentrop, Stahmer wished to know the exact status of relations between Germany and Japan, which Hitler evidently had not told him. But Ribbentrop does not seem to know a great deal himself. Although he negotiated the Italian alliance and the Soviet agreement, Hitler apparently is anxious to manipulate this arrangement with Japan himself.

One of Stahmer's questions was really a surprise, for I am sure that he could not have discussed such a subject with Hitler. Stahmer observed that the handling of the Jews and other minority groups by the Nazis had contributed largely to Germany's unpopular status in the United States. He contended that American influence was still strong in Tokyo and that the United States was using the treatment of Jews in Nazi Germany as a means of preventing a Japanese alliance with Germany. He told Ribbentrop that he would not know how to handle the situation if he came across obstacles such as this.

Ribbentrop who, as you know, is not one of the rabid Jew-baiters here, was quite frank with Stahmer and that, too, surprised me greatly. The Foreign Minister said that if an alliance with Japan were concluded the Nazi racial theory could no longer be tenable, if it ever had been. Although, he said, anti-Semitism was still a fairly effective propaganda weapon, he felt it should no longer interfere with realistic appraisals of world tendencies. In theory, he explained to Stahmer, there is only one type of Jew, but in practice there are two. First there is the Jew who is persecuted and dispossessed as a political expedient or for financial profit. The other kind of Jew, he said, you permit to work for you because you can make good use of his abilities. Ribbentrop then admitted that quite a number of this second type of Jew were working in the Foreign Office. There was no need to molest them, since it was so simple to pretend that they were not Jews at all.

If this question should arise in Japan, although Ribbentrop doubted that it would, he advised Stahmer to be quite realistic about it. Stahmer should explain to the Japanese that to fulfill his program Hitler was forced to unite the German people solidly behind himself. In this kind of politics it was not sufficient to point out deplorable conditions, it was necessary to have a scapegoat or whipping-boy. And this scapegoat would necessarily be the smallest minority in Germany, meaning the Jews. The sins of a few were vastly expanded by the propaganda shouters and pinned on the entire Jewish minority. To pick on the Jews was politically convenient because they could not defend themselves. It was financially profitable because their property could be confiscated. Since the Japanese were realists themselves, and quite expert in the persecution of minorities under their own rule, they would readily understand.

I thought it would be of interest to you to know of this conversation. I hope to have more news shortly.

Your friend,
WOLFGANG.

All this was not exactly news either to van Narvig or myself, but the fact that Ribbentrop had said it made it quite significant. Van Narvig had previously told me that he had encountered this feeling among many of the Nazi officials.

Together with Wolfgang's report, we also received one from Manfred, who wrote:

Dear Willy:

I have just spent several days at Berchtesgaden. Hitler had intended to journey to France again and I had to join the detail. But something arose to prevent his departure and now I expect to return to Berlin and the customary routine.

While here, I made certain observations that have escaped the attention of both Clara and Gottlieb, probably because they did not witness the scene of the crucifix gift to Hitler at Eupen nor the alleged conversation between the Fuehrer and the spirit of Napoleon.

Upon his return from France, Hitler set aside one of the Berghof rooms close to his study and had it converted into a private chapel, quite small. This is generally known here; also, that Hitler spends a short period each day in that chapel, alone. No one but an old servant of Hitler's and Evi Braun, who has returned to the Berghof, has seen the chapel's interior.

Whatever Hitler is doing in the chapel, personally I am certain that it is not praying—at least not in the sense that ordinary people pray. Considering the man's great acting abilities, I am convinced that he is preparing some new sort of deviltry that must concern the Church.

You will recall that he told Jodl that Napoleon's spirit had advised him to proceed cautiously with the Church of Rome. This may be the idea behind building the chapel. Hitler now appears to be seeking an understanding with the Vatican. In fact, a few weeks ago, he sent a request to Mussolini asking the Italian to intervene for Hitler at the Holy See in the interests of closer relations between himself and the Roman Catholic Church. But Mussolini, still concerned about the unsatisfactory armistice terms, let it be understood that his services in this connection are unavailable at present.

Then someone of Hitler's entourage—perhaps Jodl, whose advice Hitler accepts more and more—suggested using King Leopold of the Belgians as mediator between Hitler and the Vatican. The Belgian King, a devout Catholic, is highly regarded by the Pontiff and probably would receive more sympathy than would Mussolini. But the King would not easily allow himself to be used by Hitler for tricking the Church. Hitler's sudden affection for the Church would certainly not sound reasonable to Leopold.

However, some sort of approach to the Vatican is being planned since Henri Le Man, at present head of the civil administration in Belgium under the occupation, visited the Berghof a few days ago. For several years Le Man has been confidant to Leopold and he played a large part in the surrender of the Belgian army. Hitler's departure for France, and possibly Belgium, where the King—officially a prisoner-of-war—resides at Laeken Castle, was arranged at the time of Le Man's visit. Since the journey has been cancelled, or at least indefinitely postponed, it is my opinion that Le Man could not persuade Leopold to participate in such an affair. You can be certain, however, that this is not the end, for Hitler will try again.

I should now like to call your attention to the fact that with the exception of Gottlieb, the other members of our group are taking what I consider unnecessary and foolhardy risks.

Although I do not know how important the figures and statistics on aircraft production are to you, I feel certain they are not important enough to risk losing Linda, and perhaps jeopardizing all of us through her. I know for a fact that she was caught leafing through the latest set of statistics and making notes. It was only her ability to act stupid that saw her through in that instance.

Over at Fuschl, Wolfgang almost got himself in a jam when listening to Ribbentrop's opinions of the Jewish problem. This certainly was not worth a risk such as that. He was well aware that Clara had already sent you the report on Stahmer's mission and he actually escaped by sheer luck. After this, however, I am sure that Gottlieb will be able to handle him.

Clara, I fear, is not much better. She spends entirely too much time at her ventilator listening-post, hearing gossip that is hardly worth repeating. Since Gottlieb is in a position to tell her when she should listen—that is, whenever an important visitor arrives—there is certainly no point in her staying glued to the spot. In the long run such action is bound to arouse suspicion.

Incidentally, Gottlieb tells me that he expects Klausmann to arrive shortly with the power of attorney from you to take care of the inheritance. And I, for one, shall be very happy when a sizable fund is established in Switzerland, for the way some of our people take risks, we may face a bad situation soon where one or the other will be forced to flee Germany.

While in Berlin I shall have little to report except, of course, the usual Gestapo violence in which you are not interested. If I am detailed again to Hitler's retinue in the near future, however, you may expect to hear from me again.

In warm friendship,
MANFRED.

CHAPTER 13

AFTER RECEIVING this report, van Narvig came into my office, jittery and upset.

"Those damned fools!" he said. "I told them to be careful and not expose themselves to danger."

He appeared extremely afraid that grief might come to all of them and I tried to reassure him.

"From what Manfred writes," I said, "I am sure that Gottlieb will take the situation in hand and give them all a good dressing down."

With Hitler's protracted stay at Berchtesgaden, our little organization grew very active. Reports came in quick succession, sometimes even in batches. Here is an interesting one from Gottlieb:

Dear Willy:

Last night I had a really unique experience. I listened to an interesting conversation, which I am certain you will want to know about. Since Manfred told me of his writing you about the risks which some of us have been taking, let me assure you that I was completely in the open on this.

I shall explain. As you perhaps remember, the salon of the Berghof adjoins an open terrace, facing the Obersalzburg. Some time ago I discovered that due to the peculiar natural accoustics of the terrace, it is easy to hear a conversation there a considerable distance across the lawn, whenever the wind blows from the west. Those on the terrace do not realize that they can be heard and think they are out of earshot.

It had been a hot day, even for this altitude, but as twilight descended a brisk westerly breeze sprang up. I had come from the village on my bicycle and as I rode through the gate I saw two men walk through the French windows onto the terrace and settle down in steamer chairs.

It gave me an idea. I walked toward the lawn where a gardener was still busy with the hose and dismissed him quite obviously before the two. I then sat down on a bench, ostensibly to enjoy the evening cool in full view of the men who therefore could not even suspect that I might be spying.

The two were Rudolph Hess and Alfred Rosenberg and they immediately plunged into a spirited discussion. The topic aroused my interest at once and I prefer to repeat the conversation to you as I remembered it, with perhaps only nonessentials omitted.

Rosenberg: "I cannot understand Hitler. Certainly, this sudden religious fervor must be false. I do not see how it can be otherwise."

Hess: "I fully agree with you but I advise you not to mention it before Hitler, certainly not in the way you did just now. It may have unhealthy consequences for you."

Rosenberg: "Please, Rudi. You must know what it all means. You are closest to him."

Hess: "I used to be, once, but I am no longer. Now he is listening to his soldiers, especially Jodl."

Rosenberg: "The Party will have something to say about it."

Hess: "I am the Party, and I prefer to say nothing. There is a time for everything. When the Army has won such victories it certainly is not the time to provoke resentment on the religious issue."

Rosenberg: "The Army cannot dictate to the Fuehrer."

Hess: "The Army is not dictating to the Fuehrer, it is playing up to him. Today Hitler believes that he is the Army."

Rosenberg: "Rudi! Is the Pope now to become all-powerful in our Europe after we have shown him that he does not mean a thing to us?"

Hess: "If you think the Pope will become all-powerful anywhere, then you do not know Hitler."

Rosenberg: "But why all this wooing of Rome? Why all these concessions? Two hundred Catholic churches on wheels * for districts where the Catholic population is sparse."

Hess: "That is why the churches are on wheels. They fulfill their temporary assignment. Mobile churches can be withdrawn unnoticed when they have completed their task. To erect permanent churches and then raze them would be quite a different matter."

Rosenberg: "I believe I know the real aim. Do not try to sidetrack me, Rudi. I have a way of getting news. To attempt to force all Europe back under the Church of Rome is fantastic. It is bound to have the most serious repercussions. It should never be tried. Once the Pope is given full power over men's souls, the State will take a back seat."

Hess: "So long as Hitler heads the State it will never take a back seat."

Rosenberg: "Still, I cannot understand Hitler. We had worked out such a perfect scheme. You were all for it. Hitler was all for it, at least in private conferences. The Party was all for it. It was attuned to the warrior spirit of the Germanic race. Then came the war and the scheme was thrown in discard. I was told to forget all about it."

Hess: "What you seem to forget, my dear Rosenberg, is that while the war lasts the people long for peace. They admire their victorious leaders but more than ever they pray to God. Your scheme did not fit in."

Rosenberg: "Look here, Rudi. We all agree that there should be but one Church and that it should be the pillar of the State."

Hess: "We have gone all over that a hundred times. Your Teutonic philosophy might have worked so long as we dealt only with Germany.

*Rosenberg here refers to churches, or rather chapels, mounted on trucks, which were instituted by Hitler throughout the Warthegau and other territories annexed from Poland, to counteract reports to Rome that the Catholic clergy of these districts were being persecuted.

Now we have to consider all Europe and this changes matters. You know very well that Europe is predominantly Catholic. You might be able to sell your philosophy to Germany, but Europe will reject it. If we tried to destroy the Catholic Church and impose your philosophy instead we would have a religious war on our hands that would ruin us. You ought to know that."

Rosenberg: "Are you all blind? At least the Lutheran Church makes the head of the State also the head of the Church. The Catholic Church acknowledges no other head but the Pope. Where the Lutheran Church is national, the Catholic Church is universal. As between two evils at least you should choose the lesser."

Hess: "Not if you expect to turn the greater evil into no evil at all."

Rosenberg: "You talk like a fool, Rudi. If Hitler thinks he can out-smart the Vatican he is mistaken. He should know that the Vatican is the shrewdest diplomatic institution in the world. It will never enter-tain a deal unless certain that it gets the better end of it. If you do not want to talk to Hitler, let me do it."

Hess: "I most certainly will not talk to Hitler on the subject. If you insist, go and talk your head off, but after you are through talking you will find yourself behind bars as surely as you sit in that chair. Let me give you this advice. If you can work out a scheme that guarantees that Hitler will emerge as the head of a new European Church, you may present it to him and be certain of a sympathetic hearing. Otherwise, do not touch the subject at all, with Hitler or anyone else."

With this, Hess got up and went inside.

Manfred tells me that he has written to you on his personal observa-tions, and also communicated to you his suspicion that Hitler is plan-ning some sort of religious coup. I felt definitely that Manfred was on the wrong track and even now I am inclined to doubt it. But inasmuch as the conversation which I overhead had a direct bearing on this sub-ject, I thought it best to report on it as closely as possible.

I hope that you and yours are getting along well.

Grüss Gott!
GOTTLIEB.

After we received this report, I was puzzled as to its presenta-tion on the radio. I knew, of course, that the station censor would object, which he did. But I felt, too, that it was important for this sort of information to reach not only the Catholic laymen and the Church, but also the general public. I had no desire to offend, of course, only to help. Politics was a simple matter to discuss on the air compared with religion.

My assistant, reared in the tenets of the Roman Catholic faith, found nothing objectionable in the story and felt it would be received in an understanding fashion. I was determined to broadcast it and I won my battle with the station censor. To my considerable surprise I received literally hundreds of letters from laymen and even from high churchmen, commending my broadcast and thanking me for publicizing Hitler's attitude and plans concerning the Church of Rome.

About this time we received another long report from Clara. It proved one of the most difficult to decipher because it was written on used brown wrapping paper, creased and oil-stained, which frequently caused a blur in her stubby shorthand. She wrote:

Dear Willy:

I had quite an argument with Manfred and Gottlieb. They remonstrated with me, accusing me of taking too many risks. However, I feel that at times a risk is necessary if results are to be obtained. I am certain that my letters to you so far have shown that the risks were not unnecessary ones. I hope that you agree with me. I proved it to my satisfaction the other night when Hitler had visitors. Gottlieb insisted that the conference could not be an important one, and for me to stay away, but I did not agree with him and went to listen in as usual. I think the result will justify my attitude.

The visitors were Rudolph Hess and Professor Haushofer*. It is really seldom that Haushofer is seen at the Berghof, but he has great influence over Hess and through him over the Party doctrines. You know of course that Hitler did not write "Mein Kampf," except for the autobiographical parts. Hess really wrote the book, but the principal ideas in it emanated from Haushofer. And since Haushofer's visits to the Berghof are so rare I had a feeling that this one might be of considerable importance.

The three spent almost two hours in Hitler's study. It was Haushofer who did most of the talking, which is a surprising thing when you consider that Hitler was in the same room with him. Frankly, I was rather confused by many of the things which Haushofer brought up, and so I shall simply repeat them to you in the hope that you will understand.

Haushofer began by saying that now that French military power was

*Dr. Karl Haushofer, exponent of the German theory of geopolitics, from whom Hitler obtained much of the material for "Mein Kampf" during the Munich days.

destroyed, the time had arrived to think concretely of a European racial reorganization, to end once and for all, the incredible Wirrwarr* that has been the continental scourge ever since Napoleon failed in his attempt to reorganize Europe. Artificial barriers between economically interdependent countries must be scrapped. Linguistically homogeneous groups must be merged irrespective of the wishes of their selfish political leaders. Past errors must be corrected and the various peoples of the continent must receive the economic means for existence in accordance with their importance and predestination.

The French case, Haushofer said, was a relatively simple one. All French-speaking districts, including those of Belgium and Switzerland, must be incorporated into the new French State. The Dutch and Flemish populations are actually of Germanic stock and their inclusion into the Reich proper is furthermore dictated by the necessity of having just two large states—Germany and France—on Europe's western ramparts. The Scandinavian countries, being inhabited by the same Nordic race of which Germany is the leader, must affiliate with the Reich in one form or another. The political anomaly of Switzerland must disappear. Not only do the German Swiss districts belong to the Reich proper, but also the Alpine barrier constitutes an important link in the German line of defense.

The problems of the west and north are simple compared with those of the east, continued Haushofer. The Slavs are the greatest enemies of the Germanic race. Past errors that have permitted deep Slav penetration into the German community, must be corrected. This can be done by two methods. One is the Germanization of Slav populations with advanced cultural standards such as the Czechs, Slovaks and Croats. The other is to force back the Slav peoples into eastern geographic confines and to establish their economic dependence on the Germanic race. Those Slavs who cannot be dealt with by either method must be exterminated.

Almost all European disturbances of the past hundred years, Haushofer pointed out, have been caused by the mutual gravitation of the Russians and the Balkan Slavs toward each other. To check this mutual attraction it is first necessary to drive a strong wedge between the two groups. Once this is done, this wedge must be spread in both directions.

This wedge, according to Haushofer, is represented today by Hungary and Rumania, both of them inhabited by non-Slavic peoples. The Hungarians are strongly nationalistic but if forced to make a choice they will prefer a Germanic affiliation to one with the Slavs. Besides, Germany can promise them a growth of their particular domain within

*Jumble.

the Germanic orbit. The Rumanians are fearful of being engulfed by a Slav tide from both sides and, after all, they are just a mongrel race. They represent excellent material for Germanization. Furthermore, geopolitics dictates the incorporation of Rumania's economy within Germany's sphere.

Once the wedge has been driven, continued Haushofer, the question of the next turn will arise. The southern Slavs are easiest to deal with, but encroachment might easily bring the eastern Slavs—the Russians— prematurely into the scene. Therefore, since the Russians represent the gravest potential danger, they should be dealt with first.

Haushofer pointed out that, after all, Russia is not a single nation, but just a tremendous conglomeration of many nationalities that the Czarist government had failed to unify, but which were being swiftly assimilated by the Soviets. In the Baltic provinces of Estonia, Latvia and Lithuania, Germanic civilization had taken roots long before the Russians moved in. Properly they belong within the direct sphere of the German Reich. In the south the Ukrainian nation, although conquered by the Russians two hundred years ago, continued to maintain strong separatist tendencies. Again from the viewpoint of geopolitics, the Ukraine should be made part of the Reich. Its fertile soil would, under scientific cultivation, provide sufficient food for the German people and still leave enough to feed the local inhabitants. If Russian influence could be forced back beyond the Volga barrier the Slav danger to the Germanic race would become merely academic.

Haushofer went on to say that the southern Slavs present a favorable situation in that their principal subdivisions—the Bulgars and the Serbs —are mortal enemies. This can be used to great advantage in keeping the two separate and their differences can be exploited for their piece-meal assimilation.

The Turks, Haushofer explained, present a totally different situation, principally because Turkey is the leading Moslem nation. But this also has its favorable aspects. If the Turks can be persuaded that the Germanic and Moslem worlds really belong together, the other Moslem countries would quickly follow Turkey's example. The Germans and the Turks have an affinity because their basic philosophy subscribes to warrior courage. Both place the sword before the plough.

Hess did not say much. Undoubtedly he and Haushofer have discussed this philosophy many times. He observed once, however, that an armed showdown between Germany and England should be avoided. The other two made no reply to this.

Hitler added little to the conversation, simply asking occasional questions. He seemed especially interested in Haushofer's theories on the Slav problem and how to deal with it. At the end of what really amounted to a lecture by Haushofer, he expressed no opinion and merely thanked the professor.

I have left out much of Haushofer's presentation because, to me, it went rather into the abstract. But on the whole I believe I have given a fairly representative synopsis.

With cordial regards,
CLARA.

CHAPTER 14

THIS REPORT WAS vitally interesting and I used a great deal of the material in several broadcasts. More and more I realized that Clara was an extremely intelligent woman, despite her protestations that much of the political discussion at the Berghof went over her head.

About this time, I hinted in my broadcasts that a gradual deterioration in relations between Germany and Russia was taking place. In my broadcast of October 3, 1940, I said:

"According to a confidential report from my continental source the oil supplies now at the disposal of the two Axis powers will be exhausted within another six months of intensified warfare. That the war will last much longer than that is already accepted as a certainty in both Berlin and Rome. Germany has the Rumanian oil fields in her hands, but production here could not possibly provide enough. Hittler wants the oil of Russia."*

After that and subsequent broadcasts on the same subject, I began to receive threatening letters from persons who obviously were Nazi agents in America. I turned over some of the letters to the police and was advised by them to carry a revolver. I went as far as getting a permit, but the realization that anyone attempting to "get" me would have the first advantage, and the fact that a revolver is a heavy object to carry about, helped me to forget the matter very soon.

We already had received from Linda the third monthly report

*German and Rumanian armies invaded Russia on a 1,200 mile front from the Baltic to the Black Sea, at dawn on June 22, 1941.

on aircraft production in Germany which I promptly transmitted over the air. More letters arrived asking for the source of my figures. For an entire year thereafter these accurate plane production reports continued to come in and I shall not mention them further, except to say that later I was informed that they checked exactly with the figures obtained by the British Intelligence through their own sources. Now we had another interesting letter from Linda, who had already picked up so many Nazi secrets. This time she wrote:

Dear Willy:

I am back at Karin Hall and the wild parties at St. Germain are merely an unpleasant memory. But the gowns I picked up in the shops of Paris are definitely real. I am back at the old routine. Goering is very busy these days, planning a gigantic air assault against England. He wanted the job, and he got it. Heinrich has given me little in the way of important news lately, for Berlin is rather quiet so long as Hitler remains at Berchtesgaden.

The other day Field Marshal Milch visited at Karin Hall and I chanced to overhear parts of a discussion between him and Hermann. Unfortunately it had nothing to do with the projected assault on England. That is discussed behind closed doors and windows. This matter concerns the French and I know that you will want to hear about it.

I wrote you from Paris that Goering and Laval were attempting to arrive at some sort of peace that would make Germany and France potential, if not actual, allies. Goering is enthusiastic about it for he is contemptuous of the Italians. His secret agents work overtime in Italy and their reports on the Italian air force confirm his low opinion. The only Italian whom Goering considered able and trustworthy was Marshal Italo Balbo, and the story of his death is simply fantastic.

Goering knows it, of course; you may not. It happened this way. Balbo had inspected the Italian positions around Tobruk and on his return trip to Bengasi decided to stop over at Derna. Meanwhile Derna had been attacked by a British bomber squadron that was beaten off. When Balbo's plane appeared in the sky the Italians on the ground thought that the British were coming back. They ran to their flak guns and started popping away at Balbo's descending plane. It was squarely hit by an exploding shell and broke apart in midair. Everyone in it was dead. Goering said this sort of thing could never happen to anyone but Italians.

Hermann has been trying to convince Hitler that the Italians will be more of a hindrance than a help in fighting the war. With England's refusal to negotiate a peace—a development that Goering had predicted—the Reichsmarshal is of the opinion that France will make a more effective partner than Mussolini, especially since the present French chiefs are anxious to salvage something from the wreckage. His conferences with French politicians at St. Germain convinced him that such an alliance is possible. As I wrote you before, Laval, who is the supreme opportunist, is more than eager to collaborate.

Now it appears that Laval has little positive influence in Vichy, much less than even he suspected. The army and navy clique there—especially Weygand, Huntziger, Mittelhauser and Darlan—are in favor of a strict military dictatorship, contending that parliamentary misrule led to the ruin of France. They generally distrust politicians and they appear especially to dislike a politician of the Laval type. They are trying to hide from the French people the fact that it was the outdated military precepts which lost the war before it had ever started, and when Adrien Marquet* voiced his opinion to that effect he was immediately expelled from the Vichy government. They are afraid they will lose their present control of affairs if Laval negotiates an advantageous peace settlement with Hitler. For this reason General Huntziger, who is the chief French representative on the armistice commission at Wiesbaden, was told to extend peace feelers of his own.

Laval discovered this and told Goering. Our Hermann related to Milch how he flew to Wiesbaden, walked in on the deliberations of the commission and asked what was going on. Within two days Goering had the ear of Hitler with the result that the Armistice Commission was virtually exploded and is now lingering with no power at all. General Stuelpnagel was instantly sent to Paris to occupy himself exclusively with the tasks of the German army of occupation. Huntziger returned to Vichy, nothing achieved. The French now must negotiate through Laval or not at all.

I gathered that Laval is expected to visit Karin Hall shortly to resume his conferences with Goering. If the Vichy clique will support him I understand that he will be permitted to speak with Hitler. He will bring him a request from Marshal Petain for a personal meeting with Hitler, and after some hesitation Hitler will agree. All this will be done for the mere purpose of strengthening Laval's stand. They believe that if Petain once commits himself personally he will be unable to retreat.

---

*Adrien Marquet, who broke with Leon Blum to form the Socialist opposition later headed by Deat. He was Mayor of Bordeaux and by profession a dentist. He was a member of the Vichy Cabinet and after his removal went to Paris where he has been prominent in collaborationist circles.

It is rather ironic in a way, for, as you well know, Hitler himself stole into power by similar methods.

I expect to write you another letter soon again. Meanwhile, I hope you will think of me occasionally.

Affectionately,
LINDA.

Although this information was highly interesting, it was practically impossible to use it over the air. Linda had been too indefinite about dates and details. The most we could do with it was to reveal Laval's activities and hint that a meeting between the Fuehrer and Petain would probably soon take place. We also gave the details surrounding the death of Marshal Balbo.

The next report to arrive came from Wolfgang. It read:

Dear Willy:

We have had a rare visitor here at Fuschl—the Fuehrer himself! Although it is less than two hours' drive from the Berghof to Fuschl, Hitler has come here on only a few occasions, but each of them has been memorable. This time he lingered almost the entire day, but he was not alone. With him were the two Goering brothers, Hermann and Albert. The latter has been chief of the War Industries Board in the Protectorate of Bohemia and Moravia ever since the Nazis took over Czechoslovakia. It now appears that he will be in a new position soon.

I do not know whether you saw the map of the proposed New Order in Hitler's study. If you did you will remember that Rumania has been chosen as the next victim after France. Frequently I overheard statements that Rumania was one of the principal objectives of the Nazi Wehrwirtschaft if its program was to meet with success. Obviously the reasons for this are Rumania's oil and wheat, especially oil. The oil properties have been the greatest source of illegal revenue for successive Rumanian governments. This includes, of course, the present regime of King Carol and his mistress, Magda Lupescu. The properties are almost completely dominated by British and American capital. German investment is represented only in a few small wells. Carol, ever since his accession as King, has been quite occupied with the oil fields, planning constantly on how to gain more and more for his personal interests. After the fall of France he realized that he was supporting a loser and ever since he has sought to ingratiate himself with our Nazi wrecking crew. Three weeks ago he made a secret trip to Berchtesgaden but Hitler was quite cool in receiving him. On his return to Bucharest he subjected oil production, including British and American holdings, to strict government control. He has promised large quantities of oil to Germany and some of it has already been delivered. But the Nazis consider him utterly unreliable—in fact, it has already been decided here that he must be eliminated.

I had my usual opportunity of discovering some of the goings-on between Hitler, Ribbentrop and the Goerings, and I shall give you a resumé of the conversations.

According to the four, there is only one practical way to obtain Rumania's economic resources for the use of the Reich, and that is to occupy the country and install a puppet regime. One difficulty of this, however, is that Rumania cannot be reached by German troops except through Hungary and to occupy Hungary by force would be politically unwise. It might easily force the current pro-German government in Budapest into the anti-Nazi camp, and Hitler is most definitely not in favor of that. Also, it might toss a firebrand into the already restive Balkan countries. This would immediately cramp the German Wehrwirtschaft, which is largely dependent on its Balkan storage bin.

It was decided then, that discretion in the Hungarian case would be the better part of valor. Some inducement must be offered to Hungary in order to gain her secret acquiescence for the transit of German troops bound for Rumania. Goering has volunteered to attend to this because he has been cultivating the friendship of Admiral Horthy, Regent of Hungary, for many years. Horthy has been a frequent guest at Karin Hall and has accompanied Goering on many hunting parties. That this friendship was maintained for ulterior motives is now perfectly clear. Goering, like Hitler, lays his plans far in advance.

Goering is convinced that he can persuade Horthy to agree to the transit of troops, but he also contends that Horthy will have a difficult time holding his intensely patriotic people in check unless he can convince them that their future lies with Germany. Although Hungary, through German action, has re-acquired parts of her former territory at the expense of Czechoslovakia, this was some time ago. It will be utterly forgotten if German troops seize Hungarian lines of communication as a necessary preliminary for a push into Rumania. They plan, therefore, to offer Hungary a bribe in the form of a territory that she has coveted for a number of years—Transylvania.

There is also another factor involved, strictly a military one. Ever since Russia seized northern Bukovina from Rumania, Soviet troops have been stationed so that they can instantly march into northern Transylvania if it becomes apparent that Germany intends to drive a wedge between Russia and the Balkans. Certainly, Moscow will not approve of such a German move.

For this reason any such action must be guided first by German strategic considerations rather than Hungarian national ambitions. German troops marching in under the pretext of maintaining order must instantly form a strong counterwedge against the Russian position in northern Bukovina. Second, a plausible political pretext must be invented to make the occupation not only acceptable but even desirable to the Rumanians. Only in this manner can the seizure of Rumania become a success.

The result of all these deliberations is this: Berlin will suddenly provoke a non-existent Hungarian-Rumanian crisis over Transylvania. Then Germany, acting in concert with Mussolini, to prevent Il Duce's dissatisfaction, will intercede in the interests of preventing war between the two countries and preserving the peace of the Balkans. Ribbentrop and Ciano will go to Vienna and summon Hungarian and Rumanian delegates for a conference. They will award to Hungary a northern sector of Transylvania that extends like a solid pincer deep into Rumania and includes the protective salient of the eastern Carpathian Mountains.

This will be subject to immediate occupation by Hungarian troops accompanied by German units under the pretext of supervising the transfer of territory under the award. These German units will remain and occupy the line of the Carpathians as a barrier against possible Russian intervention, thus leaving the actual policing of the transferred territory to Hungary. This will automatically insure German control of all communication lines through northern Hungary.

To make the cession of part of Transylvania acceptable to the Rumanians, they will be offered a joint German-Italian guarantee of their remaining frontiers. Since the Hungarian award will arouse fear in the Rumanians of a complete partition of their country, this guarantee by Europe's leading military power will be welcome. The guarantee is to be principally a warning to Russia, but that of course will not be mentioned, merely understood between Germany and Russia. To carry out this promise, it will be necessary, of course, for German troops to move into Rumania, ostensibly for the purpose of protection.

This is where Albert Goering will fit into the picture. After the amputation of northern Transylvania, Rumania will be advised to marshal all her remaining economic resources for a great national effort, in view of her territorial losses. Under the present Rumanian government there is no one who could be trusted not to favor his friends and indulge in petty stealing. Therefore a co-ordinator who is above graft will be imposed upon the Rumanian government as Director of Rumania's economy. He will be Albert Goering. With German troops on Rumanian soil and the Reichsmarschal's brother in full charge of economic affairs, the gradual Nazification of that nation will become quite simple.

King Carol, as I have already told, will be eliminated, and that seems also to be a simple affair. The Rumanians will be informed, through fifth columnists in Nazi pay, that Carol, his mistress and the entire corrupt regime are wholly responsible for the loss of Rumanian territories and prestige. This will pave the way for a pro-Nazi faction to send Carol into exile and take over the government. The Nazi tool for a coup d'etat has already been selected. He is Rumanian General Ian Antonescu—quite a hero among the younger officers of the army, presumably because he has been kept from all lucrative sources of graft by Carol's and Lupescu's appointees.

Antonescu has been outspokenly opposed to Carol and at one time was imprisoned by him. He was released a few weeks ago, however, on German representation. He will meet the two Goerings within a few days to receive his instructions.

Of course, the Fuehrer is looking beyond Rumania. It appears that Bulgaria is next on the occupation schedule, but only after the German army has established strong bases on Rumanian territory. It is to be a friendly occupation, similar to that planned for Hungary. On Hitler's private map Hungary, Bulgaria and Turkey have a privileged status. Since they fought on Germany's side in the last war and were severely amputated as a sequel to Versailles, Hitler intends to win them over by the promise of territorial restoration. On the other hand, Rumania, Yugoslavia and Greece fought on the side of the Allies in the last war, and Hitler intends to treat them perfunctorily, when their day arrives.

Hitler desires Bulgaria in his camp for two reasons. First, it will enable him to reach Yugoslavia along her weakest frontier, so that that country may feel the Nazi wrath by next spring, or earlier. Second, it will bring him to the borders of Turkey where Franz von Papen is already trying to undermine the British and Russian positions. His aim is to neutralize Turkey by diplomatic action.

Compensation for Bulgarian co-operation was also discussed at this conference. She will be given the Rumanian Dobrudja outright, up to a line extending from Silistria on the Danube to Mangalia on the Black Sea. She will also be promised satisfaction of her national ambitions at the territorial expense of Yugoslavia and Greece. After Bulgaria has been attached to the Axis, Yugoslavia will be dealt with. This accomplished, Mussolini will be given a free hand to jump on Greece. No plans beyond this were under discussion.

I am glad to give you all this information. It is the first real piece of work that I have accomplished. As soon as there is more which might be of value to you I shall let you know.

Your friend,
WOLFGANG.

This report was exciting, for now we really had a line on Hitler's program of conquest for the next few months. I gave parts of it in a number of broadcasts. When the report reached us, the conference in Vienna, of course, had already begun, but we were in a position to beat the announcement of the award of northern Transylvania to Hungary by just twelve hours. We could not give the exact new boundary line between Hungary and Rumania because Wolfgang had not sent such detailed information. But we were able to announce the presence of German troops in Transylvania and along the Carpathians ten full days before the world received official confirmation. We also gave the news of the proposed award of the southern Dobrudja along the Silistria-Mangalia line to Bulgaria eight days before it actually occurred. *

For several weeks Wolfgang's report formed the basis for our broadcasts. We called the turn on General Antonescu's ascension as Little Fuehrer of Rumania and on the occupation of Bucharest and other towns by German troops. Berlin and Bucharest at that time admitted only the presence of a "German military mission" in Rumania. We were also able to give the news of Albert Goering's appointment as economic dictator for Rumania. We warned of an imminent attack on Greece by Italy. In all, the events of the next six months wholly confirmed the information contained in Wolfgang's letter.

Meanwhile the Nazis were battering at England from the air, bombing every foot of ground they could. Each day brought

---

*Williams' broadcast on October 8, 1940, contained the following passage: "Another German army, likewise of unknown strength, is assembling along the Danube in Rumania whence it could march through friendly Bulgarian territory, no doubt in exchange for Hitler's impending assignment of the southern Dobrudja to Bulgaria."

news of air action that sounded like fantastic nightmares. These
air assaults were conducted on a hitherto unknown scale and
it was obvious that Goering was making his great attempt to
erase the Royal Air Force and obtain for Germany air superiority
over England, preliminary to the planned invasion of the United
Kingdom.

Official reports on air losses, from both Berlin and London,
were so contradictory that it was virtually impossible to get at
the real facts. We had no definite idea of what was happening
until we received a report from Linda on the subject. She wrote:

Dear Willy:

I feel like a goddess of Fate. Across the English Channel the great
air war has been under way for weeks and the most fantastic reports
are being spread all over the world. The German people, especially,
are being fed stories about air victories and enemy losses, which no one
is in a position to check. Yet sitting here at Karin Hall, where all factual
information is coming in daily, all I have to do is dip into it and copy
the figures. It gives one a peculiar feeling.

At any rate, this phase of the air war is about over, for Goering has
just called off his squadrons. Three complete air fleets were engaged,
commanded by Field Marshals Sperrle and Kesselring and General
Keller. This, according to the records, means that something like 7,500
combat planes have been in intermittent action. Of these, we lost 2,876,
—one-third of our strength. Goering considered losses at this rate
prohibitive. According to figures at Karin Hall—which are the real
ones, not those inflated by Goebbels—the British lost 1,360 planes,
about half of our losses. Practically all British air fields as far north as
London were knocked out, but the British simply withdrew their
remaining squadrons to northern air bases where our assault squadrons
could not follow, as it would have meant even greater losses. While
British planes damaged in combat could land on their own fields, our
damaged planes became total losses. The increasing distances made
it impossible for our fighter pilots to reach their continental bases and
the crews were forced to bail out over England or over the Channel.
This meant that both planes and crews were lost.

Goering has stated in a report to Hitler that he still can erase the
Royal Air Force, but if he does this he will be left with an insufficient
number of planes to protect German invasion forces on British soil.
This, Goering pointed out, would mean that the British navy would
be in a position to cut the communications of any of our troops that

landed in England. Therefore, an invasion of England must be considered out of the question for the time being. Von Brauchitsch has positively stated that he will not move one German soldier across the Channel unless the Luftwaffe can guarantee complete air protection.

It is impossible for me to say what will be attempted next. No decision has been made. After Goering halted the air war, he arrived here with Milch and a number of other leading air generals for a discussion prior to submitting the entire subject to Hitler. Their unanimous opinion was that some other tactic must be found which would not involve such a tremendous sacrifice of fighter planes and pilots. I understand that while we have a great number of bombers, our reserve in fighter planes is running dangerously low because several models that were put in mass production recently have proved inadequate under combat conditions over England. Their complete discard will be recommended. These disqualified planes, together with the losses suffered in the Battle of France and over England, make the Luftwaffe losses approximately 12,000 aircraft of the fighter, pursuit and interceptor types, to date.

Kesselring made the suggestion that the Battle of England hereafter should be fought with night bombers. The British have proved that night bombing is far less costly than daylight raids, and Kesselring argued that there is no reason for the Luftwaffe to ignore this lesson, particularly when it could be used as an instrument in destroying industrial and communication centers. The only reason that the British did not have greater successes in night bombing, contended Kesselring, was because they did not use sufficient numbers of planes.

Goering reserved his opinion but promised to discuss the matter with Hitler. Milch and his air staff will submit plans for future air action.

Meanwhile I have learned something from Heinrich. He has been in Sweden and Finland for several weeks as a member of a mission. In Sweden arrangements were made for the transit of supplies for German troops stationed in Norway, near Narvik. In Finland there is a diplomatic game being played for quite high stakes.

When Finland accepted peace terms from Russia in March, it was done on secret recommendation from Berlin. As you know, the former Finnish President, Per Svinhufvud, was then received by Goering at Karin Hall. He was privately assured that if Finland accepted the Russian terms, Germany would see to it that the Soviets made no further encroachments on Finnish territory or Finnish independence. It soon became apparent that the Russians were constructing railroads and highways through sparsely populated and economically insignificant wilderness and that these communications, which all led to the Finnish border, were for purely strategic purposes. The Finns want

German help and that was one of the reasons for the mission of which Heinrich was a member.

Negotiations were conducted at Helsinki and the following agreement was reached. Germany will reinforce her garrisons in the northernmost section of Norway—at Hammerfest, Kirkenes and Vardoe. These bases are close to the Russian Arctic coast, notably, the port of Murmansk. The best way to send these reinforcements is through Finnish territory. Therefore, Finland concluded a similar agreement to that with Sweden concerning the German garrisons at Narvik and Tromsoe.

There is this difference, however. The Swedes conceded only transit rights along their railroad from Lulea to the Norwegian border. The Finns, on the other hand, have assigned the ports of Raumo and Pori as well as considerable surrounding territory for the exclusive use of Germany. These areas will be guarded by German troops and the German military commanders there will have the right to exclude all civilians, including Finns. This is, naturally, a guard against Russian spies.

In practice, Heinrich explained, it will amount to this. The Germans have undertaken the task of rearming and re-equipping the Finnish army with standard equipment seized from the Czech army in 1939. In addition to this, the Germans will accumulate large stores of supplies and munitions for their own future use at Raumo and Pori. The permanent German garrisons on Finnish soil will consist of at least two complete combat divisions. In the event that Finland is again attacked by the Russians, these troops will immediately join the Finnish army for defense purposes and more will follow. In brief, while this part of the agreement is secret, Germany has actually given Finland a guarantee against Russia similar to that extended to Rumania.

According to Heinrich, Hitler has actually launched a military encirclement of Russia from both south and north under the guise of German friendship to Rumania and Finland. He intends to station large forces on both flanks and thus be prepared for the day when he makes additional demands—or even war—on Russia. The general comment here is that Germany is merely safeguarding her position in the east, but Heinrich is convinced that it means much more than just that. The Russians, of course, will know of it and it will be interesting to watch Hitler justify these movements and make them conform to the Soviet-German pact.

Just what are you doing at present and to what extent has our information proved helpful? It is rumored here that in some unexplained fashion, vital information is reaching the United States. I wonder if it is ours? We here have no indication, I am happy to say, that anyone of us is under suspicion. Meanwhile, Himmler has ordered that all Americans are to be closely watched, particularly American correspondents. Please let me hear from you.

Affectionately,
LINDA.

CHAPTER 15

THIS INTERESTING REPORT was a very welcome supplement to the one we had received from Wolfgang. We released the information gradually, a bit here and there, fearful that our revelations to the American public might cause severe repercussions among our friends in Germany, especially since the air information could easily point to someone close to Goering as the source of the leak.

Another item that demanded discreet handling was the information concerning developments in Finland. That country still rated very high in American public esteem for its heroic stand against recent Russian aggression. Also, some of Linda's references to the Finnish situation dovetailed with news received in this country to the effect that Russia was in fact preparing another invasion of Finland for the coming winter. What with the Russo-German situation remaining unclear and the ever-present possibility that Hitler and Stalin might combine in another sell-out of a small European nation, we did not want to stress the Finnish angle too much.

Something else claimed my attention at this time. Linda's letter was delivered by Klausmann, who had returned from another of his periodic visits to Germany. It turned out that Klausmann had disposed of van Narvig's inheritance, converting Eugen's property into cash. By some method which we preferred not to inquire into, he converted the realized sum into dollar exchange aggregating something like $12,000. Of this he had established in Switzerland a fund of $6,000, which could be drawn upon by any of our six friends, should they be forced to flee Germany. This part of the transaction could meet with no possible objection. But the rest of the money he kept, having spent a great deal on bribes to make these arrangements successfully. I considered this a rather stiff fee.

I expressed myself along these lines to van Narvig, but he simply said that he had not wanted the inheritance anyway. Besides, he pointed to another consideration. We had both observed that our own State Department always released information on secret Nazi designs soon after Klausmann's return from one of his mysterious trips. Van Narvig suspected that Klausmann was engaged in undercover work, directly or through intermediaries, in the interests of the United States, in which case he was welcome to the money. As time went on, this feeling on our part increased, but we considered it none of our business and we never attempted to find out about it. Meanwhile we had the satisfaction of knowing that our friends would have adequate financial protection if they were forced to flee their country.

Our next report came from Manfred and read:

Dear Willy:

I have just returned from a trip to Belgium with Hitler. It was a hurried journey and also an enlightening one. During our railroad dash toward the Belgian frontier through the night, we passed quite a number of hospital trains filled to capacity with wounded German soldiers and I was completely at a loss to explain this phenomenon to myself. Since the signing of the armistice no fighting had taken place in either Belgium or France, except for sporadic night bombings by the British. This certainly could not account for the trainloads of wounded. If they had been civilians it would have been a different matter, but our troops are always well protected by flak artillery and fighter squadrons.

At the Belgian border another hospital train had pulled up, to let our train pass, and Hitler himself got out to inspect it. I then made the amazing discovery that none of the wounds was connected with fighting; they were all the result of horrible burns.

It was at Antwerp, our destination, that the mystery was solved. Perhaps you have heard from one of the others that preparations for a land invasion of England were actually under way until Goering admitted that the Luftwaffe could not guarantee sufficient air protection. Meanwhile all flat-bottom barges from the Dutch and Belgian canal systems had been collected and many were equipped with air propellers driven by airplane engines. I have no idea just how many of these engines were used but they must have numbered thousands, and perhaps this accounts for the fact that we did not have enough spare plane motors when they were really needed.

At any rate, hundreds—perhaps thousands—of these barges were assembled in the inlets, straits and canals of the Scheldt River delta and some twenty to thirty divisions were being trained in embarkation and debarkation tactics. Most of these maneuvers were under cover of night, since the invasion of England would naturally have to be a nocturnal job. It is fairly obvious that the British Intelligence learned of these activities from informers among the Belgians and Dutch. A number of arrests were made, but nothing could be proved.

One night several squadrons of British bombing planes flew over just as the maneuvers were under way. To supply the invasion barges with the necessary fuel a number of temporary oil storage tanks had been placed near the training grounds. They were expertly camouflaged, but it is evident that the British had precise information on their location, for they scored a number of direct hits on the oil. The tanks exploded, flaming oil flowed into the straits and canals, and within the briefest imaginable time the troops on the barges were surrounded by a sea of flames. The scene was described to me by one who saw it as one vast flaming hell. According to official computations more than ten thousand men lost their lives, literally burning to death in a gigantic pyre of oil. The number of wounded is twice that. In brief, we have approximately thirty thousand casualties, more than we had in the entire Polish campaign, and this without a military engagement.

On our return trip, Hitler stopped at Laeken Castle, residence of King Leopold of Belgium. The two met, but I can tell you nothing of it except what I heard later from members of Hitler's staff. According to them, Hitler and the King spent about four hours together, actually one half hour alone. They were later joined by Henri Le Man, Keitel and Jodl.

The conversation after Hitler and Leopold joined their advisers may give you an idea of what was discussed between the two in private. The King was sounded out on a political move. He was told that there was a suggestion—as vague as that—that Belgium and Holland be merged into a Kingdom of the United Netherlands, repeating history of more than a hundred years ago. At that time, both countries were under the rule of the Royal House of Orange, the present ruling Dutch dynasty. The current idea is to unite them under the Royal House of Saxe-Coburg in the person of King Leopold.

The King was quite reserved. He answered that with both countries under German occupation and the Netherlands' queen a fugitive in

London, he could not very well discuss the matter. If this subject were to arise at a general peace conference he might consider it, but with matters as they are, he could not very well express an opinion.

I have an opinion of my own about this. I believe that the whole scheme was presented quite boldly as a bribe to induce Leopold to undertake the mission Hitler would have him perform at the Vatican. It is highly significant that Hitler is testing Leopold while at the same time Goering and Laval discuss the partitioning of Belgium in a new geopolitical Europe.

Whether or not Leopold was able to see the plot behind this, I cannot say. It is very probable that the Vatican mission was not discussed after Leopold had shown coolness to the United Netherlands scheme. Perhaps it is significant that during the return trip to Berchtesgaden Hitler was in one of his ugly moods.

If Hitler should continue to travel you will hear from me soon again.

In warm friendship,
MANFRED.

We did not doubt that Manfred was keenly aware of the situation and knew that Hitler was working on some scheme with regard to the Church, but upon thorough discussion we decided not to use this material on the air. Religious matters have a tendency to become delicate and frequently controversial subjects. As I observed before, I had received a tremendous amount of mail after my first broadcast about Hitler and the Vatican. While these letters were written in a friendly tone, many of them, expecially if answered over the radio, would have started a heated controversy—and this we wanted to avoid.

Soon we received a stirring report from Clara, stirring not only because of the information it contained, but also because van Narvig instantly recognized the great risks the girl had taken to procure it. Here it is:

Dear Willy:

By the greatest stroke of luck, I am in a position today to write you on the results of Stahmer's mission in Tokyo.

The Japanese have specified a number of conditions which must be met before Japan will enter into a military alliance with Germany and Italy. I shall list them, for it is simpler that way.

1. Russia must be neutralized in eastern Siberia because Japan

cannot at present attempt another major war effort in addition to that against China. It is up to Germany to arrange such a neutralization.

2. Before Japan can strike in southeast Asia, bases must be established from which such operations can be undertaken with a minimum of risk. The only logical place for the establishment of such bases is French Indo-China. Since both Great Britain and the United States would very likely protest if she were to seize Indo-China by force, and might even declare war on Japan, it is imperative that Germany persuade France to permit Japan to make use of Indo-Chinese bases under some sort of agreement. Indo-China must be penetrated in a peaceful fashion, as were Austria and Czechoslovakia.

3. Japan is still lacking in sufficient machine tools. She must have these in order to intensify her war preparations and it is up to Germany to furnish them.

4. A successful war in the southwest Pacific will require unquestioned Japanese air superiority, not only in quantity of planes, but in quality of air personnel. Japan is particularly lacking in dive bombers —a German specialty. Therefore, Germany must give access to all secrets of German air power to a Japanese air mission. Japan must receive technicians and instructors from Germany. The same applies to the German panzer technique. In return for all this, Japan would willingly release her military secrets to Germany, which might prove valuable in the European war scene.

5. Since Germany holds the Netherlands by right of conquest and can legitimately claim the Dutch East Indies, these claims must be ceded to Japan. In return, Japan will agree to mutual exploitation of specific East Indies resources, but under Japanese sovereignty.

There is a great deal more, but it was impossible for me to get this at the time. Let me explain how I obtained this information. When I learned that an important message from Stahmer had arrived and Hitler summoned his aides for consultation, I went immediately to my listening post. But I had scarcely arranged myself when I heard someone entering the filing rooms. I had barely time to push the cabinet in place.

The girl who had come in remained to complete some work. I dared not arouse her suspicions because Gottlieb had told me that she was a Himmler spy. I began to file various documents, hoping that she would leave, but she didn't.

I kept racking my brain, and an idea came to me. I remembered that one of the girls had been told to prepare a set of documents that Hitler would want in the morning. As she shared the same office with me, I went there, unlocked her desk and took out the papers. Then I made my way to Hitler's study. I really had no plan beyond that. I simply prayed that good fortune would be with me.

The guard in the vestibule let me pass when I explained that the Fuehrer had asked for the dossier which I carried. I passed into the study, which I found deserted. But voices carried from the veranda through the half-open French windows. On Hitler's desk were some papers. I tiptoed across the heavy rug. At a glance I could see that there was a translation of Dr. Stahmer's code message. I read as much of it as I dared. The material is the summary I have given you. I could not read on, for a scraping of chairs on the veranda indicated that someone might return to the study at any moment.

I had to think and act fast. I stepped to the French windows and knocked on the pane. A voice from the veranda demanded, "*Wer ist da?*"

I stepped onto the veranda where I found myself confronted by Hitler, Ribbentrop and Jodl. Hitler demanded, "*Was wuenschen Sie?*"

I acted quite stupid and confused, stammering something about having heard that the documents I carried were required by the Fuehrer. The girl who had been preparing them had been called to other duties and I had taken the liberty of bringing the dossier upstairs.

Hitler glanced at the documents and said that actually he had wanted them delivered in the morning, but the situation had changed and he needed them immediately. He thanked me for bringing them and even praised my initiative. I curtsied and left immediately. Back at the office, I wrote a note for the girl, telling her that Hitler had asked for the papers that night and that I had delivered them. Then I went home, utterly exhausted from fright and nervous strain.

I wanted to write you immediately, but just couldn't. In fact, I did not sleep the entire night. In the morning I was immensely relieved when the other girl told me that Hitler had sent the dossier back and everything was all right. I pretended to be ill, returned home and wrote you this letter. I haven't told Gottlieb anything about this experience, as he would only give me a good scolding.

I regret that I could not learn more, nor is it likely that I will. Papers of this sort are usually kept in the private files upstairs until they are well dated.

I heard from my boy today. He is in good health and doing well. After his recent illness I thought you might want to know. He also received your package and I cannot tell you how I appreciate such favors.

With my warmest regards,
CLARA.

Clara had procured this information at great personal risk and we determined to use it cautiously. My first broadcast on the subject simply mentioned that Hitler's special emissary, Dr. Heinrich Stahmer, was trying to negotiate a treaty of military alliance between Germany and Japan.

After that broadcast, however, the greater part of Clara's splendid work was relegated to the files for quite a different reason. Official Washington, although it never actually censored my broadcasts, preferred that all mention of Japan as a potential Axis ally be omitted. Far East observers presented Japan's economic status as on the verge of collapse as a result of the protracted war in China. Reports contrary to these observations were considered rank sensationalism. And so we were unable to warn the American public that Japan was growing more menacing daily.

We soon received another report, even more illuminating than Clara's, this one from Linda. She wrote:

Dear Willy:

Karin Hall is currently dull. All this time Goering has been in Berlin, which he detests because of the great heat in the capital at this after-summer season. However, I have something interesting to tell you, thanks to Heinrich, who told me the story for transmission to you. It is the first time he has done it. Before this, I had to pry the information from him. In a way, I still cannot understand him. He likes me, of course, but I do not think he would pass on the information merely on that account. I am beginning to think he is doing it because of his diabolical sense of humor. He is lazy and this is one way in which he can derive a sort of amusement without exerting any physical effort. We drove to the Grunewald, where Heinrich keeps a small yacht, and went sailing on the Havel. It was there that Heinrich gave me this story.

According to Heinrich, we are headed straight for a military alliance with Japan, and it may come sooner than even the initiated expect. Hitler has been in Berlin for five days. Also Goering, Hess, Ribbentrop, Himmler, Goebbels, Frick, Funk, Ley, Keitel and Jodl—in short, everyone who counts. At this season, too.

It is generally believed that their presence in Berlin is due to the current visit of Ramon Serrano Suner, General Franco's brother-in-law and head of the Spanish Falange party. He is trying to persuade our people that Spain should receive her share of the war plunder. Many banquets have been held in his honor, but Heinrich believes that these banquets will be all the Spaniard will get.

The really important man in Berlin these days is the Japanese Ambassador, Saburo Kurusu, who has been calling at the Reich Chancellory day after day, holding private meetings with Hitler and Ribbentrop for hours on end. The lights in the Japanese Embassy are on practically all night, indicating a continuous exchange of code messages with Tokyo. Ribbentrop has left hurriedly for Rome, probably to arrange for Italy's participation in the proposed alliance.

Heinrich does not know yet what the terms of the new alliance will be, and he probably will not until the documents have been signed. But he contends that the Dutch East Indies will be assigned to the Japanese. I expressed my doubt that Hitler would renounce such a treasure house, but Heinrich says that an entirely different policy is behind the move. By having them lose their Asiatic possessions, Hitler expects to make the Dutch so dependent on German economy that they will accept incorporation into the Reich as a blessing.

While the Japanese alliance will be made for the primary purpose of breaking up the British Empire, it is also directed against the United States. Hitler fears that unless this new treaty is signed quickly, the United States will enter the war to preserve Anglo-Saxon domination of the world's sea routes, raw materials and gold. He is prepared to bargain with the United States, but if this should prove impossible and American participation in the war becomes a definite threat, he wants Japan allied with the Axis for the two-fold purpose of shutting off the United States from her supply of rubber and tin in Southeast Asia and of dividing the American war effort so that Germany will not be the sole enemy of the United States.

This is the plan he intends to use in bargaining with the United States. The British Empire is to be divided. The United States will receive all British possessions in the Western Hemisphere, including Canada, and possibly Australia and New Zealand. The United States will be offered complete control over Central and South America, subject to favorable trade agreements with a German-dominated Europe. From what you told me of America, I am certain that Hitler's disappointment will be great, although he firmly believes that he can induce your country to adopt an imperialist policy within the borders he is willing to assign.

Incidentally, Heinrich told me that Hitler—and the whole Nazi clique, for that matter—is intensely interested in the American presidential election. Bohle is getting complete reports from his men over there and both Hitler and Ribbentrop consult him frequently on the subject. At first they hoped that an extreme isolationist would be nominated to oppose Roosevelt, in which case they would have poured funds into America to insure the isolationist's election.

News of Willkie's nomination was first received with elation, for they felt that a German-American would be in sympathy with German interests and conduct himself accordingly. When Willkie, however, went even further than Roosevelt in his anti-Nazi speeches, their elation turned into rage. Hitler states that Willkie is a traitor to his blood, a man who has no right to live. After this, the Nazis decided to keep aloof from the elections, but this attitude changed when a long report from Fritz Wiedemann arrived. Nazi agents in the United States are now instructed to campaign, and violently, for Roosevelt. The reason behind this move is simple.

According to Wiedemann's report, there are many divided factions in the United States, all of them bitterly fighting each other. The factions are capital and labor, interventionists and isolationists, as well as various other groups, and their controversies have been brought about by Roosevelt's policies. Because of this, Hitler believes firmly that the American people are in a deep muddle and very much confused. He believes that if Roosevelt continues in office, these controversies will not only continue, but will grow in intensity. As a result the government will not be able to adopt a definite foreign policy, and certainly not an openly belligerent one. Second, Hitler feels that if Roosevelt makes his own decisions and ignores those of the warring factions, there will be revolution in America and this he fervently wishes.

The Nazis are thoroughly contemptuous of the Roosevelt administration. They believe that Washington officials, especially those in accord with Roosevelt, are idle Utopian dreamers who are content to be dilettantes and dabble ineffectually with plans for social betterment. The Nazis believe that Washington officialdom is completely lacking in realism because, although these officials supervise and administer the richest country in the world, they still have been incapable of bringing the country successfully out of an economic depression. If Germany and the United States go to war against each other, Hitler prefers to have these men in governmental control. He believes they will cripple the nation with their degenerate idealism, rather than stimulate it.

A new administration, Hitler fears, might produce strong men capable of organizing the high industrial potentialities of the United States for a powerful war effort. From what you have told me of the American people, I think that the Fuehrer's arithmetic has been taken from the wrong text book.

This is all I could learn from Heinrich at this time, but he has promised to get in touch with me as soon as something breaks. I shall keep you posted.

I only hope that we shall not have to fête another delegation of Nipponese at Karin Hall. The way things look we may be overrun by missions from the East and it will be part of my work to entertain them. What a life!

I have not been at Berchtesgaden since my return from Paris. If things quiet down a bit I intend to run up there and present Clara with one of my Parisian gowns. She may not have a chance to wear it, but she will get a kick out of just trying it on. Please write me as soon as you have a chance.

Affectionately,
LINDA.

Linda's letter was as complete and interesting a document as we ever received from Germany, especially with regard to German reactions to the political situation in the United States. Unfortunately, the larger part of it did not fit into our broadcasting scheme. Mention of the Japanese situation was still officially taboo. And the section dealing with American politics was sure to be misunderstood, by both Democrats and Republicans. The country was in the midst of one of its most bitterly-contested election campaigns, and under the circumstances we simply did not dare use the information.

Above all, my position in radio was that of a reporter. I presented the facts as they came to me. If one of my stories represented a certain person's opinion, I was careful to state the fact that it was an opinion, and rigidly restrained my own thoughts on the subject. One of the prime reasons for my remaining aloof from domestic politics was the fear of confusing the public and giving the impression that an American election might be decided by Hitler.

However, it seemed too bad that Linda's splendid work should be wasted. We felt that the American public should know the workings of Hitler's machine. Therefore we used Linda's information as the basis for a magazine article entitled, "Why Hitler Watched Our Election." This was published in one of our national weeklies* and appeared on the newsstands the morning after election day. It had been held back until it could do no harm.

Our female contingent in Germany seemed to be working overtime, for the next letter to reach us came again from Clara. She wrote:

Dear Willy:

We just had a foreign visitor at the Berghof—Ramon Serrano Suner, Spanish Minister of the Interior, head of the Falangista party and brother-in-law of the Spanish dictator, General Franco; all of which may mean a great deal in Spain but seems to be quite unimportant here.

He was brought here by Hess. A dinner was held in Suner's honor and the Spaniard presented Hitler with a decoration from the government of Spain which Hitler probably will toss into a drawer. He never wears these things. After the dinner all retired to the study and so I was able to hear parts of the conversation.

Suner evidently came to Germany feeling that Hitler intended to distribute riches at the expense of France and England. He conveyed Spain's wish to share in the spoils of conquest—specifically Gibraltar, Tangier and a considerable part of French Morocco. These were the official requests. Privately the Spaniard admitted that Spanish aspirations go much further. The Falangista party aims at regaining Spain's historical status as a world power. Spanish culture, he explained, is deeply implanted in Central and South America, and while Spain does not expect to re-establish political domination of the Latin American republics, she hopes to bring about a reorientation of public opinion toward the former mother country. The Falangista idea has been well received in many South American countries, he said, and the Party has established numerous affiliates throughout that continent. Suner predicted that Spanish influence would become particularly strong in Argentina and Chile. He considered a politically-united bloc of Spanish-speaking countries a distinct possibility. If this happened, it would mean the entrenchment of the Fascist ideal in South America as against the money democracy of the United States.

Hitler listened to Suner without interruption and with what for him must have been unusual patience. After the Spaniard's speech the Fuehrer said that he would have no objection to Spanish possession of Gibraltar and Tangier, but it would be Spain's own problem to go ahead and take them. As for Spanish wishes regarding a part of

Liberty Magazine, issue of November 16, 1940.

Morocco, Spain would have to take the matter up with the Vichy government.

Hitler evinced great interest in the question of South America. He said that inasmuch as South America's natural trade outlets had always been in European countries and in this industrial age politics are controlled by economics, the establishment of a political bridge between South America and Europe via Spain would be a logical development. He felt that Spain's national interests pointed entirely toward South America, but that Spain must be prepared to combat American dollar diplomacy. But, he cautioned, Spain must bide her time. After South America had drained the United States of money, the Latin American republics would find that their economic interests had little in common with Washington's. Then, if Spain followed a wise policy, South America would naturally turn to the former mother country.

To prepare for the future, Hitler advised that there should be a strengthening of ideological ties between the Falangists and the Nazis. He suggested that large quantities of Fascist propaganda should emanate from Spain and be directed toward South America. In fact, Hitler promised that he would be happy to send his foremost propagandists to Madrid to advise the Spaniards. He also suggested that Spain send promising young men to Berlin in order to study the methods of Dr. Goebbels. He stressed that it was vital to prepare for the future, since the events of today were merely a painful transition from a decadent world order to a new strong order based on a completely revised economic and political foundation.

That is all Suner could get out of Hitler. That he was disappointed was quite obvious, although he assured the Fuehrer that he was immensely impressed by the conversation which had given him a completely new outlook. He departed the same night for Rome, probably to see what could be done with Mussolini.

For the time being this is all. However, the tension here is strong and we are expecting a climax of one sort or another. I shall keep you posted.

With warm regards,
CLARA.

Another letter from Linda arrived with Clara's. She wrote:

Dear Willy:

It has happened! The tripartite pact between Germany, Italy and Japan has become reality. Ribbentrop returned from Rome with Count Ciano. According to Heinrich, Mussolini agreed to the Asiatic Alliance less than three hours after Ribbentrop arrived in Rome. The treaty was signed with great ceremony on the morning of September 27, 1940. Hitler was tremendously pleased and he and Saburo Kurusu were rivalling each other in smiles and handshakes.

But it came as a great shock to a number of Nazis. I doubt that Goering is pleased with the new alliance and I know that Hess is positively unhappy about it. This means that Hitler's official heirs fail to see eye to eye with him on the subject. Heinrich is furious. As you know, he was a follower of Kaiser Wilhelm's ideals and therefore to him an alliance with Japan is criminal.

Incidentally, you will be pleased to know that Heinrich has changed. Instead of having to be persuaded to give me information, he readily volunteers it. And here is something quite interesting.

Of course, you must already know the official text of the pact, which has been widely publicized. But the officially proclaimed document was not the only one signed. Before the official ceremony took place Ribbentrop, Ciano and Kurusu affixed their signatures to a set of secret articles, which supplements the pact. These articles are the substance of an agreement between the three countries to go into effect at the end of the war, when the world has been conquered by the new Axis.

Heinrich has given me most of the terms and, needless to say, they are fabulous. This is the agreement.

1. Germany agrees that Japan's predominant influence shall extend to all territories in Asia and Australasia to the east of a line formed roughly by the Ninetieth Meridian and to be determined in detail at a later date. The exercise of this domination shall be determined by Japan's national interests.

2. Japan agrees that Germany's and Italy's predominant influence shall extend to all territories to the west of a line formed roughly by the Seventieth Meridian and to be determined in detail at a later date. The exercise of this domination and its division between Germany and Italy shall be determined by a separate agreement between the two powers at a later date and is no direct concern of Japan's.

3. The status of territories between the two lines mentioned in paragraphs One and Two, shall be determined in due time.

4. The territories now forming the Union of Soviet Socialist Republics are exempt from this agreement and the relations of Germany, Italy and Japan to these territories will be the subject of subsequent agreements.

5. The contracting parties agree that each shall be free to establish its domination over the territories mentioned in paragraphs One and Two, by its own means and methods.

6. If in the process of extending their domination over the territories mentioned in paragraph Two, Germany or Italy, or both, should be subject to openly hostile acts on the part of the United States of America, or to a declaration of war by the United States of America, Japan agrees to come to the assistance of Germany and Italy with all her armed forces, but the time of her doing so shall be determined by her military preparedness to do so.

7. If in the process of extending her domination over the territories mentioned in paragraph One, Japan should be subject to openly hostile acts on the part of the United States of America, or a declaration of war by the United States of America, Germany and Italy agree to come to the assistance of Japan with all their armed forces immediately.

8. To facilitate Japan's preparations for carrying out her part of the agreement, Germany and Italy agree to prevail upon the government of France to open her ports and other facilities in French Indo-China to Japan under an agreement to be worked out between Japan and the government of France.

This is all that Heinrich gave me. He also told me that a separate agreement was signed between Germany and Japan. This agreement dealt with the exchange of military and naval missions between the two countries and also concerned mutual exchanges of patents and similar rights. A trade agreement was appended.

There you have it. As Heinrich says, Hitler—the self-appointed Aryan—has betrayed the White Race. He has sold out to the arch-enemy of Western Civilization. Heinrich calls it the Goetterdaemmer-ung* of the Occident.

Many here feel, like Heinrich, that Hitler has committed the gravest error of his career, and I am among these. But personal sentiments are out of place. I have matters of greater importance to write you about. These are a few conversational bits that I overheard at Karin Hall.

Goering, Milch and Udet have been engaged in discussions for a number of weeks. Most of their conversations were too technical for me and I can only give you the gist of them. The Luftwaffe failed to knock out the Royal Air Force because it was not sufficiently equipped for the task. Udet has been experimenting with new types of Jagdflugzeuge, Zerstoerer and Kampfflugzeuge†. He and Goering have inspected and tested a number of them and some new models have gone into mass production. The winter production drive will be intense, but even so, the Luftwaffe is not expected to have a sufficient number of combat squadrons for major air operations until May, 1941. As soon as I can

*Title of an opera by Richard Wagner meaning, "The Twilight of the Gods."

†Fighter planes, destroyer planes and bombing planes.

get hold of details on the new types I shall forward them to you.

I have gathered this much. The short-range, level-flight bomber with a flying radius up to 750 miles has been found unsuitable. Except at night, when specific targets do not have to be taken into consideration, it is too dependent on fighter plane support. As a result, losses in fighter planes have been out of all proportion. The place of these bombers will be taken by two new types. One will be a long-range fighter-bombing plane capable of shifting for itself in combat and at the same time carrying a considerable bomb load. The other will be a larger and faster Stuka with a crew of three or four, a special gadget to elude barrage balloon cables and with a flying range of up to 750 miles.

The level-flight bombers now available in large numbers will hereafter be used for night bombing exclusively, except where antiaircraft defenses are sparse. Since night bombing against specific targets has proved ineffective, operations will be carried out hereafter in the form of mass raids on general targets. In other words, there will be an indiscriminate demolition of large population centers.

While Udet has worked on the production angle, Milch has devoted himself to organization. A special Kuestenseeflugkommando has been created. To it have been assigned all long-range patrol and bombing planes of the new Courier and Condor types, all flying boats and amphibian bombers. Its planes are to patrol the ocean and form a team with the submarine fleet, much along the same lines as the Panzer-Stuka team in the army. The planes will also bomb ships at sea.

A separate bomber command has also been created for the organization of mass night raids. It has no fighter planes at its disposal. Inasmuch as they operate at night exclusively, these bombers must shift for themselves. All these organizational changes were considered necessary because of the new and radically different problems presented by the war against England.

This is all for today. I am fed up with things here. I should like to be in America and have you show me your country from one end to the other.

Affectionately,
LINDA.

Needless to say, we used Linda's information on the changes in the Luftwaffe set-up immediately in our broadcasts. As for the secret agreement with Japan, its terms stunned us. But we could go no further. We did not broadcast this information because we knew that it would immediately bring a tide of disbelief, and the station censor grew more rigid daily. We could not prove our assertions even if we had broadcast the information, without involving our friends in Germany. Therefore I simply gave a brief resumé of the general situation.

We next received a letter from Gottlieb, from whom we had not heard for quite a while. The Gestapo man wrote:

Dear Willy:

For the past month or more the best I could do was to forward the correspondence of our friends. In between I had a two-week vacation, my first in twenty months. I spent it with my folks. It was a relief to get away from the witches' cauldron, from spying and being spied upon, from seeing the same faces every day and wondering whether they could see through me. I gave my young sister away in marriage, did some fishing and generally tried to forget the rest of the world.

Now I am back again and in harness. In fact, it was a good time to return. On the third day after I got back, I had to be on Hitler's armored train as it left for the Brenner Pass and a meeting with Mussolini. *

Il Duce's train had already arrived. The two dictators met, shook hands, and seemed especially tense. Although each of the two men had brought a numerous retinue with him, the actual conference was attended only by the dictators themselves, plus Ciano, Ribbentrop, Badoglio, Keitel and Jodl.

All I can tell you is what I learned from others on our way back. The discussion concerned mainly a new war plan. Since England has refused to sue for peace and since the Luftwaffe failed to destroy the Royal Air Force, Hitler and his generals are preparing for a difficult battle. Mussolini seems to waver and our men are sure that he is not prepared for hard fighting.

The new plan calls for the breaking up of England's colonial empire. The argument is that an invasion and eventual subjugation of the British Isles would be so costly that it might leave Germany too weak to engage in an eventual war with Russia and at the same time continue the quest for important raw materials in the East. Furthermore, an invasion of England would still leave the British Empire intact and there is the likelihood that the British fleet and government would escape and continue the war from overseas with the assistance of the United States.

On the other hand, if the colonial empire is broken first, the British

*Hitler and Mussolini conferred at the Brenner Pass on June 2, 1941.

homeland will be so weakened that it will abandon a hopeless struggle. It was with this purpose in view that the deal with Japan was made.

The war is now calculated to last at least into 1943 for the simple reason that Japan will not be ready to fight until a year from now, or late in 1941. It was for this reason that Goebbels and Pavolini—the two propaganda ministers—were brought along. They are to co-ordinate their respective propaganda machines in order to prepare the people of Germany and Italy for the prospect of a long war.

The grand strategy aims at cutting the British lifeline with simultaneous drives by the European part of the Axis eastward and the Japanese westward. It is calculated to solve two principal problems: first, to tear from the Empire structure such important units as Egypt, Iraq, India, Malaya and possibly Australia and New Zealand, at the same time destroying all investments by British capital in the East; second, to obtain for the Axis, and at the same time deprive England of, such important raw materials as oil, rubber, tin, manganese, jute, hemp and others. This would reverse the economic picture as it looked during the first phase of the war.

To succeed, both drives need well-prepared *Ausgangspunkte.* * For the Japanese, this would mean French Indo-China and Thailand. For the European Axis coalition, Libya and the Balkans must be the logical starting points. Libya is already under Axis domination. The Balkans must be penetrated in such a way as to be quickly converted into bases for a push into the Levant. It is also necessary to eliminate any possible Russian interference.

The Balkan push will take a concentric form. This means that a simultaneous enveloping movement must begin from the north and south until the two pincers meet and encircle the central Balkans. The northern pincer must secure Rumania and then move into Bulgaria. The southern pincer will obtain Greece and move up to Bulgaria. This will encircle Yugoslavia. Germany will move with one arm into Rumania and hold Russia with the other. Italy must seize Greece with one arm and hold her Libyan position with the other. Germany's next maneuver will be to win the Turks and proceed to Syria and Iraq.

For this purpose Germany is already training troops for desert warfare. Lieutenant General Erwin Rommel has been assigned two stretches of land—one along the Baltic coast and the other in the Austrian plain —where desert conditions have been artificially created in tremendous, heated hangars. Germany's desert armies will extend one pincer through Palestine for a meeting with the Italian armies driving east-

*Starting points, meaning bases.

152

ward from Libya, while the other pincer will be thrust into Iraq and Iran for a junction with the Japanese arrival from the East.

All this will, of course, take time, and with all these preparations in the east, the west will not be neglected. There remains the possibility that the British, with American assistance, will involve the European branch of the Axis on a western front. Hitler has undertaken to guard against this. The Atlantic coast line now under German control will be strongly fortified. Farther to the south, Hitler will attempt to form a defensive bloc composed of France, Spain and Portugal to guard against any invasion attempt through their territories. At the same time, England herself will be subjected to intensified night bombing by the Luftwaffe, to destroy, or at least disrupt, her industrial and communications centers and render her incapable of any offensive operations.

This is the general outline, the best I could obtain. I hope to give you more information on this new war plan as soon as I learn it.

Grüss Gott!
GOTTLIEB.

CHAPTER 16

APPARENTLY THERE WAS A BREAK in our communications, something that had delayed our messenger, for Gottlieb's report did not reach us until after German troops had moved into Rumania. This was not important, however, since we had already forecast the Rumanian move from Wolfgang's latest letter, although that one had not contained the complete motivation. We still hesitated to use the information about Japanese intentions, but we availed ourselves of the remainder of the Axis plans, involving the overrunning of the Balkans by bloodless conquest, the extension of pincers from both sides toward Suez and a drive against the oil fields of Iraq and Iran. In my broadcasts I also repeated the warning that Mussolini was preparing to march into Greece. *

We carefully considered the involvement of America in the war foreshadowed in Gottlieb's report. As a matter of fact, months earlier, during the Battle of France, when practically all America

*Williams' broadcast of October 8, 1940, stating, "A Blackshirt army in Albania, a quarter million strong, is ready to move against Greece." Actually, the Italians invaded Greece on October 28, 1940.

believed that Hitler's army would be defeated, we decided to sound out American public opinion on the question of national defense. We began an intensive radio campaign advocating a strong U. S. Army, equipped for modern mechanized warfare and recruited on the principle of selective conscription. For a period of months I finished each broadcast with a recommendation for this plan. I quote from the initial suggestion made over the air on June 11, 1940:

"Therefore, I advocate a standing army of at least 700,000 soldier mechanics recruited and maintained by selective conscription. I should like very much to get the reaction of my radio audience to this proposal. I should like especially the opinions of our young men who would be directly affected and of the mothers of these young men. Please write me in care of this station, WOR, in New York."

I had a stiff battle with the station censor over this proposal. He argued that it fell under the classification of personal opinion and that commentators were not allowed to present personal opinions over the air. It was only after my refusal to go on the air unless I was permitted to broadcast this patriotic appeal that I won out.

The reaction from this audience was spontaneous and encouraging. Letters poured in by the hundreds from all parts of the country. With but a few exceptions, the writers were enthusiastic and promised full support of my proposal. Many letters were from women who were anxious to know how they could help our country while their husbands and sons served in the army.

Then the Burke-Wadsworth bill for Selective Service was introduced in Congress. All through the Congressional debate I kept plugging the bill in my broadcasts. Later Senator Burke sent me a letter of appreciation for my work in the bill's behalf. Van Narvig and I felt that we had helped get the national defense program going, and naturally were proud of the part we had played. As soon as the legislation was passed, both van Narvig's son and mine entered the United States armed forces. Eventually both went overseas to fight the Jap.

Gottlieb's latest letter left us with no doubt that Hitler intended to involve the United States whenever it suited his purpose. This was a difficult matter to handle, for we could not urge the United States' entry into the war at a time when the country was totally unprepared for such a venture. Furthermore a bitter battle between isolationists and interventionists was raging, and so I remained a factual reporter and did not take sides.

Finally we struck what seemed to us the proper method of handling this situation. We kept urging the enlargement of the United States armed forces and increased production of modern armament, especially planes and tanks. Eventually we predicted that the United States would become involved in the war by the spring of 1941*.

Our next letter from abroad came from Linda. She wrote:

Dear Willy:

I have spent two days with Clara at Berchtesgaden. Hitler and his staff were absent, so we had a really good time. Wolfgang came over from Fuschl. Something is going on between him and Clara and I should not be surprised if the two got married. Clara is not exactly in love with him, but she is very fond of him. I advised her to wait at least until spring, winter in wartime being such a miserable season here. I gave her several things from my Paris loot and she was very happy.

One thing worries Clara and that is this work of ours. It seems that it just would not fit in with married life. At present all of us are either spinsters or bachelors. Marriage imposes responsibilities that are incompatible with the risks that we simply have to take at times. At least, if I were married I certainly would not do anything that might land my husband in a concentration camp, or perhaps worse. But enough of personal matters.

The Japanese alliance is beginning to be more in evidence. We are now lending some of our best Luftwaffe men to the Yellow Peril. The other day Milch spent two days at Karin Hall in conferences with Goering. Now he is on his way to Japan, and with him is a large staff of experts. Others are to leave in groups over a period of the next thirty days, traveling across Russia via the Trans-Siberian railway. They will

*Williams and van Narvig understood that United States involvement would be gradual because of the country's military weakness. The first step in the direction of war was actually taken in March, 1941, with the passage of Lend-Lease legislation.

total more than 750 men—designers, aviation engineers, special crafts-
men in the instrument field, test pilots and flight instructors. Their
assignment is to help organize Japanese production of dive bombers and
fighter planes along German mass production methods. The Japanese, I
understand, have constructed a number of new factories but are unable
to get them into real volume production. Milch is expected to return
some time before the New Year, leaving behind those of the technicians
whose help is still needed in Japan.

We are also committed to the delivery, via Russia, of considerable
numbers of Zeiss bomb sights and numerous other instruments which
Japan as yet is unable to produce in quantity. In brief, we are handing
over to our new partners virtually all our secret devices. In return,
Milch is supposed to be given some special Japanese inventions, but
just how valuable these will be remains to be seen. Goering is rather
skeptical about the arrangement. The only thing he and Milch think
may be worth having is the design of a torpedo-carrying plane developed by the Japanese navy which, we have been told, is superior in
maneuverability to anything similar we have.

I have not heard from Heinrich in more than two weeks, but I am
quite certain he would communicate with me if he had anything of
importance to tell. However, I expect to go to the Reichsluftminis-
terium* in Berlin next week, to deliver some things for Goering, and
then I will have a chance to talk with Heinrich.

Affectionately,
LINDA.

Linda's letter arrived simultaneously with one from Clara, she
wrote:

Dear Willy:

Linda was here from Berlin on a two-day visit. She recounted much
of her experiences in Paris and presented me with some of her new
Paris clothes. It was fortunate that she described some of the leading
French politicians so vividly, including their favorite mannerisms, as
otherwise I might not have recognized Pierre Laval when he arrived
here, unheralded and incognito, yesterday.

With Laval came Otto Abetz, whom I had never seen before. I
found out who he was when he was addressed by his last name during
the discussions upstairs. Goering had arrived earlier the same day, but
he has been here so often of late that his visit occasioned no particular
excitement.

*Air Ministry.

I recognized Laval the moment he entered the large downstairs hall. His manner was fidgety, just as Linda had described it to me. I was surprised at the courtesy and friendliness with which Hitler greeted him. I had expected something quite the contrary, but apparently the Fuehrer had good reasons of his own for putting on this most agreeable manner.

The conversations centered on the possibility of concluding a permanent peace between Germany and France to replace the armistice agreement. Hitler said he was not anxious at this time to discuss peace terms, stating that relations with France under the terms of the armistice agreement were quite satisfactory. That is easy to understand since Germany holds a highly productive and strategically important part of France and the costs of the occupation are being paid by the French government, imposing no burden on the Reich for its maintenance. The armistice also provided that almost two million French prisoners of war were to remain in German hands until three months after a permanent peace was concluded. Since most of these prisoners are now working for the German war economy they represent no burden. Hitler told Laval that he realized that some of the armistice conditions imposed great economic hardships on France, but this was part of the price of defeat.

The Fuehrer agreed with Laval that at the time the armistice was concluded, neither France nor Germany expected the war against the British to continue for long. That it had continued, he said, was the fault of London entirely, and now that it appeared likely to go on for at least another year, France was facing a much heavier burden than her leaders had calculated. While he sympathized with the plight of the French people, Hitler said, and would gladly help ease their situation, he could only do this if reciprocal advantages were offered him in the war against England. If Laval were in a position to suggest any such advantages, Hitler promised to weigh the question carefully.

Laval replied that he fully appreciated the Fuehrer's attitude, but found himself in a rather peculiar position. He had always stood for a policy of closer understanding between France and Germany and had his advice been heeded, the war would not have taken place. Now he was entrusted with the responsibility of directing French foreign policy in the most trying period of France's history. He was a Frenchman, first and last, and it was up to him to obtain the most favorable possible conditions for his country.

As matters stood, the armistice burden was ruinous to France. The maintenance of the German army of occupation was a completely unproductive expense. The best farm labor was in German prison camps and French agriculture was virtually at a standstill. If this continued another year, not only would France be unable to deliver agricultural products to Germany but she would even be unable to feed her own population. French industry was completely disrupted because several million skilled workers had fled to the south where they remained unemployed, while factories in the north stood idle.

German hegemony in Europe was already established, asserted Laval, and both he and his colleagues in the French government were convinced that Germany would be victorious in her war with England. Its entire policy was based on this conviction. Germany had undertaken to organize Europe and he had been assured by Reichsmarshal Goering and others that France would be accorded an important position in the New Order. In the interests of continental organization, he maintained, an economically re-established French nation would be advantageous to future German plans, especially in view of further and possibly far-reaching military operations.

Laval contended that the re-establishment of French economic life depended on certain changes. First, he said, it was impossible to govern France, from Vichy. It amounted to the same thing as trying to govern Germany from Karlsbad or Innsbruck. Paris was not only the political and economic hub of the nation but it was a symbol in the eyes of every Frenchman. Only after the French Government was re-established in Paris could it really begin the economic re-organization of France. Second, the farm workers now in German prison camps must be released to undertake the rehabilitation of French agriculture. Third, France could not possibly put her financial house in order so long as she had to pay the tremendous cost of supporting the German army of occupation. Fourth, the French government must have sufficient civil power in the occupied zone to direct French industrial production. He, Laval, understood perfectly that under existing conditions French industry must work largely for the German war effort, but even this would be better than the present situation. At least it would keep French industrial organizations intact, the French worker would make a living, and the French government would be relieved of its present colossal burden of caring for millions of unemployed. If Hitler could grant these adjustments France would quickly become a distinct asset to Germany.

Hitler approved greatly of this. He said that if this plan could be acted upon immediately, Germany's New Order in Europe would have a real beginning. He asserted that he had devoted a great deal of thought to the French problem, and because he wanted to establish a new friendship and understanding between the French and German

158

peoples he would go even further than the proposals made by Laval. In fact, he could make France a very advantageous offer.

Now, this is the offer and its terms. First Hitler spoke of the territorial adjustment regarding Alsace and Lorraine which must become provinces of Germany. In return, the French-speaking sections of Belgium would be given to France. In the event of a later re-organization of Switzerland, France would also be given the French-speaking districts of that country. With regard to colonial possessions, he was willing to guarantee the integrity of the French colonial empire as currently composed, with the exception of those African territories which were German prior to the Versailles Treaty*. He would also undertake to obtain the consent of Italy to this guarantee, provided that France would sign a trade agreement that would provide for the division of certain essential colonial products among the three countries.

Referring to Paris as the seat of the French Government, Hitler pointed out one difficulty. Paris is the hub of the French railroads and highways. So long as the war with England continued, German military authorities must have control over these communications lines. There could be a compromise, however, reached by removing all German troops from the central parts of the city to the outskirts and altering the present demarcation line so that the Unoccupied Zone would include Versailles. Hitler said he was also willing to release French prisoners of war as soon as a definite understanding on future European policy is reached between the two countries. With regard to the costs of the German army of occupation, Hitler expressed himself willing to reduce them by seventy-five per cent.

Hitler went on to say that he saw no objection to the restoration of French civil authority in the occupied zone, with the exception of the coastal stretch which must remain exclusively under the jurisdiction of the German army. He said that Germany is fully prepared to win the war against England without outside help. She needs no military or naval aid from France and would consider such help undesirable for reasons of prestige. However, France must establish absolute political and economic collaboration with Germany. This means that so long as the war continues, French industry and agriculture must work in the interests of the German Wehrwirtschaft, and that French foreign diplomacy must be within the framework of the New Europe.

Hitler launched an idea concerning the creation of a Latin Defense

*German East Africa, divided between Britain and Belgium, now administered under a mandate; Togoland, divided between Britain and France; and the Cameroons, likewise split between Britain and France. Part of French Equatorial Africa ceded to Germany in 1911, was returned to France under the Treaty of Versailles.

Bloc consisting of France, Spain and Portugal. France would assume the leadership in this union and, as the leader, would undertake the defense of southwest Europe and northwest Africa against all aggression by any power at war with Germany. Hitler expected soon to meet with General Franco of Spain for a discussion of this project. He would then hold another meeting with Laval, after the latter had reached a full understanding with Marshal Petain. Then the articles of peace could be signed. Naturally, the proposed Latin Defense Bloc would be required to use its naval forces to protect its shipping against interference by the British blockade. This would apply especially to the French navy, which would thus be placed in the service of the Latin Bloc—entirely under French command, however.

This was the essence of the discussions. They continued throughout the day and it was impossible for me to hear everything. But I believe that I have covered all the important points.

With sincere regards,
CLARA.

Political events moved so rapidly that Hitler's meetings with General Franco and Marshal Petain had already made the headlines by the time Clara's report reached us. We were able to broadcast, however, a comprehensive picture of the general policy then pursued by Hitler. In this we were considerably aided by a report from Manfred which came to us at a moment when the nature of Hitler's political manipulations was still a matter of speculation in the United States. Manfred wrote:

Dear Willy:

I am in Berchtesgaden, writing this to you before leaving for Berlin. I have just returned from one of the most hectic journeys yet. A detail of Gestapo men was ordered out of bed at four o'clock in the morning and told to be in Berchtesgaden by noon. The instructions were signed by Himmler himself on a special new form bearing the heading, "Sicherheitsschutzdienst des Fuehrers."*

We were at Berchtesgaden at the designated time, but the armored train did not leave until late that afternoon. We were going toward France. I believed then that our destination would be the Channel coast, to get first-hand information on the London bombings. I was wrong, however. We arrived in Paris the following morning and were driven to the Crillon, staff headquarters of the army of occupation.

*Security Service of the Fuehrer.

At noon Pierre Laval, who had just arrived by special train from Vichy, presented himself. Clara had told me of his visit to Berchtesgaden less than a week before. He was certainly not here merely to pay his respects.

I was very much surprised when Hitler emerged from his suite to greet the Frenchman and shake hands with him most cordially. Hitler then led Laval into his rooms where the two remained closeted for more than a half hour. I learned what had been discussed, later, when I overheard General Jodl mentioning it on the train after Hitler had confided the details of the meeting to him.

Laval informed Hitler that he was meeting many difficulties, especially with Petain, in accomplishing the plans which had been decided upon at the Berchtesgaden meeting. Petain, it appears, had refused to believe Laval and wished reassurances from Hitler, personally. He had sent Laval to ask that a meeting between Hitler and the Marshal be held. Hitler agreed to this and promised to inform Laval of the date and place later on.

Laval, however, had something of his own to say to Hitler. He asked that the Fuehrer restrict his conversation with Petain to generalities and then imply that Laval, informed in complete detail of the plans, would be acceptable to assume charge of negotiations on the French-German collaboration agreement. If Laval were given such undisputed authority there could be no interference from the army clique in Vichy.

That same night we were traveling again, this time proceeding south on the Angoulême Railroad. We crossed the Gironde at Bordeaux and stopped for refueling. When we passed Biarritz it was quite evident that we were headed for the Spanish frontier. There was no longer any doubt that Hitler was on his way to meet General Franco.

We stopped for more than an hour at Hendaye and I was sure that we were waiting for Franco to arrive. But again we started to move, quite slowly though, and within twenty minutes we arrived at a small mountain station, heavily draped with swastika flags and the red and gold colors of Fascist Spain. We were actually on Spanish soil. No civilians could be seen on the station platform, only Spanish troops and several Gestapo men. The first to enter Hitler's car was Baron von Stohrer, our ambassador to Spain, dressed in full diplomatic regalia. He acted quite excited and a few minutes later he and Hitler emerged from the car, to be greeted on the platform by Franco and his staff.*

With Franco were Serrano Suner, General Varela, chief-of-staff of the Spanish army, Count de los Monteros, Spanish ambassador to Berlin and several others who do not matter. With Hitler were Keitel,

*Hitler and Franco met at the French-Spanish border on October 23, 1940.

161

Jodl, Stuelpnagel, Ribbentrop, Dietrich and Schmidt*. A Spanish guard of honor was drawn up on one side of the station, a similar German guard on the other. Hitler and Franco inspected both, the others following closely behind.

After this ceremony, Franco and Hitler, accompanied by Schmidt, retired into the Fuehrer's car. The military of both sides formed one discussion group, the diplomats another, until both were invited to join the dictators. I can tell you a great deal about this meeting for the details were freely discussed on the train during the return trip.

Franco asked Hitler if Germany intended to push south and, in that case, what position he expected Spain to take? Hitler, I might add, is well informed on the domestic situation in Spain. He knows that the people of Spain are hungry, that their cities, railroads and highways are largely destroyed and that no real attempt at rebuilding has been made. He also knows that a German army in Spain would be of little use.

He likewise knows that Franco is seeking food. He had been receiving some from the French, but that source was cut off when Germany entered France. The only source now open to Franco is the Western Hemisphere and to obtain from there the food he needs, it is necessary that, at least on the surface, Spain remain neutral. Hitler agrees fully with this tactic.

Without hesitation he informed Franco that he does not want to see Spain involved in the war, at least not until Hitler can provision not only the Spaniards, but also a German army of assistance in Spain, with the necessary supplies.

Hitler, however, expects Franco to pay for the German assistance which Franco received in establishing his regime. He wants to be sure that no one enters through the Iberian back door and threatens his hold on the continent while he is busy in the east. While he is fairly certain of Spain he is wary of Portugal's long-standing alliance with England. He wants Franco to lure Portugal away from her British tie-up.

He explained his ideas regarding a Latin Defense Bloc to Franco. That is why, he explained he is permitting the French to build up their West African defenses. Apparently, after the British attempt to seize Dakar, Hitler gave the French the choice of reinforcing Dakar's defenses or letting him do it.

Hitler told Franco that, in his opinion, the weakest point in Europe today is Portugal; not only the country itself, but also her island possessions of the Azores and Madeira. He wants to be sure that the British will not establish themselves on these islands. Therefore he wants

*Dr. Otto Dietrich, Nazi Press Chief, and Dr. Schmidt, Nazi Propaganda Ministry Official.

Franco to negotiate a military alliance between Spain and Portugal, and by this means wean the latter country away from Britain.

Since he still feels that the British fleet is a menacing power, he wants particularly to have Portugal fortify and garrison the Azores and Madeira against any surprise attack by the British. He has also asked Franco to impress upon the Lisbon government that if the islands should be occupied by a power at war with Germany, Hitler would be forced to send his armies through Spain to occupy Portugal.

Spain is also to keep the Canary Islands well garrisoned and on guard against British seizure. If Spain is still interested in Tangier, she is at liberty to seize this territory whenever she pleases. Germany and Italy will support her after the fait accompli. Gibraltar will be awarded to Spain at the conclusion of the war. In the meantime the Spanish press, which Franco rigidly controls, will raise demands for Gibraltar, to keep the British guessing in the war of nerves. A special trade agreement between Germany and Spain will also be concluded. Germany is particularly interested in Spanish cork and oranges.

In return for all this, Hitler will guarantee to keep Spain and Portugal out of the war.

This is all I can tell you concerning the Hitler-Franco meeting. Our propaganda machine will probably blow up the results of the conference to elephantine proportions, but do not let that fool you. Hitler is definitely not going into Spain, nor is he intent on seizing Gibraltar. His only present concern in this part of Europe is to erect reliable guards in the west, so that he can attend to his eastern plans without any fear of interference.

We left Spain late in the afternoon, after luncheon was served in Hitler's dining car. Once again we passed through Biarritz and Bordeaux, and northward along the Angoulême Railroad. Hitler seemed impatient and we assumed that he wished to be back at Berchtesgaden. We were quite surprised—the entire trip was a series of surprises— when the train stopped early in the morning at a small French station called Montoire and remained there for some time.

The station was heavily guarded and there were even flak guns posted in a number of places. A squadron of Messerschmitts hovered overhead. About nine o'clock Keitel and Jodl appeared on the platform. They were soon joined by Hitler and the three walked back and forth briskly. Meanwhile a guard of honor made its appearance from somewhere. I was still speculating on the possible significance of this when a motorcade approached from the east. As it drew up I saw that the first car was filled with Gestapo agents. From the second Pierre Laval and Marshal Petain emerged.

The situation was truly ironic. For, as the men stepped from the car, the guard of honor snapped to attention. A military band struck up the Marseillaise. Tricolors suddenly swayed with the breeze. Hitler himself stepped forward, grasped Marshal Petain by the arm and helped him solicitously up one step. There was an inspection of the guard. Although France had fallen in defeat and shame under the Nazis, Marshal Petain was treated with great respect as the head of a government.

The conference between Hitler and Petain was not so private as those held between Hitler and Mussolini, or even the one between Hitler and Franco. In fact, at no time during the meeting did the two confer alone. Laval and Abetz were always present and others entered and left during the meeting. Under a very flimsy pretext, even I managed to get in.

Evidently the entire procedure had been carefully planned in advance by Hitler and Laval. With Laval speaking fairly good German, and Abetz fully conversant in French, Dr. Schmidt's services were rarely resorted to.

Hitler told Petain that while Germany and France were at war it had naturally been his most important aim to defeat the military power of France. Now that hostilities were a matter of the past, he felt very friendly toward the French. In fact he had always had a kind feeling for France because he believed that the war had been largely the result of British machinations. As long as the war between Germany and England continued, Germany was forced to take every precaution and maintain her defensive and offensive bases on French soil. Hitler said he felt certain that an experienced soldier like Marshal Petain would well understand this. Petain agreed that he understood very well.

Aside from these forced military considerations, Hitler continued, Germany had only the best intentions toward France. He was not concerned with the system of government by which France was ruled, as this was a purely French affair. It was his conviction, however, that amicable relations between chiefs of state reflected favorably on the relations between the peoples governed by them. With this, too, Petain agreed. The Marshal then said that Pierre Laval had submitted for his consideration certain proposals aimed at regulating relations between Germany and France, and his reason for wanting to meet the Fuehrer was to discuss them. He also wished to know exactly what attitude the Fuehrer took with regard to France's position in the New Order.

Hitler replied that he had undertaken the Gargantuan task of building a new Europe, completely unified in its purpose to establish a happier European community than had ever before existed. This new

Europe, he said, must be based not on bitterness and intermittent wars, but on co-operation and prosperity. This could not be realized, however, unless France, one of the most important nations in Europe, occupied her rightful place in it; which required, as Marshal Petain no doubt could well understand, full collaboration between Germany and France in the economic and cultural spheres.

Hitler asserted that he did not want to see France a weak nation. While military necessity dictated that he hold the rebirth of the armed power of continental France in temporary abeyance, he considered the French African colonies a vital outpost of European defense. He wanted France to be strong enough in her overseas possessions to repel any possible aggression against the West African shore. He felt that if France had not sufficient military power to undertake the defense of these shores, he must do this himself, although he had not the slightest inclination for the task. The history of England, he pointed out, proved that the British invariably extended their own colonial empire at the expense of their one-time allies and he did not want to see anything like that happen in the case of France. It was here that German and French military policy met on common ground.

Petain agreed to this. He declared that the French government was determined to defend its African possessions at all cost, as had been done at Dakar. It was for this purpose that General Weygand had been commissioned by Petain to organize African defenses. However, Petain explained, France was severely handicapped in that her principal armament industries were in the occupied zone and that the few still remaining in the area governed from Vichy were controlled by German military commissions. Unless France were in a position to keep her African forces equipped and supplied, what chance did she have to resist a really strong attack?

Other considerations, Petain said, were the Italian demands. As yet there was no assurance that Italy would modify her inflated territorial claims. If, in the end, France were to lose part of her colonies to Italy, what reason could she have for defending them now?

Hitler carefully replied to these arguments. He said, first, that Germany was prepared to release to the French government all captured and controlled French war equipment which, upon mutual agreement, would be considered necessary for French defenses in West Africa. France still had her fleet and Germany would be willing to grant its remobilization. He reminded Petain that it was England and not Germany who had attacked and damaged the fleet. In regard to Italian claims, the situation now was quite different than what it had been under the nationalist concept. A united Europe would mean the exploitation of all colonial holdings for the common good. Since Italy would be assured of her share of economic gains, there would no longer be any reason for her to demand political domination over French territories. Therefore he would not work against the interests of his Italian ally if he guaranteed France the political integrity of her colonial holdings on the basis of full collaboration between Germany and France.

Hitler said he had already discussed a number of aspects of French-German collaboration with Laval whom he accepted as an authorized representative of Marshal Petain. Hitler understood that Petain and Laval were in complete accord and he congratulated Petain on his choice of Laval as principal aide in the restoration of France. From what Hitler had seen, Laval had the interests of France at heart. Of course, he added, time is necessary to complete all the details of this new relationship between two former enemies, but so long as it is done on the principle of mutual respect, the results surely will be beneficial to both. He said he had agreed to this meeting with Marshal Petain so that the two chiefs could agree on the principle of this new collaboration and he trusted that their principal aides could study the details and complete them successfully. If Petain agreed to collaboration and appointed Laval to represent France in the working out of details, Hitler felt that both countries would soon be facing a truly happy future.

Petain, apparently delighted with Hitler's surface cordiality and frankness, heartily shook hands on the idea of collaboration. He promised to explain the greatness of this plan to the French people in a personal broadcast within a day or two. He also promised to invest Laval with full authority to carry out the collaboration plan for France. He departed feeling, so he said, that the days of tribulation for his beloved France were at an end.

Frankly, I do not know what to say. One thing is certain—Hitler and Laval put on a perfect show. It was quite evident that Petain was sold.

Two questions sprang to my mind. First, did Hitler really mean everything he said? Second, is Laval really devoted to Petain, as he pretends, or is he simply making use of Petain's prestige to build himself up as the Fuehrer of a Fascist France? The answers to these two questions will really decide the relationship between the two countries.

When our train left Montoire that evening, I felt certain we were going home, but again I was wrong. We stopped in Paris for a day while Hitler conferred with Abetz, Stuelpnagel and others. In the afternoon we were traveling again and the following morning we reached Berchtesgaden, at last. We expected to return to Berlin, but received orders from Himmler to remain stationed with Hitler. That same evening the Fuehrer boarded the train again with his party and this time we went south, unquestionably on our way to meet Mussolini. We were puzzled by this. On previous occasions, when Hitler and Mussolini met at the Brenner Pass, local Gestapo men from Berchtesgaden accompanied the Fuehrer. The solution came when we did not stop at Brennero but continued into Italy.

The weather was very bad and when we came out on the Lombardian plain it poured harder than ever. Toward noon we arrived at the great new station in Florence where we were greeted by the news that the Italian army in Albania had marched into Greece that very morning. Two of our party received the news quite glumly—Field Marshal Keitel and General Jodl.

On the platform, protected by the train shed, Mussolini stood waiting. I had never seen the Italian leader before. When he shook hands with Hitler his countenance was beaming. After the reception ceremonies were over at the station, members of the party were driven off in automobiles. The one that the two dictators used looked as if it were built of heavy armor plate and bullet-proof glass. As we were driven through the streets I was surprised to find hordes of people braving the downpour, shouting their welcome to Hitler and giving the Fascist salute. I had to take my hat off to the Italian police. If Mussolini had visited a German city in such a heavy rain as this, I doubt very much that we could have gotten out so large a crowd to greet him.

At last the motorcade entered the wide Piazza della Signoria and we all filed into the sinister-looking and gloomy Palazzo Vecchio. Hitler and Mussolini retired into one of the vast rooms, all by themselves. We joined the Italian secret agents guarding the doors and so I can tell you that during the two hours and fifteen minutes that the two dictators spent in secret conference no one entered the room. There were no staff conferences between German and Italian generals; therefore I assumed that Il Duce's blackshirts were acting independently in their Greek venture.

When the discussion between the two dictators was over, the entire party was driven to the Palazzo Medici-Riccardi, where a sumptuous luncheon was served. We Gestapo men were excused from duty and were well served in one of the smaller rooms. I shall long remember that meal. If the Italians eat like this they cannot feel the pinch of war.

The luncheon ended late in the afternoon and after that the entire party was driven to a concert hall. It was a gala occasion. All seats were filled with Fascist dignitaries and their wives. Of course Hitler and Mussolini were given a stormy ovation. After the concert we returned to the railroad station, Hitler made his adieux to Mussolini and a few minutes later we left for home.

During this part of the journey I was able to learn something of what took place during the conferences. Hitler confided to his closest aides and subsequently the story was told in turn to all of us.

Hitler reported to Mussolini on his whirlwind tour of France and Spain. He said that Franco had pledged full co-operation with regard to Portugal and throughout the entire conference had been quite agreeable, and even eager, to enter the proposed Latin Bloc. He also said that the French situation was promising since Laval had been authorized by Petain to negotiate a peace with Germany and Italy. One of the conditions made by Petain, Hitler told Mussolini, was that France should lose no territory to Italy and Hitler had promised this. At this point Mussolini was angered. He insisted that Italian demands for Tunisia and French Somaliland must be met, especially since Italy was now carrying her burden of the war. Hitler could not persuade Mussolini to reduce his demands and the question had to be left open.

Mussolini stated bluntly that Italian rewards must be given in proportion to Italian contributions toward victory. His armies would have the Greek mainland occupied within a month and the Greek islands, with the exception perhaps of Crete, within another. Marshal Graziani was making final preparations in Libya for launching a desert drive that would carry him far into Egypt, possibly even to Alexandria. The British forces in Egypt were numerically weak and unable to resist. Italy would establish advance bases on the Greek islands by April 1, 1941, and be prepared to give Germany effective assistance in a concentrated drive against the Near East, provided German preparations in Rumania and Bulgaria were completed by that time.

Hitler asserted that the German army would keep its schedule as it always had. Rumania was being converted into a strong base. King Boris of Bulgaria would be invited to Germany shortly. Franz von Papen was preparing the foundation for the Germans in Turkey. The Syrian situation would be handled efficiently at the proper time and full co-operation by the French there would be assured. In Iraq all was ready for an overthrow of the pro-British government and establishment of a pro-Axis regime. A Persian mission would be received in Berlin before the end of the year.

The only remaining problem for discussion at this point was Russia. Moscow had been dubious ever since the occupation of Rumania, but Hitler felt that he could buy off the Soviets a second time. Russia was aware that the German army was now free to strike on a front of its own choice. Plans were being readied to receive a special Russian mission in Berlin to define the new situation created by the Tripartite Pact, which apparently was worrying Russia. Hitler confidently expected that he could handle the Russians, and he certainly would not permit any Russian participation in the Balkans, except on terms favorable to the Axis.

Meanwhile, the bombing of England would proceed according to schedule. Before spring arrived, Hitler felt, British industry would be paralyzed. He said that British shipping was already driven from St. George's Channel. Passage through the North Channel would be made equally unsafe so that supplies from the United States could not easily get through. This would force the British fleet to remain idle. If the Italian armies did their share, everything would be ready for a paralyzing blow against the British Empire.

This is the substance of the talk between the two dictators. But I have learned another important detail. It appears that Hitler approached Franco, and without success, to intercede for the Fuehrer at the Vatican. He was forced to accept Franco's suggestion that the matter be postponed until a more propitious time. I still contend that there is a sinister purpose behind these persistent attempts to draw the Vatican into Hitler's circle.

All members of our party aboard the train seemed very happy at the outcome of the Fuehrer's extended journeys, with two exceptions. The sour note was struck by Keitel and Jodl. I overheard the two in a talk with some other Nazi dignitaries, and they expressed the feeling that the Italians would never carry out their part of the bargain. Keitel declared that the Italian army was incapable of the task it had so confidently undertaken. Jodl added that he considered the Italian plan of an invasion of Greece strategically wrong, and he evinced little faith in Graziani's Libyan army. The Italians, he contended, have no flair for military organization and go about their business in too haphazard a fashion. The Nazi dignitaries simply laughed at this, declaring that Hitler had little doubt that the Italians would win in their relatively easy assignments. To which Keitel replied that his and Jodl's opinions on the subject were shared by von Brauchitsch and Halder. He feared that time would prove them correct.

I am back in Berlin now and rather tired from this journey. I am also tired of guarding Hitler, of roaming all over Europe and of witnessing pompous ceremonies that do not mean a thing. I wish I could be far from it all. I hope you will find this useful. I cannot tell when you will next hear from me.

In warm friendship,
MANFRED.

CHAPTER 17

The information contained in Manfred's long letter, although certainly significant, was overshadowed by a radiogram that van Narvig received the same day that Manfred's report arrived. The message said:

"The mountain is coming to Mohammed."

We were in my office. Van Narvig, looking at both documents, said, "Connecting this message with Manfred's letter, it can mean only one thing—Moscow is coming to Berlin."

"Not Stalin himself?" I asked.

Van Narvig shook his head.

"I don't think so," he said. "You remember that Ribbentrop, not Hitler, went to Moscow to negotiate the Soviet-German pact. It stands to reason that the Soviet visitor in this case will be Molotov."

I agreed with him and went out on a limb to this effect in my next broadcast.*

This broadcast caused something of a sensation and in the excitement, Manfred's report, which I broadcast in its entirety, was practically ignored.

We soon received further proof that our German friends were really working, for eight days after Molotov departed from the German capital,† a detailed report came from Linda. It read:

Dear Willy:

I have something choice for you this time, and you can thank Heinrich for it. As soon as I learned that Molotov had arrived in Berlin and that the conferences were taking place at the Reich Chancellory, I felt certain that Heinrich would know all about it. And he did. We met in a wine cellar the morning after Molotov's departure and there

*Williams' broadcast of November 5, 1940, in which he said, "Apropos the Russian mystery, I reported two weeks ago that an important diplomatic conference between Germany and Russia was being planned for November. The Kremlin's representative at this powwow will be Comrade Molotov who is expected to come to a still undetermined point in Germany."

†Foreign Commissar Molotov of the U.S.S.R. was in Berlin on November 12 and 13, 1940.

he told me many of the details. He said it was comparatively simple for him to get this information because he was frequently called into the conference room with various documents in his charge, and also because the official protocols covering the conference went through his hands.

The fact is that Hitler has very neatly double-crossed the Russians, whether they know it or not. It appears that ever since the signing of the Tripartite Pact and the stationing of German troops in Finland and Rumania, Moscow has been constantly bombarding Berlin for an explanation of the Russian status in view of these developments. Moscow also kept reminding our ambassador, Count von der Schulenburg, that a clause in the Soviet-German treaty of last year stipulated that both signatories consult each other in matters of mutual interest. Moscow was informed that all these explanations would be given as soon as plans for the establishment of the New Order in western Europe were completed.

Therefore, when Molotov was invited to come to Berlin, he brought with him a staff of more than sixty experts in anticipation of a new treaty to be signed with regard to additional spheres of interest—this being the diplomatic name for "loot." But events took an entirely different turn.

Molotov first wanted to know the real significance of the Tripartite Pact. When Russia entered into her agreement with Germany, he said, it was understood that neither party would enter any other alliance with a third party that might be interpreted as inimical to the interests of the other contracting party. Since Japan was a powerful neighbor of the Soviet Union and relations with her in the past had been none too friendly, Moscow had every reason to feel anxiety over the military alliance between Germany and Japan.

Hitler assured Molotov that the Tripartite Pact was aimed mainly at England and, indirectly, against the United States, which showed an increasing disposition to espouse the British cause. He then produced clause Number Four in the secret agreement with Japan which stated that all relations of the new allies with Soviet Russia were exempt from the Pact and subject to later definition. He said he knew that General Tatekawa, the new Japanese Ambassador in Moscow, had made advances toward the signing of a friendship pact between Russia and Japan. Therefore he could see no reason for anxiety on the part of Moscow.

Molotov next brought up the question of German troops in Finland. He said that it had been understood a year ago that Finland belonged in the Russian sphere of influence. He insisted that this was of particular importance to Russia inasmuch as Finland represented a salient from which Russia could be menaced by an unfriendly power. It has also come to Russia's attention that the Finnish army was being re-equipped with weapons received from Germany. While Russia was not concerned with the internal affairs of other nations, it was necessary for her to keep close watch over the security of her frontiers. For this reason a final settlement of the Finnish question in the Russian direction was extremely desirable.

You will understand that all this was not brought forward by Molotov at one time. There were long debates and counter-debates on every separate question. I am simply condensing things by confining myself to the important facts presented by each side.

But to go on. Hitler told Molotov that the presence of German troops in Finland was necessitated by the war with England. Germany had to relieve and reinforce her garrisons in Norway. She could not expose her troops to attack by superior British naval forces along the Atlantic and Arctic sea routes. For this reason Finland had agreed upon military transit facilities to Norway. It simply was a geographic necessity created by war conditions that did not exist when the agreement between Berlin and Moscow was negotiated. Inasmuch as Russia had a similar transit agreement with Finland for reinforcing and supplying the Russian garrison at Hangoe, Hitler again could see no reason why Moscow should feel perturbed.

It was quite true, Hitler admitted, that Finland was purchasing military equipment from Germany. Rather, it was being traded in exchange for goods sent to Germany. It consisted exclusively, however, of material taken over from the Czech army in 1939. None of it suited German army requirements. It was in the open market and could be purchased by any country that could use it. If Russia desired this material she was perfectly welcome to it on the same terms that any other country would have to meet.

Hitler said it was quite obvious that Russia had special interests in Finland. But, he saw no reason why Russia should consider Finland as a likely locale from which to attack the Soviets. Under existing conditions the only country that could make use of Finland in such an attack would be Germany. But Germany, after all, had a long direct land frontier with Russia and she certainly would not need Finland for a front in any proposed war with Russia. If the Soviet Union felt that England might attack her through Finland, this could be prevented by Germany's occupation of Norway and her use of the Finnish transit facilities. After the war, Hitler said, Germany would gladly consider the Finnish question in a manner favorable to Russia, but for the present Germany's own military considerations demanded that the matter be postponed.

Molotov then discussed the Balkans. He referred to the German army of occupation in Rumania. This had already led to chauvinistic demonstrations by Rumanian nationalists, who were demanding the return of Bessarabia by Russia, and Moscow was gravely apprehensive of this situation. Certainly, something must be done about it.

Hitler replied that Germany had vital economic interests to safeguard in Rumania. The German war effort depended greatly on oil. Russia possessed all the oil she required in her Caucasian fields, but Germany's only available major source was the Rumanian properties. Germany could under no circumstances relinquish her control over this oil while she was at war. Hitler said he did not see where Russia need feel concerned over the activities of a mere handful of Rumanian nationalists. Russia well knew that no German army units were near the Russo-Rumanian border. All German forces were stationed in the Ploesti oil region and along the Danube for the obvious reason that England had units of her air force in Greece. Germany must be prepared in the event that England should attack her from Greece.

To this Molotov replied, significantly, that Bulgaria was between the German units in Rumania and the British forces in Greece. Russia would be perfectly willing to send an army of occupation into Bulgaria and thus interpose an effective barrier between the German and British forces now in the Balkans. This drew the remark from Hitler that Germany could not possibly speak for Bulgaria, and that Russia might more properly take this matter up with the Bulgarian Government. If Bulgaria felt that her interests were at stake and asked for Russian protective occupation, then Moscow and Berlin could discuss the subject.

Molotov next raised the question of the Dardanelles. Now that Germany had occupied Rumania and was poised on the Black Sea, England might strike with her naval power at the new German positions. Inasmuch as Turkey was a military ally of England she might open the straits to let British naval forces into the Black Sea. This would bring the war into an area absolutely vital to Russia. Therefore Moscow thought that a temporary occupation of Istanbul and the Dardanelles would prevent a broadening of the conflict. These forces would be withdrawn after the war was over. It would be merely a precautionary operation.

Hitler's reply was that the possibility of British naval forces moving into the Black Sea had already occurred to him and he had taken precautions against it. He had warned the Turks that if they permitted

British warships through the Dardanelles, Turkey would automatically find herself at war with Germany and Italy. He did not think that Turkey would risk this. However, since the Straits were Turkish territory, it would be appropriate if Russia made her suggestion to the Ankara Government. Personally, he did not believe that Russian occupation of the Straits would be an ideal solution, but if Turkey proved amenable to the Soviet suggestion, some sort of workable solution might be found. In any event, Moscow's first move should be to consult the Turks.

Hitler then reached for a map of Central Asia and India that he placed on the conference table. He said that he appreciated Russia's apprehension over the question of the Dardanelles. From his study of Russian history he assumed that the question of direct outlets to the ocean highways of commerce had always been the guiding consideration of Russian foreign policy. Russia felt that she was imprisoned in the Black Sea so long as she had no control over the Dardanelles. But even if Russia obtained this control, she would still remain a prisoner because the Dardanelles led into the Mediterranean, which was closed by British sea power at both entrances, Gibraltar and Suez.

However, said Hitler, if Russia obtained an outlet directly on the Indian Ocean, she would gain undisputed access to the ocean highways. It was none of his business to point the way for Russian foreign policy, but it had simply occurred to him that the Soviet Union had a very large Moslem population. In India there is the centuries-old dispute between the Hindu majority and the Moslems in the western provinces, which extend to Karachi and the Persian Gulf. If a way could be found by which this Moslem minority could be persuaded to affiliate itself with the Soviet Union it would also solve the Russian problem of direct access to the sea. He advanced this idea merely as something which had occurred to him, but felt that if Moscow were interested, an understanding between Germany and Russia would be a simple matter. After all, he added, England was not a neutral country, and Germany could look only with approval at any action that would weaken the Empire's position.

Molotov seemed disconcerted by this. He admitted that he had come to Berlin totally unprepared for anything of this sort and that it was a subject which he would first have to take up with his government. Hitler said he could understand this and repeated that if Moscow considered this move worth discussion, he would be most happy to join Molotov in another conference, at which time a number of the other questions raised by Molotov might be settled.

And so, without accomplishing a thing, Molotov and his staff departed. He was not exactly rebuffed, but was simply outmaneuvered.

Heinrich also gave me a few side-stories. He said that Hitler brought up the Indian matter because if Molotov actually believed that this idea was a good one, the Red Army would be seriously involved at a great distance from the German borders. It could not interfere, therefore, with any of Hitler's own plans in the Balkans and the Near East. At the same time it would relieve Japan of any fear of Russian interference when she undertook her program of conquest in Southeast Asia.

At the outset of this report I told you that Hitler had pulled a neat double-cross on Molotov, and here is how it was done. Heinrich says there were microphones concealed in the conference rooms and all that Molotov said was electrically recorded, as you might guess, for the benefit of Turkey, Bulgaria and Finland. In fact, almost immediately after Molotov's departure, an invitation was sent to King Boris of Bulgaria to visit Berchtesgaden for information of a very confidential nature. Similarly, Franz von Papen is to take the recordings of the Dardanelles discussion to Ankara. This, in addition to arousing Turkish suspicions of Russia, is to convince Turkish leaders that Germany has the interests of Turkey close to her heart, and that, since she must realize it now, it would be a good idea if Turkey were to withdraw from her British commitments and join the Axis.

And there you have the story. I may have missed a few points but on the whole I think Heinrich gave us marvelous information. Until next time.

Affectionately,
LINDA.

Linda's report, added to the others, gave us a comprehensive picture of Hitler's military and diplomatic strategy. His plans were almost perfect—indeed, too perfect. All that remained was the execution of them. And this execution was already under way, as we learned from a letter sent by Wolfgang. Our friend at von Ribbentrop's estate wrote:

Dear Willy:

I am still alive and trying hard, but my trouble is that I am in a place where little is happening. Ribbentrop is in Berlin for the most part, and whenever affairs of state are handled here in the south, it is usually done over at the Berghof where you have excellent correspondents. But yesterday a break came my way and the news of it goes to you promptly.

Franz von Papen, Hitler's chief trouble-shooter in Turkey and the

Arab countries, stopped over at Fuschl before returning to his Ankara post. He had been expected to go to Berlin, but Molotov was still there and it was thought better that von Papen remain unseen, as otherwise the Russian might have become suspicious. Therefore von Papen pretended illness and remained at his estate in Upper Austria for a week. Yesterday he came here for instructions and I can tell you exactly what happened. Ribbentrop came straight from Berlin to meet him.

Ribbentrop explained that Turkey must be kept out of the war when German troops move into Bulgaria. This event is evidently scheduled to take place within the next two months. Turkey's full neutrality can be brought about only by instilling in her a fear of Russia. The Turkish government must be made to realize that Russia has of late become an enemy of Turkey with intentions of seizing control of the Dardanelles. Turkey must also be made to feel that Germany is ready to befriend her, in spite of the fact that she foolishly entered into an alliance with Great Britain. She must be reminded that she and Germany were comrades in the last war, and it is because of that comradeship that Germany is warning Turkey now.

Von Papen said that the assignment of embroiling Turkey with Russia was a tall order. The Russian Ambassador in Ankara, Terentiev, was one of the most respected members of the diplomatic corps in Ankara. He had made many personal friendships with high officials in the Turkish government. The Turks would definitely be suspicious of anything that emanates from Berlin. They would listen to him, of course, but they would never believe him unless presented with tangible evidence.

Ribbentrop promised that von Papen would have all the evidence required. Ever since Germany concluded her treaty with Russia in 1939, asserted Ribbentrop, Moscow had tried to use Germany in order to bring Turkey under Russian domination. Specifically, Russia has always desired to occupy Istanbul and the Dardanelles. Heretofore, Moscow's inquiries had been couched in vague terms, but when Molotov was in Berlin he made positive statements to this effect. Since the remarks were made by Russia's Foreign Minister, the Turks could scarcely doubt Russia's intentions. Von Papen could prove this to the Turks by showing them copies of the protocol covering the Molotov conference and by playing a recording in which Molotov raises the question of Russian occupation of the Dardanelles.

Von Papen grew quite excited. He said that what had been done in Berlin was a master stroke of diplomacy. He assured Ribbentrop that with these means at his disposal it would not be difficult to inflame the Turks against the Soviets. He agreed that if Turkey were in fear of

Russian aggression, she would never implement her treaty with England by entering the war against Germany unless she were directly attacked. He emphasized that on this last point there must be the most definite reassurances from Berlin. Ribbentrop replied that these reassurances would be forthcoming at the proper time. Meanwhile von Papen could tell the Turks that so long as he, von Papen, remained in Ankara, nothing would happen to Turkey so far as Germany was concerned.

This is all I have today. I understand that visitors from Yugoslavia are expected here shortly. I do not know exactly when, but I shall keep my eyes and ears open. Regards.

Your friend,
WOLFGANG.

Simultaneously with Wolfgang's brief report we received a letter from Clara which contained similar information. This is what she wrote:

Dear Willy:

Hitler has entertained a royal visitor at the Berghof, King Boris of Bulgaria. The King crossed the Danube incognito into Rumania, whence a Luftwaffe plane flew him to Munich. From there he was driven to Berchtesgaden.

Boris came alone. The German Minister in Sofia had an audience with him, assuring him that the Fuehrer would prefer to confer with him personally, man to man. Immediately after Boris' arrival at the Berghof, luncheon was served. The only ones present at this meal, aside from the two principals, were Jodl and Boris' father, the former King Ferdinand of Bulgaria, who had come from his estate in Thuringia at Hitler's special invitation. After luncheon, Hitler and Boris withdrew for a private conference.

Hitler started out by saying that since Boris had so excellently administered his country, it would be a pity if he were to lose his throne. Boris, highly astonished and even disturbed at this inference, asked just what Hitler meant. The Fuehrer said that the Russian system did not permit retention of the monarchial form of government in any territory forming part of the Soviet Union. He went on to say that he was quite aware of Russia's intention to occupy Bulgaria and then annex the country.

The King was utterly amazed. He asserted that this was the first time he ever heard of such a thing. To which Hitler replied that there could be no mistake, and asked if Boris was certain of the loyalty of his ministers? Perhaps, suggested Hitler, some of them were plotting

177

in concert with Moscow. The King insisted that his ministers were all completely trustworthy, and that he could not imagine that any one of them could take part in any such scheme. He knew, of course, that a minority among the Bulgarian population had racial ties with Russia, but that was all.

Hitler then stated flatly that during the recent conferences in Berlin with the Russian Foreign Commissar, Molotov had directly asked for Germany's acquiescence in a Russian occupation of Bulgaria. Boris would be shown copies of the official protocols of these conferences as well as being permitted to hear straight recordings of Molotov's request. The Fuehrer went on to say that he could not see how Molotov could have raised the matter at all, unless preliminary negotiations had taken place between Russian and Bulgarian officials. Therefore it was high time that King Boris be informed of the scheme. Because of the delicate nature of the subject, Hitler had taken it upon himself to inform the King in all confidence and without any ministerial go-betweens.

Boris thanked Hitler and promised to look into the matter the very first thing upon his return to Sofia. He was still certain that none of his ministers was involved. On Hitler's request he agreed to treat the subject with the strictest confidence.

Hitler then said he would like to discuss with Boris the political implications involved in this situation. Of course, he added, all this was strictly off the record. The Baltic states presented an example of what to expect if Russia seized influence in any country. When the governments of Estonia, Latvia and Lithuania originally accepted occupation by Russian troops they were solemnly assured that their political and social systems would be respected. Yet today these countries were communistically ruled units of the Soviet Union, undergoing the most ruthless process of Sovietization. If Russian troops were allowed to undertake a protective occupation of Bulgaria, the inevitable result would be the abolition of the present system of government in favor of a direct Soviet regime under the notorious Bulgarian Communist, Dimitroff, who was already in Moscow arranging for just such an eventuality.

Entirely apart from the fact that Germany regarded Bulgaria as a comrade-in-arms since the First World War, the Reich government could not permit the establishment of a Soviet regime in that country. When Germany and Russia signed their treaty of non-aggression in 1939, Russia was granted a preferred status in certain territories that she claimed were essential for her security, but Bulgaria most definitely was not among them. The present attitude of Moscow was entirely new. It only proved that Russia could not be trusted any further than the eye could see. Germany was allied with Italy, and both were at war with England. Any action undertaken by Germany, such as the occupation of Rumania, was merely a case of military necessity. Russia was not at war with anyone and her actions were dictated simply by the desire to extend the Soviet domain.

Hitler said that undoubtedly a special envoy of the Soviets would arrive in Bulgaria shortly, to present Moscow's views directly to the Bulgarian Government. Hitler could not prevent this, nor would he presume to advise the Bulgarian Government. Russia was a sovereign state and as such not subject to German dictates with regard to her diplomatic negotiations. However, he would give his own diplomatic representatives in Sofia orders to watch the situation closely. He would also instruct his army command in Rumania to hold its forces available. If King Boris should find, as a result of Russian pressure, that strict measures were in order to prevent Russian encroachment, he could rely implicitly upon the German army to maintain the integrity and independence of Bulgaria.

After this visit, King Boris left for a short visit with his father, at the latter's estate.

This development is far beyond me, for I have no idea of what happened during the Molotov conferences in Moscow. The evidence that Hitler presented to Boris might be authentic or a fraud. However, I cannot see how Hitler could practice a deception on the King, especially in a strictly personal conversation. It would be utterly stupid, and Hitler is anything but that.

You might like to know that Wolfgang has asked me to marry him. I am rather in a quandary about it. If I married I would like to be reunited with my son. I have asked Wolfgang to wait until May and see how things turn out. In these cataclysmic times it is very difficult to make up one's mind.

With warmest regards,
CLARA.

In the same mail with Clara's and Wolfgang's letters we also received one from Linda. She wrote:

Dear Willy:

Something important is going to take place shortly and I hope this letter reaches you before it happens. Goering has just returned from a short trip to Paris where he met Laval. I understand that the Spaniard, Serrano Suner, was also present at the meeting. Everything is ready for a peace treaty with the French along the lines that Goering and

Laval have discussed from the very beginning. France will receive part of Belgium. Then France and Spain will conclude a defensive alliance with the approval of Germany and Italy. Portugal may also be taken into this alliance, but that is not yet certain. France and Spain will then declare their non-belligerency in the war.

It will be brought about in this fashion. As you know, Napoleon Bonaparte's son (from his marriage with Marie Louise of Austria) was the Duke of Reichstadt, or L'Aiglon, as the French called him. He died in exile and was buried in Vienna. As a gesture of friendship for the French, Hitler has decreed that the remains of L'Aiglon be disinterred and taken to France so that they may rest beside his father, Napoleon. The ceremonies will be conducted in Paris with great pomp. Hitler will proclaim himself heir to Napoleon's great ideal of uniting all Europe and freeing the continent from English vassalage. Germany and France will be united in reviving this great ideal.

Marshal Petain will be present at the ceremony, of course, and he and Hitler will clasp hands over Napoleon's sarcophagus to symbolize the new solidarity of the French and German peoples. The world will be very much impressed, so the Nazis believe, by the spectacle of Germany and France forgetting their enmities for all time and hereafter marching together toward a united destiny.

As positive and immediate proof of this new and wondrous friendship, Hitler will inform Petain that Germany relinquishes her right to further payment of the costs of occupation. He will consent to an enlargement of the French army under Petain and will proclaim immediate deliverance of all French prisoners of war. He will revise the demarcation line so as to include Versailles in the Unoccupied Zone. Petain will establish his official residence as French Chief of State at Versailles, where suitable quarters have already been prepared for him. The French government will return to Paris.

These are the prospects. I have not seen Heinrich lately and do not know what he thinks or has learned. I have this information from the unguarded conversations of Goering, who is quite elated. To him, this is a great achievement for which he has diligently worked these past six months, at times in opposition to both Hitler and Hess. Perhaps he expects to receive a French decoration from Petain.

It seems as if we are headed for better times, doesn't it? Perhaps, if this scheme works out, we may not even be so far from a general peace. Then you and I could meet again. Wouldn't that be fun!

Affectionately,
LINDA.

CHAPTER 18

ABOUT THIS TIME, a unique opportunity presented itself to us. Klausmann, who continued to commute between Germany and America, called it to our attention. He told
us that a batch of very important and highly confidential documents had been brought to Washington by the same Spanish
diplomatic courier—at least he traveled under a Spanish diplomatic passport—who also had carried the reports from Wolfgang, Clara and Linda. The documents in question, Klausmann
intimated, might be seen by us for a brief moment or two. He
said they were to be forwarded to Heinrich Stahmer, Hitler's
envoy in Japan, to aid Stahmer in his further negotiations with
the Japanese.

Of course we were intrigued. However, both van Narvig and
I understood the pitfalls awaiting the trustful in this sort of game,
and while we had every reason to trust Klausmann, despite his
mysterious ways, we had no means of knowing whether he was
being deluded by a Gestapo agent who might have discovered
his connection with us. We wanted more information on the
nature of the papers, and the circumstances surrounding them,
before we made a move. Especially, we wanted to know why
these documents, destined for Japan, were routed the long way,
via the United States.

Klausmann told us that relations between Germany and the
Soviet Union had become less friendly. The documents in question contained important military information. If by some chance
they were to fall into Soviet hands while crossing Russia on their
way to Japan, there might be dangerous repercussions. For this
reason, they were being sent via America.

The documents, Klausmann said, were in the German Embassy in Washington. He had a friend at the embassy. With the
help of this friend and the Spanish courier it would be possible
to give us access to the papers. He insisted, however, that the
documents must not leave the embassy. Also, his friend and the
Spaniard would expect a financial consideration.

Van Narvig and I discussed the matter at length. The fact that money was involved somewhat allayed our original suspicions. Since I was kept in New York because of my broadcasts, I felt that it was my partner's job to go to Washington and inspect the entire deal. To my great surprise, he balked at the job. He pointed out that surreptitious acquisition of secret information within the embassy premises of a foreign nation was a risky business in which he might run afoul of the law. We made careful inquiries on this point. Provided with a high-speed camera and the necessary cash, van Narvig and Klausmann departed for Washington.

It was early forenoon the following day when van Narvig telephoned from the capital. Klausmann's friend was Heinrich Nostiz, an administrative clerk at the German Embassy and at heart decidedly anti-Nazi. The Spanish courier, who spoke fluent German, was found amenable. Van Narvig had already had a glimpse of the documents. There was one hitch, however. They would not permit photographing the papers. They explained that there were several sets of these documents. Other sets had been forwarded to Rome and elsewhere, and therefore it would be quite safe to show them. But photographs could be easily traced to this particular set, and this was a risk that they simply would not run. I suggested that van Narvig copy as much as he could and let it go at that.

The following morning he was back in New York with forty pages of closely written shorthand. The documents, it turned out, consisted of copies of a series of reports made to the Reich Chancellory. The most important ones were from the Reich Air Ministry, the Reich Defense Ministry, the Great General Staff and the chairman of the Four Year Plan. They contained vital statistics covering the composition and equipment of Germany's land and air forces as well as valuable data on the economic aspects of Hitler's war effort. In them we found confirmation of some of the information that our friends in Germany had sent us piecemeal.

This information was immediately given by us to U. S. authorities and we received permission to publish some of it in a series of magazine articles. One periodical, when approached by our literary agent with these articles, decided against using them, although several associate editors had been outspokenly enthusiastic. The editor gave as his reason for refusal to print them that, "such information is too frightening to give to the American people." However, a more courageous editor, Fulton Oursler, believed that the American people could take the information reasonably and without panic. The articles were then printed in Liberty Magazine and ran for several weeks. An unfortunate selection was made, however, when we decided on the general title of the series, which we called, "Hitler's Secret Plans for the Invasion of England." We did this because much of the information pointed directly to preparations for an island invasion. As it developed, later on, these measures had actually been planned for an invasion of Crete.

On the same day that van Narvig returned from Washington the sensational news broke that Pierre Laval had been dismissed from his post as Vice Premier of France and arrested on orders of Marshal Petain. Unquestionably something had occurred to upset Hitler's plans, for all the information we had received previously about Laval pointed to his rise, with the reluctant approval of Petain, as a political power in France.

"There's no sense speculating on a thing like this," van Narvig said, after we had deliberated for hours. "We can make any number of guesses and they all may be wrong. The best thing is to sit tight and wait. Our friends will let us know."

In the meantime I had to broadcast that night and I would have liked to tell my audience some facts. Since I had none, I told them so, adding that I expected my sources to come through with some shortly. I would not speculate.

Our friends did not let us down. The information came in the form of a long letter from Clara. She wrote:

Dear Willy:
We are all in a dither. The nearest thing to hell has broken loose all over the place. Hitler is in a fury and at times shouts like a madman.

This is one time when there is no need for eavesdropping. Things are shouted for all to hear. This letter contains the combined observations of Gottlieb, Wolfgang and myself.

For almost two weeks Hitler has not been himself. First he was upset by the Italian failure in Greece. Then came the British raid on Taranto which, we understand, has about immobilized the Italian battle fleet on which Hitler had been counting for effective service in the Mediterranean. What particularly annoyed him was that Keitel, Jodl and von Brauchitsch were right when they practically forecast that the Italians would be beaten if permitted to go about things in their own sloppy way. But from Rome came assurances that these setbacks were only temporary and would be remedied. Mussolini declared that he had absolute confidence in his newly-appointed generals.

Hitler was preparing to go to Paris for the transfer of the remains of L'Aiglon and to perform the sham ceremony with Petain. He felt that now that the French situation was well controlled, he need not worry too much about Italy's bungling, at least for the moment. Then came the news from Vichy, and it produced the nearest thing to an earthquake. Hitler was having fits. Physicians from Berlin were summoned post-haste, as well as Evi Braun, who had been visiting in Munich. At one time it was feared that the Fuehrer might suffer a stroke. When he regained his power of speech a summons was sent out to all the Nazi chiefs and they all came running—Goering, Hess, Goebbels, Himmler, Keitel, von Brauchitsch and all the rest.

By the time they had assembled, Hitler was raging again. He became quite hysterical and accused Petain of having broken his solemn pledge given at Montoire. He declared that Petain would suffer greatly for this misdeed—this traitorous act. Hitler swore that he would sweep the traitors from the surface of the earth. He demanded that the army bear down on France immediately and grind her into dust. He cried that he would prove to them that one does not make commitments and then idly break them. He wanted the army to be sent to occupy all of France and said the Gestapo should institute a reign of terror.

It was von Brauchitsch who literally took his life in his hands by setting out to show Hitler that all these ideas were ridiculous. He was so insistent that Hitler finally calmed down and was persuaded to behave.

Von Brauchitsch pointed out to Hitler that not only were his orders impractical, they were actually impossible to carry out. Sixty per cent of the army, von Brauchitsch said, was now in Germany, working in the munitions factories for the duration of the winter. Of the remaining forty per cent, one-half had already been given Christmas leave. All panzer units had been transferred to the east for reorganization and replenishment. The bomber command of the Luftwaffe was engaged in its operations over England. Two-thirds of the combat squadrons were at eastern bases for their winter overhaul. Even if all the units had been on call, it would require at least two weeks to work out a comprehensive plan for an operation such as Hitler demanded.

In the midst of this discussion Ribbentrop and Prince Otto von Bismarck burst in, both in a state bordering on hysteria. Prince Otto has been pinch-hitting in Rome during the illness of the regular ambassador, van Mackensen. It appears that we had military observers with Graziani's armies in Libya. One of them had succeeded in getting a plane and flying to Rome. The information which he brought with him was so important that Prince Otto had instantly flown to Salzburg to convey personally the news to Ribbentrop at Fuschl. From there the two had sped to the Berghof.

Prince Otto's report was a black one. Mussolini either did not know the actual extent of the debacle in Africa or he has been concealing it. Graziani had not suffered just an ordinary defeat. It compared, on a smaller scale, with the Allied debacle in Flanders. With only two divisions the British had not only routed an Italian army five times the size of the English, but had actually annihilated it. No Italian combat unit was fit for action anywhere east of Bengasi, even though the British were still three hundred miles from that point. Not enough serviceable equipment was left to fit out one brigade in the whole of Cyrenaica. The Italians had been so surprised by the British attack that they had not even put up a fight. They had surrendered by the thousands, with all their artillery and equipment intact. The Italian air force was swept from the African skies, with British combat squadrons roaming far and wide with no opposition.

What was still left of Graziani's armies was falling back in panic, with many units throwing away their arms and waiting for the British to take them prisoner rather than flee across the Libyan desert. The fall of Bardia, Tobruk and Derna, perhaps even Bengasi, was simply a question of time, depending on how quickly the British could organize their pursuit. Given the time they could probably sweep all the way to Tripoli. The Italians could not send any reinforcements to Libya for weeks because the passage across the Central Mediterranean had been under British control ever since the raid on Taranto. The Italian navy was so frightened that it did not dare sneak out of whatever port the ships happened to be in. If any part of Libya was to be held as a base for future operations in Africa it was definitely up to German forces, because the Italians were through.

Hitler remained speechless for so long a period that it was feared once more that he might be suffering a stroke. After a long, very long, silence, he demanded to be connected with Mussolini in Rome by telephone. The conversation between the two dictators lasted almost half an hour. Hitler discovered that Mussolini had no actual knowledge of the extent of the catastrophe in Libya, for his own generals had failed to appraise it correctly, whereas, the German military observers had required but one glance to evaluate the entire situation. They knew that when an army does not want to fight it is finished. What Hitler told Mussolini about his Italian generals and soldiers is not fit for repetition.

As he turned back to his aides he kept repeating, time and again, *"Dieses Italienische Lumpenpack!"* *

But the catastrophic news had a sobering effect on those present. When von Brauchitsch returned to his argument with Hitler he was wholeheartedly supported by the army faction, including Jodl and Goering. With the Italian collapse in Africa as well as in Albania and the Italian fleet condemned to impotence, von Brauchitsch said, the war plan, as it stood, was built on false premises and must be completely changed.

This, he said, would take much time. It would require new diplomatic preparations. Realities must be faced, now that the Italian pipe dream was exploded. It was a good thing, at least, that the Italians had refused German advice on the subject of their military operations and had insisted on acting independently. This way, said von Brauchitsch, their disgrace would at least cast no reflections on Germany's armed forces. But it certainly would lower Axis prestige, and diplomatic negotiations would become more difficult. The French case was an example, for it was more than likely that Petain's sudden change of mind was a direct result of this new situation. And this was an even greater reason why Hitler should take no precipitate action in France.

Goering took up the argument from this point on. He said that before any decision could be arrived at, it would be necessary to make a thorough investigation. For this purpose the first thing to do was to make contact with Laval and find out through him what had actually happened in Vichy. Only after Laval had presented his version of the story, could any effective action be decided upon. Furthermore, Goering said, the liberation of Laval was a question of maintaining Reich prestige.

At the conclusion of these deliberations Otto Abetz, who had been called immediately from Paris, was summoned. Abetz was frightened and not sure what to expect. He was instructed to proceed to Vichy,

*This ragged Italian rabble.

accompanied by an armed guard, and demand an explanation of Petain's actions. Whatever the explanation, he was instructed to demand that Petain free Laval and permit him to return to Paris. It was to be made perfectly clear to Petain that Laval was to present his case to Hitler personally. When Abetz left the room, it was obvious that he did not relish the assignment. However, he could not argue about it with Hitler.

You can be certain of one thing. Even though Hitler is acting on the common-sense advice of the army and his other aides, his bitterness toward Petain will have repercussions. He has sworn never to look upon the Marshal again. Whatever turn the affairs of France may take, the French will be oppressed so long as Petain is head of their government. France will be treated as a conquered nation from now on.

This is all that I have to report on these exciting events. Christmas is only one week off and from the looks of things it will be pretty quiet here. Hitler has already declared his intention of spending the holiday with the army in France. He may see Laval then.

I hope that Linda will have a chance to come here and spend Christmas with me. It probably will not be anything like last Christmas when you were here and had just returned from Switzerland after seeing my son. Eugen, too, is gone. We shall miss the cozy Christmas Eve celebration at his house. But such is life—we come and we go.

With all our best wishes for a merry Christmas and my warmest regards,

CLARA.

Shortly after Clara's letter arrived, we received two more. One was from Linda, and she had this to say:

Dear Willy:

I am writing from Berchtesgaden. Arrived here on the morning before Christmas after a miserable trip. Never saw anything like it. Had to stand up most of the way. The train was crammed like a can of sardines. So many people are traveling for the holiday, principally soldiers who want to spend Christmas with their folks. Who knows? It may be the last time for many of them.

It is quiet at Berchtesgaden. Hitler is somewhere in France. They say he is spending the holiday with the army, but this may be just a pretext. There is not much of the army in France just now. Perhaps he is meeting with Laval. Clara told me that she wrote you all about the French and Italian situations.

Clara met me at the station, and who do you think we ran into but Colonel Wartenburg. He was surprised to see me and made a joking reference to the night when he came upon the two of us. He asked if I had any news from you. I thought it wiser to say I hadn't heard from you for a long time.

Clara and I decorated the Christmas tree which Gottlieb had cut down. At nine o'clock in the evening Wolfgang arrived from Fuschl and we lighted the candles on the tree. Clara sat at the piano and we all sang, "Silent Night" and "Oh, Tannenbaum!" When we exchanged gifts, I had the surprise of my life, for there was that package from you with mementos for us all. Clara had not mentioned one word about receiving it. We all appreciate it very much, and we remembered that you were with us last Christmas. Then we sat down to a meal of Polish carp, which Wolfgang had brought from Ribbentrop's well-stocked larder. On Christmas Day we had goose with apples and sauerkraut. The goose was my contribution, brought from Karin Hall. Goering will never miss it.

This was the first time we were all together since the time when you were here. Only Manfred was missing—he is somewhere in France, guarding Hitler. We exchanged experiences, did some planning, and paid heed to Gottlieb, who warned us to be very careful hereafter.

Before I came here, I had a talk with Heinrich in Berlin. There was nothing really new, he just gave me a general outline of the situation as it is viewed by the Wilhelmstrasse. A month ago they believed themselves sitting on top of the world. Today they are deeply worried. There are some who go so far as to say that Mussolini has already lost the war for us by destroying the carefully built-up story of Axis invulnerability. Perhaps there is something in that.

For one thing, Heinrich said, there is this nasty French business. Everything had been arranged so nicely, from the Berlin point of view, when Petain smashed it to pieces. Heinrich said there is no chance that relations with France will return to a friendly basis. Hitler will never again deal with Petain. To Hitler, anyone but Laval will be unacceptable as the head of the French government, and Petain could not possibly reappoint Laval without resigning himself. Probably the Gestapo will be sent to crack down on France, in which case the French are bound to hit back, at least from the dark. It will breed hatred between the two peoples that will preclude any chance of ever reaching an understanding. This makes it look very bad for the New Order.

The Bulgarian affair is not going smoothly, either. During his visit here, King Boris had virtually agreed to join the Axis, but meanwhile Russian and British influences in Sofia have pooled forces and now the Bulgarians do not know what to do. They do not want our armies to move into their country, but they want the Russians even much less. They're walking a tight rope and will continue to, as long as they can.

Relations with Russia, while they appear amicable on the surface, are actually in their worst shape since the signing of the 1939 pact. Heinrich says Hitler will abide by the pact so long as he can keep the Russians frightened or guessing, or both. But some of the opinion on the Wilhelmstrasse has it that the Russians cannot be fooled much longer. The conference with Molotov showed plainly that Russia is beginning to get wise to Hitler's game.

It all goes back to the Italian defeats. Today, everyone realizes that Goering, Keitel, Jodl and von Brauchitsch were correct in their appraisal of the Italians. It is plain that the Italians are of no help— rather the contrary—unless organized and supported by the Germans. But Mussolini has insisted to Hitler that he intends to play his part in the war. Heinrich said that the Wilhelmstrasse is more worried about the Italians than about the Russians or the French, and the same goes for the army's feelings on the subject. I heard Goering say to Udet the other day, "Between a reluctant Frenchman and an Italian hero, give me the Frenchman any day."

There is really nothing more for the present. I thought that perhaps you would like to have a general picture of the situation as Heinrich sees it at the Chancellory. Things are in a state of flux. The old plans have been abandoned, but no new ones have been arrived at as yet.

Just one more item. Goering had a talk with Lieutenant General Rommel the other day. I do not know whether you know about Rommel. He is a panzer expert who led the dash to Abbeville last spring. For the past months he has been experimenting with special panzers for desert warfare. He has a huge laboratory and training ground in southern Austria. His special troops have been training for desert fighting in Mesopotamia and Palestine. Goering told Rommel that he may have to take his brigades to Libya instead.

I conclude by wishing you a very happy New Year.

Affectionately,

LINDA.

The other letter that we received with Linda's, came from Manfred, who wrote:

Dear Willy:

I am on the move again with Hitler. I had figured on spending Christmas with our friends at Berchtesgaden, but I had to spend Christmas Eve in Cambrai. Hitler spoiled the holiday for others too, among them Keitel, Jodl and von Brauchitsch, who had to accompany him.

At Hitler's headquarters there was a tremendous Christmas tree, filling a hall two stories high. It was decorated with artificial snow and white candles. Hitler presented each of his generals and aides with an autographed picture of himself in a silver frame.

Christmas Day was spent in lengthy consultation with Goering and Sperrle*, who were summoned for the day, as well as Milch, who had just returned from an inspection trip in southern Italy. He had previously spent two months in Japan.

Milch's report was bad. He said that the Italian air force was practically destroyed by the British. The air force had lost more than a thousand planes in Libya, seventy-five per cent of them on the ground, and more than six hundred were lost in Albania. The flying personnel was completely demoralized. Cases of insubordination were common. In Libya, Graziani was already evacuating Bengasi, although the British were still two hundred miles away. Milch confirmed everything about the Italian situation that Prince Otto von Bismarck had previously reported. Mussolini wanted his air squadrons from the English front to return to Italy without delay, but Milch's opinion was that unless a strong German air unit went with them they would merely face disaster.

Hitler made some strong remarks about the Italians in general and Mussolini's air force in particular. Goering observed that, after all, one couldn't expect much of pilots who had been brought up as individuals and trained for spectacular publicity flights across the ocean. If Hitler wanted the Italians to fight the war as it should be fought, he must teach them first. Milch said the first thing to do, if the Libyan situation was to be saved, would be to close the Central Mediterranean to British naval squadrons and establish a safe convoy route for Italian shipping to Tripoli, over which reinforcements could be sent. This could be done only by sending a Luftwaffe fleet. The Luftwaffe must dive-bomb the British in those waters as they had in St. George's Channel. He declared that Mussolini had made a big mistake by not invading Malta immediately following his declaration of war. In the intervening months the British, with free access to Malta, had reinforced the island to such an extent that now prohibitive losses would be entailed in a sea and air assault.

Hitler's decision was that he could not afford to let Mussolini lose Libya, especially in the light of the French situation. If the British were allowed to push as far as Tripoli, General Weygand might easily join forces with them, in which case the Axis could never hope to regain a

*Field Marshal Sperrle, chief of the Luftwaffe bomber command.

foothold in Africa. Milch was told to let the Italian air squadrons in France proceed to Italy. In addition, a Luftwaffe corps was to be sent to Sicily along with German ground personnel in sufficient numbers, for Milch said he would not trust Mussolini's demoralized ground organization.

As you know, Pierre Laval was released from prison, following Otto Abetz' visit to Petain. On the day after Christmas Hitler received Laval with Goering as a witness. Laval expressed his appreciation for having been rescued by Hitler's orders, but the Fuehrer waved all this aside, snapping, "Vergessen Sie das. Was ist denn passiert?" *

Laval began by explaining that he had made personal enemies in Vichy who feared that he would become dictator in the event of Petain's death or removal. His enemies, said Laval, were scattered among the politicians and the army and navy clique. The latter especially desired one of its own men as official successor to Petain. General Huntziger had never forgiven Laval for bringing negotiations in Wiesbaden to an abrupt end. All this had not concerned him, Laval said, for Hitler had assured him that he was the only man through whom the Fuehrer would deal with France. All would have gone smoothly, had not the Italians been defeated in Africa.

When he returned to Vichy from Paris, Laval related, after arranging for the L'Aiglon celebration, he was informed by his own men that General Weygand, in Africa, had had a long telephone conversation with Petain. Weygand was well informed on the Libyan situation, the information having reached him even sooner than it had Berchtesgaden. He told Petain that, with her navy crippled, her air force destroyed, and her armies in Libya and Albania demoralized, Italy would cease to be a factor in the war. If Mussolini was forced to make a separate peace with the British, Hitler would have his hands full. Weygand cautioned Petain not to make any definite commitments under the circumstances.

On hearing this, Laval went to see Petain immediately. He told the Marshal that the ceremony at Les Invalides would take place on December 20th and that he, Laval, was making special preparations for a train to carry Petain and the entire French government to Paris for the occasion. Petain replied that he had reconsidered the matter and decided not to go. Laval requested an explanation. Petain stated that Laval had neglected to inform him of all the details. Laval pointed out that the Marshal had agreed to the arrangement in principle and had given him carte blanche to work out the details as he saw fit. Petain accused Laval of having overstepped the authority delegated

*Forget all that. What happened?

191

to him. Laval then demanded pointblank whether Petain intended to go to Paris as arranged. Petain intimated that he might be arrested while in Paris, or be subject to an accident, and then Laval could conveniently step into his place. Laval shouted that Petain was insane. Petain shouted back that Laval had betrayed him, called the guards and had Laval arrested.

Hitler, who knew all this from Abetz, said, "*Das ist eine alte Geschichte. Was wird nun getan?*" *

Laval said that he was solely interested in striving for French-German collaboration, but that nothing could be done with the Vichy clique until the German army had won new victories. He added that Petain now had his doubts if Germany could win the war.

Hitler said, "*Mit dem Mann spreche ich nicht mehr!*" †

Laval said that he would form a committee in Paris that would organize opposition to Petain's policies, first in the occupied part of France and later in the Unoccupied Zone. He added that if Hitler would support such a committee, the time would come when Petain could be forced out of office. Then matters could be easily arranged.

Hitler said, "*Tun Sie das.*" ‡

Meanwhile, Hitler has given orders to treat Occupied France as a conquered nation and to have no further intercourse with Vichy. In practice this means that the demarcation line will be drawn so tightly that no traffic of any kind, not even mail, will get across it. Members of the Vichy government will be prohibited from visiting their ministries in Paris and all stocks of food and other commodities will be seized by the occupation authorities. The population will be deprived of ration cards if there is the slightest opposition. What a Christmas gift for the French!

There is nothing more to report. Hitler will soon be back at Berchtesgaden and I shall be in Berlin. I hope that you, at least, will have a happy New Year.

In warm friendship,
MANFRED.

Two weeks passed before we received another letter. It came from Linda, who wrote:

Dear Willy:

We have been entertaining quite a few more inquisitive Oriental visitors. This time it is a mission consisting of some 140 Japanese officers

---

*All this is history. What is to be done now?
†I shall deal no more with that man.
‡Go ahead with it.

from all services, led by Lieutenant General Tomoyuki Yamashita.* He is a personal friend of the new Japanese ambassador, General Oshima, who always pays a personal call on Hitler when the Fuehrer is in Berlin.

Oshima brought Yamashita to Karin Hall and warmly recommended him to his honorable friend, Goering. Yamashita is a broad man, rather stocky and short, with shrewd eyes. His physique is that of an ox. He is exceedingly deferential to Goering and very polite to everyone here, even the help, which is more than can be said for some of his underlings.

Yamashita is interested in everything about him, but wants to study specifically the tank and dive bomber teams. He expresses great admiration for the Luftwaffe and declares that he and his aides have much to learn. They want to know all about the weapons and the organization that have made the German military machine unbeatable, and they are especially interested in observing our army in action against the enemy.

It is hard to believe, but Goering took this man Yamashita up in a Junkers 97 bomber and flew with him over London while the city was being pounded by the Luftwaffe. When they returned, Yamashita said that seeing the smoking ruins of the big city was one of the great thrills of his life. What would happen if these savages ever gain the upper hand in this world?

Back at Karin Hall, Goering held a large reception for the visitors. Among the guests were Ribbentrop, von Brauchitsch, Keitel, List, Guderian, von Reichenau, Hess, Goebbels, Himmler, Frick and Ley, and they all treated the Japanese like long-lost friends. I noticed that the Japanese warriors did very little drinking, scarcely touching their glasses even when Hitler and Hirohito were toasted. They danced a bit, were very gallant to the ladies, and listened intently to all that was said. The great moment of the evening arrived when Yamashita produced a velvet box, stepped up to Goering and decorated our Hermann with the Grand Cordon of the Rising Sun as "a small token of esteem from my exalted Emperor." Goering beamed at everyone.

The next morning a conference was held in Goering's study. Present, besides Goering, were Milch, Udet, Dr. Todt, von Kleist, Yamashita and three other Japanese whose names I cannot spell. Yamashita had already seen the Luftwaffe in action. He was excited over its function as heavy vertical artillery moving faster than the wind. He asserted that he was thrilled with the performances of Stukas over the English Channel. Their incredible maneuvers had fascinated him. He ap-

*General Yamashita conquered Malaya and Singapore in the spring of 1942.

plauded the performances of the Messerschmitt 110 fighters and the new Focke-Wulf destroyers.

For hours they sat and talked over sketches, blueprints and plans, with Udet and Milch explaining and the Japanese devouring every word and asking occasional questions. Then Dr. Todt explained at length the function of big Junkers transports as a method of ferrying supplies. The Orientals were intent but when it came to glider trains and their utility they did not seem particularly interested. Yamashita explained that in Japan's prospective war theater she would have complete domination of the sea and would not need gliders. Furthermore, the glider problems involved long studies of winds and air currents. The Tokyo war office had little time for this because they had to prepare quickly.

Yamashita explained that he intended to remain in Germany at least five months. He wished to see everything, including Germany's next campaign, and he wanted all the advice that could be given him. He asked for additional German technicians and instructors for the new Japanese air force. He also asked for certain patents, licenses and manufacturing rights, especially for the 800-horsepower B.M.W. 132 radial engine. He was promised all that, and more. The visitors then were turned over to Vice Admiral Grassmann and General Keller with orders to be shown the whole works.

In our opinion our men have gone utterly mad. Nothing good can come of this. How I wish I were far from this land of war madness!

Affectionately,
LINDA.

Our next report came from Manfred and was one of the most revealing that ever reached us. Earlier, he had called attention to Hitler's curious behavior in matters of religion, and many of his later reports dealt with this subject. Heretofore, everything he had written on the subject was, more or less, personal deduction based on his observations. Now, for the first time, he gave facts that could no longer be disputed. He wrote:

Dear Willy:
On Hitler's return from France I was ordered to remain in Berchtesgaden and within a few days a rare opportunity presented itself that I would not have missed for anything.

It happened like this. Additional space was needed in the filing rooms downstairs and Clara received instructions to have the entire place rearranged. Actually she volunteered for the job because she wanted it done in a manner that might prove useful on future occasions. She asked Gottlieb and me to help her. It was a Sunday, and most of the staff were away. Hitler was here, but no unusual developments were expected. He had invited a few personal friends for a quiet afternoon. They were Hess and Max Amann, who was Hitler's top sergeant in 1917 and 1918. The two, as you must know, remained friends and, in the early days of the Nazi movement, Amann was among Hitler's advisers. Eventually, he became the big fund-getter for the Party. He is a shrewd and efficient executive. Hitler put him in charge of the Eher Verlag, which gradually brought under its control not only most of the book and periodical publishing firms in Germany but also all the important daily papers. In brief, the Eher Verlag has become the Publishing Trust of the Reich and a deciding factor in the molding of public opinion in Germany, insofar as the printed word is concerned. Amann has nothing to do with the propaganda angle, which is Dr. Goebbels' job. Amann is the financial boss and, with his control of the purse strings, he has the whip hand over Goebbels. Since the publishing business is one of the most profitable rackets in Nazi Germany, Amann has made himself indispensable to Hitler, who is the principal stockholder in the Eher Verlag.

In political and military matters Hitler asks the advice of experts like Keitel, Jodl, Halder and von Brauchitsch, or Goering and Ribbentrop, but none of these, with the possible exception of Jodl, is really his close friend. Whenever the Fuehrer wants a purely personal exchange of opinions, he falls back on his old cronies from the early days of the Nazi movement—Hess, Amann and Wilhelm Brueckner. Brueckner is Hitler's personal adjutant and he, too, was present at this Sunday gathering.

Our eavesdropping was really accidental. While rearranging furniture, Clara showed me her listening post, and the first words I heard interested me so much that the three of us took turns in writing down the conversation. At times, when someone entered to see what was going on in this part of the basement, we had to shut off the connection and all three of us devoted our energies to shifting file cabinets and other furnishings. Naturally, we heard only part of the *Kaffeklatsch* upstairs, but I give it to you just as we jotted it down. First we heard Hess.

Hess: "While I concede that some features of Rosenberg's philosophy are of merit, I do not think that as a whole his ideas are practical."

Amann: "From a business organization point of view they are preposterous. Nothing but theory, which could not even finance itself, much less yield profits. I would not touch the scheme."

Brueckner: "The man lacks all sense of reality."

Hitler: "Precisely. Rosenberg means well, but he is just an impractical dreamer. Had I let him handle foreign affairs, instead of Ribbentrop, we would have wound up in a mess. The same goes for his religious theories. He simply cannot shake off the impressions he collected from the Greek-Orthodox Church during his early days in Russia. He fails to understand the one cardinal point in which the National Socialist doctrine and the Catholic Church meet. Both have the same dogma for a basis—implicit faith and unquestioning belief. In Catholicism, if the Pope proclaims something it is so, and there can be no questioning by Catholics the world over. In National Socialism, when I proclaim something, it must be so and there can be no questioning. From the outset I realized that to make our movement a tower of strength it needed something more than an appeal to reason. People who reason are hard to convince. People who follow in blind faith are the best tools. I told myself that I could do nothing better than take over this dogma of blind faith from the Catholic Church."

Amann: "The Catholic Church has been, and still is, the greatest financial success in the world."

Hitler: "Correct, but in our present discussion that is beside the point. Before you can think of reaping financial profits from a mass movement built on hypnotic suggestion you must build up a lasting psychological effect in the mass mind. This is what the Catholic Church has done, and it is also what we have accomplished in large measure. It is where the Bolsheviks made their mistake, or at least Lenin did. He and his associates went out of their way to destroy all religious belief because it conflicted with their theory of Internationalism based on cold-blooded materialistic reasoning. Their ideas were basically correct, but they tackled the whole problem from the wrong end. You cannot take religion from the masses without giving them something in exchange which the mass mind will accept. If your goal is Internationalism and World Revolution you must begin by building up a strong core of Nationalism and proceed from there."

Hess: "As Stalin has done."

Hitler: "You mean, as Stalin is on the way to doing. And just because he is on the way to doing it he presents a much greater potential danger to us than British and American plutocracy, whose gods are the dollar and the pound sterling. If you want to hold on to the masses you must give them something more than just the chase after money. It is not good for the masses to have more than just a nibble of material wealth. The Church understands this perfectly, which is why it has always fought material wealth as a sin and is trying to siphon the money from the masses by every conceivable device. In this respect the Church is the natural ally of the State. The two belong together, in that religion is a great factor as a builder of morals in the interests and for the use of Nationalism."

Brueckner: "Early Protestantism did it by combining the functions of the Chief of State and the head of the Church in one person."

Hitler: "That was only a compromise. In itself Protestantism is a creed of rebellion. It is responsible for the so-called liberal minds. In the final analysis it is a destroyer of Nationalism. It is a maker of Sectarianism. Where the Catholic Church gravitates toward one pole—the Pope, the various Protestant sects represent a centrifugal force scattering in all directions. It is a waster where the Catholic Church is a gatherer. If the Catholic Church could be harnessed in the service of Nationalism, it would be a great achievement. Only one thing is wrong with it—it has lost its militancy. It gives too much allegiance to the cross and too little to the sword. The two should be made one."

Brueckner: "As Mohammed did it."

Hitler: "Ah! There was a man! And there is something for us to consider, my friends. Islam is the only religion which owes its success almost entirely to the sword. It became, and in a way still is, the greatest supporter of Nationalism. Even today the dream of all faithful followers of Islam is the creation of a great Moslem State. Now, if you combine Islam and Catholicism into one great religious faith in the service of Nationalism, you have something."

Amann: "Looks to me like a tall order."

Hitler: "I am surprised at you, Max. Your great imagination is failing you. Consider this: Mohammed was an accidental being. By sheer will power he proclaimed himself the tool of God. When people refused to take his word for it, he made them taste the sharpness of his sword, and they promptly accepted him as the Prophet. He built up something that has lasted a thousand years."

Brueckner: "I am beginning to see."

Hitler: "Of course. I have elevated myself from an accidental being to the tool of God. I have created my German nationalist core just as Mohammed created his Arab nationalist core. I am branching out into my world revolution, in the same way as he branched out into his world revolution. I am a prophet in my own right—a second Mohammed! It was the element of distance that stopped Islam short of world conquest—it had to move on horseback. Distance cannot stop me, I have the airplane and the radio. Napoleon relied only on the sword. Mohammed used the sword merely as a means in the service of Faith. That is precisely what I can do after I have proclaimed a new universal faith."

Hess: "That means the destruction of the Church."

Hitler: "Not to begin with. The wise man takes what is on hand and places it at his service. The Catholic Church is based on blind faith. There you have your dogmatic connection. The man who can plan one solid structure out of these ingredients is the man I am looking for. That man is not Rosenberg. He may be in Rome, or he may be in Bagdad. Perhaps there will be two or three men. They will pool their resources and place them at my disposal. Then we shall have a new universal faith. We shall have the millenium!"

As you will understand, this is simply an excerpt, or rather, several excerpts from the conversation. As I explained, we were interrupted several times. However, this confirms all that I have suspected of Hitler's designs on the Church of Rome. Thus far, he has not gone very far with his ideas, for he still cannot get close to the Vatican. But no doubt, he will keep trying.

I expect to return to Berlin shortly and you may not hear from me for some time.

In warm friendship,
MANFRED.

Here at last, voiced by Hitler himself, was the ultimate aim of the obscure corporal in Kaiser Wilhelm's army. There have been countless speculations as to the final Nazi aim, and they have not been flattering. The Nazis, however, always have insisted that such somber word and picture sketches of their character and intentions were the inventions of degenerate and usually Jewish minds.

From Manfred's report for the first time emerged a picture so definite and so precise that no doubt could remain about the fate of the civilized world, should Hitler emerge the victor in this war. Not only does he want to become master of the world's wealth, but also master of men's souls.

The next report contained a partial answer to how Hitler might make a start toward realizing his monstrous ambition. It came from Clara, who wrote:

Dear Willy:

There have been a number of events at the Berghof that few of us will ever forget. One who will remember them longest will be Mussolini. I do not see how he can ever forget the fact that he went to Canossa.*

---

*Reference to German Emperor Heinrich IV's pilgrimage to Pope Gregory VII. The Pope let the Emperor stand for three days in the yard of the castle of Canossa before he granted him an audience.

Il Duce arrived at Berchtesgaden in the armored train that Hitler had once presented to him when times were different. At the station there was no ceremony, no special greeting. The train simply arrived, Mussolini and his party entered waiting automobiles and were driven to the Berghof. It was only there that Hitler extended his welcome. How the mighty have fallen!

At times it will seem to us that Hitler must be carrying some sort of charm on him—a rabbit's foot, as you call it in America. The man has really become great principally through the mistakes of others, his enemies and friends alike. Whoever fights Hitler may have a chance, but whoever embraces him is definitely lost. Who is there left in Europe to oppose him? Eight months ago he conquered France. Now he has conquered Italy, and this without moving a single soldier or even leaving the Berghof himself.

But let me start from the outset.

Mussolini tried to smile when he clasped Hitler's hand, but the best he could bring forth was a sour grimace. He was taken to the apartment assigned to him where he waited for the ordeal to come. When Il Duce returned to the salon, Hitler was waiting for him. He took Mussolini through the various rooms, showing this and that, for this was Il Duce's first visit to the Berghof. Presently Hitler led his guest into the private study where the two remained alone for quite a while. For Mussolini, it must have been like being led to the guillotine.

And I listened. I wouldn't have missed it for anything. Fortunately, Mussolini speaks fluent German and so I was able to understand every word.

Hitler started out by saying that things were rather different now from what they had been when the two last met in Florence. Il Duce said that, yes, that was true. Hitler stated that all previous plans must be discarded, or at least drastically revised, as Il Duce must understand. Mussolini admitted that he understood it perfectly. Hitler pointed out that, after all, the Germans had accomplished their part of the general plan, to which Mussolini replied that war was like a game of cards. You guessed at the hand which your opponent held, and if your guess was wrong you lost the game.

Hitler said that that was true to a certain extent, but that one never guessed at the cards in one's own hand. If one had not a sufficient number of trumps in one's own hand, one passed and let one's partner play the hand. One certainly did not mislead one's partner by pretending to hold the high cards that were actually not there. Then, bringing the facts of war into this, Hitler said any general could lose battles; it was part of war; but if a general had only a bogus army, it was much better not to send him out at all.

Mussolini retorted, somewhat testily, that he had not come to be told things he already knew. To which Hitler replied that he was stating facts that Mussolini did not know. If a country chose total war, it was the first requisite to send party leaders and ministers to the front to set an example. To keep the hierarchy at home where it could continue its graft and easy living while the soldiers at the front gave their lives, was the wrongest possible way to conduct a war. It produced apathy among the population and resentment among the front line soldiers. The trouble with the Fascist hierarchy, said Hitler, was that its members had been living too easily too long. Their militancy had been expressed in words, not deeds. He, Hitler, had definitely earned the right to give advice, and it was entirely up to Mussolini if he chose to accept it. If he did then he would clear out the soft, prosperous leaders surrounding him so fast they would think a tornado had struck them.

Mussolini agreed that something along these lines had to be done, and would be done immediately. On his part, Il Duce wanted to know what could be expected of the French situation. Hitler replied positively that nothing could be expected so long as the Italians were being routed time after time by inferior enemy forces. He pointed out that as a result of Italian failures they now had a real war on their hands, and that it would last at least one year longer than originally foreseen. It also meant that Mussolini would lose Ethiopia unless the Italian troops there were incomparably superior to those in North Africa which, according to Hitler, was highly doubtful. It meant that France, which by this time would have been in the Axis pocket together with her colonial empire, had slipped out of it. It meant that there was no chance now to obtain the co-operation of the French fleet, and with its help to drive the British from the Mediterranean. It meant that the Axis war plan was shot so full of holes that it must be abandoned. A new one could not be planned until the Germans knew definitely just how much Mussolini could contribute to the common war effort.

Mussolini asserted then that Italy was prepared to give all. He said he had joined with Hitler because he had implicit faith in the power of the German army. He still had that faith, he assured Hitler. Italian defeats had been due to poor generalship and a breakdown of organization. This was being remedied, but Italy needed help. She needed planes and tanks. She also needed aid in retaining Ethiopia. He did not want to lose his East African empire.

To this Hitler replied, "I do not belong with the fantastic dreamers. The conquest of India and Arabia occupies an important place in the realm of propaganda, but there is no room for it in realistic war planning. Neither is there for the defense of Italian East Africa by forces other than those already isolated there. Dispersal of military effort carries the germs of defeat. I do one thing at a time. Today we must confine ourselves to the objectives nearest to us and easiest to achieve."

Hitler went on to discuss the inefficiency of Italian fliers, ground personnel and tank forces. He claimed that the Italians had no sense of mechanics. He pointed to the way Marshal Balbo had met his death. He said, "My people have been tightening their belts for years in order to build the best air force and panzer divisions. I trust that you do not expect me to put the products of my people's toil into incompetent hands. If German planes are to help Italy maintain her fronts they will be flown by German pilots and serviced by German ground personnel. If German panzers are to stop the enemies of Italy they will be operated by German soldiers."

Mussolini conceded that German fliers and panzer troops had displayed greater efficiency than their Italian counterparts. But he pointed out that there were certain inner political considerations that he had to take into account. His secret police could cope with growing discontent within the country, but only to a certain point. Fascism was sustained on a strong nationalist feeling among the Italian people. They would stand for defeats in battle if told that past mistakes were being remedied. But if Italian troops were placed under German commanders it might arouse such resentment that the Italians might turn against their friends and allies instead of the common enemy.

By this the shrewd Roman probably anticipated Hitler's next demand which he had already sensed.

And it came. Hitler stated that, as Mussolini knew, he had dispatched his Lieutenant General Rommel for a first-hand study of the situation in Libya. He had deferred this meeting with Mussolini until Rommel's return, and now he was in a position to discuss the African military situation with perhaps a better knowledge than Il Duce. The German air corps stationed on Sicily had already closed the Central Mediterranean to the British convoys. It would be augmented and it would secure passage for Italian supply ships to Tripoli. Hitler had two panzer divisions specially trained and equipped for desert warfare. He would send these two divisions to Africa. They would accomplish what an Italian army of more than twelve divisions had failed to do—chase the British back into Egypt. But to accomplish this they could not depend on inefficient Italian organization. They would not fight under the command of incompetent Italian generals. The Libyan army and its supply services, including whatever Italian contingents were available, must be placed under General Rommel's command. Mussolini could take it or leave it.

Hitler then said he would respect Mussolini's inner political difficulties so far as the war in Albania was concerned. He realized that the Albanian front was too close to Italy and it might injure Italian sensibilities if the German command tried to interfere directly. Furthermore, the Albanian situation was not so important to him at the moment as holding the North African position. He would approach the war in Greece in an entirely different way. However, while he was prepared to let the Italians fight alone on the Albanian front, they would have to co-ordinate their movements with the requirements of the German General Staff when the German army would be ready to strike. This, too, Mussolini could accept or not, as he pleased.

The third point, said Hitler, was production. Germany was winning the production battle, Italy was losing it. This would not do. Italy's production was far below her capacity to produce. The fault lay with organization. If German production were to supplement Italian production hereafter, the two had to be closely co-ordinated. Wherever productive facilities were available in Italy these had to be connected with the German Four-Year Plan. It would require a German-Italian commission on production. Since Italy had a surplus of man power compared with her production facilities, idle Italian workers must be sent to Germany to work in production there. Order had to be established amid the chaos of Italian production.

Il Duce was given time to think about these things. The remainder of the day was devoted to a state dinner. After this, Mussolini was allowed to retire for the night. The next morning he gave his answer.

It was an acceptance of all of Hitler's terms. Then followed a general council of war. Mussolini was assisted by Count Ciano, General Cavallero and others. Hitler, of course, had Ribbentrop, Keitel, Jodl and Rommel with him. About this meeting I can tell you only what I have been able to glean from other sources.

Rommel's two divisions, to be called hereafter the Afrika Korps, are to depart immediately for southern Italy, there to embark for Tripoli. To safeguard their passage another Luftwaffe corps will be sent south. The Italian army in Albania will hold a specified defense line until German forces operating from Bulgaria go into action against the Greeks. Bulgaria is to be occupied without delay. A German industrial commission under Dr. Schnurre will go immediately to Rome to prepare the organization of Italian industrial production for war.

I was at the station in Berchtesgaden as Mussolini's train left. Not far from me stood Colonel Wartenburg, who commanded the Schutzstaffel guard. As the departing train rounded the first curve I heard the Colonel very distinctly say, "There goes our latest Gauleiter. I certainly would not like being in his shoes."

This is all I have to tell you at the moment. Warmest regards,

CLARA.

Here was something that we could use, and use well. The report reached us two weeks after the meeting and we covered it thoroughly in broadcasts. In spite of the lateness of the report's arrival there was still a great deal of public interest in the Hitler-Mussolini meeting and rumors were flying wildly about, so that our broadcasts were timely.

The next letter to reach us came from Linda. It read:

Dear Willy:

Germany has seen a great deal of official entertaining lately. We have had important callers from Russia, Italy, Japan, France, Spain, Bulgaria, Hungary, Yugoslavia and Finland. At present there is a Persian [Iranian] mission here.

Heinrich has given me the information on the latter. It appears that, in secret at least, both Iran and Iraq have joined with Hitler. This was arranged by von Papen, operating from Ankara. It was accomplished before the Italian defeats that have altered the previous program considerably. However, von Papen's arrangements could not be cancelled entirely because these people in the Middle East are supersensitive, according to Heinrich. Therefore Berlin has assumed the attitude that nothing of great importance has really happened in Libya and Albania. It is a problem of saving face. Something is about to happen in Iraq and it has been arranged by Jah Amin el Husseini, former Grand Mufti of Jerusalem* who is now being paid substantially by Hitler. Heinrich does not know yet exactly what it is all about.

The business now being done with Iran demonstrates quite clearly that Hitler intends to double-cross the Russians if they should refuse to agree with him. This Persian mission, on the surface, is strictly economic, but actually some very important politicians from Teheran are

*Jah Amin el Husseini, Grand Mufti of Jerusalem who, as a paid agent of the Nazis, was guilty of inciting the Arabs to riot against the Jews in Palestine and was responsible for the circulation of Fascist propaganda in the Middle East. He was forced to flee British territory and for a while was the "guest" of Mussolini in Italy, where he continued to serve the Fascists by broadcasting propaganda to the Arabs. He was president of the Supreme Moslem Council and as such was the country's highest religious and judicial officer of the Arab community. Lately he has gone to the German-occupied Crimea where he is helping to organize a Tatar Republic for Hitler.

among its members. Rhiza Pahlevi, the self-made Shah of Persia, has lent a very receptive ear to Hitler's proposals. The Shah has always been suspicious of England and Russia. He is particularly afraid of Russian Bolshevism and Hitler has taken full advantage of this fear. Von Papen has convinced the Persians that Russia will overrun their country and they are here to learn how Hitler intends to protect them. So far they have been heaped with promises which may turn out quite empty. For, as Heinrich told me, Hitler's previous plans with regard to the Middle East had to be discarded as a result of Mussolini's military failures, and since there is as yet no good substitute, Hitler will make no definite commitments.

This is fairly evident because the members of the Persian mission were not taken directly to Hitler, who is now in Berlin. He is quite busy, of course, for Mussolini's capitulation has opened new opportunities for action. At the Chancellory one conference after another is being held. Goebbels confers with Hitler almost daily, discussing plans for a new propaganda program to be directed at the United States. Halder, Goering, Milch, Keitel and von Brauchitsch are rushed with new campaign plans. These are not known yet, but we do know here that General Rommel is already in Tripoli with two panzer divisions that were rushed across the Mediterranean in one week. The men went in transport planes. Their equipment goes by ship and may not yet be there. Heinrich heard that Rommel was training his troops between Tripoli and the French Tunisian border where they are considered safe from British air reconnaissance. In a few days Hitler is scheduled to deliver a speech at the Sportspalast, and will promise new great victories to the German people. However, he expects certain diplomatic developments that may have a bearing on the speech. That is why everybody is frantically working, especially Ribbentrop, who is in daily communication with our ambassador in Moscow. Perhaps it is connected with Molotov's visit here last year, or it may concern Bulgaria.

Goering came out to Karin Hall for just one day. He was accompanied by Milch and Udet and they discussed some new Stuka models. At coffee after dinner—there is still real coffee at Karin Hall—I heard Goering refer to Ribbentrop in rather harsh terms. Hermann has always considered the Foreign Minister a party upstart. I remember once when Hitler was here and referred to Ribbentrop as a "second Bismarck," Goering could hardly control his laughter. He insists that Ribbentrop owes his solid position with Hitler merely to his good fortune in 1938 when he informed Hitler of his conviction that England would not go to war over Czechoslovakia.

On this particular occasion, however, Goering observed that Ribbentrop was standing under the gallows and did not realize it. He had got himself into such a complicated situation in the Russian affair that he could not right it. He had assured Hitler, Goering said, that he would be able to convince Russia of Hitler's power and bring her to terms. Now, it seems, Moscow is raising many unexpected difficulties in our policy in the Balkans. This seems to fit in with Heinrich's ideas on the subject and we are fairly sure that Hitler is impatiently waiting for developments from Moscow.

This is all for the moment. We are all tense and you shall hear from me as soon as something happens.

Affectionately,
LINDA.

The girl kept her word. In less than a week we had another letter from her and the "something" had certainly happened. She wrote:

Dear Willy:

I am writing you from Berlin where I have been for a few days. Heinrich suggested that I stay where he could reach me quickly because the big things are really happening. It appears that, following his conversations with Molotov, Hitler has actually been pressing Stalin for an orientation from Central Asia in the direction of India. Perhaps this is one of the reasons why the question of India was not settled in the secret clauses of the Tripartite Pact.

The Russian reply came. The new Soviet Ambassador, Dekanosov, called on Ribbentrop and presented him with Stalin's decision. Ribbentrop hurried to the Chancellory to give the message to Hitler and it must have been an unpleasant task for him.

Dekanosov had informed him that the Russian government could not see its way clear to enter into additional international commitments at this time. The situation in the Soviet Union is such that the people need rest and peace. Russia has undertaken to deliver considerable quantities of commodities to Germany and to do this she must stay aloof from military entanglements. A difficult campaign could not possibly be undertaken now. All of this was, of course, the usual diplomatic language and probably none of the reasons advanced was valid.

That same evening Hitler completely scratched Russia from the picture and, for Hitler, in a peculiar fashion. He invited the Japanese foreign minister, Yosuke Matsuoka, to visit Berlin as soon as it would be possible to do so. The provisions of the Tripartite Pact will now be pressed for all they are worth, and the attitude of the European and

Asiatic Axis partners toward Russia will be closely defined. As you recall, the pact stipulates that Germany is to neutralize potential Russian interference with Japanese expansion southward. Hitler's first attempt to weaken the Soviet Union by involving that country in an aggressive military adventure against India, has failed. Now, I suppose, he will try a different policy. Hitler is furious with the Russians because they have failed to comply with his wishes. Once again, the Soviet Union, to him, has become an uncontrollable monster. Once again, he speaks of Stalin as a fiend. All this, of course, in strictly private conversation.

Now I shall give you the next development resulting from Stalin's refusal to fall in with Hitler's wishes. As you probably know, a number of Indian radicals who have been here ever since the war began, have been permitted to engage in radio propaganda advocating an independent India. Actually, they were minor figures. In January, however, they were joined by an important man, Subhas Chandra Bose, former president of the All-India National Congress Party who resigned on April 30, 1939, after a disagreement with Mohandas Gandhi. Bose wanted a program of direct action against the British bordering on open revolution, while Gandhi insisted on a continued program of passive resistance.

Bose was originally a Communist and for years maintained relations with certain Indian Communists then in the service of the Kremlin. Bose had also visited Moscow some years ago and for this reason he was carefully watched by the British. When Hitler was victorious in Germany, Bose thought the new movement might be more suitable for conditions in India than Communism. He actually advocated adoption of an Oriental variety of Fascism as "a system which gives us an example of what can be accomplished by vigorous action and unity." When England declared war in September, 1939, and forced the British government in India to join in the declaration of war, Bose, together with Pandit Jawaharlal Nehru, who was also at odds with Gandhi, denounced the action and both were jailed by British authorities. Presently they were released and Bose arrived in Germany early this year.

On his arrival, Bose immediately tried to see Hitler. However, while still uncommitted to an Indian policy and at the same time suggesting aggression against India to Stalin, the Fuehrer would not see Bose. He was treated quite courteously by the smaller fry and asked to wait until a more propitious opportunity arrived. But immediately upon Hitler's decision to invite Matsuoka, Bose was turned over to Baron von Weissaecker, one of Ribbentrop's assistants. The following day he was presented to Hitler.

In the course of a two-hour conversation with the Fuehrer, Bose, who speaks fairly fluent German, outlined his views on the situation in India. He explained that Gandhi and his policy of passive resistance were outmoded. The present, he said, calls for direct, vigorous action aiming at the liberation of the Indian people not only from the British, but also from the slavery of their ancient philosophy of life. With a world revolution on the way, India must grasp her chance now or be forever doomed to her present shackles. The caste system, together with other impossible relics of the past, must be broken. The sixty million Untouchables must be given human rights. India must belong to the Indian masses, not to the British and their obedient vassals, the Indian princes. Bose claimed a personal following of at least thirty per cent of the All-India Congress Party. He explained that if he received substantial support for the liberation of India, the others would quickly fall in line with him. But he said he wanted action, not mere words and promises.

The outcome of it all is this: Bose will be permitted to organize a provisional Government of Independent India in Berlin. He will be recognized by the Reich Government as the President of such a government. In this capacity he will be allowed to sign a treaty of alliance with the Reich as soon as the time for such action is ripe. The alliance will be a pledge to wage war against the British. On his part Hitler will pledge to send a German army to co-operate in the liberation of India as soon as the military situation permits.

Now I have a few words about the latest French developments. Otto Abetz was in Berlin and conferred with Hitler. Petain's new vice-premier is Admiral Darlan, who has approached Abetz with a plan of his own for French-German collaboration. In fact, Darlan intimated that he would like very much to confer with the Fuehrer himself.

To this Hitler replied, "Dieser Darlan kann mir den Puckel hinunter rutschen."* He then gave Abetz full authority to negotiate with the French on whatever questions they may raise, but to concede nothing unless he gets ten times the amount in return. Hitler added that until Laval is returned to power in Vichy he, Hitler, would have no intercourse with the Petain crowd. He would not discuss any terms with an outfit of selfish French politicians, who have no sense of world realities. Meanwhile, Abetz was to play a cat-and-mouse game with them.

That is all for this time. I am going back to Karin Hall. Hitler, I understand, is returning to the Berghof, and there is no sense in my remaining in Berlin. I am still working for a living, you know.

I like to know what you are doing, I have not heard from you for a

*This Darlan is welcome to slide down my back.

long time. Are you satisfied with the kind of information that I have been sending you? Please write me soon and make it a nice letter. God knows, I need some encouragement.

Affectionately,
LINDA.

CHAPTER 19

THE OUTSTANDING FEATURE of Linda's excellent report, of course, was the news that Hitler had issued a call for Japanese Foreign Minister Matsuoka. Because of the general attitude in Washington and among the American press on the Japanese situation, I had broadcast nothing on the German-Japanese alliance for quite a long period. In this instance, however, after a long discussion with van Narvig, we decided to go to town on the subject, and we did. *

As a matter of fact, this news was accepted very skeptically in the United States, for it was not until twelve days after my first mention of Matsuoka's impending journey that the teletype confirmed my story. The official confirmation from Tokio announced that Yosuke Matsuoka had prayed before the shrine of his honorable ancestors for the success of his journey to Berlin.

During my broadcasts of this period I also stated plainly that the "friendship" between Berlin and Moscow had cooled considerably.

The next letter from Germany came from Gottlieb. It read:

Dear Willy:
For quite a while Clara has been incorporating my information in her reports, and now I am doing the same for her in this letter. She is

*Williams started his broadcast of March 9, 1941, with the following: "As the clock strikes tonight, The Rome-Berlin-Tokyo Axis is clearing the decks for a worldwide diplomatic offensive on an unprecedented scale, as a prelude to Hitler's 1941 blitz-krieg. In my broadcast of February 25th, I reported that Japanese Foreign Minister Matsuoka was preparing for an important trip to Moscow and Berlin. I called it important because this is the first time in the history of the Empire of the Rising Sun that one of her ranking statesmen is going abroad under such momentous conditions as the present. Yesterday, positive confirmation of my report came from both Tokyo and Berlin."

down with a cold—nothing really serious, but persistent. Wolfgang rushes over here almost daily to see her. I have tried to keep him away, because it is indiscreet, in my opinion, for the two to be outwardly associated together. But Wolfgang is in love and there is little I can do about it under the circumstances.

I want to tell you about a visit to the Berghof by two statesmen from the Balkans. They were Premier Cvetkovich and Foreign Minister Cincar-Markovich of Yugoslavia. They came here in response to an invitation from Hitler, but I doubt very much if they enjoyed the journey. However, there was little else that they could do, what with approximately forty divisions of German and Italian troops stationed in the vicinity of their country's frontiers.

Since Clara was confined to bed and since I could not avail myself of her listening post without a great deal of risk, I cannot give you any first-hand details on the conference. But from several sources I have learned in general what took place.

Hitler, as is the custom on such occasions, joined the two visitors at luncheon. After that, he told them that he wanted to discuss, in friendly fashion, the perilous situation of their country. He explained the differences between his Balkan policy and that of Prime Minister Churchill and President Roosevelt. The difference is that he, Hitler, desires peace for the Balkans, whereas England and America are anxious to entice the Balkan peoples into a disastrous war, not for any benefit of these Balkan peoples, but for entirely selfish Anglo-Saxon reasons. He referred to Colonel Donovan's* mission in the Balkans and then asked, pointblank, what Yugoslavia could gain by declaring war on Germany. His visitors promptly replied that their country had not the slightest intention of fighting Germany.

Hitler then said that he could see only one way for Yugoslavia to escape battle. Greece, he declared, had been foolish enough to fight Italy. She had won at first, primarily because of poor Italian preparation. Had it been simply an issue between Italy and Greece he, Hitler, would have waited for an eventual overpowering of the Greeks by the Italians. But Greece had given the British a new foothold on the European continent and this Germany could not tolerate. The British must be kept out of Europe, if Hitler had to drive them out time and again.

This meant, Hitler went on, that he simply had to take a hand in the Greek war, and the Greeks certainly could not hope to hold out against

*Colonel William J. Donovan, now a brigadier general and director of the Office of Strategic Services, made an extensive tour of the Balkans and the Near East on a fact-finding mission for President Roosevelt early in 1941.

the Germans. His armies, however, must pass through Yugoslav territory. If Yugoslavia were to permit this arrangement, then it would automatically involve a certain amount of German military control over the country. If Yugoslavia were to refuse, it would become necessary for the German war machine to bear down on her. In that case a partition of Yugoslavia would become inevitable. His visitors knew of course, he stated, that Pavelich* was in Rome with his own plans for an independent Croatia, and that he enjoyed the backing of Premier Mussolini. In the process of dividing Yugoslavia into her Serb and Croat components, other parts of the country would disappear. He, Hitler, was in favor of retaining Yugoslavia as a whole.

One way was still open for the Yugoslav nation to avert this disaster. If the Belgrade government could persuade the Greeks to make peace with Italy before Germany entered the fight, then the Balkans, and especially Yugoslavia, would not become involved in any fighting. Certainly it would be better for Greece to preserve her fields and valleys from destruction by panzer divisions, and her population from consequent starvation. At this time Greece might be able to buy a relatively easy peace by merely placing her outlying islands under the occupation of German troops as a token of good faith.

Hitler assured his Yugoslav visitors that, from a military point of view, it made little difference to him whether or not reluctant portions of the Balkans were drawn into the war, because he had the power to crush them quickly and easily. He merely had the interests of the Balkan peoples at heart. Of course, he would prefer to settle the Greek affair peacefully in order to devote his full attention to other objectives. For this reason, he had extended this invitation for a realistic discussion of the problem.

The Yugoslav statesmen assured Hitler that their government would do everything possible to persuade the Greeks to accept whatever terms might be offered. If under British pressure they refused, it certainly could not be the fault of Yugoslavia.

Two days later Hitler had Field Marshal List at the Berghof for what evidently was a preliminary council of war. This indicates that the Greek campaign will soon begin. List, it is understood here, will command any Balkan campaign that takes place. He is a specialist in mountain warfare. In the Polish campaign he broke through the Carpathian Mountains from Slovakia with the Fourteenth Army, forced

*Ante Pavelich, Croatian anarchist, who organized the assassination of King Alexander of Yugoslavia in Marseille. He had sought refuge in Rome where Mussolini befriended him for political reasons. Pavelich now heads the puppet regime in Croatia.

the strong Jablonka Pass, then, over exceedingly bad roads, occupied the fortress of Przemysl, all in three days. This foiled any Polish retreat southward. In the French campaign, List, with the Twelfth Army (consisting of mountain troops from his native Swabia and the Tyrol), forced the heretofore impenetrable Ardennes Forest in two days and accomplished the break-through at Sedan that sealed the doom of the Allied armies in Flanders. Like Hitler, he loves art, likes to travel for pleasure and favors Wagner and Goethe. He is the field commander in whom Hitler places his greatest faith.

In the presence of Keitel, von Brauchitsch and Jodl, List outlined his plan for a Balkan campaign. He assumed that Bulgaria would permit herself to be used as a German advance base. Hitler replied that that question had been favorably settled months ago. He was greatly amused by the astonishment of his generals and informed them that two weeks after the visit of King Boris to Berchtesgaden, in November, the monarch had signalled his affirmative answer. The matter had been kept secret for diplomatic reasons, especially in connection with Russia. Hitler then asked the generals if they recalled the incident in Sofia when Colonel Donovan's wallet was stolen.* Photostatic copies of the contents of that wallet, said Hitler, had been in his possession for some time.

After this, List explained his plan. He showed on a map just how his troops would be deployed. A panzer division racing down the Maritza Valley would reach Dedeagach on the Aegean Sea in twenty-four hours, thus eliminating the possibility of a Greek retreat into Turkish territory. Another panzer brigade would cross the Rhodope Mountains through two narrow passes and occupy Kavalla in less than three days. A division of mountain troops assisted by a panzer brigade would move down the Struma River against Rupel Pass where he expects stubborn resistance. Therefore he thought it advisable to send a third panzer division across the mountains into the southeast corner of Yugoslavia to make a dash down the Vardar Valley toward Salonika, which it could reach in three days, compelling a surrender of the Greek army at Rupel Pass. The Yugoslavs would have to let this division pass through their territory unopposed. If Yugoslavia resisted, List said, he would be compelled to make slight changes in his plan and use additional troops. With Salonika occupied, a junction with the Italians driving from Albania would bring about the capitulation of the remaining Greek forces. Hitler expressed his belief that the Yugoslavs would

*On January 22, 1941, Colonel Donovan announced the loss of his portfolio containing his diplomatic passport and various other documents. It was later returned intact at Sofia to George H. Earle, then U. S. Minister to Bulgaria.

not resist, but he instructed von Brauchitsch and List to make their preparations in case of resistance.

This is all for now. I hear that Hitler will go to Vienna shortly. If he uses his armored train I shall probably be on it. In that case you will hear from me again.

Grüss Gott!
GOTTLIEB.

This report had evidently been delayed for several days, for with it we received a letter from Wolfgang, who had this to say:

Dear Willy:

I am writing about an occurrence at Fuschl that may not be very significant, for it does not directly refer to any of the current events. It is actually a character study and I thought it might provide extra material for you.

Ribbentrop has purchased—or perhaps pilfered—a collection of old weapons that he wants to exhibit here. I was busy cataloguing them in the designated exhibition room. In the adjoining study were Ribbentrop and two of his close friends, Foreign Gauleiter Bohle and Press Chief Dietrich. They expected to go to Vienna for a state occasion of some sort in a few days, and in view of the strenuous work of the past few days, they were relaxing. The door was open, and since I was moving about they were aware of my presence.

Bohle commented on Ribbentrop's diplomatic coups and mentioned rather casually that except for sheer chance, Rosenberg might be foreign minister. From here on I made notes of their conversation, which ran like this:

Ribbentrop: "Rosenberg would have been impossible at the Foreign Office. Hitler understands this. Rosenberg is the dreamer type with no sense of realities and practical expedients."

Dietrich: "Still at one time he virtually dictated our foreign policy. He had more to say than von Neurath."*

Ribbentrop: "Von Neurath, in his way, was a good diplomat. But he had two cardinal faults. For a nation bent on aggrandizement by every available means, he was too scrupulous, and he placed a wrong interpretation on the meaning of honor. He did not understand that a promise was valid only so long as the circumstances under which it was given remained the same. This did not go with Hitler. The greatness

*Baron Konstantin von Neurath, who was Reich Foreign Minister during the early years of Hitler's regime, and later was appointed Protector of Bohemia and Moravia, a post which he had to relinquish to Reinhardt Heydrich in September, 1941, because he was considered too easy-going on the Czechs.

of a man does not lie in his keeping a promise under any circumstances, but in his strength to break it as soon as the national interest demands. The inability to comprehend this cost von Neurath his job."

Bohle: "Still, I remember that you had a rather difficult time eliminating Rosenberg from the competition."

Ribbentrop: "I used the right approach. I pointed out to Hitler how impossible Rosenberg would be for the post because of his background. In the first place, the man is not even a native German. While he comes from German stock, he was born in the Russian Baltic Provinces and did not see Germany until after the Bolshevik Revolution. In Russia he was a dyed-in-the-wool monarchist and reactionary. He belonged to the Black Hundreds and organized many Jewish pogroms. While this might be an asset from the anti-Semitic party view, it certainly would be a terrible handicap for a Foreign Minister who has to deal with international situations. This Jewish business has caused our Foreign Office plenty of embarrassing situations. Both von Neurath and I could tell you volumes about what we went through because hare-brained idiots did not know where to draw the line."

Bohle: "I do not think that the anti-Semitic background would have made much difference with Hitler."

Ribbentrop: "In the early days it would not have, but Hitler too has grown in stature since he developed from a common demagogue to dictator of the most powerful nation in Europe. However, I had still another lever to use. The story is little known, but based on fact. At one time Rosenberg was actually a Bolshevik. He was in Moscow during the Bolshevik Revolution and managed to get close to Lenin. But he wanted an important job with the Bolsheviks and did not get it. Then he came to Germany and joined the Nazi movement. When I presented these facts to Hitler they destroyed every chance Rosenberg might have had. Can you imagine a Foreign Minister of Nazi Germany who once was a Bolshevik!"

Dietrich: "This is the first I have heard of it."

Ribbentrop: "Only a few know. Among them are Goering and Hess. They confirmed the facts to Hitler and that was sufficient. Not that I exactly like either one of them, but 'man muss mit den Woelfen heulen'." *

Bohle: "Do you think that Hitler will spare the Yugoslav Kingdom if Belgrade joins the Axis?"

Ribbentrop: "Frankly, I do not think that Yugoslavia will retain all her territory. In the beginning, yes. But later there are bound to be territorial adjustments. Don't forget that Yugoslavia is one of the Versailles nations, and definite commitments have been made to Bulgaria

*One must howl with the wolves.

and Italy. If Belgrade goes all the way with us, Yugoslavia may be given Salonika as compensation for the loss of her Dalmatian harbors. But Croatia is a big problem. Ante Pavelich is a protégé of Mussolini, and Hitler has made certain promises to the Italian. However, it is too early to consider the subject. The chances are that Mussolini will take what is given him, and like it."

At this point Ribbentrop rose and closed the door to the exhibition room. I instantly occupied myself with my work.

This is all I have to write at present. Over at Berchtesgaden, Clara has been ill, but she is better now. I hope to find a way of looking through Ribbentrop's private files. They should be interesting.

Thanks for your friendly note. I shall try to be careful if you will tell me how.

Your friend,
WOLFGANG.

This letter was quite an interesting one, but we could find no way to use it without involving Wolfgang, inasmuch as he was the only known witness to the conversation. Now, unhappily, this no longer matters.

Gottlieb soon made good his promise to send a story from Vienna. His letter read:

Dear Willy:

The old saying that all roads lead to Rome certainly does not hold for the Balkan nations. In their case, all roads seem to lead to Vienna.

Today, Bulgaria came to Vienna in the person of her Premier, Bogdan Philoff. From what I saw of him he is quite a decent chap. He appears to believe that under the present circumstances an alliance with Hitler is about the best possible thing for his country.

At that, the Russians blundered clumsily in the Bulgarian affair. They actually barged in after everything had been settled between Hitler and King Boris. They should have understood that at the time Hitler had reinforced his garrisons in Rumania. If they weren't prepared to fight, as is plainly evident now, they should have kept out altogether. Instead, they stirred up a lot of trouble in Bulgaria, first trying to undermine Boris' position, and then offering a Russian army of occupation. Such an offer in itself is sufficient to drive any of these small nations straight into Hitler's arms.

Anyway, here was Philoff in the Belvedere Palace, with Hitler, Ribbentrop, Count Ciano and General Oshima of Japan. As they all affixed their signatures under an appendix to the Tripartite Pact, the others congratulated Philoff on his astuteness which seemed to make him feel particularly good. I should like to say now that anyone who naïvely believes that Japan is a minor power with hopes of remaining on the sidelines in this war, is utterly misinformed. I hope you can make that clear in your country.

Hitler's presence at this ceremony was unusual in itself. It is the first time that the Fuehrer has condescended to appear in person when a small country joins the Axis. This was a signal honor and Philoff accepted it as such. But then, Bulgaria's adherence was actually Hitler's personal job. He also feels that from the military point of view, Bulgaria is a very important ally. She gives easiest access to recalcitrant Greece and also is right next to the still uncommitted Turks. Moreover, if Bulgaria had resisted, there would have been a great deal of trouble with the Soviet Union and Hitler wanted to avoid this, at least for the present.

After the alliance was signed, there was a state banquet. Here I saw Hitler do something that I do not believe he has ever done before. He raised a glass of champagne and offered a toast to King Boris. Philoff, beaming, countered with toasts to Hitler, King Victor Emmanuel and Emperor Hirohito. The other allies—Hungary, Rumania and Slovakia—were somehow forgotten.

Before the ink on Philoff's signature was dry, German troops were crossing the Danube into Bulgaria and proceeding southward to the borders of Greece and Turkey. Field Marshal List was already in Sofia. This surprised no one. Labor battalions of the Organization Todt have been in Bulgaria for two months, repairing roads and strengthening bridges. Luftwaffe ground personnel in Bulgarian uniforms has been installing flak guns and air field equipment. German naval personnel has been surveying port facilities in Burgas and Varna. Today's signing was actually a mere formality.

Hitler is staying here overnight and tomorrow we shall be on our way back to Berchtesgaden. Other things will certainly happen. You are lucky to be where you are.

Grüss Gott!
GOTTLIEB.

Bulgaria's adherence to the Axis made headline news the very day it occurred. Dr. Goebbels saw to that. When Gottlieb's letter reached us, the information was stale. The best we could do with it was file it for the record.

Not long thereafter we received the following letter from Clara:

Dear Willy:

As you have probably heard from Linda, Japanese General Tomo-yuki Yamashita has been in Germany for some time as the head of a large mission of officers who are making a detailed study of the Wehr-macht. The General had wanted for some time to be presented to Hitler, but for some unknown reason this occasion was continually postponed. Now, at last, the General's wish has been granted.

It has become a practice here to make every presentation to Hitler a major event. The build-up for these affairs has become simply colos-sal. Foreign visitors especially are given the impression that they are about to be confronted with a representative of the Almighty. Perhaps next Hitler will install himself in some sort of shrine.

Yamashita arrived in the company of Goering and Japanese Ambas-sador General Oshima. The Berghof was covered with swastikas and the emblems of the Rising Sun. I understand that the General had brought a decoration for Hitler, but he was informed that the Fuehrer does not accept any.

Goering introduced Yamashita to Hitler. As Hitler clasped Yama-shita's hand, the General muttered confusedly that next to being pre-sented to Emperor Hirohito, this was the greatest moment of his life.

Hitler patted him on the shoulder, insisting that he is no different from any other human being. After the preliminary build-up, this was a cleverly calculated gesture. Hitler invited Yamashita to sit next to him on a settee, then started a conversation along lines so shrewdly con-ceived that anyone who does not know Hitler for the great actor he is, would have been instantly impressed. Hitler began in a spiritual vein. He said that a people's rise to power does not spring from material desires but from the urge of a national spirit that far surpasses anything which the world has to offer. It was only a Japanese or a German who could express himself thus and be sure of understanding, because of the deep spiritual kinship between the Japanese and German souls.

"Japan is no stranger to me," Hitler continued. "Ever since my boyhood I have been attracted by the spirit which manifests itself through the Japanese people, and their unshakeable belief in their ulti-mate destiny. I made it a point to read every report covering the war between Japan and Russia. While people around me could not under-stand how Japan was able to deal annihilating blows to the Russian colossus, I even then realized that Japan's strength came from some-thing far greater than guns and battleships. As I grew older this impres-sion increased. In many respects I have followed Japanese precepts in building up the national consciousness and strength of Germany.

It is my inner conviction that Japan represents the race to be placed in charge of Asia, as Germany is the race to take charge of the European sphere."

After more of this, the conversation reverted to its proper level with talk of tanks, guns, planes and the disciplining and educating of a people for total war. Yamashita expressed his appreciation for the assistance and advice he had received during his stay in Germany. He asked to see much more and was assured that everything that Germany had to show was at his disposal. In closing the conversation, Hitler said:

"Both our nations are in the midst of a great national war effort. Our peoples are pledged to each other to see it through. Great difficulties lie ahead until the common goal is reached. Whatever happens, Germany and Japan stand together. I do not know how long I have to live, but when I pass I shall remember Japan in my will. I shall call upon the German people to bind themselves eternally to the heroic Japanese."

So much for Yamashita's visit. That Japan has long been planning to conquer her part of the world has been clear to everyone here for some time. And if the day arrives when she drives the white race out of Asia the responsibility will rest with Hitler, who not only is giving her the opportunity but is pointing the way.

I have only one thing to add. Grand Admiral Raeder has just returned from Italy, where he inspected Mussolini's navy. What he told the Fuehrer did not sound encouraging. It will take from four to six months to repair the battleships which the British damaged during the Taranto raid. Until then, the Italian navy cannot be counted on for any important naval operation. Admiral Raeder considered it problematical that the British could be driven out of the Mediterranean before 1942 at the earliest.

He had no criticism of morale among Italian navy personnel, which he found to be higher than he had expected. But the basic training, he said, was all wrong. The Italian navy is trained in hit-and-run tactics, but its attempts to surprise any part of the British fleet in order to make use of such tactics have failed, because there is practically no naval air force, and naval reconnaissance is virtually nonexistent. Raeder expressed his opinion that the Italian navy would never be able to match a British force of equal strength, and at best could be used only in auxiliary operations.

I have been in bed for more than a week with a cold, but I am back in shape and again on the lookout.

With warmest regards,
CLARA.

This letter was almost immediately followed by another, also from Clara. She wrote:

Dear Willy:

I should have waited one day before sending off my last letter. Heinrich Stahmer has returned from Japan to give Hitler all possible information on how to deal with Japanese Foreign Minister Matsuoka, who is expected in Berlin shortly. It was Stahmer, you will recall, who actually arranged for Japan to enter the Tripartite Pact with Germany and Italy.

Stahmer reported that the Japanese situation on the whole looks promising. Preparations are proceeding rapidly toward the transformation of Japan for total war along the same lines as Germany. A great deal has already been accomplished, but there are hurdles still to overcome, particularly in the production of aircraft. However, it is expected that upon General Yamashita's return he will proceed instantly with the reorganization of ground and air forces with a view of co-ordinating their operations on the pattern mapped out for him in Germany.

The Japanese expect to move into Indo-China some time in July. Before his departure from Tokyo, Stahmer was reminded that Germany had pledged her co-operation in the matter. With relations between Berlin and Vichy somewhat strained, as they became after Laval's dismissal by Petain, Tokyo feared that Hitler might not be able to prod the French into submission. Japan does not want to use force in occupying Indo-China, as this might provoke action by Great Britain or even the United States before Japan was fully prepared.

Meanwhile, Japan is readying herself for the coming struggle in her own way. After his return from Germany, Count Terauchi transferred six divisions of picked troops to the island of Hainan. They are secretly undergoing intensive training with special weapons for jungle warfare for the coming campaigns in Malaya, Burma and the Dutch East Indies. In July the Japanese general staff intends to send these divisions into Indo-China and replace them on Hainan with other divisions to be trained in the same way.

Japan is also busily engaged in organizing fifth columns in the territories she expects to invade. Special attention is given to sending into these countries large numbers of pangees—Buddhist monks who are either Japanese or have been eduated in Japan. They are expected to be especially useful in influencing the native populations and in gathering military information.

With regard to gathering geographic and strategic information,

Stahmer told Hitler a story that I will try to put down in detail because it is genuinely interesting.

According to Stahmer, the Japanese General Staff dispatched a Colonel Yakematu to Singapore a year ago. There he hired himself out as a coolie on a small rubber plantation and worked at menial jobs on Singapore Island until he had learned the lay of the land. Then he obtained a job as longshoreman in Keppel Harbor, receiving point for all supplies for Fort Canning headquarters, fortress of Singapore, nearby. Next he hired out as a construction worker at the principal naval base on Johore Strait. Eventually he became foreman on a Japanese-owned rubber plantation near Tampin, in the Malay state of Negri Sembilan, where he established secret headquarters. Colonel Yakematu's actual job was collecting and mapping all information of military and economic interest to the Tokyo General Staff.

The colonel was not alone in his work. Actually he headed a secret mission composed of about 180 Japanese army and naval officers who, in turn, recruited numerous aides among the native population. These men hired out as sailors on coastal ships in Singapore, Port Dickson, Port Selangor and Penang. Some established themselves as captains of sampans, junks and tugboats. They charted the channels along the Strait of Malacca. They worked as fishermen along the South China Sea coast, out of Mersing, Kuantan, Patani and Singora—the last named in friendly Siamese territory where a transmission base was established. They studied the beaches with regard to possible landing operations. Supervision of all these tasks was assigned to the naval contingent of the mission.

The army officers pursued different assignments. They and their native aides worked as coolies on rubber plantations in Kedah, Selangor, Johore and other strategic locations. They became hunting guides in the jungles of Pahang and Trengganu, particularly for British officers, whose habits and characteristics they studied. They hired out as switchmen, conductors and shop workers on the Singora-Singapore railroad. They became truck drivers in Wellesley and Malacca. They labored in the Perak tin mines around Ipoh. They became construction workers on the new airfields which the British were building at Kota Bahru, Alor Star, Kuala Lipis, Kuantan and other places. Some were dock workers along the Singapore and Penang waterfronts. They wormed their way into every place where important information might be gleaned, employing means such as driving delivery trucks to Fort Changhi, which guards the entrance to Johore Strait and to the naval base, or becoming watchmen at the Singapore waterworks, or doing repair work on the causeway connecting Singapore Island with Johore Bahru on the Malayan mainland.

They were subject to the strictest military discipline. If one failed it meant that he had to pay with his life. They operated in groups, each composed of from six to twenty members under one of Yakematu's officers. Some of them, especially those operating along the coast, came from the Japanese merchant marine, while others were recruited among dependable native Malays and Tamils. The information they gathered was forwarded by Colonel Yakematu to the Tokio army and navy staffs, giving them a picture of conditions in Singapore and of Malaya which they claimed was better than anything the British themselves possessed. Stahmer declared that when the time arrived to strike, the Japanese would know even more accurately where to go and what to do than did the Germans in the Norwegian campaign.

Stahmer remained for two days and I did everything possible to get complete information. The feeling here is that Americans still think the Japanese are bluffing. I assure you that this is definitely not the case. The Yellow Peril today is more real than it ever was, largely owing to Hitler's machinations. If something is not done to check it in time, the negligence will prove very costly, more costly than even you might imagine. This is not just a woman's intuition. I know precisely what I am talking about.

Hitler is leaving for Berlin. I understand that the conferences with Matsuoka will take place there and so I shall not be in a position to find out anything about them. I am certain that you will get complete information from Heinrich and Linda.

With my warmest greetings,
CLARA.

This letter confirmed our worst suspicions—van Narvig's and mine. We had felt all along that the Japanese were not, as the commentators and officials repeated time and again, on the brink of economic catastrophe. They were not weak, and they certainly were not near-sighted. The information supplied by Clara was made the basis of one of my broadcasts.*

I approached authorities in Washington with my information,

---

*Quotation from Williams' broadcast of April 17, 1941: "I have . . . received a comprehensive report dealing with Japanese Foreign Minister Matsuoka's activities during his extended stay as a guest of the Soviets . . . . I am also in receipt of information that six Japanese divisions are on the island of Hainan, training in the complexities of jungle warfare. Since the terrain of Hainan is very similar to that of Malaya, the conclusion is obvious."

trying to warn them of the steadily growing Japanese threat. I must say that I was only scoffed at. I was told that the whole story was probably a fantastic concoction of my "mysterious informants." A report such as this, I was told, was not worth reading, let alone imparting to the American public. I had best forget all about it, I was advised. There was nothing we could do but file it away for future reference. This future was not too far away, as our country discovered less than eight months afterward.

The next letter we received came from Linda. It read:

Dear Willy:

Yosuke Matsuoka, Foreign Minister of Japan, is expected to arrive in a few days. Heinrich is positively rabid on the subject. He regards the German-Japanese alliance as the first step in the fall of Western Civilization. He says that Hitler has the German people completely dazzled. That is not new of course, but he accuses the Americans and British of being completely blind. Heinrich has promised to give me complete information on the Hitler-Matsuoka conversations.

Meanwhile Hitler, who is already in Berlin waiting for the arrival of his Oriental guest, made a speech at the Zeughaus on our Heldenge- denktag in commemoration of the German war dead. Since it was not broadcast, except in Germany, you may not have the text. Hitler's one significant phrase was, "Spring is here!" This means that the German army is ready to strike again. In view of the developments of recent weeks, certain passages of his speech, according to Heinrich, were also very significant.

For the first time, Heinrich said, an open threat was directed against the United States when Hitler thundered, "No power and no support coming from any part of the world can change the outcome of this battle in any respect!" Homage was paid to the Italians, probably be- cause of Mussolini's submission, when Hitler said, "This winter our allies bore the brunt of the whole power of the British attack, but from now on German forces again will resume their share of this load."

Very likely the Fuehrer referred to General Rommel's Afrika Korps, which is expected to strike any day. Most significant was the absence of all mention of relations with Russia, friendly or otherwise. Heinrich thinks that Hitler has tacitly informed the German people that the Russo-German alliance is a thing of the past. Vitriolic attacks were made against France, which Hitler had studiously refrained from men- tioning in any of his speeches since the Montoire meeting.

It appears that we now are able to understand Hitler's motives and are able to interpret his words and deeds. Unfortunately, we have learned this lesson too late.

The other day Goering and Udet were engaged in a rather frank discussion while I was attending to some work nearby. As you know, Udet is Goering's best friend and the two keep very few secrets from each other. This time they were discussing Goebbels. Goering never has liked Goebbels, but his real antipathy for the man began at the time of Goering's second marriage. Emmy Sonnemann was courted by Goebbels before she decided to become Frau Goering. I do not know if she was particularly attracted by Goering at the time, but I can state definitely that she is deeply attached to him now.

Since it was well known at the time that Evi Braun would never be elevated to the position of the Fuehrer's official consort, Goering's wife would automatically occupy the position of the first lady of Germany. This was a prospect which Emmy could not very well refuse, so she accepted Goering. However, she actually is a very swell person and I am rather fond of her. It appears that Goebbels, who probably sensed Emmy's principal reason for accepting Goering, felt that he could easily carry on an affair with her after her marriage to Goering. As you know, Goebbels' sense of morals is about on a par with his sense of truth. I know for a fact that he tried to seduce Emmy before her marriage but failed.

After she and Goering had returned from their honeymoon, Goebbels again started making advances. Emmy told her husband that she was in fear of Goebbels, and the lid was off. Goering rushed straight to Goebbels' residence. The swine barely managed to escape through a back door. He ran to Hitler and appealed for help. Hitler finally straightened the matter out by sending Goebbels on a two-month "vacation" after warning him to behave in the future. Udet knows all this and if it were left to him, he would have liquidated Goebbels personally a long time ago.

It appears now that Goebbels is in trouble once more, this time over the young wife of another Nazi dignitary, but one who is not as important as the Reichsmarschal. It was in this connection that Udet said to Goering, "I should like to have the swine at a barbecue and roast him to a crisp before I tossed him to his porcine relatives."

Goering replied, "I should not mind helping you with that, Ernst, but we must face realities. In spite of his indecency, he is doing an excellent job at his post. In fact, no one could do as well. So let time do its work."

Udet asked, "Do you think time will take care of Hitler?"

To which Goering replied, "Tut, tut, my friend. It is all right to be frank with me, but take care of that tongue of yours. It has a tendency to slip. Speaking of Hitler, I agree with many of the things you'd like to say. He has developed a Caesar complex. At times I am afraid he will succeed in utterly corrupting the moral standards of the German people.

"But we must give credit where credit is due," Goering continued. "Hitler lifted Germany from mental lethargy and physical misery. He created unity from chaos. He stopped the process of German disintegration. He made Germany the strongest power in the world. In the final analysis it matters little what means he has employed. He has accomplished all these things. Like other builders of empire he cannot stop now. It is in the nature of things, you know. *Der Appetit kommt mit dem Essen*."*

So there you have it. Our Hermann is rather a philosopher in addition to his many other accomplishments.

Come to think of it, I never really got my meal. Perhaps that is why I am still able to suppress my appetite. Your stay in Germany was too short. Please do not wrinkle your brow if I have spoken out of turn. At times we just cannot help wishing, especially when we know that it does not get us anywhere.

Affectionately,
LINDA.

Another, and very exciting, letter from Linda followed this one almost immediately. In it she wrote:

Dear Willy:

For once, believe it or not, I am in a daze. So much has happened in the past few days that I hardly know where to begin. Matsuoka was here, of course, and although that is very important, I shall leave it for last. This is one time when I cannot attempt to report events in their chronological order without getting all mixed up, so you will have to bear with me.

The day before the arrival of the Japanese, as no doubt you know, Yugoslavia signed her adherence to the Axis† in Vienna and so became one of the chosen nations in this part of the world. The following morning Matsuoka arrived. As the little top-hatted man stepped from the train "smirking like a misshapen baboon" (Heinrich's personal description) all the ambassadors and ministers of Axis countries, including

---

*The appetite develops with the meal.

†The Yugoslav Government of Prince Regent Paul signed Yugoslavia's adherence to the Axis in Vienna on March 25, 1941.

the Yugoslav Minister, were there to shout a great welcome to him. The Yugoslav, poor fellow, was one of the most enthusiastic among the welcoming group. What must he have felt when he was forced to go into hiding barely twenty-four hours later?

Dawn had scarcely broken when the electrifying news came that the Serbs had jailed their Regent, Prince Paul, had overthrown his government and established a pro-British regime. The new regime declared that Yugoslavia's having signed up with the Axis meant nothing. The general public did not hear of it until late that afternoon, but Heinrich had to jump out of bed at daybreak. Hitler got the news just as he stepped from his shower and the story is that he rushed half the way to his office before remembering his clothes. By the time he had slipped into his uniform and boots he was raging. Ribbentrop was already there with the few details he had and he is said to have been scorched by Hitler's diatribe against him.

After thus venting his first wave of wrath, Hitler paced the huge room for a few minutes like a caged animal, then shouted,

"Yugoslavia will cease to exist. Belgrade must be destroyed!"

Von Brauchitsch had been with him last winter when Hitler decided to destroy the French. This time von Brauchitsch was not anywhere near, nor anyone else who had the courage to talk sense. Hitler demanded to be connected by telephone with Field Marshal List, who was in Sofia. He then shouted his orders that the armies were to be concentrated against Yugoslavia. He would see to it that the Italian armies followed.

You may hear all sorts of stories about diplomatic exchanges. You will hear that Ribbentrop already has begun negotiations with the new government in Belgrade, and Goebbels will back up this story with his usual propaganda line. Do not believe a word of it. All this is trickery to screen the real preparations. War on the Balkan nation has been definitely decided.*

Please think back to your friendly get-together with Colonel Wartenburg, the day after he had surprised the two of us returning late at night from our skiing tour. You told me that he had outlined to you the strategic situation in the Balkans.

Colonel Wartenburg once toured Bulgaria and southern Serbia for the General Staff. He was greatly commended for a report that he sub-

*General Dusan Simovich staged a successful coup in Belgrade on the night of March 27, 1941, forcing the Regent, Prince Paul, now interned in Kenya Colony, British East Africa, to flee the country. Simovich sought to maintain Yugoslavia's neutrality in the crisis and resisted as best he was able when German armies crossed the frontier on April 6, 1941.

mitted on his return. This report, I am told, has been made the basis of the Wehrmacht's strategic considerations for that region. If Wartenburg outlined to you how a blitzkrieg in the southern Balkans should be conducted, take his views for a pattern and you cannot go wrong.

Before telling you about Matsuoka, I must ask you to be very careful in the way you mention the information I give to you this time. I have never asked that before, trusting your own judgment, but now there are reasons. Heinrich is beside himself over this Japanese business, and very careless with anything connected with it. He may have left some loose ends. If the information I give you now should ever be heard here, it is not at all impossible that it might be traced to him. So please be careful. I am sure I can depend on you.

Here are the facts. Matsuoka has conferred with Ribbentrop several times and he had two personal meetings with Hitler before he left for Rome. The Rome trip may be considered a mere courtesy visit. Heinrich does not know what occurred at the Ribbentrop conferences, but he thinks that only details were discussed, while the really important talks were those with the Fuehrer. The Japanese scheme, after all, is Hitler's personal idea.

Matsuoka stressed that he had not come to discuss military matters, which are entirely the affair of the Imperial army and navy. He knew that General Ott (German Ambassador in Tokyo who returned to Berlin prior to Matsuoka's arrival) had conferred with Japanese army leaders. He was informed of these discussions, but they did not concern him directly. General Yamashita, who represented the army, was in Germany for the discussion of such matters. Matsuoka stated that he desired to confine himself exclusively to the political aspects of the situation. He made this perfectly clear at the outset of the conversations.

He was both polite and methodical. He declared that the principal objective in his making this long journey had been to meet, in person, the great man who had recreated the German Empire. Alliances worked far more smoothly if the ranking statesmen of the allied countries knew each other. Of course, he had a secondary reason for crossing all of Asia and half of Europe. In pursuance of this, he wished to ask four questions, vital ones.

The first concerned Russia. Under the terms of the Tripartite Pact, Germany had undertaken to neutralize Russia in the event of a Japanese move southward into the areas assigned to Japan under the pact. His stay in Moscow had been brief, but he had noticed that the Kremlin had exhibited a definite coolness in regard to Berlin. He was very anxious to know if there had been any material change in relations between Germany and Russia.

Hitler replied that Russia had shown herself unreceptive to German proposals that would have accomplished such a neutralization. He suggested that during Matsuoka's return, he stop again at Moscow and intimate that a friendship and non-aggression pact with the Soviets would be desirable to Japan. This would not be difficult, Hitler pointed out, if Matsuoka pretended that a coolness had crept into German-Japanese relations and that the Tripartite Pact was actually a disappointment to Japan. If Hitler understood the Russians, they would believe this easily.

Matsuoka said this was a helpful suggestion and he would avail himself of it. He observed, however, that some non-aggression pacts belonged in the category of temporary expedients. They were entered into merely to be abrogated when conditions changed. A non-aggression pact was a very fine thing for filing purposes, but it did not contain practical guarantees such as the Tripartite Pact called for. Hitler agreed with Matsuoka's interpretation. He then said that while he, Hitler, was not yet in a position to indicate just how it would be done, Germany would stand by her commitments. Japan could be certain of that.

Matsuoka's second question concerned France. Japan, he said, would soon need French Indo-China for an advance base. The army felt certain that it could be seized without difficulty, but the Foreign Office was forced to consider diplomatic complications. Indo-China was French and France, so to speak, was under German protection. Japan did not presume to interfere with Germany's treatment of France, but the situation appeared to have reached a stalemate and Japan wanted to know just what her position was.

Hitler replied that his French policy was dictated by reasons that he preferred not to discuss. For the present he was concerned with the Balkan question since it was a necessary preliminary to others. When this was disposed of he would again turn his attention to France. When Japan was ready to proceed into Indo-China she had only to notify him in advance, and he would see to it that Vichy raised no difficulties. Between allies, he said, he was in the habit of fulfilling his commitments.

Matsuoka's third question concerned Great Britain. Japan did not presume to ask questions concerning the war in Europe. But her proposed advance to the south would largely depend on successful naval operations. It was likely, indeed almost certain, that the United States would interfere with Japan's venture, for economic reasons, if not for others. The Japanese Admiralty did not fear the United States fleet, alone. But if, in addition, Japan would be forced to face large British naval forces, this would definitely upset the balance of naval power. It was vital to Japan, therefore, to ask Germany to hold the British fleet in European waters.

Hitler replied that the transfer of any sizable British naval force to the Pacific was extremely unlikely, because the British were kept under the constant threat of a German invasion. The German air and submarine campaign against British shipping lanes held additional British forces in the North Atlantic. The Italian fleet, in spite of reverses, could still hold the British Mediterranean fleet where it was. The German army in Libya, with its threat to the Suez Canal, was another reason for the British not to release any important naval units from the Mediterranean. In view of all this, Great Britain could not possibly dispatch strong forces to the Far East without leaving herself open to crippling attack.

Matsouka's fourth question concerned the United States. The lend-lease legislation that had been passed, he said, had made America an open ally of England. The implications were plain. The United States would not send billions of dollars worth of war materials to Great Britain without protecting their transit overseas. War between Germany and America was merely a question of time. Germany could then invoke Japan's aid under the Tripartite Pact and Japan, too, would stand by her commitments to an ally. But Japan still needed time.

Hitler went deeply into this question. Here are direct quotes. They are from Heinrich's memory and you must make allowances if they are not literally exact, Hitler said:

"The implementation of the lend-lease act by the United States will be a direct act of war against Germany and Italy. Heretofore President Roosevelt has hidden behind a screen of trickery in his aid to England, but now he has, at last, come into the open. I never doubted that this would happen. I never left Japan in doubt on this point. Since the last war, economic domination of the world, based on mastery of the seas, has been shared by the two Anglo-Saxon nations. If one is destroyed the other cannot maintain herself. For all practical purposes Germany and the United States are at war right now. The open declaration of war will be a mere formality. With due regard to Japan's wishes I shall attend to that formality at the proper time.

"During negotiations leading to the Tripartite Pact," Hitler continued, "the question of the United States was exhaustively considered by both Japan and Germany. Complete agreement was reached. The United States alone blocks the path of Japan's achievement of her legitimate aspirations. The United States alone has made it possible for England to continue at war with Germany. The United States is the principal enemy of both Japan and Germany. . . . .

"The American question has been considered thoroughly," Hitler said, "from its military angle. America does not realize the meaning of total war and it will take her years to learn. You know how long it took your own country. Granting America's greater potentialities, she will require a minimum of three years to organize for total war production. She will require at least that length of time to build the ships without which her war potentialities would remain nil. We will be sinking many of these ships. By the time America has fully organized herself for total war, the British Empire will be destroyed and America will face our victorious alliance alone. . . . .

"President Roosevelt," Hitler went on, "has created the greatest split in American opinion since the Civil War. No national leader can work entirely alone. He must delegate authority to trained and qualified men capable of leadership. Yet Roosevelt cannot tolerate anyone in his government who is better qualified than himself. He is intensely jealous of his reform program and will not allow anything—even a war emergency—to interfere with it. He has surrounded himself with personal cronies who have proved themselves utterly incapable of solving even the simplest economic and social problems. He does not trust anyone but these friends. We need not fear America under that kind of government. . . .

"The United States is a pacifist state," Hitler declared. "The nation is honeycombed with peace advocates and world improvers. War is anathema to them. In the eyes of the average American, a soldier is a waster, a parasite who consumes taxes and gives nothing in return. He is looked upon as a rowdy, a hoodlum. He is in the army because he is not fit for anything else. Officers of the United States Army are compelled to play up to loud-mouthed politicians. They have no hope of promotion for real achievement. A powerful army such as that of Japan or Germany is not pulled from a magician's hat. A competent officer corps is not created overnight, out of nothing. It requires years—many years. . . .

"The American people," said Hitler, "are, for the most part, Fettwanste.* They are gluttons for good food, fine clothes, amusements, luxuries and comforts. Their women dote on film stars, divorce cases, fur coats and silk stockings. Their wasting of material values is prodigious, their sense of saving virtually non-existent. They swarm into churches to display their finery, but their real God is money. Those wasters would rather cut their throats than be required to submit to the same hardships, sacrifices and privations that our peoples have endured for years, and without which total war is utterly impossible."

These are just a few of the things that Hitler told Matsuoka on the subject of the United States. When I recall our talks together, it appears

*Fat bellies.

that you and Hitler are far apart in the appraisal of your country. You are there. You should know. But, according to Heinrich, Hitler sounded very positive and Matsuoka was definitely impressed.

I am afraid I have nothing more to write this time. Somehow, I am unable to concentrate. We are all quite jittery over here. I suppose it is nerves. How I wish that I were with you in America!

Affectionately,
LINDA.

There was no broadcast for us on the day this information arrived. The following morning the news broke that Hitler's panzer legions in the Balkans were on the move against Yugoslavia and Greece. Van Narvig and I sat in the office, carefully reading Linda's report. One passage in it struck me. We were too late to beat the news of the Yugoslav invasion, but perhaps there was a possibility of broadcasting a complete picture of Hitler's plan of attack.

"What's this?" I asked, after rereading the passage carefully. "You never told me one single word about discussing Balkan military operations with Wartenburg."

"It was not important then," van Narvig answered. "At the time it was more of an academic discussion. Under today's conditions it may assume a different aspect."

"It's certainly a boon to us that Linda has such an excellent memory," I said. "Let's go over it now."

We got out a detailed map of the Balkans.

"Southern Serbia is the most difficult part of the Balkan terrain," van Narvig explained. "I know it from my own tour of the country, years ago. In the present case it is of immense strategic importance because it borders on Greece. It is mountainous throughout. If the Yugoslavs are given a chance to consolidate there they may be able to hold out for months. That is why Hitler must strike there first."

"And just how will he do it?" I asked. "What did Wartenburg tell you?"

Van Narvig took a letter opener and pointed at the map.

"Here is the southwest corner of Bulgaria. Here is the Struma

229

River, flowing from north to south." The point of the paper knife moved. "Remember Field Marshal List's plan. He has one mixed column of panzer and mountain troops striking down the Struma at Rupel Pass and into Greece. But that would not be his principal force. If Wartenburg's recommendations are being followed, List's shock troops are disposed all along the western bank of the Struma. Here are the Belasitza Mountains, largely in Yugoslav territory—in fact, forming the border between Yugoslavia and Greece. Here, to the north, are the Malesh Mountains. Between the two flows the Strumitza River, a tributary of the Struma. To both sides of the mountain chains are two smaller rivers. All three break through the mountains. It is up these river valleys that List's panzers will break into southern Serbia from Bulgaria.

"Still farther north," van Narvig continued, "is the Vinnitza River, flowing into the Vardar. It is through the Vinnitza Valley, from Kuestendil in Bulgaria, that a fourth Nazi column will strike."

The point of the knife kept moving over the map.

"Still farther north, here, you see Dragoman Pass," van Narvig went on. "Here a fifth Nazi column will strike toward Nish, the old Serbian capital. The Yugoslav southern army will be cut into small groups by these five separate spearheads. The Nazi columns will pour into the Vardar Valley. One will swing south, down the Vardar, and race for Salonika. Two columns will cut right across to Albania and make a junction with the Italian army there, severing every connection between Yugoslavia and Greece. The fourth column will race northward to Kachanik Pass and attack the main body of the Yugoslav army from the south, coming from a direction where the Yugoslavs are entirely unprepared to meet a powerful enemy. The fifth column will take Nish and cut all communications between north and south. Result—no more Yugoslav army in two weeks."

Personally, I knew nothing of the Balkan terrain, but I had spent the previous evening with a group of military men whose arguments had impressed me.

I said to van Narvig, "Our experts contend that those mountains are too rugged to be crossed by either tanks or armored cars."

"Of course," he replied, tossing the paper knife on the desk. "Our experts also contended that Hitler's panzers could not scale the Norwegian mountain roads, especially over snow. Yet they did, because it was the snow that helped them. Remember that the Balkan mountains are still covered with snow."

"Still," I maintained, "it is all a matter of opinion."

"Quite," said van Narvig coolly. He lit a cigar, folded the map and put it back on the desk.

"What it all amounts to," he said, "is that some of the brass hats here have quite a few things to learn. But we have a few officers in Washington who have studied the German army, and they'll tell you the same things that I do. As for the Yugoslavs, some Serbian units may escape into mountain hide-outs and operate as guerrillas for many months. It's that kind of country. But the Yugoslav army, as such, is doomed. If it had prepared for this thing, it might stand a chance today. But it didn't. As I said, I give it two weeks."

I had considerable respect for van Narvig's opinions on military tactics and strategy. In the past he had disagreed with the opinions of military men of my acquaintance and events had proved him correct. The following night I stated in my broadcast:

"From what I have learned of the Nazi plan of attack, German operations to the west of the Rhodope Mountains will be the deciding factor. Nazi panzer forces are pushing over mountain roads covered with snow from Bulgaria into southern Serbia with the objective of reaching the Vardar Valley, where some will swing south to reach Salonika and outflank the strong Greek position at Rupel Pass. Other columns will push westward from the Vardar through the mountains to the Albanian border and a junction with the Italian army there. If this is accomplished, Yugoslavia will be cut off from Greece and the Yugoslav army will face encirclement."

The next morning I received a number of vehement telephone calls, all asking sarcastically if I really knew what I was talking about. One of my critics advised me to consult qualified military men before making an ass of myself. Other commentators and military experts predicted that the Germans would be inevitably stopped cold in the mountains. I felt sure of my ground, but the next few days brought no decisive news from this new front. On the contrary, persistent reports came in that the Yugoslav army had invaded Albania from the north and that the Italians there were facing annihilation. I pointed out all this to van Narvig, adding that this time I hoped we had been wrong.

He remained unperturbed.

"Wait another day or two," he said. "As for the Yugoslav army occupying all of northern Albania, don't let anyone kid you. The Yugoslavs have too much on their hands without thinking of an Albanian invasion. You watch Ante Pavelich rush from Rome to Zagreb and proclaim an independent Croat State without the slightest difficulty."

The following morning brought the news of the Nazis' entry into Salonika* and their capture of the Greek army that had defended Rupel Pass. The next day it became officially known that the Germans had effected a junction with the Italians in Albania and that Yugoslavia was cut off from Greece. And the day following that came the announcement that Ante Pavelich was in Zagreb where he had proclaimed a separate Croat State. On the twelfth day of the Balkan campaign, the Yugoslav army capitulated. Van Narvig had given it two weeks.

Back home in New York, both van Narvig and I were bitterly disappointed because we had not been able to get anything at all on the Balkan campaign through our special radio receiver, as we had during the Battle of France the preceding year. Van Narvig tried fruitlessly many times to pick up the German code signals. Once or twice he caught a few signals but found himself unable to decipher them. Finally he came to the conclusion that the Nazis must have changed the code of their Supreme Command.

*The vanguard of German troops entered Salonika on April 9, 1941.

As we had half expected, knowing that Hitler had gone to the front, we soon received a letter from Manfred, who wrote:

Dear Willy:

The great conqueror is traveling again, with a heavier guard than ever before. In addition to us of the Auslandsschutz, two companies of the Schutzstaffel and four batteries of flak artillery are seeing to it that nothing happens to our modern Ghenghis Khan. This great roundup of manpower is stationed at the Fuehrerhauptquartier auf dem Balkanishen Kriegsschauplatz*, which is rather far from the actual Balkans.

During the first week of the campaign we remained on German soil near Graz in Styria. Now we are at Maribor (or, as it is now called, Marburg) in the northwest corner of what was once Yugoslavia. Last week Marburg, which has a predominantly German population, was reincorporated into the Reich with all the ceremonial pomp displayed on such occasions. There is no fighting here of any kind. The Germans simply marched in without encountering a single Yugoslav soldier. It is as close as Hitler will advance to this new war front. To the south lies the newly formed Croat State under the ex-anarchist Ante Pavelich, who has proclaimed himself the Poglavnik† of all Croats. Since the new Croat state will be placed under Italian protection, Hitler considers that he cannot very well go there without making Mussolini a complete public fool. Although Il Duce is now entirely controlled by Hitler, political niceties are to be preserved, for the present anyway.

Hitler expressed a desire to move closer to the fighting front, but to do this it would be necessary for him to pass through Hungary, Rumania and Bulgaria. Although these are called our loyal allies, the army has flatly declared that it cannot guarantee the Fuehrer's safety within these frontiers, and in order not to arouse the native populations, especially in Hungary, the Gestapo has been kept out of those countries for the time being. So, for the rest of the campaign, we will remain in Marburg, which is only 170 miles from Berchtesgaden.

We are stationed outside of Marburg itself, with Hitler's armored train remaining at the platform of a small railroad station and two protective trains on the sidings. Flak guns surround us, although the location is kept a secret, and even if it were not, it is most unlikely that British or Serbian bombing planes would fly this far north.

I have never been here before and I find it magnificent country. The Styrian Alps are in the background and the picturesque river valley of the Drava is beneath us. The Backer Mountains are on the other side.

*The Fuehrer's headquarters in the Balkan Theater of War.
†Croatian for Chief.

If it were not for continuous arrivals and leave-takings of the infernal dispatch riders, it would be an enjoyable place to stay. Hitler has a huge map of the lower Balkans on one wall of his car and spends much of his time, quite childishly, shifting small swastika flags on it as the news of troop movements comes in over the wires.

Yesterday, Hitler celebrated his fifty-second birthday. It began with a brief concert played by a military band, followed by a review of a mixed echelon of troops which then goose-stepped past Hitler along the station platform. Then a sort of reception was held in the salon car. Among those who attended were Goering, Hess, Himmler, Ribbentrop, Goebbels, Rosenberg, Frick, Keitel, von Brauchitsch, Milch, Halder, Raeder, Kesselring, Jodl and the members of Hitler's staff. List was not present. He is well occupied on the Greek front, but he sent his congratulations together with a special gift. The gift was a piece of rock from Mount Olympus and the message read: "This comes from the seat of the ancient Greek gods who welcome you, my Fuehrer, into their eminent domain."

Hitler was toasted with French champagne, although he himself abstained.

Goering, in raising his glass, declared, "May you, my Fuehrer, live long for the continued glory of our great German Vaterland."

Hess, next, proclaimed, "God protect our Fuehrer during this and many other years to come."

Keitel followed: "I raise my glass to your new colossal successes!"

Ribbentrop exclaimed, "To the greatest statesman and war lord of the German race!"

Von Brauchitsch simply said, "To new and greater victories!"

Himmler pronounced, "To my great and glorious Fuehrer, now and always!"

Goebbels piped, "To my beloved Fuehrer, who will go down in history as the greatest empire builder of all times!"

And so they went on. When it was over, Hitler retired with Keitel and Jodl to study war maps, discussing the latest front developments. He has every reason to be satisfied with the progress of his new venture. Yugoslavia, which dared to defy him, is obliterated. She is the last of the hated Versailles States to be wiped out. Large parts of her territory will be distributed among Italy, Hungary, Bulgaria and Rumania. What will become of old Serbia, we do not know yet, although there is talk of a Serbian puppet regime.

As for Greece, Hitler appears to have done equally well from a conqueror's point of view. One Greek army was encircled and captured in the Struma Valley. The other surrendered in Epirus. British troops in

Greece have lost all their equipment and are desperately trying to reach their ships, presumably to be taken back to Egypt. Hitler has sworn to drive the British from the European continent and apparently he has succeeded. That he is undisputed master of continental Europe no one doubts any longer, and the future looks darker than ever before.

I shall not waste space with direct war news, for you are doubtless receiving daily press reports. However, I want to point out this: While the clergy of the Greek-Orthodox Church in Serbia, which opposed submission to Hitler and was instrumental in accomplishing the Simovich coup d'état, is being severely treated in many cases, the Roman-Catholic Church of Croatia is not only escaping such treatment, but is being accorded special privileges. Doubtless, this is for the benefit of the Vatican. I am still convinced that Hitler is attempting to draw the Catholic Church into his schemes.

That will be enough for today.

In warm friendship,
MANFRED.

It was quite a time before we received the next report. As always when Hitler was at the front, there was little for our friends in Berlin and Berchtesgaden to communicate to us. This new letter came from Wolfgang at Fuschl Castle, and it really gave us something to think about. He wrote:

Dear Willy:

At last I have the opportunity to send you information that is better than that contained in the ordinary letters I have previously written.

Count Werner von der Schulenburg left Moscow when the Soviet Government intervened in Bulgaria and when the Soviets encouraged the Simovich coup in Belgrade. The count has remained in Berlin ever since. Whether this is a sign of Hitler's displeasure with Moscow—a sort of small-scale war of nerves directed at the Kremlin—I do not know. Officially, Schulenburg has been recuperating from a breakdown caused by overwork, but I happen to know that he is as healthy as I am, and I feel fine. Once he paid a brief visit to field headquarters in the Balkans and there has been much talk to the effect that he may not return to his post. Doubtless, this talk was created to impress the Russians, for I know that Schulenburg will return to Moscow. But he will carry with him a neat diplomatic package that I am sure the Russians will not like.

Yesterday he passed some time at Fuschl with Ribbentrop, who has just returned from conferences with Hitler. Ribbentrop and Schulenburg held their discussion in the library where I have an excellent opportunity to observe.

It appears that of late relations with Russia have been quite strained. Stalin was angry when Molotov returned from Berlin and reported that the Germans were quite cool in regard to Russian ambitions in the Balkans and Finland. The Kremlin sensed that in extracting Mussolini from the Greek debacle, Hitler might venture too far. Hitler had assured Molotov that he would not interfere with the Dardanelles so long as the Turks behaved, but Stalin was inclined not to believe him. Rather, he feared that Hitler might take possession of the Straits and then use his position to force Moscow into far-reaching commitments.

Stalin attempted negotiations with King Boris of Bulgaria after Boris had already entered a secret agreement with Hitler. When it became known in Moscow, through Schulenburg, that Hitler had asked the Yugoslavs to exert pressure in Greece for a total submission to Mussolini, Stalin became more hopeful. But when the Greeks refused and a German invasion of the Balkans became a foregone conclusion, the Russians, according to Schulenburg, encouraged the Simovich faction to seize power in Belgrade and maneuver Hitler into protracted negotiations, in which Moscow expected to take a prominent part. Stalin was further angered when Hitler did not negotiate, but promptly answered the Yugoslavs with an invading army.

Second, Stalin definitely did not like what was going on in Finland. The Kremlin has excellent spies there. They knew that a strong faction in Helsinki was working desperately for an alliance with Berlin. They knew, too, that the number of German troops in Finland was far in excess of the requirements of the Norwegian situation.

After discussing the foregoing, Ribbentrop gave the returning ambassador certain instructions which make it quite clear that Hitler intends to remove the mask and get tough with his eastern neighbor. He explained to Schulenburg that a showdown between Germany and Russia is inevitable unless the Kremlin quickly makes up its mind to co-operate with Germany's war effort all along the line. Schulenburg is to tell this to Molotov as his personal impression.

This is what Schulenburg is to make the Russians understand. Hitler is very displeased with the Kremlin's action in extending immediate recognition to the revolutionary Simovich government in Belgrade, without even bothering to consult Berlin. Such action was entirely in violation of the clause in the Russo-German pact which stipulates mutual consultation before taking action where the interests of the other contracting party—in this case Germany—are affected. While

Hitler and Molotov discussed the Bulgarian question at great length and Russia was free to act there, Yugoslavia had not been mentioned in the Berlin conversations.

Hitler is further displeased with Russia's action in raising the freight rates on the Trans-Siberian railroad five hundred per cent on all transit materials for Japan and instituting other domestic measures contrary to the spirit of the Russo-German trade agreement. Hitler feels that Russia is not complying with her part of the agreement.

Schulenburg is also to tell Moscow—and this officially—that Germany is resolved to fight the British Empire to the finish, and is firmly determined to employ every method to gain complete victory. This was made perfectly clear to Molotov during the Berlin conversations. Germany can only take the stand that whoever is not for her is against her. Germany is perfectly willing to let Russia have her living space so long as she does not interfere with Germany's plans for winning the war against England. Russia was offered an opportunity to profit handsomely from the collapse of the British Empire but did not react to this suggestion. From this point of view, Germany is willing to strengthen her ties with a friendly Russia, even to the extent of a military alliance. But Russia must make up her mind definitely, and Berlin is open to concrete suggestions from Moscow.

This is the gist of the message that Schulenburg was instructed to take to the Kremlin.

Just now I must be very careful here. I do not know what prompted the idea, but last night one of the Gestapomen, who are always interested in the affairs of others, asked me where I had been the greater part of the day. I managed to explain things to his satisfaction, but I had best be careful for a while. I am not afraid so much for myself but, as you know and I am sure that you will understand, there are other considerations.

Your friend,
WOLFGANG.

By the time Wolfgang's letter reached us, the world knew that Stalin had assumed the office of Premier of Soviet Russia—an event that aroused much speculation. To us it was obvious that it was a result of Count von der Schulenburg's mission. However, since Wolfgang had told us of the suspicion cast upon him, we felt it was out of the question to broadcast details of the conversation. I simply stated at that time that negotiations were about to get under way concerning a military alliance between Germany and Russia.

Simultaneously with Wolfgang's report we received a letter from Linda. This is what she wrote:

Dear Willy:

Goering has not been at Karin Hall for some time. He dallied at the Balkan front, then went to France in order to meet Admiral Darlan somewhere. No details on that yet.

The information I have for you today comes directly from Heinrich. While Goering went to France, Hitler returned to Berlin for a while. There he had a series of conferences with Himmler. It appears that there are not sufficient trustworthy men available for important diplomatic missions. Goering is in France, Hess in Spain, Frick has gone to Rome, and Ribbentrop is busy with Moscow and the Turks. Therefore Hitler has selected Himmler to go to Madrid, of all places!

Heinrich has more than a suspicion that Himmler is being sent there to keep an eye on Hess. His official reason for going is entirely different. General Franco is opening the House of America. This is supposed to be a select institution for the maintenance of cultural and spiritual relations between the Spanish mother country and the Spanish-speaking republics of South America, principally Chile and Argentina. Actually it will be a propaganda nest, also a convenient clearing house for Gestapo activities and espionage on the other side. For some time Franco had about one hundred Falangists in training with our Propaganda Ministry and also with the Gestapo. All these have returned to Madrid to become section chiefs for the House of America. Moreover, Himmler is taking with him a score of his own agents, all trained in Spanish, to work with the men in Madrid. Himmler will also represent Hitler in the dedication ceremonies of the House of America. Just why Hess, being in Madrid, could not represent Hitler on this occasion, Heinrich cannot understand. He suspects that something must be behind it.

Meanwhile, Goebbels has received special orders. Through his agents in neutral countries he is to create the impression that Hitler will undertake a push through Spain for Gibraltar and across into French Africa. Official denunciations of these rumors will be made from Berlin, but these will, of course, merely intensify the rumors abroad, leading to a belief that Spain is preparing to join the Axis. Heinrich contends that it is all a screen behind which to hide Hitler's actual intentions which, as yet, are unknown to either of us.

In closing, I must tell you that I am very much disappointed in you. I have had no direct word from you in almost three months. I do not think this is fair. Even with conditions as they are, you should not neglect keeping hope kindled. What more is there to live for, these days, but hope? It is principally the hope for a brighter future that keeps us going.

Please keep this hope going in all of us, and particularly in me.

Affectionately,

LINDA.

CHAPTER 20

FOLLOWING THIS BRIEF MESSAGE from Linda we received in rapid succession a series of sensational communications from our German friends that kept us in a constant state of excitement. However, in many cases the time element was against us, for by the time these reports reached us through the mysterious channels maintained by Gottlieb and Klausmann, the developments foreshadowed in them by our friends, had usually already occurred. Hitler was moving fast in those days. At that, while in many instances we were unable to beat the actual news, our inside information enabled us to interpret the news correctly.

Our first report in this series came from Clara. She wrote:

Dear Willy:

I have a fantastic story to tell you. Events may move faster than this letter, but if you get it ahead of developments, you will have a good inside story on what may be the greatest melodrama of the century.

Last night Rudolph Hess had a long conference with Hitler in the latter's study. Hess returned from a trip to Madrid only a few days ago. He traveled incognito and no one here had the faintest idea of what it all meant. The first clue I obtained of these doings was through Hess' talk with Hitler.

Hess went to Spain on his own initiative. The alliance with Japan had irritated him tremendously, for he feels that Japan is aiming at nothing less than the humiliation of the white race. He had always felt that the white peoples of Germany and England should join in the domination of the world. He had expounded this theme when he wrote Hitler's "Mein Kampf." Hess wished to make one more attempt to unite England and Germany.

He went to Madrid for the purpose of reaching Sir Samuel Hoare, British Ambassador there. While he had discussed the project with no one, not even Hitler, the Gestapo apparently had gotten wind of it. Anyway, Hess has complained to Hitler that Himmler was dispatched to Madrid hurriedly so the Gestapo chief could spy on Hess. Hess said he would have remained in Madrid if Himmler had not urged him to return to Germany.

While in Madrid, Hess did not see Sir Samuel Hoare, but he contrived to reach the British through friendly Spanish sources. He explained his ideas to them, but was told that the matter was too dangerous for any British statesman to be linked with it. Hess gained the impression, however, that his suggestions might meet with consideration if he could get them to the direct attention of certain circles in England. He mentioned several names to Hitler, but pronounced them so hurriedly that I could not get them.

Now, this is what Hess proposes to do. He wants to fly to England alone. This undertaking in itself, he contends, would be so spectacular that the war mongers now directing British policy could not keep it a secret. As one of the principal figures of the Nazi regime he would be treated with respect and was certain to obtain a hearing. Since it would be a peace mission in the interests of both England and Germany, he believed that he would be accepted as an ambassador plenipotentiary and provided with the means of return to report on British reaction. He appealed to Hitler to permit this mission.

Hitler admitted that it would be a spectacular thing to do. But, said Hitler, we must be realists. The undertaking might be a glorious achievement, but one also had to consider the possible failure of this mission. There was the Japanese alliance, which held every promise of success, to be considered. There was the Russian situation. Hitler could not possibly be connected with a project of this kind, since in the event of failure it might easily lead to the destruction of everything he had built up. Moreover, there were the personal chances Hess would take. He might be shot down long before he reached England. There was no guarantee that he would obtain a hearing or even be permitted to return. The British war party was firmly entrenched and in an ugly mood, especially since America had promised aid on a large scale.

Hess said he had a plan by which all these objections could be met. He had specified in Madrid that he was acting on strictly personal initiative. Hitler had not been mentioned and there would be no need for him to enter the picture now. No one need know of their conversation. In the event of failure, Hitler could easily disavow any knowledge of the matter. Hess would leave letters behind him showing that he had embarked on a personal venture. If he were well received in England, as he believed he would be, he would simply state that he had sufficient influence in Hitler's councils to convert the Fuehrer to his views. As for the personal risks, what did they matter when one thought of the possible achievements?

Hitler began warming up to the idea. He and Hess have always been very close to each other except in military matters. In their personal relations he trusts Hess more than any other man. During this conversation, he forgot realism and became quite sentimental for a moment. He complained that the British and Americans did not even try to understand him.

"They call me a demagogue and think they insult me with it," said Hitler. "To be a demagogue is no dishonor. Roosevelt and Churchill are demagogues in their own right. I am a demagogue, but I am also a genius. In politics demagoguery is necessary until one achieves the power which allows one to dispense with it.

"They jeer at me for not establishing the New Order while the war is still going on, but at the same time they cannot achieve any sort of order among themselves or their subject peoples. I never undertook to cement the New Order while the war was in progress. It is impossible to accomplish it so long as war economy and restrictions last. This is merely a transition period. These European peoples are so imbued with the old order that it must be ripped from them. I never resort to half-measures, and this certainly is no place to start. Like every major operation, the inculcation of the New Order is a very painful process. Old conceptions must be cut out like infectious boils. There is only one thing to do with these peoples—one must browbeat them into submission, starve them to utter apathy, root out all seedlings of opposition. Only when this has been done can we gradually give them the better things that will be part of the New Order. Then they will understand and appreciate what is being done. All this takes time."

Hitler then returned to political realities. Since the British refused to listen to sensible suggestion, they had to be beaten into listening. The Japanese alliance was the best available means of doing this. Hitler said he well knew that the Japanese would conduct their own war aiming at the realization of their own nationalistic ambitions. He never expected them, he said, to do otherwise. It was a Vernunftsehe* in which considerations of sentiment played no part. The British, who had been realists themselves for the past three hundred years, refused to recognize realism in others.

Hitler conceded that Hess' idea had certain merits. At the least, he could explain their present position to the British. He could tell them that they were about to lose all their Asiatic possessions with no prospect

---

*Common sense marriage.

of regaining them ever again. They would lose all their investments in other countries of Asia, such as Iraq and Iran, and also in the Dutch East Indies. They would lose their command of the Middle East and Suez. They stood to lose their African possessions. Their remaining dominions would break away from them and place themselves under the protection of the United States. Finally, they would be restricted to the British Isles, where they would face the onslaught of a united Europe. If they desired to accept this fate, that was their affair.

On the other hand, if the British listened to the voice of reason, they stood to lose very little. Their homeland would be saved from further destruction. Naturally, they must restore to Germany her former colonies and acknowledge Germany's economic and political leadership on the continent of Europe. They must give Gibraltar to Spain and Malta to Italy. The Suez Canal would be internationalized. England would assign to Germany one-half of her oil holdings in Iraq and Iran. The British navy would have to be the same size as Germany's. In exchange, they could have a military alliance with Germany for the preservation of their remaining overseas possessions.

Hitler then told Hess that he would instruct Himmler to assist in procuring the proper plane and have it equipped according to Hess' instructions. Hess would give Himmler whatever explanation he cared to, except the right one. There was no need of taking Himmler into full confidence. Hess was to make all his other arrangements in secret. Whatever letters he left behind were to be delivered after his departure.

Hess thanked Hitler for accepting his plan. Hitler replied that he had agreed to the scheme under the strictest understanding that he be considered to know nothing about it. He would have to disassociate himself completely from the venture unless and until Hess had made sufficient progress in England to assure success. If Hess wanted it different, he had better drop the whole idea.

Hess declared that this was precisely how he wanted it. He expected to be back in several weeks. But if something should happen to him, he entrusted Ilse—Frau Hess—into Hitler's care. Hitler promised to take care of Ilse. On this note the two parted.

There you have it. If Hess really flies to England in the near future, you will know that my story is valid. If he does not, then simply assume that I have dreamed it, for I am almost willing to believe that myself.

I am too upset emotionally to write on any other subject.

With my warmest regards,
Clara.

As the whole world learned, Hess did fly to England, but not until after our friend at the Berghof had dispatched to us a report covering another significant development. Unfortunately, this batch of letters from our friends reached us only two weeks after the events foreshadowed in them had taken place. As for the Hess story, it was too late for broadcasting when it reached us. However, we incorporated parts of Clara's report on it in an article for a national weekly.*

In her second letter Clara wrote:

Dear Willy:

There have been no further developments thus far in the Hess matter on which I wrote you only a few days ago. However, there are many other events taking place at the Berghof these days. Today we had a French visitor, Admiral Jean François Darlan, Vice-Premier of France.

I am told that Darlan came by German transport plane to Munich, whence a train brought him to Berchtesgaden. The good people of the town were shown a spectacle that they will not forget very soon. A company of German marines lined up at the station as a guard of honor, which is in itself unusual, for the marine unit was brought here from Hamburg for this occasion. But what completely confounded us was the sight of the Tricolor waving in the wind at the station.

Ribbentrop arrived at the station for the reception. A band played the Marseillaise and Darlan was evidently surprised at this attention. He inspected the guard of honor and then he drove off in an automobile with the Tricolor triumphantly waving on it.

There was the usual build-up for a foreign visitor coming to the Berghof. Introductions, light talk on frivolous subjects, an official luncheon followed by the withdrawal of the conferring parties to the study. There Hitler turned immediately to the business at hand and said, "I understand you expressed a desire to see me, Herr Admiral?"

Thus Hitler dropped the burden of the discussion squarely on Darlan. The Admiral began by saying that since the day he was appointed Vice-Premier it had been his urgent wish to bring about normal, friendly relations between Germany and France. These relations were still being guided by the conditions of the armistice which, at the time of its conclusion, had been considered simply a temporary expedient, to be followed by more definite arrangements. These were still in abeyance. In the meantime, France carried a crushing burden. His purpose in asking an audience with the Fuehrer was to arrive at a closer understanding that would bring certain easements for France.

Liberty Magazine, issue of July 19, 1941.

Hitler replied that these matters had been discussed several times last year with Laval.

Darlan then said that the misunderstanding between Marshal Petain and Laval had been unfortunate. It had been completely cleared up, however, and Laval had, in fact, been offered a post in the French government which he had seen fit to decline for personal reasons. He, Darlan, then undertook the task of clearing the atmosphere between Germany and France.

Hitler replied that he understood perfectly. At that time Italian armies had suffered a series of defeats by British and Greek forces. Now the German armies had once more been victorious.

Darlan then proceeded to try to convince Hitler that he, Darlan, was the man with whom Hitler could negotiate successfully. He was quite skillful at this. He averred that there had never been any doubt in his mind, nor in Marshal Petain's, that Germany would be victorious in her war with England. He pointed to the good will that France had shown toward Germany in the last few months. French factories were working for the German war machine at a greatly increased rate. Deliveries from French Africa had been stepped up. France had shown a conciliatory spirit toward Japan in settling the dispute between Indo-China and Thailand. France was sincerely interested in becoming a major factor in the new European set-up.

At last Hitler began to talk. He said that Germany did not expect military help from France. Germany was fully prepared to win the war against England without any help from others. If France doubted that, she could simply sit back and wait. He understood that France was having a difficult time, but that was her own fault. He, Hitler, had once extended his hand to France. It had been rejected. Petain had personally subscribed to a policy of collaboration with Germany, then made a farce of the agreement. In Europe today one must deal only with realities. Naturally he, Hitler, had the best interests of Germany at heart, but he had tried to combine these with the best interests of France. Germany wanted nothing more from France than what she already had. Why, even today he was willing to guarantee the territorial integrity of the French Colonial Empire. He was in a better position to do this now than before because, in the meantime, compensations had been found for Italy elsewhere.

Darlan expressed appreciation, saying that the Fuehrer's promise would hearten both Marshal Petain and the French people.

It was then that Hitler brought up his reservations. He said that his promise could be applied only to such French colonial possessions as France undertook to defend against British aggression. There were already certain French colonies that had passed into British hands by the convenient method of assigning them to the traitorous group led by de Gaulle.* Hitler said he was reliably informed that the British would soon attack French Syria with the object of adding that country to their colonial loot. Needless to say, the French could not expect him to recover their lost colonies for them. That was a French task. They would also have to defend their remaining colonies. If, for the purposes of such defense, France should need an increase of her armed forces in excess of the armistice stipulations, he would instruct his ministers to receive this request in a friendly manner and to deal with it in a similar fashion.

Hitler then introduced the French Indo-China situation. He said he was particularly interested in having France preserve her sovereignty over that Asiatic colony. He noted with satisfaction that Japanese garrisons were already in the extreme northern part of Indo-China by arrangement with the French government, to protect the colony against a possible Chinese invasion. However, there still were the rich southern provinces and it was quite possible that England might seize them in order to isolate Thailand and gain control of that country. Hitler said this would be disastrous.

Darlan replied that he shared Hitler's apprehensions with regard to Indo-China, but there was virtually nothing to be done about the situation in view of the great distance between it and France. Whereupon Hitler promptly suggested that France make arrangements for the common defense of Indo-China with the only power in a position to help—Japan. He understood that it would be rather awkward for the French government to approach Japan on the subject, but he, Hitler, was in an excellent position to suggest this move to his friends in Tokyo. France could then make her own arrangements with Japan.

Hitler then said he would make a gesture of good faith. He would instantly order the release of 50,000 French prisoners of war. He would order the release of an additional 200,000 prisoners as soon as arrangements for the safety of Indo-China had been made. He would also at that time cut the cost of the German army of occupation in France by twenty-five per cent. Moreover, he would make the reduction retroactive to this date. He would also instruct the German occupation authorities in Paris to give favorable consideration to the other easements that Darlan had in mind. Details of these could be discussed with Otto Abetz in Paris.

*General Charles de Gaulle, leader of the Fighting French.

I was prevented from obtaining more information on these conversations between Hitler and Darlan, so I am sending this off.

With warmest greetings,

CLARA.

For the moment Clara seemed to have assumed the entire burden of keeping us informed on events in Germany, for a few days later we received still another interesting letter from her. This time she wrote:

Dear Willy:

I have been in luck lately. Today again I have something of interest. I stumbled on this one by mere accident. The latest caller at the Berghof was Franz von Papen, our ex-Chancellor and now Ambassador to Turkey. He came with Ribbentrop. Both had dinner with Hitler and then retired with him to the study.

Hitler wanted von Papen to give him his latest impressions on the Turkish attitude. Von Papen stated that the Ankara government is more favorably disposed toward Germany now than at any time since the outbreak of the war. The information that he had been able to give the Turks regarding Russia's designs on Turkey had contributed a great deal toward this change. Turkish fears had been aroused and the new Soviet ambassador, Vinogradov, had not been able to dispel them. The Kremlin had played into German hands by replacing its former easygoing envoy, Terentiev, who had won himself many friends in Turkey, with Vinogradov, who was known as one of Moscow's experts in the arts of pressure diplomacy. The Turks as a whole, and especially President Inonu, view every new Russian move with suspicion.

Turkey's relations with the British, von Papen told Hitler, also had deteriorated. The British-Turkish alliance, which the Turks had held in abeyance after the fall of France, could be considered as good as dead. It provided for the supplying of armaments to Turkey by the British, and up to the present the Turks had received nothing. The promises that Eden* had repeated on each of his visits to Ankara had become a standing joke. It can be regarded now as certain that Turkey will not enter the war at the behest of England.

The fact is, von Papen continued, that Turkey now regards England as less of a friend than Germany. The Turks are perfectly aware that England wanted to draw them into the war while their own policy was to remain neutral. He, von Papen, had assured Turkey that Germany's

*Anthony Eden, British Secretary of State for Foreign Affairs.

246

own interests called for keeping Turkey out of the war, and after the Russian story they had come to believe him. But, he continued, future relations would have to be handled carefully. To press for Turkey's adherence to the Axis now would be a mistake. It would serve only to rouse old suspicions that now have been almost completely allayed. If Germany gains a decisive victory over England in the Eastern Mediterranean, that will be another matter. While there are many important personages in Ankara who favor tying up with Germany, they prefer not to express their opinions openly until they are reasonably sure that in doing so they are casting their lot with the winning side. Another German success in the Mediterranean would most definitely swing the balance in Germany's favor.

Hitler said that what he wants particularly at this time is a pact of friendship and non-aggression with Turkey. Such an arrangement would give him an entering wedge, he said, that can be exploited later. He wants to have this pact negotiated as quickly as possible. He had already written President Inonu, assuring him that as a comrade-in-arms from the first World War, Turkey occupied a privileged place in his, Hitler's heart. Germany valued Turkey's friendship and would support her in any restoration claims that she might decide to bring up later on. He wanted von Papen to take this letter to President Inonu and then press for a pact of friendship. He gave von Papen one month— no more—in which to bring such a pact about.

This is all I can tell you on the subject. I do not think that anything more of importance occurred because I saw both Ribbentrop and von Papen leave the Berghof a half hour after they completed their conversations in Hitler's study.

It may be that I will take a trip to Switzerland to see my son if the opportunity arises. If Hitler embarks on another campaign I may be able to do so. I should like to do it before I give my final decision to Wolfgang, who has become rather pressing.

With my warmest regards,
CLARA.

This report was followed almost immediately by a letter from Gottlieb, who wrote:

Dear Willy:

We have had quite a time. The excitement all over the country was greater than at any time since Hitler's accession to power.

It began when Goebbels announced that Rudolph Hess had crashed in a plane and had met his death. All flags in the Reich were instantly lowered to half staff. The Ministry of the Interior had already prepared for Hitler's signature a decree proclaiming three days of national mourning.

Then came the big denouement. The British announced that Hess had landed by plane in England [Hess actually landed in Scotland] and had been taken prisoner. Goebbels had made the biggest mistake of his career.

Despite all of the Gestapo's efforts to prevent this news from reaching the people of Germany it rapidly became public knowledge. A flood of rumors spread throughout the country. One was that Hess had been shot by the Gestapo and that a double had been sent to England to cover the deed. Another said that Hess had been kidnapped by a British agent posing as a Luftwaffe pilot. A third claimed that Hess had fled the country because he had learned he was about to be purged and he had beaten Himmler's executioners to the Augsburg airport by a mere fifteen minutes.

A fourth rumor which, incidentally, gained widespread credence, was that Hess and Himmler had been seen together at the airport. Himmler, so the story went, had been ordered to arrest Hess. Then Hess had convinced Himmler what a demoralizing effect this would have on the German people and that since he had to die anyway, wouldn't it be better if he were to be allowed to take a plane and crash to his death? It certainly would meet the requirements of the situation, without causing any blow to public morale such as having him shot would. Himmler consented to this and escorted Hess to the airport, so the story continued, and Hess double-crossed the Gestapo chief and flew to England. Those subscribing to this version of the event argued that the very fact that Goebbels had announced the death of Hess in a plane crash barely twelve hours after the take-off, in a measure substantiated it.

I am afraid that in connection with this story there has been a slip-up. Clara neglected to tell anyone of us about overhearing the private conversation between Hitler and Hess. Since she had gone to Switzerland for a few days just before the Hess flight occurred, we had no idea of the true circumstances. Klausmann was here and he insisted that this was a story on which you must be fully informed immediately. Inasmuch as this last version was accepted as true even by quarters close to Hitler, we decided to send it to you. With Wolfgang's assistance, Klausmann slipped into nearby Liechtenstein* and sent you a wireless message to the effect. It was only after Clara's return that we learned

*The Principality of Liechtenstein, a very small neutral country situated between Germany and Switzerland.

the true circumstances of the case, but then it was too late to rectify the error. I hope it has not caused any inconvenience.

To continue with my account. Goebbels, whether on his own account or at the urging of Himmler, came out with still another story. Hess was known for some time to have had hallucinations and it was during one of these spells, according to this explanation of Goebbels', that he flew to England. This served only to increase the spread of rumors. Too many people knew that Hess was perfectly sane. He had spoken at a party rally only two days before the flight and had been seen by several thousand people, all of whom were willing to swear to his mental stability.

Thus far, Hitler had kept himself aloof, but now he took a hand himself. Himmler was summoned to the Berghof and, after a terrible dressing down by Hitler, was given his orders. Within six hours Frau Hess, Haushofer, Messerschmitt [Willy Messerschmitt, plane designer], Bohn and other personal friends of Hess were rounded up and on their way to the Berghof, to be questioned by Hitler himself on what they knew about Hess' flight and the various rumors. Frau Hess and Haushofer produced letters received from Hess in which he informed them that he was going to England on his own initiative because he believed that he would be able to bring about peace. Beyond this they knew nothing. Hess had passed the night before his flight at home but had not given his wife any inkling of what, apparently, he was about to do. Frau Hess was given over to the care of Evi Braun for three days, but the others were permitted to leave, having been admonished not to discuss the matter. Goebbels was ordered to cease all propaganda releases connected with the Hess flight.

In the light of what Clara knew about the conversation between Hitler and Hess all of this, of course, was sheer farce. But what followed was deadly serious. Three days after Hitler's questioning of Hess' friends, all Gauleiters were summoned to the Berghof, including even Terboven from Norway, Seyss-Inquart from Holland, Frank from the Gouvernement General and Buerckel from the Westgau.* When they were assembled in the Great Hall, Hitler came out to talk to them. He announced that he was shocked by what had happened to his dear friend, Rudolph, who was an idealist. He had thought that he could talk peace with the British. They had encouraged him, telling him that if he went to England, Winston Churchill would gladly discuss terms with him. He, Hitler, had forbidden Hess to make another move in the matter, because he knew that the British could not be trusted. Hess, following his fixed ideas, had defied orders and gone just the

*Westgau is the present German name for Alsace-Lorraine.

same. As it turned out, the whole thing had been just a trap set by the British, who had wanted to lay their hands on Hess in order to find out from him something of Germany's future war plans. But the trick had failed because Hess was completely uninformed about the plans of the German Supreme Command.

Then Hitler got down to business. He told the Gauleiters that Martin Bormann, lately administrative assistant to Hess, would be in charge temporarily of party affairs. The Gauleiters were to see to it that the news which they had just received from Hitler was to trickle down through regular party channels to the lowliest party worker. Hitler wanted them all informed on what actually had happened to Hess. Any other rumors in circulation were to be discredited and countered with this, the true explanation.

So far as Hitler was concerned, this was to be the end of the Hess affair. As you will notice, Hitler took good care that his personal connection with the Hess mission remained a secret. Of course there is the chance that Hess, now in England, may tell about it, but that is hardly likely. As for Bormann, ten Hesses would be preferable to this man as party head. He is a common Brown-Shirt thug who participated in the beer hall putsch of 1923 and was sentenced to one year in jail together with Hitler and Hess. It is common knowledge that his present wealth comes from his manipulations of party funds. If he should ever be invested with the succession and some day occupy Hitler's place, then God help us all.

I am getting this off in a hurry. Perhaps it will reach you in time to counteract Klausmann's wireless message on the Hess affair.

Grüss Gott!
GOTTLIEB.

Unfortunately, Gottlieb's letter was delayed in transit and did not reach us in time to prevent us from using the information contained in Klausmann's wireless. It was used as the basis for an article on the Hess affair published in a national weekly.* We saw at once, of course, that the wireless conflicted in certain essential details with the information contained in Clara's letter on the conversation between Hess and Hitler. But since the wireless was of a later date than the letter, we felt that the situation probably had undergone some changes since Clara had written us. As it turned out, we were wrong, but the harm was done.

*Liberty Magazine, issue of July 19, 1941.

It was this same article which almost led to a break between van Narvig and myself. As a rule it was van Narvig who prepared our article material. He had done so in this particular case and then left for the South, to visit his son at the army training center at Fort McClellan, Alabama. While going over the article it occurred to me that the information contained in it would gain in authenticity if I introduced part of the code text of the wireless message and mentioned the place from which it was sent—Vaduz, the capital of Liechtenstein. The story was printed in this shape.

When van Narvig saw the article in print he was furious. He said that quoting of the code text was all right, but to mention Vaduz in the same connection had been a grave mistake. With both these items for a lead, he said, it would be an easy matter for the Gestapo to trace the sender of the message.

I admitted the error which, of course, could not be undone. At the same time, however, I pointed out that at the time of publication of the article Klausmann had already returned to the United States, and so the message could no longer be traced to him.

What neither van Narvig nor I knew at the time was that the wireless message had been actually filed in Vaduz by Wolfgang, who had accompanied Klausmann on this mission. For months we remained in complete ignorance of the part which this message played in a later tragedy.

We next received a letter from Linda which gave us a great deal to think about. It read:

Dear Willy:
This Hess business came as a distinct shock to many of us here. It started an abundance of rumors. There were even whispers of a purge that would put the Army back on top, and many party leaders started treating army men with a respect and consideration which they had not shown for some time. However, eventually the storm blew over.

The other day Goering came to Karin Hall with Udet and Milch and they started talking about Hess. Goering referred to him as "*ein verrueckter Kerl.*" * This really surprised me, for Hess and Goering had

*A crazy fellow.

always been on good terms. In fact, at one time Hess visited Karin Hall more often than any other party leader.

Goering and his visitors retired to the smoking room and closed the doors. At times I could hear their raised voices—they were drinking. But all I could make out was that they were arguing the question of Russia. I gathered that something must be afoot, and the following day I arranged to go to Berlin.

Heinrich, as I hoped, had the story, or at least most of it. I take it that you know that von der Schulenburg was sent to Moscow to convey Hitler's great displeasure with Moscow and the reasons for it. This sent the Kremlin into a flurry of action. Stalin left the Commissariat of Foreign Affairs to Molotov and assumed the Premiership himself. One of his first acts was to call von der Schulenburg and inform him that Russia would recognize our puppet government in Iraq headed by Rashid el Gailani and would withdraw recognition from the fugitive governments of Norway, Greece and Yugoslavia. As you know, Stalin had signed a friendship pact with Belgrade only twenty-four hours before Hitler's army marched in.

Von der Schulenburg also reported that immediately upon Stalin's recognition of the Iraq regime, Sir Stafford Cripps, the British Ambassador in Moscow, asked to see Stalin for the purpose of protesting this action. Stalin merely replied that Russia had to mend her own fences and could not take account of British sensibilities. Cripps then let it be known that he would return to London, because his position in Moscow had become intolerable. It was in this connection that Goering expressed himself thus: *"Der Russe kommt zu Kreuze gekrochen."* *

So much for that. Here is some straight news from Heinrich. The Russian Ambassador, Dekanosov, paid a long call on Ribbentrop at the Wilhelmstrasse and the message he conveyed was so important that it brought Hitler up from Berchtesgaden. There are many rumors here concerning Dekanosov. Some say that he is a close relative of Stalin's. Others even maintain that he is Stalin's son, but there is of course no way of checking any of this. However that may be, it is definitely known that Stalin trusts him implicitly and often sends him on confidential errands.

Dekanosov delivered an oral message and this is it. The Soviet government regrets that its actions in the Balkans caused inconveniences to the Reich government. The Soviet wishes to explain that the pact entered into with the Yugoslav government of General Simovich was not a new venture, but the outgrowth of negotiations conducted with

*The Russian comes crawling.

252

the former Yugoslav regime. That it was signed by a representative of the new regime was merely a coincidence.

The re-establishment of peace, said Dekanosov, has been a cardinal policy of the Soviet Union. For this reason the Soviet Union is most eager to preserve its neutrality. Since the suggestions of the Reich offered to Foreign Commissar Molotov during his conferences in Berlin would have led to Soviet aggression, the Soviet Union did not at the time find itself in a position to follow these suggestions. However, since there are indications that the war may spread to new territories in which the U.S.S.R. has a paramount interest, the Soviet Union is inclined to reconsider its previous position.

Dekanosov continued that the policy of the Soviet Union has been, and will continue to be, the cultivation of friendly and neighborly relations with the Reich. Guided by this desire, the Soviet Union believes that personal exchange of views between the heads of the two governments and their foreign ministers would result in more rapid and amicable agreements than would cumbersome diplomatic negotiations. If such a proposal was acceptable to the Reich, the Soviet Government would be prepared to dispatch its Premier and its Commissar for Foreign Affairs (Stalin and Molotov) to confer with the Reich Chancellor and the Reich Foreign Minister (Hitler and Ribbentrop) at a designated location along the Russian-German frontier, perhaps at Brest-Litovsk or nearby.

All this is of course diplomatic language. The gist of it is that Stalin is more than anxious to continue living in peace with Hitler, even at the cost of some minor inconveniences.

Heinrich said that Ribbentrop was elated over the Russian message. Hitler, too, is not exactly displeased. Ribbentrop's idea is to press Stalin for the conclusion of an outright military alliance with Germany. He believes this can be done if Russia is permitted to participate in the resulting spoils. Under such an alliance, Ribbentrop figures, considerable economic advantages could be obtained for the Reich. It might also bring about a new world alignment powerful enough to prompt Great Britain into suing for peace. If not, the Russian army would become an additional factor in breaking up the British Empire. Hitler has gone back to Berchtesgaden to ponder the Russian bid.

Heinrich also said that, so far as he knew, there have been movements of our troops from the Balkans toward the Russian borders. However, since we have always maintained from thirty to forty divisions in Poland, Rumania and East Prussia as a sort of safety measure, he saw no immediate significance in the strengthening of these garrisons. It is more likely that Hitler is conducting a silent war of nerves against the Russians in order to force them to greater concessions. Prevailing opinion here is that Stalin will sign any agreement rather than fight, especially if given a consolation prize that will enhance his prestige both at home and abroad.

I received your letter a few days ago. It was very nice of you to write as you did. I was beginning to think that you might have forgotten. Please write me again in the same vein.

Affectionately,

LINDA.

Events in Germany seemed to be moving apace. We had scarcely digested the information sent by Linda, when we received a letter from Wolfgang that tossed all our previous calculations into a cocked hat. Wolfgang wrote:

Dear Willy:

I have come across some very important news. This morning a special courier from our embassy in Moscow arrived here. He had flown from Koenigsberg to Salzburg because the ministries in Berlin were closed for the week-end and Ribbentrop was known to be at Fuschl. From this I gathered that he was carrying something of great importance. Of course it was up to me to find out what it was, for an opportunity like this does not come to me every day.

It appeared that Count von der Schulenburg had sent a voluminous report. The moment I read the introduction I realized its great importance. It seems that for a considerable time our intelligence service has been trying to find out what was really going on in Russia. Schulenburg himself had some undercover men planted in the Kremlin to keep him posted. One of these, during a drinking bout with a Kremlin key man, had been successful in eliciting vital information.

Schulenburg's report dated back to the Russo-German pact. According to it, Russia knew that England and France would declare war on Hitler if he attacked Poland. It was this knowledge that convinced Stalin at the time to accept Hitler's proposals. Stalin had counted that Germany would exhaust herself in the war with the two Western powers and become so weak, militarily, that she would be ripe for Communism. France and England likewise would emerge thoroughly exhausted from the struggle, and Stalin would then emerge as the dominating factor in Europe.

The Kremlin had figured that the war on Finland would be a simple affair, the preamble to Schulenburg's report continued. It would present an excellent chance to extend Russian influence into the Scandinavian countries. Instead, the Finnish war opened Stalin's eyes to the deficiencies in the Red Army organization. When, immediately thereafter, Hitler invaded Norway, Stalin grew anxious because this was a development he had never taken into consideration as being possible.

The complete collapse of France in six weeks, which also prompted England to relinquish her hold on northern Norway, came as a terrific shock to the Kremlin. More than that, it revealed the crushing efficiency of the tank and dive bomber combination. The Red Army had counted on the tank and level-flight bomber exclusively. Stalin then gave immediate orders to Marshal Shaposhnikov to reorganize the entire Red Army set-up with an eye on Hitler's method. This reorganization, Stalin was told by his generals, would require at least two years. In the meantime, the generals counseled him to keep out of Hitler's way.

The Tripartite Pact with Japan proved a new worry for the Kremlin, for now Russia would have to be on the alert on two important fronts. Therefore Stalin dispatched Molotov to Berlin with instructions to obtain an agreement whereby Russia would undertake to safeguard the Balkan countries while Hitler turned to an invasion of England. This did not work, because Hitler saw through the Russian intentions. Instead, Hitler tried to lead Stalin in the direction of India, but Stalin wanted none of that. His idea was to secure the Balkans with Hitler's knowledge and thereafter block any German push to the east. But Hitler once more proved too clever for the Russians.

When Matsuoka visited Moscow, Stalin was convinced that Japan and Germany would soon attempt a large-scale play against the British Empire in Asia. This suited him perfectly. In a drive of such gigantic proportions both Germany and Japan would have the wind taken out of them, while he would be building up. Stalin virtually pushed Japan toward southeast Asia by suggesting to Matsuoka a friendship and non-aggression pact with Russia.

But Hitler completed the initial part of his squeeze drive by overrunning the Balkans with an ease that startled Moscow. Stalin was well aware that in this strategy, Japan would not be ready for some time to start her own push. He watched closely the various military missions that crossed Russia, commuting between Berlin and Tokyo, and made his own calculations accordingly. Meanwhile, Hitler had a tremendous army on his hands with apparently no immediate job to do. He could easily throw this force against Russia if he wished. Being a supreme realist, Stalin well knew that non-aggression pacts meant little.

With an abruptness characteristic of Stalin when paramount issues are at stake, he assumed official leadership of the Soviet Union, realizing that only he had the necessary prestige to force a complete reversal of Russian policy if the situation so demanded. He knew, reported Schulenburg, that he could carry on an outward appeasement policy toward Hitler while building and planning secretly. He intended to accept a military alliance with Hitler and even pledge himself to co-operate actively in the destruction of the British Empire. But he would see to it that Germany and Japan did all the hard fighting while keeping his own forces away from costly ventures. Schulenburg concluded that if a military alliance with Stalin were entered into, Germany would have to see to it that Russia did a proportionate part of the war work.

After this general background, Schulenburg gave an account of current conditions in the Soviet Union. Stalin, he said, had withdrawn eight divisions from the Far Eastern Army on the Manchukuo border and had concentrated them in Central Asia, evidently for the ostensible purpose of a push into Iran and India if an alliance with Germany were concluded. But at the same time Stalin had removed eight divisions from Central Asia and was secretly transferring them to the Baltic Coast. In other words, the new troops in Central Asia represented no real concentration, but just a replacement. Russia was erecting new fortifications along the Bug River and in Lithuania, also farther east. Russian factories were feverishly producing war materials, especially tanks and planes. A new type of fighter plane, as well as a dive bomber, had been developed and were about to go into mass production. The reorganization of the Red Army from its old bulky formations into streamlined units was proceeding rapidly. A fair appraisal was that within another year Russia would be ready to contest German military power.

Schulenburg's report contained a supplement of military statistics, but this is being copied by Ribbentrop's secretaries. I shall try to get access to it and send you this additional information. You will hear from me again shortly.

Your friend,
WOLFGANG.

Little did we know by what risky means Wolfgang had obtained this secret information and that this was the last letter we would ever get from him.

At this time flagrant rumors insisted that German troops were concentrating along the Russian border. These rumors were promptly denied by both Berlin and Moscow. However, we knew that they were true. Linda's report had informed us of new units along the Russian frontier weeks earlier. Presently official news came from London that Ambassador Sir Stafford Cripps had arrived from Moscow with the discouraging story that Stalin was about to line up definitely with Hitler. Sir Stafford at that time said there was little reason for him to return to his post. This tallied precisely with the information contained in Linda's last letter and we felt no hesitancy in using her information in a broadcast.

There were several points in Wolfgang's letter, however, that made us think hard.

"It looks to me as if Stalin, too, has been double-crossing his alleged friend in Berlin," I observed to van Narvig.

"There is no honor among thieves," he replied. "If two strictly imperialist regimes make a deal it is usually with the intention of robbing some weaker party, or perhaps each other."

"What do you think the chances are of Russia and Germany going to war against each other?" I asked.

"They might," he said, "if the loot over which they quarrel is sufficiently important. As I see it, only the Balkans are of real importance to Russia. Stalin tried to get in there in a timid sort of way, but Hitler was too fast for him. That's all washed up now. Stalin would be a fool to believe that Hitler would disgorge anything that's safely in his pocket. And Stalin has proved himself anything but a fool."

"What about Finland?" I suggested.

"Now there's a case," van Narvig said. "Unquestionably Hitler has deceived Stalin in the Finnish business. When I was in Moscow at the time of the Hitler-Stalin deal I found out for certain that Finland was assigned to Russia. But Stalin played the Finnish game stupidly. First he made a poor military showing. Then he blundered further when he concluded a makeshift peace with the Finns and so provided Hitler with a technical loophole. Hitler simply picked up the cards that Stalin dropped."

"Suppose Stalin should want to get these cards back?" I said.

"If you mean that Stalin might go to war with Hitler over the Finnish issue," van Narvig said, "forget it. Stalin is an even greater realist than Hitler. In the Balkans much greater Russian interests are at stake. I wouldn't have been a bit surprised had Stalin started fighting there and then. The very fact that he didn't proves more than anything else that he does not consider himself strong enough to fight Hitler, even in company with the British, who certainly would like nothing better than to see Russia in the war on their side, and would be glad to forget Communism for the moment. Remember that Stalin practically handed Cripps his walking papers. No, Stalin is not going to fight Hitler so long as there is another way out. Of course he's got to counter Hitler's technique and he ought to know it by this time."

"Just what have you got in mind?"

"Hitler's time-tested technique," said van Narvig, "is to add to his demands when his opponent in a pressure game shows a tendency to weaken. But he has also a time-tested technique of lowering his demands if the opponent stiffens. In that case he takes what he can get and comes back for more later on. Stalin must estimate how much he can concede to Hitler without weakening himself. Hitler must find a compensation for Stalin that will not conflict with his own or Japanese aims. Somewhere in between they may strike a bargain."

"Suppose Hitler decides to go to war on Stalin?" I asked. "He always wanted the Ukraine."

"If Hitler could get this much talked-of Ukraine without firing a shot," van Narvig said, "it would be one thing. But to fight a bloody war all over that territory is quite another. The country would be ruined, the crops trampled, the industries destroyed. To conquer the Ukraine by war would only result in Hitler's having forty-five million more people to feed from his own resources, without getting anything out of the country for at least a couple of years. If Hitler goes to war over the Ukraine, he will be a fool."

I could see the logic in that.

"If only we had more direct news on this," I complained.

"Our friends will keep us posted," van Narvig said.

For once he was wrong. For several weeks we received no reports—not one word! It was as if our people on the other side had suddenly ceased to exist. When the news broke of Hitler's invasion of Russia, we had absolutely nothing to go on. In fact, I had gone out on a limb on the strength of Linda's last letter, and now found myself caught.

Van Narvig concentrated on his receiving set. For days on end he fished among wave lengths and code signals, then passed nights trying to decipher what he had intercepted. After almost two weeks of this, he came to the office one day, gaunt and hollow-eyed, and threw up his hands.

"It's no use," he said. "I've tracked down their new wave lengths. I'm catching their signals from time to time in spite of distance, but they're using a brand new cipher based on a principle unknown to me and I cannot break it."

"Then we're licked," I said.

"For the time being it looks that way," he admitted.

"Do you think anything has happened to our friends?" I ventured.

"Frankly, I don't," he said. "The most likely explanation is that the transmission belt has broken down."

"I still do not know by what system these reports have been reaching us," I observed.

"Neither do I, with any certainty," van Narvig said. "Gottlieb and Klausmann worked this out between them. Had I asked questions I wouldn't have got an answer. In this game, you know, when you're caught it's for keeps, and these men have their own scalps to protect. My idea is that the diplomatic courier service was used by them in some way that I never bothered to figure out. Our government has closed down all consulates and other German agencies in this country. This has killed the courier service. That's probably why the reports don't come through any longer."

He lit a cigar and went on, "It's only a guess on my part, of course. At present there's no way in which I can find out. Klausmann is on one of his mysterious trips to Germany and until he returns I'm afraid we'll remain in the dark."

CHAPTER 21

THANKS TO VAN NARVIG, my broadcasts included a number of inside stories on military strategy on the Russian front. Van Narvig was familiar with that theater of war. He had been there in the fighting during the first World War, and he had covered most of the territory during his extended Russian trip in 1938. With his military knowledge it was comparatively easy for him to analyze the progress of the fighting. His familiarity with the territory even enabled him to penetrate beyond the terse official communiques.

One day we sat on the lawn at my home in Greenwich, discussing the European scene and, as usual, argued about Hitler's chances.

"It is a question of the winter," van Narvig said. "Beyond doubt the Germany army is engaged in the toughest job it has tackled so far. Tactically, the outcome before the advent of winter depends on gun power. I don't count much on the Russian tanks or the Red Air Force. Hitler is unquestionably superior in striking power. But gun power is a different matter in this case. The Russian army has always placed special emphasis on artillery. The Russians are among the best gunners I have ever seen. If the Red Army is amply provided with heavy guns and ammunition it will be a hard nut to crack."

"Unquestionably," he continued, "Hitler's strategic aim is not territory but the destruction of the Russian field armies. Just what the strategic plan of the German Supreme Command is I haven't the slightest idea. This angle was never touched upon during my stay in Germany. At the time all preparations were for a campaign in the West and, again, Hitler always tackles one thing at a time."

"Can't you make a good guess?" I asked, and looked at him. He laughed.

"The trouble with guesses is that they are more often bad than good," he answered. "I can only give my opinion as to how the Germans may proceed in Russia, but it may not be worth a plugged nickel."

"Let's have it just the same," I said.

"From what little I was able to learn of the outer Moscow defenses," he said, "they are the most formidable anywhere. The Russians have always been great at building fortifications. It is the old Totleben* tradition with them. I don't think a frontal assault on Moscow can succeed except at terrific cost. I rather believe that the Germans will try to encircle the southern Russian armies and seize the Black Sea coast.

"We can forget the Ukraine, the bread basket, the granary, and all other such slogans," he said. "It is not likely to deliver much bread for the next couple of years, hardly enough to feed the local population. I'm looking at the subject from the strategic angle exclusively. The Russian south, including the Donets Basin, holds virtually one-half of all Russian war industries. If Hitler succeeds in seizing it, he will have dealt Russian resistance a crushing blow.

"Furthermore, he will then be able to advance on Moscow through the open plains leading to the rear of the Soviet capital, where permanent defenses are virtually non-existent, instead of coming at it from the west, where Moscow is protected by dense forests difficult to penetrate. If he reaches the line of the Don River and follows this up by an occupation of Moscow before the advent of winter, the question of further Russian resistance will become academic. If Hitler does not reach this line, he will then have an awful headache. He may even have to revise his strategy completely."

"You mean, he will suffer the fate of Napoleon?" I asked.

"Not at all," van Narvig replied. "All this talk about Napo-

*General Totleben, defender of Sevastopol during the Crimean War of 1855–56.

261

leon's fate in Russia is just another cliché. There is no parallel between the two situations. Napoleon advanced into Russia on a thin line affording a most precarious means of communication with his rear. His campaign was an outright gamble with a view of catching up with the only Russian field army then in existence and annihilating it. When he failed to catch up with that army his goose was cooked and he had no other choice but to retreat all the way back, against the most formidable odds.

"Hitler is not dependent on just one field army pushing forward on a thin line easily cut," van Narvig continued. "His armies are advancing on a broad front. He has a safely consolidated rear and his flanks are protected by the Baltic and Black Seas. The Russians may dent one or more points on this long front, but that will not bring about its collapse and compel a general retreat. No, Hitler's headache will be of a different sort.

"If he should not reach the objectives that I have just outlined, it will mean that the Russians have preserved, at least, part of their field army. Winter in the Russian plains demands a stabilization of the front. But a modern army cannot dig in on a front more than 1,500 miles long. It can only occupy certain key sectors of such a front and leave long stretches between them practically unprotected. This will give the Russians an opportunity to push into these open stretches and wreak havoc with railroads and other communications. Should they have enough punch left in them, they could even reduce some of these key sectors. But even if they don't they will have a winter to make new preparations of their own. There will then be no more surprise attacks on Hitler's part. He may still go on from where he stopped for the winter, but his task would be much harder than it is right now. And he will hardly be in a position to keep his rendezvous with the Japs in India. But all this is mere opinion. We'll just have to wait and see which way the rabbit jumps."

We still felt that our friends in Germany were safe. We suspected that the reason reports did not come through was because Klausmann had not yet returned. The next few days, however, made us realize the grave dangers with which all those connected with our enterprise were threatened.

One morning, as van Narvig entered the office, I sensed immediately that something had gone wrong. He looked positively sick.

"What is it?" I asked.

He dropped into a chair.

"Remember Heinrich Nostiz?" he asked.

I could not place the name. Then van Narvig told me.

"He's the chap in the German Embassy in Washington who helped us copy those confidential records sent to Heinrich Stahmer last December."

Of course I remembered him.

"What about him?" I asked.

"He's dead!" van Narvig said. And I could tell from his tone that some unusual fate had befallen this friend of ours.

Van Narvig told me about it.

"It happened in the embassy building," he said. "First they claimed it was death from heat prostration. The story did not hold water. Corpses with bullet holes in them have a different sort of heat turned on them than that of the sun."

"You mean . . . ," I began, and stopped abruptly. Then, "Not on account of those papers?"

"Probably in part," van Narvig answered, and the corners of his mouth twitched nervously. "Nostiz hated Hitler and the Nazis. From what I understand, the information he let us have was not all that he allowed to filter through. He and Klausmann were close. I suspect that together they were responsible for considerable information on German conditions that reached our State Department from time to time. There can hardly be any doubt that the Gestapo caught on to him. He was ordered to return to Germany. He preferred to put a bullet into his head, or perhaps someone did it for him."

I did not like this at all. If the Gestapo got Nostiz, it was fair to assume that they would corner Klausmann too, especially since he was in Germany. Both of us were in a state of nerves for several days.

But the Gestapo did not get Klausmann. A week later he turned up in New York, quite safe. He did not know of Nostiz's fate and was deeply upset when he heard of it. We never knew by what mysterious route he shuttled across the Atlantic, and we did not inquire. It was sufficient for us that he had brought with him a number of letters from our German friends.

However, the first of these, from Gottlieb, was a horrible shock to us. He wrote:

Dear Willy:

Wolfgang is dead. It is bad to be the transmitter of tragic news and you must understand how I feel. I have tried to get all the details of his death, but if they are a bit scrambled you will know why.

As you had been told many times before, Wolfgang was the most enthusiastic of our group. He took risks constantly and never seemed to care for his own life. Always he felt that he was not sending enough important news to you. I understand, however, that his last letter concerning a report to Ribbentrop from our Moscow Ambassador was vital. I also understand that he promised to send additional information on this Moscow business. It was while he was trying to get this that Wolfgang betrayed himself.

One thing is not quite clear to me. I understand that Wolfgang had been watched for quite a while. I learned of this only after the tragedy, or I would have warned him in time. I am told that it had something to do with that trip to Liechtenstein that he and Klausmann made together, and whence they sent you an important wireless message. Are you sure that no indiscretion in connection with this message was committed on your side?

Anyway, to go on with the story.

You know the type of place that Fuschl is. A medieval castle, several hundred years old. There are secret passages, staircases, maybe a tunnel or two, and while many of them are known, there are some that are not. Wolfgang lived at Fuschl from the day of his birth. He knew every corner and cranny, and once he told me that he could get into the weapon room, the library and some other places, with no one knowing it. There were some passages that only he and his brother knew.

It was by some such means that Wolfgang obtained the information he sent you in his last letter. In his excitement over getting such important information he must have slipped up, for it was quickly discovered that the papers in question had been handled by some unauthorized person.

The Gestapo men at Fuschl were shrewd enough not to give an alarm or take open measures that might have warned the culprit. The existence of as yet undiscovered passages was generally suspected, but it was not believed that anyone in Fuschl knew of their location. Now that they realized someone was familiar with the passages, special guards were posted. Those under suspicion were carefully watched. I had repeatedly advised Wolfgang to join the Gestapo, and had he been one of them he would have known of these measures. But he refused to join because he hated them.

In trying to obtain the additional statistics, Wolfgang was tailed without being aware of it. He was caught in the act, so to speak. He managed to escape from the room, but when he emerged from a secret exit on the castle grounds, he met Gestapo guards who were combing the area. Wolfgang was armed. He shot it out with them, but they were too many. He was killed immediately.

Unfortunately the matter did not end there. Whenever the Gestapo catches anyone, his connections are immediately suspected and run down. Wolfgang's frequent trips to Berchtesgaden to see Clara were of course known. Word was sent to the Berghof to apprehend Clara. I was among those who received the order.

It was Sunday morning and Clara was not working, nor was she home. I knew that she had gone on a hike and I also knew her favorite trail because we had covered it together on occasions. Since there are still folk here who value friendship more than allegiance to Hitler, I managed to have Clara intercepted and she took refuge in a safe place. The Gestapo waited in vain for her return and when she failed to come back their suspicions were really aroused.

Of course there was the chance that Clara could have convinced them that she was innocent, but I am familiar with Gestapo methods. Clara is a smart girl, but frail, physically, and I doubt that she could have gone through the torture methods that I felt sure would have been applied. Then there was her child to consider, as well as Linda. I arranged that Linda be warned and I am certain that she will succeed in fooling the Gestapo. However, if Clara had uttered one unguarded word under questioning, Linda might have become so deeply implicated that she would not have escaped. I could not risk that.

We kept Clara in hiding for four days, then we managed to get her into a motor van bound for Friedrichshafen. The driver is a friend of mine. He made a short detour and delivered Clara to a family I know very well. They live in a village not far from Immenstaad on the Bodensee. These people are fisherfolk who at times run errands the nature of which need not be mentioned here. We wanted to get Clara across the lake into Swiss territory where she would be reasonably safe. The lake is rigidly patrolled and a crossing of this sort can be made only under favorable conditions. Clara stayed with this family a week, then on a dark, stormy night the men managed to get her across. That is all I know of that phase of it.

You will understand that Clara's disappearance, together with the circumstances of Wolfgang's discovery and death, have sent the Gestapo here into working overtime. All possible leads are being run down. Someone recalled that you and Clara were friends. All your movements during your stay in Germany are being checked. I know of your trips to Switzerland to visit Clara's child, and I hope that you left no trail to follow. If they discover the child they will certainly find Clara and it would not be the first time that Germans in Switzerland had mysteriously disappeared. It is also possible that they will look you up in America. They have men there, you know. They may not harm you there, but nevertheless I would be careful of the people you talk to. The Gestapo has a long memory and an equally long arm.

I cannot tell at this time what possible consequences this will have on our work here. At present we must take every possible precaution and you will probably receive much less information than heretofore. The method of transmission has also become a problem. We who remain here are just as involved as we ever were, but there is little to gain by jeopardizing our lives without accomplishing enough to make the gamble worth while.

I regret I had to send such bad news. It does not make any change in our friendship.

Grüss Gott!
GOTTLIEB.

The Nostiz business had shaken us quite a bit, but the picture of Wolfgang perishing in a gun fight with Gestapo agents showed us in all its terrifying clarity what a dangerous venture we had engaged in. But reflections at this stage were of no help. We were in it and there was nothing we could do but carry on. It was evident from the other letters that Klausmann had brought with him that our other friends in Germany showed no inclination to retreat from the path on which their steps had been turned. One was from Linda and she wrote:

Dear Willy:

The news from Gottlieb was a great blow. Poor Wolfgang! He always wanted so much to help and he felt he was restricted to a place where opportunities to be of use did not occur as often as for us others. When he saw a really big chance he made the mistake of allowing himself to be carried away by his enthusiasm beyond the limits of the necessary caution.

We owe thanks to Gottlieb for having acted so promptly. It chills me to think what those beasts might have done to Clara had she fallen into their clutches. It is lamentable that we lost her services, but this is one of the things for which we all have had to be prepared. I shall miss Clara a great deal. We were almost like sisters. But it is comforting to know that she is safely out of all this. She is where she belongs—with her child—and for the first time in years faces the prospect of leading a normal life, raising her boy to be a champion of the freedom that we all hold so dear.

The Gestapo displayed their usual thoroughness in investigating Wolfgang and Clara. Two Gestapo agents were here to question me, but it so happened that Goering was here when they called and they had to obtain his permission before interrogating me. He insisted that the questioning be done in his presence, for which I am grateful. I managed to convey the impression to them that I was very stupid and entirely concerned with emotional attachments. I told them I knew nothing about Wolfgang except that I had met him once or twice socially while visiting Clara. I said that Clara was an old friend of mine and that I understood she and Wolfgang were to be married sometime in the future. I had not heard from Clara for months, I told them, and had no idea where she was now.

Then they asked me about you and whether I knew about the connection between you and Clara. I said I knew plenty, and at this they perked up instantly. I told them Clara was enamored of you in a silly sort of way, but that I too had found you interesting and had snatched you from her. Friendship between women was all very well, I said, but it stopped where a man was concerned. They asked when I had last heard from you and I said not since your departure for the United States, but that I should like to lay hands on you because you had promised faithfully to write. At this Goering laughed and told them to get out and not bother his employees. They went and that was that.

But enough of personal matters. Since I wrote you last there has been an unexpected turn in events.

Hitler and Ribbentrop had a series of consultations at the Chancellory on the subject of a report sent by Ambassador von der Schulenburg from Moscow. The gist of it was that while Moscow was anxious to make a new agreement with the Reich, Stalin was also making feverish preparations for war.

The report gave Hitler his first comprehensive picture of the strength of the Red Army. According to this report, Stalin's mobilized forces now consist of 250 combat divisions (including infantry, cavalry, artillery and engineers), and 34 armored brigades, which are far in excess of Russian needs under normal peace-time conditions. The distribution of these forces is as follows: 28 divisions and four armored brigades in the Far Eastern Red Banner Army, garrisoned in Siberia between Lake Baikal and Vladivostok; twelve divisions and two armored brigades in Central Asia; another twelve divisions and two armored brigades in Transcaucasia, close to the Turkish and Persian [Iranian] borders; eighteen divisions and two armored brigades in the Leningrad military district, including the border with Finland; forty divisions and eight armored brigades in the former Baltic states of Estonia, Latvia and Lithuania, on the approaches to East Prussia; in the interior of Russia, twenty divisions and no armored forces. The entire remainder of the Red Army—120 divisions and 16 armored brigades—is quartered within less than 200 miles of the frontier of German-controlled territory in Poland and Rumania.

Von der Schulenburg reported that while Stalin was eager to avoid war he would not recede from certain basic conditions. He would insist upon complete Russian military control over Finland. He would demand Russian control of the Turkish shore of the Black Sea as far east as Sinop and to achieve this, he would propose the division of Turkey into Russian and German spheres of influence. He would not agree to demobilization of the Red Army, nor a withdrawal of the considerable forces now stationed along Russia's western frontiers. He would agree to participate in a war against England, but only to the extent of Russian military operations from Central Asia and Transcausia into Iran and India, and even these would be limited in scope. He would agree to increase substantially deliveries of essential raw materials and foods to Germany, but would not permit German control commissions or other supervising bodies on Russian territory.

Hitler did not regard these concessions as at all satisfactory. His ideas go far beyond the limits that von der Schulenburg believes Stalin will agree to. He wants among other things, reduction of the Russian army to a peace strength of 120 divisions, of which not more than 40 divisions be stationed west of Moscow; transfer to German control of the shipyards in Libau, Riga and Talinn for the duration of the war; German control over Russian heavy industry west of the Ural Mountains as well as control over the Caucasus oil fields, with one-half the oil production to go to Germany; increase of Russian grain deliveries to Germany to 10,000,000 tons annually; German supervision over Russian railroads in the Ukraine. Besides all this, Hitler will not concede Russia anything in Finland beyond her present holdings and certainly not so much as a square foot of ground in Turkey.

Ribbentrop advised direct conversations between Hitler and Stalin. He believed the Soviet Premier would be impressed by what Hitler has to say and that an acceptable compromise could be worked out. He said he would not be surprised if Russia accepted the larger part of Hitler's demands rather than risk war. Hitler finally decided to leave the matter in abeyance until after he had consulted with his military advisers.

To this end, several conferences were held. Among the conferees were Colonel General Halder, Field Marshals von Brauchitsch, Keitel, List and Milch and, of course, Jodl and Goering. Halder gave a cautious and deliberate opinion. He viewed a campaign in Russia as consisting of three main phases and three main objectives. The first phase would have as its objective the annihilation of the Russian frontier armies. He was confident that this could be successfully accomplished. The Russians, if they anticipate a German attack at all, would look for it along the Rumanian border and into the southern Ukraine, and it was in this sector that they had made their strongest defensive preparations. Their strategy in case of an attack in the south would be a counter-offensive of their own from the Bialystok region in northern Poland with the objective of cutting off East Prussia from the remainder of the Reich, Halder believed. Most of their offensive strength was concentrated in that area. By striking in two pincers on both sides of this Russian army group, powerful German armies could encircle it, pushing all the way to Minsk and even beyond, and the battle of the frontiers would be over.

The second phase would consist of a series of separate operations, according to Halder's view. In the north, German armies would drive to the east of Lake Peipus, heading for Leningrad, to cut off the Russian forces in Latvia and Estonia. In the south, German armies would slice off a large Ukrainian pocket extending across the Dnieper River or, if this could not be accomplished in one powerful blow, then in a series of offensives. In the center, German armies would force the Dnieper at various points and converge on the Russian main army guarding the Smolensk approaches to Moscow.

The third phase would demand a large concentration of striking power in the south for the purpose of occupying the Crimea and driving through the Ukraine to emerge to the rear of Moscow from the southeast. If this operation could be completed before the heavy autumn rains, Moscow would become untenable and the campaign would, for all practical purposes, be concluded.

Success of these operations, Halder explained, would depend on the speed with which the Russians could bring reserves into action. By this he did not mean freshly recruited armies so much as large contingents of the Far Eastern Red Banner Army which Halder considers the best troops at Stalin's disposal. If these should reach the European front soon enough in sufficient numbers, the Russian defense might stiffen considerably and the German plan would have to be revamped. When asked by Hitler for a timetable he said the first phase should be carried out in two weeks, but refused to commit himself further.

Goering said that war against Russia in the air would be complicated by one unfavorable factor that has been absent in all previous German campaigns. This was the vastness of Russia and the secrecy that has surrounded the Russian military establishment. The Luftwaffe went into all of its previous campaigns, he said, with full knowledge of the air strength of its opponents. In this case, all that was known with any degree of certainty was that the Russian field army could count on the support of approximately 10,000 combat planes. The Luftwaffe, Goering said, was perfectly able to cope with these, but the big question was the extent of Russian air reserves secreted deep in the interior of the country. From the viewpoint of the Luftwaffe, he concluded, a campaign against Russia contained a strong element of chance.

Keitel, by contrast, was strongly in favor of going to war against Russia. He said that von der Schulenburg's report left no other choice. Stalin's unwillingness to consider further concessions must be regarded as a Russian attempt to play for time. Germany could not concentrate her full efforts on the British Empire so long as there was a Red Army waiting to pounce upon Germany from the rear at the first sign of German weakness. Keitel said he certainly would not subscribe to either an invasion of the British Isles or to an all-out effort in the Middle East so long as the threat of the Red Army remained. In Keitel's opinion, it was either a case of forcing demobilization of the entire Russian army or of destroying it. Since it was perfectly obvious that Stalin would never agree to the first solution, further negotiations would merely give him additional time to prepare. Germany must strike first and negotiate later.

Keitel did not agree with Halder's estimates and called them extremely conservative. Halder's plan was properly conceived, he said, but it allowed too much time for the various phases of the operations. He presented a detailed timetable of his own, which allowed three months for completion of the three phases, setting the end of September

270

for the start of an assault on Moscow from three sides. He did not believe that the Russian transportation system would be able to move the Siberian armies to the front in time to save Moscow.

Von Brauchitsch offered no comment except to say that the Wehrmacht stood ready to execute orders, whatever these may be.

Following these conferences, Hitler again met with Mussolini at the Brenner Pass, his mind already made up on attacking Russia. The purpose of the conference was to define Italian participation in the campaign. I can give you no details of what took place, but Heinrich was given to understand that, aside from an Italian token contribution of four divisions toward the Russian campaign, Mussolini is to continue providing for the defense of the Mediterranean for the duration of the war in Russia. Italian forces are to occupy Greece and the Greek islands to relieve German garrisons now stationed there, so that they can be transferred to the Russian front. Mussolini was likewise to supply whatever reserves Rommel needs in North Africa.

This is the extent of my information on these events. Needless to say, there is a great deal of military activity, but as to this our information is scanty. We know that the war on Russia has definitely been decided upon. It may come any moment. It will be highly popular with the army, with the exception of some of the conservative elements in the higher command. Men like Halder and von Brauchitsch are not so certain this time as they were last year, before the campaign in the west. At that time they knew all there was to know about the French army. But Russia to them is a closed book. They are wary of miscalculations that may force a complete change of plans. However, they are agreed that since war with Russia could not be avoided in the long run, it is better to strike now.

Once the war on Russia begins I shall probably be of little use, for there will be virtually no activity here. However, I shall do my best. Of one thing you may rest assured—I will not fall down on the job because of what happened to Wolfgang and Clara.

> Affectionately,
> LINDA.

Had Linda's letter reached us a few weeks earlier it would have given us a series of great radio scoops. But it had suffered a very long delay in transmission. This was evident from the fact that at the same time we received a letter from Manfred. His dispatch said:

Dear Willy:

Events have moved fast. I am at Hitler's headquarters here at Allenstein in East Prussia, but it is unlikely to remain here long, as we understand the Fuehrer is moving early next week to new headquarters across the Russian border. He is just waiting until the Army considers it safe enough for him to go there. I probably will have nothing of consequence to tell you until then.

At last the reason for Hitler's past overtures to the Vatican has come into the open. Scarcely had our armies marched into Russia when Goebbels, following Hitler's orders, proclaimed a Holy Crusade by the Church and State against godless Bolshevism. Hitler is now being portrayed as the great savior of religion, as the holy crusader against the Bolshevist peril, and all European states are asked to send contingents of volunteers to participate in the great and holy struggle. Both Mussolini and Franco have been asked to intercede at the Vatican and to have the Pope proclaim a holy war against the Soviet heathen or, at least, to give Hitler's crusade the official blessing of the Catholic Church.

So far the war is only a week old and the Vatican has not reacted at all. I do not think it will, for I cannot see how the Pope, who is supposed to symbolize peace above all, can give his blessing to a war, when such action might conceivably result in bitter factionalism in the Church.

I was grieved to hear of the tragedy at Fuschl. I feared that some day Wolfgang, who was always an impetuous person, might take too great a risk that would result in his undoing. Of course his personal hatred of Ribbentrop was very deep and he did not always consider the risks. It was more difficult, too, for Wolfgang to obtain information than it was for us others.

I understand that Clara is safe in Switzerland and is taken care of financially. Gottlieb was very good in that and his help to Clara is admirable. If we go into Russia it may be difficult to transmit my letters to Gottlieb. Therefore, if you do not hear from me for some time, do not think that I am not working with you.

In warm friendship,
MANFRED.

The same batch of reports also brought the letter we were most anxious to read. It was from Clara, written in the security of Switzerland. She had this to say:

Dear Willy:

I am sure you have heard the story of what happened to us from Gottlieb. It is now more than three weeks, but I am still stunned. It came all so swiftly, without the least warning. And it is still strange to remember suddenly that I am no longer working at the Berghof and spending hours at my listening post.

I had gone on a hike that Sunday morning. I was still a bit weak from the cold I was ill with a few weeks earlier. The weather was quite lovely and I felt that a long walk on the mountainside would do me a lot of good. Saturday night Gottlieb and I had been to the cinema and I had asked him to walk with me. But he was on duty Sunday and could not go. That is how he knew of my whereabouts.

It was early afternoon when I reached my favorite place in the mountains and I was resting after my lunch when a little boy caught up with me. He is from the family with whom Gottlieb lives and they are very good people. The boy handed me an envelope and was immediately on his way back. I found this note from Gottlieb:

"You are no longer safe at your home or at the Berghof. Do not return under any circumstances. Go immediately to B——— and remain there until you hear from me, even if it should take a few days. They have been advised by me and will care for you well. Destroy this at once."

I had not the faintest idea of what had happened but I knew Gottlieb would not take such action unless it were absolutely necessary. I burned the note. Then I went across the hills to a small mountain inn owned by the people to whom Gottlieb had sent me. They could tell me nothing except that they were instructed to hide me until further word from Gottlieb. They took me to a hay loft where I was told to remain, no matter what happened.

I spent two nights and days there and I was almost frantic with fear and uncertainty. On the third night Gottlieb arrived. He had not been able to get away from the Berghof before without arousing suspicion, because he was supposed to be among those who were searching for me. He told me the story of Wolfgang. You must know my feelings. Karl, my husband, was killed within a month after we were secretly married. Now I had agreed to marry Wolfgang and he, too, met with violent death.

Gottlieb said it was my duty to go to Switzerland, to my son. He had made preparations for my escape. Before sun-up the next morning I was to be on my way across the mountains at a certain point on the Traunstein road. A truck would come along about ten in the morning. I was to remain in hiding until the truck stopped and the driver got out to tinker with his engine. Then I was to show myself to the driver and he would know what to do.

It was a long hike and I started out before dawn. I was dreadfully tired when I reached the spot on the road, but I was almost an hour early. I hid in the underbrush close to the road and waited. Several trucks came along, but none stopped. Time was passing and I was afraid that something might have gone wrong. Finally, almost an hour late, a large, closed lorry came up the grade. It reached the top from where the road was visible for a considerable distance both ways, then stopped. The driver leaped from his seat and opened the hood of the engine. I left my hiding place and walked out on the road.

The driver, without turning, asked:

"Do you know Gottlieb?"

I answered, "Yes." He quickly glanced along the road, then walked to the rear of the lorry, opened the door and helped me climb inside. He told me to make my way to the front across boxes and bundles where I would find a space to sit down on a box. Then he slammed the door shut and I groped my way to the front end. A small window gave out on the driver's seat and it provided some light. I was surprised to find my two traveling bags in which I assumed Gottlieb had packed my most important belongings. But I did not bother looking just then. The driver asked if I was all right, and I answered yes. I seated myself on the box and the lorry rolled downhill.

The trip lasted almost an entire day. I did not know where I was going, but that did not bother me. Occasionally, when the road was free from traffic, I stood up and through the small window exchanged a few words with the driver. He was a husky Bavarian about forty years old and very decent. He said his instructions were to drop me off at a certain place and the rest did not concern him. Late that afternoon he drove up to a small inn, and before leaving the lorry, told me to be quiet. After twenty minutes we were on our way again and he shoved a package in to me which had a paper container of soup and three sandwiches. How grateful I was for that.

It was dark when we drove up to a house and stopped. The driver instructed me to wait and disappeared in the direction of the building. In a few minutes he was back and opened the door. I handed him my bags, then jumped down myself. I found myself facing a middle-aged woman who had picked up one of my bags and nodded to me to take the other. We walked around the house. I could hear the lorry starting on its way. The woman led me to a barnlike building. She opened the door and lit a lantern. In the bleak light I saw that I was standing before a ladder that seemed to lead to a hay loft. The woman whispered:

"Behind that pile of hay you will find it comfortable. Be careful not to use any light. I shall see you in the morning."

After I had climbed the ladder she handed my bags up to me and a few moments later I heard her close the door and lock it.

Clinging to my bags I scrambled across the hay. On the other side was a vacant space. In the gloom I could discern a small table, a chair and on the floor a mattress, which, when I touched it, appeared to be covered with fresh linen. A wooden wash stand was in another corner with a small mirror over it. It was evident that these good people were accustomed to giving aid to fugitives.

In the stillness I could hear the lapping of waves against wood or stone. There was a small window on the other side of the table and I stepped over to look out. I could see what was evidently a large body of water stretching far. I assumed that this must be the Bodensee, with Switzerland on the opposite shore. I felt so tired. For the first time in five days I would have a clean and decent place to sleep. I undressed, slipped between the sheets and, I think, fell asleep immediately.

I woke up when someone touched my shoulder. It was broad daylight. A slightly gray-haired woman of perhaps fifty-five stood beside the bed, smiling down at me from friendly blue eyes. She spoke in a low voice:

"Conditions must be quite bad when nice young girls like yourself are forced to flee for their lives."

Then she motioned toward the table and said:

"I have brought some breakfast. Good, plain food that will make you feel better. You will find fresh water in the pail. Try not to move around very much and stay away from the window, especially in the daytime."

My first question was, "How long must I stay here? And is Switzerland on the other side of the lake?"

She smiled and said, "Switzerland is on the other side. With God's help you may cross soon. When you will be able to cross I cannot say. It will depend on the weather."

With that she left and I was alone again.

I arose. It was a warm morning and the cold water from the pail felt good on my face and hands. I soaked a towel and rubbed down my body. It made me feel so fresh and clean. Then I realized how hungry I was. On the table were a deep plate, a spoon, a paper bag and a small dinner pail. I lifted the lid of the pail. It was filled with steaming fish soup, almost as thick as stew, with carrots and potatoes in it. The paper bag contained several slices of black bread and an apple. The soup smelled so good and I was so hungry that I just could not wait. For the first time in my life I ate a meal without any clothes on.

In one of the traveling bags I found a blouse and a pair of slacks and I slipped into them. My hiking togs had become so dusty after five days that they needed a good cleaning. I found that my bags had been packed with care and understanding. My family Bible was there and a few other mementos from my parents that I dearly cherished. On the whole I had little to complain about. Countless others had fled the country with much less.

I was forced to spend seven days at this place. Later I discovered that I had been near Immenstaad on the north shore of the Bodensee. While there I met no one except the kindly woman who came three times a day to bring my meals and other things I needed. Each night, after dark, I was permitted to spend an hour or two in the open, but always remembering to remain in the deep shadow cast by the barn. Whenever I asked about my leaving, she simply answered,

"It depends on the weather."

At times I sat, late at night, before the window. There was the lake, tauntingly before me, and I could see steam launches, motor boats and barges towed by tug boats close to shore. Frequently I could see German patrol boats armed with small guns and equipped with search-lights approach the other vessels, circle around them and occasionally stop one. I feared that I could not possibly get across with so many patrol boats in control of the lake.

Late in the afternoon of the eighth day it began to rain. The sky was a dirty gray from one end of the horizon to the other. When the little lady came with supper that evening she carried with her a dark rain-coat with a hood. She left it with me and said,

"Tonight we shall try to get you across. Be ready before midnight."

I was terribly excited and fearful and happy, all at once. I could not eat all of my supper. I packed my bags quickly and sat waiting—pray-ing. At about ten o'clock the hinges of the door squeaked and a voice called for me to come down. I handed my bags down and climbed down the ladder so quickly I almost fell. A man's voice from below warned,

"Take it easy, Fräulein, we do not want an invalid on our hands."

The woman said,

"This is my husband who will take you across. You can trust him."

I threw my arms about her and kissed her and she said, "You must not be too excited. You have a difficult journey before you."

The man, dressed in high boots, raincoat and storm hat, took my bags and told me to follow him. Outside the rain was coming down in sheets, lashing my face. Underneath the raincoat I wore my hiking out-fit, which had been cleaned. I trudged behind the man across a soggy field, stepping into puddles and trying to keep my balance in the slip-pery mud. Once I fell in the mud and my hands and face and clothes were covered with it. I did not care.

At last we reached a cove. There was a boat and another man wait-ing. It was a small boat, perhaps forty feet long, perhaps less. It had a front cabin and a mast on which the other man was hoisting the sail. The man who had guided me instructed me to go into the cabin. It was dark and musty in there and I knew I would be sick, so I begged him to let me stay in the open.

He said, "All right, but we may run into a squall or worse before we are across. If I tell you to hold, hold on with everything you have got."

The two men pushed the boat out of the cove. As the wind filled the sail, we gathered speed. I heard the rolling of thunder. Looking behind me, I could see flashes of lightning in the black sky.

The second man said, "I hope it does not catch up with us too soon."

The rain whipped against the sail, but it was not the weather that frightened me. It was the uncertainty. I prayed to be across.

We were moving rapidly, but the storm from behind us came up even faster. With every new roar the thunder sounded much closer. In the north, flashes of lightning streaked across the sky in all directions. The rain kept bearing down and one of the men was working a handpump, bailing the water. It was a night for witches and I almost felt like one.

Of a sudden one of the men shouted, "Hold!"

I had just time to grasp the railing on the cabin roof when the squall hit us. The boat reared and shook. It careened dangerously and for a moment I feared we would capsize. I clung to my hold with all my strength, till my knuckles hurt.

Then the boat righted itself. At the same time a bolt of lightning shot down with an ear-splitting roar. I closed my eyes and thought the end had come.

In another moment it was pitch-dark again, but then I heard the wail of a siren through the night. A patrol boat had probably spotted us in that flash of lightning. The searching finger of a spotlight tried to pierce through the sheet of rain. A voice shouted to crouch low, and I obeyed instantly. The siren kept wailing. But the gale that had almost capsized us took hold of the sail and was driving us through the water with amazing speed.

The two men knew their business. Probably they had made the same crossing in many a night like this. Soon the searching beam was left far behind and the siren's wail grew faint. Eventually the rain slackened somewhat and through it I could distinguish a few shimmering lights. One of the men began to haul in the sail. Presently the keel of the boat ground against a shore.

The man next to me said, "You are in Switzerland, Fräulein," and I embraced and kissed him.

He laughed and said, "It was a rough crossing but you bore it well."

I answered, "If you had locked me in that cabin I probably would have died."

I fished in the pocket of my hiking trousers for some money Gottlieb had given me, but when I handed it to him he said, "No, thank you, Fräulein. We receive our reward elsewhere."

We were expected. A male voice hailed us through the night and one of my companions answered. I heard the sound of wheels. A shape emerged from the dark and materialized into a horse and wagon. A figure jumped to the ground and the voice said, "It is an ugly night. I wondered if you could make the crossing."

"We always do," one of the men answered.

I was lifted ashore and my bags followed. I was asked to wait while the three men lifted some boxes and kegs from the wagon and stowed them inside the cabin. It did not matter to me. They could smuggle anything in the world, for all I cared. I knew that I was reasonably safe from the Gestapo.

When they had finished, the man who had taken me from the barn said, "You need not worry now, Fräulein, Joseph will see you through from here."

I could not speak. I merely shook hands with them. They leaped aboard, and in a few moments were lost in the darkness. They were brave men.

Joseph said, "Let me help you on the wagon."

I asked him where we were and he told me, "You are near Kesswil, in the Canton of Thurgau. I shall take you to an inn where you can spend the rest of the night."

He then lifted me onto the wagon, took the reins and we rolled off.

About half an hour later he left me in a clean and friendly Swiss inn where for the first time in weeks I slept in peace and comfort. The following afternoon I was with my son.

I have been here now for ten days. You have visited with these people and you know what good, kindly folk they are. I am quite safe. So long as I remain here the Gestapo will not be able to find me. Thanks to your arrangements I have no financial worries. I can draw on the fund which you established and I promise to be frugal. There will be sufficient money for our other friends if they should need it. Our requirements here are modest and the amount on deposit will last a long time.

Although I have been here only a short time, I am not accustomed to such idleness and I dearly wish I were back at my listening post. I realize, of course, that my place is with my child and, truly, we are happy together. Nonetheless I feel utterly useless. Perhaps I will be able to work further for our cause some day.

This is a nice country. Everyone here is very kind to us. I remember often, however, your stories of the United States. I am very grateful, you must know, for all the help you have provided here. But perhaps, sometime, if it is not too much trouble and it is safe for you, you will be able to bring me and my son to America. It is a presumptuous request, I know, but I long to leave here, and become active again. Thank you a million times. I shall be praying for you and for our friends back there.

With my warmest regards,
CLARA.

CHAPTER 22

WHEN WE RECEIVED Clara's letter and the other reports, we did not realize that so much time would pass before we would hear again from our German friends who had served so bravely. For almost two years our service had functioned so smoothly and with such excellent results that we had taken for granted that it would never cease. But our system was beginning to crack. Wolfgang had been first to go, then Clara. Who would be next?

About this time van Narvig and I had a serious dispute over a matter that had caused me considerable concern ever since I learned of the suicide—or murder, whichever it had been—of Heinrich Nostiz. Van Narvig had maintained a rather casual acquaintance with Tugendwald, the Gestapo representative whom he had met in connection with the Homburg letter, which eventually was surrendered to Fritz Wiedemann. Van Narvig's purpose in continuing this contact had been to gain information that might prove of interest to our authorities. However, Tugendwald was a smooth character and for a long time van Narvig could get no further than to learn a few names that he picked up during infrequent meetings with Tugendwald and others of his circle.

Among these were two who deserve particular mention. One was known to van Narvig as Theodor Gottschalk, which may or may not have been his right name as most of the German agents in the United States operated under one or more aliases. Like Tugendwald, Gottschalk had a rather tenuous connection with one of the semi-official Reich agencies in this country, probably to justify his presence and to cloak whatever activities he was carrying on. He had a desk in the German Tourist Bureau on 57th Street in New York City, but his appearances there were somewhat infrequent. At times he was not seen at the office for as long as a week. Gottschalk had a half-brother who was employed by a firm of stevedores in Brooklyn and the two had organized a gang of spotters for the purpose of collecting information on the movements of ships bound for Europe. Van Narvig was on friendly terms with Gottschalk and hoped to gain some knowledge of the operations of this group when something occurred that spoiled his chances. The State Department demanded the withdrawal of German consular and other agencies in the summer of 1941 and Gottschalk, who was carried on the official roster of the German Tourist Bureau, was forced to leave with the others. With his departure, the trail that van Narvig had been trying to follow, was obliterated.

Another of Tugendwald's associates was one Muehlendorff, who was active in New Jersey where he had established connections in shipyards and other defense industries. Muehlendorff was a field worker for the German Library of Information where he went under the rather common name of Schmidt. He was inclined to claim credit for things he didn't do if the opportunity presented itself. When part of the Hercules Powder Company's plant was destroyed by an explosion, he reported that an associate inside the plant had made it possible for him to cause the blast. Actually the Hercules explosion was the result of an accident, but Muehlendorff's claim was believed and he got himself in trouble with his superiors. Gestapo agents at that time were under strict orders to refrain from direct sabotage and to concentrate on organizing for future needs. Muehlendorff was recalled to Berlin where he apparently cleared himself, for about two months later he returned to the United States using the name of Furnesa, with, presumably, a Spanish passport. He was last reported somewhere in Texas.

Among the names that van Narvig managed to pick up were Albert Woelflein, Helmuth Federlein, Hans Joost, Wilhelm Bieder and Fritz Schmidt, who were Gestapo representatives in Chicago, Boston, St. Louis and Cincinnati, respectively. But apart from these names it was impossible, with van Narvig's slender contacts, to obtain any definite information on Gestapo activities.

During his attempts to make friends with these agents, van Narvig gained the impression that they were trying to build up a gigantic blackmail system for future use. Its foundation is supposed to be a dossier prepared by the American section of the Gestapo Foreign Department in Berlin. This is said to contain the names of some fifteen million Germans by birth or extraction now living in the United States, including citizens and non-citizens, who during the past eight years communicated by letter with relatives or friends in Germany or who received mail from them. The list contains their full names, addresses, occupations, financial status and place of employment. The Gestapo is even better informed on their relatives and friends in Germany.

The Gestapo agent first checks off the names supplied him against membership lists of local German clubs or social organizations. Where such listings are found the task is simplified, otherwise a preliminary step is required. A prospective victim is approached with the suggestion that he join such a club or society. It is pointed out to him that men and women of German blood should stick together in a foreign country, at least culturally. Where the first approach fails, pressure is applied. The victim is reminded of his or her relatives in Germany and is told they might find themselves in difficulty as a result of the refusal of the victim to associate with other German folk in America. This usually works, the victim believing that after all no harm can come from joining a cultural folk organization. The leadership of these organizations as a rule is as pro-Nazi as it dares to be without running afoul of the laws of the United States.

This done, the next step is to compromise the victim, usually by involving him in a controversial conversation in the presence of other club members. Human nature being what it is, he is reluctant to run against the expressed opinion of his associates, especially if he knows them to be devoted Germans and feels that he is regarded by them in the same light. He will voice approval of some Hitler measures, perhaps even go as far as to express the wish that Germany will win the war. With this, his doom is virtually assured.

He is next visited by a Gestapo agent, usually under an assumed name. The visit is brief and to the point. The victim is informed that he is employed by a certain factory in a specific capacity. He is a member of this or that cultural society and has repeatedly voiced sentiments that mark him as a true German patriot. The Fuehrer demands that all men and women of German blood help to establish the New Order throughout the world. The Reich is in need of certain information, which the victim is in a position to furnish. He is requested to provide this information.

The diabolical aspect of the scheme is that the initial information requested is so unimportant that the victim has no compunction about giving it because it is accessible to virtually anyone. In fact, the Gestapo does not need this particular information. The request is merely another thread in the growing net being drawn about the victim. Gradually the victim is asked for more and more information, soon of a confidential nature. If he balks at supplying this he is reminded of his father or mother, brother or sister, still in Germany and given to understand that they might come under suspicion if their close relative in America shows that he is not a good German.

Where the mere threat does not produce the desired results, the thumbscrew is actually applied. Within a few weeks the victim receives a letter from a member of his family in Germany stating that a close relative has been arrested and taken to a concentration camp, accused of conspiring with the enemies of the Reich. That the German censors permit such a letter to pass is sufficient evidence that they are under instructions to let it go through, but as a rule the victim never thinks of it that way, and anyhow, the reported arrest may be a fact.

Eventually he is again visited by the Gestapo agent who brings him confidential information that a close relative in Germany has committed a crime against the Reich and is paying for it with life imprisonment. The victim protests that his relative must be innocent, but the agent assures him that the authorities in Germany do not make mistakes of this kind. However, things can be arranged among friends. The relative's lot can be eased, or he may even be pardoned, if the pardon is won for him by the victim's compliance in the United States. At this point the victim usually becomes agreeable.

Unfortunately, all of van Narvig's information was of a general nature and purely circumstantial. He never was able to point a finger at a specific person with specific evidence. The authorities here demanded positive evidence whenever we gave them information of a circumstantial character and I saw that unless we were to go into the counter-espionage business on a large scale, nothing was to be gained. I insisted that van Narvig give up this plan, especially since a year of patient work had brought such slender results. But he continued to take a certain amount of risk in order to run down some of his leads.

About this time I experienced some difficulties in connection with my radio program. Some persons, and even organized groups, too stupid to understand what we were doing and why, protested to the broadcasting company that my work was contrary to the best interests of the United States, because I was able to give so much confidential information on what was happening in Germany, and very little about Great Britain. They did not have the sense to understand that confidential information about Britain and British plans, if broadcast, would only harm England's war effort. Some individuals went so far as to suggest that I was a paid Nazi propagandist. Much later I learned that direct Nazi influences were behind all of these persistent efforts to sabotage my work and force me off the air.

Almost two months had elapsed since we had last heard from any of our friends in Germany, and we had just about resigned ourselves to the conviction that our lines of communication had been severed and that we would receive no more news, when, one morning, van Narvig telephoned in great excitement to say that he had received some letters. He hurried over with them and we examined the package carefully. It was postmarked at Natal,

Brazil, and neither Klausmann nor anyone we knew had been involved in its delivery. However, for the moment we were not interested in the method of transmission. We hastened through the letters, one of which came from Linda. She wrote:

Dear Willy:

It has been some time since I wrote you. Gottlieb had advised me that for the time being it was impossible for him to forward anything. As it happens, little has been lost, except that I would have liked you to have personal news of me. With the war in Russia, we have been merely distant spectators and diplomatic activity in Berlin has been at an ebb.

So when Gottlieb sent word that he had succeeded in opening a new channel for you, I got busy at once. First, let me tell you that I am getting along fine. Miracles, you know, still happen. Recently Frau Goering spent a few days in Paris where she could get at whatever stocks of finery still remain. She brought a few presents for me. Among them is a swimming suit—that's what they call it, but there is extremely little of it. It has a red, white and blue color scheme—the colors of your country. I'd simply adore to have you see me in it.

But enough of frivolity. I have some serious news for you. Some of it may be dated but I am sure you would want to know it.

Some time ago Goering returned from the front long enough to give a farewell party to our Japanese visitor, General Yamashita, who had seen our panzers and Stukas hammering away at the Russians and was thrilled by the show. He remained here about six months and said he was returning with a concrete idea of what the Japanese intend to do to white imperialists in the Far East. During his stay he was given every kind of patent and manufacturing license, as well as large quantities of special flying instruments, which have already been sent to his country. The Russians were fools to let them cross their territory.

During the affair at Karin Hall I overheard a conversation between Yamashita and our Admiral Grassman, who said:

"The United States has a very strange conception of realities. She informs the world that she is building a two-ocean navy for the purpose of keeping Japan in check. Then she naïvely asks you to wait until she has this big navy ready for you."

To this Yamashita replied, "Democracies are very stupid. They think all they need to do to frighten us is to make a big noise. These foolish Americans cannot understand that we Japanese do not frighten. We are not afraid to fight and to die. And we are not going to wait until the Americans are ready for us. We are not that stupid."

In the course of the evening Yamashita asked me to dance with him and I could not refuse. We girls served as decorations and had to do our part. He was a very poor dancer. Afterward, he invited me to Tokyo.

The following morning I heard Goering and Udet discuss the various aspects of the new war. Udet is working hard, developing new plane types and aerial weapons. Among them is a larger and faster dive bomber with a device that will permit the plane to dive through balloon barrages without becoming entangled. He is also experimenting with a new armor protection for planes that is said to be lighter than aluminum yet stronger than steel armor.

Goering is not exactly satisfied with the progress of the Russian war. He confided to Udet that the German armies as a whole are considerably behind the schedule set by Keitel and that Halder's predictions are proving correct. We hear that the Russians have suffered great losses in men and equipment, but they are fighting better than any other soldiers encountered by the Germans in this war. Their fortified positions are much better defended than were those of the French. They have better equipment and more of it than our side had expected, especially in guns. Goering is afraid that unless there is a revolution against Stalin by the Russian people, the campaign may drag into another year, and in the end the Japanese will be the only ones to profit.

Goering also told Udet that Hitler is fretful and developing something of a Dr. Jekyll and Mr. Hyde complex, as Hermann called it. One day, he will tell those of his entourage how happy he will make the Russian people when they are at last under his regime. The next day, he orders wholesale executions of the populations of entire villages because some Russian guerrillas have been sniping at our supply trains in rear of the front. Goering told the gruesome story of how the entire civilian population of one village was wiped out in a few minutes, although it should have been quite obvious that the villagers could have had nothing to do with a nearby guerilla raid. The army command has no influence over Hitler now, although it is constantly pointing out Hitler's errors to him. The situation was entirely different in France. Goering is worried about Hitler.

Heinrich told me recently that serious trouble is expected in Iran. It has been known here for months that Shah Reza Pahlevi and Iranian Premier Ali Mansur are for Germany. The Iranian government claims strict neutrality, but under the surface it is not neutral at all. It banks on a German victory. The British have a monopoly on Iranian oil, which they need, but the Iranian government, lately, has been claiming that delivery of such an important war material to one belligerent to the disadvantage of another, will constitute a breach of neutrality, and has invented numerous other objections. So far as is known, only insignificant quantities of oil have been permitted to leave Iran during the last two or three months. Heinrich says it is expected here that the British will move into Iran and occupy the oil fields.

Heinrich also says that Ribbentrop is now very busy trying to control the Iranian situation. It is well known that the Iranians cannot resist Great Britain, and our people want to use certain persons now in Teheran in the future. Von Papen has notified Ribbentrop that he has permission from the Turks for Rashid Ali el Gailani, former Premier of Iraq, and Jah Amin el Husseini, former Grand Mufti of Jerusalem, both of whom had found refuge in Iran, to pass through Turkey on their way to Germany. Ribbentrop is supposed to arrange for them to reach an agreement with Subhas Chandra Bose, the Indian leader now here and who is recognized as the nominal head of Free India. The idea behind this is to form a triumvirate to sponsor a revolutionary movement against the British in India and throughout the Middle East. Ribbentrop, with little knowledge of the Orient and its peculiar ways, is in a rather bad situation.

To complicate things further for Ribbentrop, Hitler has unloaded himself of the French situation and has handed it neatly to his Foreign Minister. Ordinarily, Hitler or Goering would handle the French, but both are occupied. Otto Abetz is under instructions to delay French requests and, in reference to a peace treaty, to alternate with promises and threats, to the effect that Germany will gain all she wants and France get nothing of consequence. Hitler has definitely decided not to permit real negotiations until Laval is returned to power. On the other hand, it is quite obvious that Petain will not reinstate Laval unless subjected to heavy pressure from here. Hitler, however, deals with his problems singly, so that the French will have to wait until he reaches a satisfactory solution in Russia. This, from what we observe here, will require a great deal of time, if it ever comes to pass.

I understand from Gottlieb that he expects soon to hear from you directly, and I expect confidently that you will not forget me. Until then, this still is,

Affectionately,
LINDA.

This batch of letters also included a short one from Gottlieb, who had this to say:

Dear Willy:
After a long interval I am in a position to communicate with you again. After what happened to Wolfgang and Clara, I took it upon my-

self to suspend the activities of our group, at least for a while. I had to do this because I am in a better position to judge the situation at this end than you are. It is not that I think differently now, but at times one has to use one's head for the best interests of all concerned.

When I wrote you last I deliberately omitted several things. There were many loose ends here in connection with Clara's escape on which the Gestapo might have seized. There also must have been some indiscretion at your end. I am not certain yet exactly what it was, but it apparently connects with that wireless message which Wolfgang and Klausmann sent you from Liechtenstein after Hess' flight to England. Inasmuch as Klausmann has not shown up here again, I could not ascertain the facts. Perhaps you can.

Most of the leads from here of course pointed to Linda as Clara's closest friend, and for a time I was greatly worried. It was really fortunate that she was questioned by the Gestapo in Goering's presence and that she brushed them off the way she did. But even then I could not be sure. I know the Gestapo.

You will also be interested to know that Colonel Wartenburg was killed in action on the Russian front. I never mentioned this before, but Wartenburg was aware of some connection between you and Clara. When I arranged for her flight, I did not think of this, but later it worried me greatly. I know for a fact that Wartenburg was questioned about you and Clara. He, however, airily referred to it as just an innocent flirtation. As for Linda, he said he did not know of anything that might connect the three of you. I thought you might be glad to know this. Men like Wartenburg do not come often in our perverted world. I was sorry to hear that he lost his life.

I have nothing to report on any developments at the Berghof, for no one is here. I have this opportunity to send you these letters with the full assurance that they will reach you. There is a chance that you may experience a great surprise shortly. I cannot tell you about it now, but if you should suddenly come face to face with someone you know, do not act startled.

If I have another opportunity to communicate with you, I shall do so. Until then,

Grüss Gott!
GOTTLIEB.

The last of the letters came from Manfred, who wrote:

Dear Willy:

I have gone through the busiest weeks of my life. Hitler kept constantly moving. We stayed at Allenstein only long enough for the army to clean up scattered Russian bands in the border regions so that it would be safe for the Fuehrer to move forward. Then our travels began.

First we went to Kaunas, where a local Lithuanian government was established with great display. Needless to say, this government will exercise no more than local police power. From Kaunas we journeyed to Schaulen, to Mitau and then to Riga, where a Latvian administration was installed with similar pomp. Hitler did not go into Estonia where Red Army troops are still resisting and we went back to Windau and Libau where he inspected harbor installations with Admiral Raeder. It was decided to use the shipyards in both ports for the assembly of submarines.

For a time we remained at field headquarters, then established at Kaunas. Then we penetrated deeper into Soviet territory, to Smolensk. It was here for the first time that I realized what war is really like. I can tell you that the French campaign was kindergarten play in comparison to what is now going on in the east. To everyone's surprise, the Russians are fighting like lions, and at some places they are doing a good job. The victories in this campaign so far have been costly. Smolensk was a witness to the fury of the fighting. Three-fourths of the city is in ruins. The hotel in which Hitler stayed was the only building of any consequence in the town that showed no battle scars.

The Russians considered Smolensk the most important defense bastion on the road to Moscow. They had converted it into a fortress of a type that we had never seen before. It was not just one fortress, but an elaborate system of fortifications constructed in what is called, hedgehog fashion. It is a singularly devised defense-in-depth, said to date back to Marshal Toukhachevsky.* On a front only thirty miles wide the defense was almost a hundred miles deep, consisting of several hundred defense islands scattered over an area of three thousand square miles. There were at least forty hedgehog bodies in this area—large steel-and-concrete forts, expertly camouflaged, each garrisoned by a regiment or more, with huge underground tank garages and even plane hangars, not to mention numerous artillery emplacements. From this hedgehog body the quills shoot out in all directions. Each such quill consists of a series of smaller fortifications, starting with underground concrete blockhouses at the point nearest to the body and running out into fortified machinegun nests at the very end of the quill. The idea is that each of these defense islands composing the hedgehog quill is independent of the others. It is equipped for defense on all sides. In fact, the garrisons can sortie and attack enemy troops that have by-passed them.

*Marshal Toukhachevsky was convicted of treasonable dealings with a foreign power, presumably Germany, and was executed in 1937.

Into this Smolensk hedgehog area the Red Army had crammed some sixty divisions, or almost a million men, with large quantities of tanks and guns. They dared our armies to execute the well-known pincer movement. Field Marshal Fedor von Bock, commander on this front, did exactly that. His panzer column led by Generals Guderian and von Kleist thrust to both sides of this vast defense area. When the two pincers met at Yarzevo, about sixty miles behind Smolensk, they had accomplished nothing. Behind them was a tremendous network of Russian fortifications that could not be taken from the rear and from which Russian tank columns issued almost at will to pound our panzers. In a way, the panzer divisions found themselves cut off after accomplishing the pincers movement.

Von Bock then had to resort to another method. While the advanced panzer spearheads, reinforced by mechanized infantry and artillery, had a bad time holding off Russian assaults against both their front and rear, von Bock sent five parallel prongs from each of three different sides into this Smolensk defense zone, each of the three resembling a gigantic pitchfork stuck between the hedgehogs. Each two prongs were assigned the task of reducing, one after the other, the defense islands between them, while fleets of dive bombers continued to pound at the hedgehog bodies and quills from above. The battle turned into the most confused melee during which it was difficult to discern, at times, who were the attackers and who the attacked, because the Russians did not sit idle in the islands, but broke out with one counter-attack after another.

It was the bloodiest and most fiercely-contested battle of the entire war so far. It required eighteen days to reduce the hedgehog area and gain undisputed possession of Smolensk, which had changed hands four or five times in the course of the battle. Our total casualties were slightly under 175,000 men, or almost fifty per cent greater than during the entire Western campaign of last year. The Russians lost some 600,000 men in casualties and prisoners, with about one-third of their forces breaking through and escaping. It was the ceaselessly pounding Stukas that made all the difference. The Russians had almost no air support during the entire battle. I am giving you these details so that you will understand what sort of war this is. These Russians certainly are tough.

Hitler realizes this too. He is getting jumpy—something that never happened to him in previous campaigns. He blames his generals for this and that. He is trying to run everything himself. From the very beginning of this campaign he insisted on personally editing all communiques—a task which heretofore had been performed by von Brauchitsch's staff, usually by the Quartermaster General, Lieutenant General

Tüppelskirch. Now the communiques written by Tüppelskirch are relayed to the Fuehrer's headquarters where Colonel Thomas, chief of Hitler's headquarters staff, goes over them. Then Hitler takes a hand himself, making all sorts of changes, increasing the figures on prisoners and enemy casualties, and inserting plain political phrases.

The army command detests this practice, but nothing can be done about it now that Hitler has superimposed himself as Supreme War Lord. The generals are glad when he does not interfere with direct field operations, but even that he cannot always resist. During the battle of Smolensk he telephoned six or seven times daily to von Brauchitsch's and von Bock's headquarters, demanding to know whether the operation was concluded, and why not. If this sort of thing continues, the field commanders will be more worn out by Hitler than by the Russians. We at headquarters are sick of the sight of him and wish we had never been sent here.

I am trying to get myself transferred elsewhere and if I succeed you will hear from me shortly.

In warm friendship,
MANFRED.

There were two things about Manfred's letter we could not explain. One was that it was dated ten days before it reached us. This seemed literally impossible, especially considering the fact that the two other letters of this batch were almost three weeks old. The second was the fact that it was written in plain German, Gothic script. It had been a standing rule with our friends that all their communications be written in the code agreed upon. To us it was incomprehensible that Manfred, of all of them, should have violated this rule. Van Narvig ventured no opinion.

These three letters arrived three days before I temporarily ceased broadcasting. We were both tired. Van Narvig, who had been on constant watch for almost two years in addition to preparing the broadcasts, insisted on a long vacation. However, his idea was to combine business with pleasure.

His persistent attempts to uncover something of the Nazi machinations in the United States had brought some little success. He gained a hazy sort of knowledge that somewhere outside the United States a gathering of the principal Gestapo agents for the

Western Hemisphere would be held. He had only this vague information, but he was eager to continue the trail.

I felt it was too dangerous and asked him to forget the project, especially since we were off the air. I could not talk him out of it, but I made him promise not to leave United States territory unless he was absolutely certain that it would be safe, and to get in touch with me immediately if there was the faintest sign of danger. On this note he departed.

I did not hear from him for more than a week and I had not the faintest idea where he was. After ten days I received a telegram from him. It was from Havana!

The telegram was short and concise. It read: "Have tracked the gang down. It will be a big story."

After that one brief message days passed with no word from van Narvig. I was worried, of course, and was just ready to have him traced by American authorities when I received a long letter from him. He wrote:

Dear Wythe:

Sorry to have kept you in suspense this long time, but there was little point in communicating with you so long as I did not know very much.

I left New York with Klausmann. I told him of my suspicions and he informed me that he had heard the same rumors, but like myself he did not know where the meeting was to be held. He doubted whether any of the participants knew. So far as he knew, the Gestapo men had orders to report singly in Miami for further instructions.

Klausmann and I decided to pool our forces and we started for Miami. There I spent two pleasant days on the beach while Klausmann went about snooping. On the third day he told me that he had met a couple of men who were headed for the meeting. They had been told to report in Havana for further instructions. They were leaving that very day and he was going with them. Naturally I wanted to go along, but he dissuaded me. He had heard that Fritz Wiedemann had returned from Germany and was expected to be present, and perhaps there would be others who might know me by sight. If Klausmann and I were seen together it might be just too bad for both of us. He told me to lie low in Miami and he would let me know as soon as he thought it safe for me to come to Havana, or wherever the proceedings would take place.

Of course I did not like this, but it is useless to argue with Klausmann. He has been getting away with things ever since this war started, and he has succeeded only because he never takes outright chances. He is the epitome of caution.

So I let him go and returned to my swimming at Miami Beach. On the third afternoon I got a telegram from Havana telling me to hop across. There was no possibility of getting a plane seat that day, so I took the first plane in the morning. When I landed at the Havana airport, Klausmann was waiting for me. He led me to a closed, parked car. As I opened the door I found myself face to face with—Manfred!

For the moment I was speechless.

Manfred, prepared for this, simply smiled and said, "Hello."

I scrambled into the car. Klausmann sat beside the driver, a Cuban, who spoke English.

I asked in Russian, "Where do we go from here?" and Klausmann replied in the same language, "It's your destination. You're paying for the car."

We reached Havana in less than twenty minutes. Klausmann asked to be dropped at the Prado. He had some personal matters to attend to, he said, and further, he did not wish to be seen with us any more than was absolutely necessary.

I told the driver to take us to a nearby seaside resort. The hour was early and we had the place all to ourselves, with the exception of a few Cuban women and their children. We settled down in the shade and Manfred told me his story.

While trying to be transferred from Hitler's field headquarters, he said, he learned that Reinhardt Heydrich, chief aide of Himmler, was to make a rapid trip to South America and was looking for members of his staff who were familiar with American conditions. Manfred applied and was among those chosen.

The party went to Madrid where they were provided with Spanish passports and other necessary credentials. They flew in a specially chartered plane to Dakar in French West Africa and there boarded a Transatlantic plane of the Italian Lati line, which carried them across to Natal, Brazil. It was from there that Manfred mailed the last letters we received, but he considered it inadvisable to notify me of his nearness. They had to wait there for the arrival of Heydrich's main party, which also included Heinrich Stahmer, Erich Wendler and Fritz Wiedemann. These three, together with others, but not Heydrich, were scheduled to continue to Japan for special purposes of their own.

By various routes the different parties arrived at Havana where a Gestapo conference attended by Himmler's principal agents in the

Americas was in progress. While there, the Gestapo men were meeting in small groups to avoid attention. One meeting, which Manfred attended immediately on arrival, was held in a sumptuous residential structure owned by one of Hitler's Cuban devotees and located in the fashionable Miramar suburb.

Not having been previously connected with the foreign branch of the Gestapo, Manfred did not know any of the agents personally, but he had remembered and written down a few names. Among these were Federmann, Kempter and Bruntzer from Brazil; Sandstede and Fonseca from Argentina; Gaertner and Monteros from Chile; Osternfried from Colombia; Aziaga from Guatemala; Herrero from Venezuela; and Bedacht, Kringelein, Aussendorf, Beljitzky, Valleo and Furnesa from the United States.

Only one general meeting was held and this on the night before I arrived. It was held on a large plantation in Pinar del Rio province, about seventy-five miles to the southwest of Havana. While he had no positive evidence, Manfred had every reason to assume that this plantation served as a sort of general staff headquarters for the Gestapo in the Caribbean zone. When departing at night, he had observed over the main building the high steel mast of a powerful radio antenna, probably of a collapsible type since it had not been noticed during the day. As Manfred told me later, it must have been over this station that an order came in for the immediate return of Heydrich to Germany.

The meeting at the plantation was the only one at which Heydrich made an official speech, so far as Manfred knew. Otherwise the activity of Himmler's principal henchman consisted of private conversations with the principal sub-chiefs for the Americas at which he gave definite instructions on the new organization set-up and the policy to be pursued. Manfred had counted seventy-eight participants at the plantation meeting, who probably included all those summoned to Havana. Since the Gestapo machine in the Western Hemisphere had more than two thousand direct agents, it was obvious that only the pick of these had been summoned for the conference.

As given by Manfred, here is the organizational plan: Latin America and the United States will be two separate entities. The whole of Latin America will be divided into five separate districts of Gestapo activity. Manfred gave me the dividing geographical lines, but these are not important. Each district will be under the command of a regional Gestapo chieftain who will be responsible to the continental Gestapo leader, whose seat will be in Buenos Aires. A relative of Heydrich will occupy this post. Where heretofore the Gestapo and the propaganda bureau were handled as separate organizations, they will now be combined.

The policy will be twofold. Propaganda will concentrate on the political, national and ideological differences between Latin America and the United States, to promote bad feeling with the United States. In this the Falangist activity of the House of America will assist. In fact, the Falangists will have a major part. The aim is to lay the groundwork for a secret police organization that will be prepared to step forward the moment totalitarian governments are established.

All Gestapo and propaganda activity in the United States will concern itself with Hitler's war effort. Berlin believes that it will be only a matter of months before an official state of war between the Axis and the United States is declared. Berlin does not think that the United States will be in a position to fight effectively for at least another year. During that time there is to be only underground organization by Gestapo men in the United States. Not a single open act of sabotage is to be committed. These are strict orders, based on the theory that it is foolish to hack piecemeal and jeopardize later successes so long as the pickings are relatively insignificant. The sabotage machinery is to be organized for later action. The signal for such action will be given by Berlin at the proper time. Meanwhile no one is to make himself suspect.

This was only part of Manfred's story—in fact, the less important part. I am giving this to you first because in a way it is the culmination of our efforts of the past fifteen months in trying to find out what the Gestapo plans to do. The second part has nothing to do with the Gestapo, but it is much bigger because it deals with events that will strike seriously at our country soon, and it is not prepared.

Stahmer, Wendler and Wiedemann have no direct connection with the Gestapo meeting here. They were window dressing, so to speak, to impress the little men of the Gestapo. It happens that they are waiting about because they are not due at Valparaiso, Chile, for ten days. There they will board a Japanese steamer that will take them to the Marshall Islands whence a plane will carry them to Japan.

Stahmer will be Hitler's envoy to the Imperial Court of Manchukuo (do not forget that the Japanese armies will be in a position to strike at Russia's rear in Siberia if this should be required by Axis strategy). Wiedemann will be German Consul General in Shanghai, at least that will be his official title. Actually he will be in charge of the Gestapo in the Far East. Wendler will be German Minister in Thailand, where Japan will be master in a few months. Yes, just that.

Between Hitler and the Japs it is all set. Stahmer will be joined in Valparaiso by a special German army mission—Field Marshal Milch has been mentioned. These Germans are now dealing directly with the Jap army and navy. On their arrival in Tokyo, the present Japanese cabinet of Prince Konoye will retire, to be replaced by an outright army regime.

The Japs are preparing frantically for the next break of the season in Southeast Asia and the East Indies. This means we shall have no more than three or four months of peace at best. We will be in the war, up to our neck. The Japs will not wait for us to go to war against them. They will go to war against the United States, the British and the Dutch, all at one time. So will Hitler and Mussolini. Their plan is to catch us while we are still preparing.

I informed Manfred of the conferences now taking place in Washington, as a result of Prince Konoye's personal letter to President Roosevelt, which suggested a peaceful adjustment of outstanding differences between the United States and Japan. Manfred laughed bitterly. He asked if I remembered the Russians and Port Arthur in 1904. He said this was only a Jap appeasement move used as a blind from behind which Japan was preparing to strike. Tokyo wants Washington to believe that Japan is frightfully weakened when the exact opposite is the case.

We drove back to Havana and stopped at the place where we had left Klausmann. We entered one of those open bars and there he was waiting. While we drank the juice of three pineapples, Klausmann told me that he had arranged for the luncheon party which we had tentatively discussed while driving from the airport. Manfred said that if I got there ahead of time and played my role well I could easily verify much of the information he had given me. I had to give Klausmann money with which to pay for the luncheon party. He is a tightwad from the word go, which is why he has provided for his old age. I had paid his expenses to Miami and even his plane ticket to Havana. He wouldn't lay out a cent, though I'm certain he profits greatly from this affair in a way all his own.

I attended to a few personal matters, which included my telegram to you, and at the appointed time had myself driven to the restaurant. It was a quaint little place with a small patio, and rather exclusive. So, too, were the prices they charged, and I understood Klausmann's request for the money. Not a patron was there when I arrived, but I noticed several tables placed together and laid out for a larger party. I selected a table nearby.

I was at my hors d'oeuvres when the group arrived. There were eight; Manfred and Klausmann were among them. So was Dr. Stahmer, whom I instantly recognized from photographs. Two were definitely Cubans and they were rather prosperous-looking. The remaining three I could not place.

I remained at my table with my back turned to the party, ostensibly occupied with my food. But I could hear quite well. Stahmer was drawn into conversation by Klausmann and the two Cubans were quite attentive. From the way Stahmer outlined Hitler's Japanese policy I could easily gather that the two were considered of importance in the Nazi foreign machine. The conversation confirmed virtually all that Manfred had told me. I wish I could have had our State Department listening in.

I was seated so that I had a direct view of the entrance. I heard a strange noise outside and then two uniformed men with submachine guns marched up the flagstone walk and placed themselves on each side of the door.

For a moment I had the crazy notion that the Cuban government had learned of what was going on, on its hospitable island, and had thrown out the dragnet. This was promptly dispelled, however. An important looking man in white walked in and was bowed to a secluded table. He was President Fulgencio Batista of Cuba. I learned later that he frequently lunched here.

Presently, one of the Cubans arose with Dr. Stahmer and walked toward the President's table. The Cuban, apparently acquainted with the President, made the introductions, but I could hear nothing. The conversation among the three lasted a few moments and I do not believe that President Batista realized who Stahmer was. It rather seemed to me that the Cuban wanted to make an impressive showing before Stahmer.

Eventually, there were more newcomers. One was a complete stranger to me. Only later I learned that it was Wendler. But the other was Wiedemann, whom I knew well and who was not supposed to see me. I was in rather a bad spot. I knew the two had not been invited, nor were they expected.

If I stood up and turned directly toward the door I'd find myself face to face with Wiedemann, who would certainly recognize me. He might possibly have recognized me, just seeing the side of my face. I hoped he would leave at once, but instead he drew up a chair and asked for a glass of wine. And I had paid for that wine!

I finished my luncheon, which I had dragged out as long as possible. I then began to write post cards. I called the waiter and asked him for stamps. After that I could not very well linger more. I stood up and turned to the door. I had to squeeze past Wiedemann's chair. As I came abreast of him I stopped abruptly, looked what I hoped was truly surprised and exclaimed, "Captain! The last man I expected to meet in Havana. I understood you were back in Germany."

From the corner of my eye I could see Klausmann turning pale, almost yellow. Manfred was continuing to talk with Stahmer and the Cubans.

Wiedemann rose and I was sure that he had recognized me at the table.

He said, "Isn't it strange the way people meet in out-of-the-way places? What are you doing in Havana?"

I told him I was on my vacation in Florida and had decided to fly across to Havana to meet an old girl friend of mine. I had arrived in the morning, but the lady had not yet turned up, so I was left to my own devices. I knew this would strike a receptive note with Wiedemann, who adores the fair sex and is considered rather a gallant. Then I asked him how he happened to be in Havana.

He said he was actually on his way to the Far East, but that, with time to spare, it occurred to him that he had a few odds and ends to straighten out. Since Havana was the nearest place to the United States, that's why he was there. Then he invited me to join the party.

With a man like Wiedemann one can never tell. He may have believed my story, or he may not. I was sure that Klausmann would never forgive me if I accepted. So I told Wiedemann it was time for me to seek out my friend. He laughed and I left.

At the appointed hour, I drove up to the former meeting place and Manfred was there. Klausmann had thought it best not to come. Instead he sent a note through Manfred. In it he asked me to leave Havana that same day to avoid meeting others who might recognize me. Wiedemann, he said, had not seemed suspicious, but one could never tell. Klausmann wrote that he would meet me in New Orleans in about a week and he might have something for me there.

Manfred suggested that I follow Klausmann's advice. Anyway, I could learn nothing more in Havana. Manfred himself was scheduled to leave with Heydrich's party that same night and the other Gestapo men were about to return to their posts in North and South America. I checked timetables and found that the last plane left Havana at four that afternoon. Manfred drove with me to the airport. I caught the plane and by night I was back in the United States.

Make the best you can of this information.

As ever,
BILL.

CHAPTER 23

UNFORTUNATELY I WAS NOT on the air at this time and so I was unable to make use of van Narvig's amazing information in a broadcast. But I went to Washington and passed the report on to our authorities. They were interested in the information regarding the Gestapo, but the most important part of the report—the Japanese angle—was all but ignored. Their view was that while Hitler would like nothing better than to see Japan go to war against the United States, Japan was already negotiating with this country for a peaceful settlement of all outstanding differences and would be weaned away from Hitler. I asked permission to incorporate the information obtained in a series of magazine articles and was told to go to any length on the Gestapo business, but was advised to refrain from using anything about Japan. It would prove embarrassing, I was told, to write anything so sensational about Japan at a time when negotiations had been initiated between the two governments.

Van Narvig returned to New York one month after his departure. By that time I had a series of magazine articles virtually completed and I wanted him to go over them. I also wanted to add anything that had occurred in New Orleans.

"I'm afraid there's little to add," van Narvig said.

"Didn't Klausmann show up?" I asked.

"He did, and he gave me a few additional details on the Havana business which I have already sent you," van Narvig said. "There was nothing more worthwhile. Klausmann is winding up some unfinished business here, then he leaves for South America. He believes that will be a more fertile field hereafter than the United States. He promised to keep in touch with me. If something important turned up, he said, I might run down and get a big story."

"That would be an expensive trip," I commented. "We're only free lances and must pay our own way."

"Anyway, about New Orleans," van Narvig said, after a

silence, "Klausmann put me on the trail of a fellow who, he said, had returned from Havana. It proved a good tip, too. I followed him through Louisiana and Texas. There were army maneuvers going on in that area at the time and that may be why he was there.

"I lost him for a time but caught up with him again in Texarkana. It was there that I became certain of his mission. I saw him meet another chap and this one I knew. It was Muehlendorff, who used to be one of Tugendwald's associates in New York before he was recalled to Germany. But here I pulled a boner, and I can kick myself for it. I thought I might get close to the two, and so I walked up and said, 'Hello, Muehlendorff, glad to see you again.' He didn't bat an eye. He said I must be mistaken. His name was not Muehlendorff and he had never set eyes on me before. Before I knew it the two had disappeared and I never caught up with them again."

We made a deal with a magazine publisher for the series of articles. But a serious hitch developed. The editors wanted positive proof and demanded that we produce either Klausmann or Manfred, or if possible both. This, of course, was impossible. Neither was available. Even if they had been, it was doubtful if they would have agreed to increase the number of people who knew of their activities by even one more. Certainly Klausmann would not. And so the deal fell through and the articles were never published.

Subsequently the State Department revealed that Hitler had drawn up a plan to divide Latin America into five separate states under Nazi domination. Together with this information came a map. The boundaries on it coincided exactly with what van Narvig had learned in Havana about the five Gestapo districts that had been established. This indicated, we believed, that the State Department had obtained information on the Havana business through channels other than our own. The information could have come only from Klausmann, and this tied in with van Narvig's belief that Klausmann was engaged, directly or indirectly, in some sort of espionage work for the benefit of the

United States. This was probably the reason he was always so careful. The Government's announcement identified the districts as Nazi states when we knew them as Gestapo districts, but we felt that was to give the story added flavor.

Shortly after this, something happened that confirmed a long-standing theory held by van Narvig and myself that Nazi influence in the United States was standing in the way of my getting a new radio contract. Some old friends of mine returned from France and were astonished to find me in New York. I couldn't understand this, for I had not been out of New York. Then they told me they had heard me broadcasting for the Nazis in Occupied France just before they left for this country. They said they had heard me say over the air that I had recanted on my anti-Hitler attitude and was now wholeheartedly for the Nazi Fuehrer. They considered me a traitor and I had great difficulty in convincing them that it could not possibly have been me, because I had not been in Europe for several years.

Subsequent investigation proved that the Nazis actually had been using my name for one of their propagandists broadcasting over Hilversum and several other continental stations in Occupied Europe. These broadcasts had started three weeks after I had ceased broadcasting in the United States. The whole scheme evidently was calculated to make it appear as though I had gone directly to Germany after my broadcasts here had ceased and had sold myself to Hitler.

Van Narvig and I discussed the subject from every possible angle. There was no question in our minds that the same people who had moved heaven and earth in this country to get the network to drop my broadcasts were directly connected with that treacherous move by the Nazi broadcasters. This made it appear rather obvious that some people here who pretended to be great American patriots, probably were secretly working in Hitler's interests. Van Narvig believed that the Gestapo had been behind the scheme. He also felt certain that it was connected with that wireless message from Liechtenstein the text of which I had inadvertently revealed in that magazine article, thus giving the Gestapo a lead toward tracing the connection.

It was a long time until we again heard from our friends in Germany. Two letters arrived, once more by the way of South America. One was from Linda, who wrote:

Dear Willy:

I am in rebellion against Fate. Why doesn't the Gestapo send women on its foreign assignments? Why have other people all the luck? Why was it Manfred, and not I, who could go to America?

However, I am grateful. I found comfort in the letter and the other things that you sent through Manfred. They made me very happy, and so I shall carry on.

There is nothing to report from Karin Hall. Goering has been at his field headquarters near Dubno, or otherwise on the Russian front, all this time. I wonder how he likes it. They say that our men wade through a great deal of Russian mud. But then I expect our Hermann is flying—he never did like to walk.

The lull at Karin Hall gives me a chance to go and see Heinrich more often than before, but he too has little information. Last week, however, he told me some interesting things about the Russian war. But you probably know all about events there as quickly as we do.

On the whole the campaign is not going as expected. Keitel's time-table has been torn to shreds and discarded. Halder, events have proved, was more accurate in his estimates than any of the others, and now he refuses to commit himself to any predictions as to the time required to complete the campaign. Von Brauchitsch is a sick man—he has a liver ailment—and Hitler's constant interference in the campaign aggravates his condition. The rumors are that he may retire before long.

The army's inability to maintain the fast tempo against the Russians that it had established in previous campaigns is causing repercussions behind the front. There is serious unrest in Yugoslavia. Ante Pavelich, the Poglavnik of Croatia, is managing affairs badly and his Ustachi bands in many places have turned into plunderers who are said to be robbing the peasants of Serbia. Numerous bands of Serb Chetniks have been formed in self-defense and some pitched battles have been fought between the two groups. This has led to the formation of a Serb revolutionary army under a Colonel Mikhailovich* which has driven the

*Colonel, now General, Draja Mikhailovich, former leader of the Serb revolutionary army that has caused the Nazis and Italians no end of trouble.

Italian occupation forces from many sections of the country. Field Marshal List, who commands our forces in the Balkans, has been forced to detail some of his troops against the Serb revolutionaries, but he has few reserves to draw on and consequently has made little headway. He has asked for four additional divisions, which Hitler is not giving him.

The Communists, who have been quiet ever since the war began in 1939, are now making trouble, and numerous arrests have been made in Norway, France, and in Belgium. Even the Czechs are getting unruly. There has been considerable unrest and sabotage, and numerous strikes have occurred throughout the Protectorate. Considerable numbers of shells made in Czech factories have turned out to be duds, and this is said to have affected the progress of the army in Russia. Things do not look too well. There is talk that the war against the Russians may have been a mistake.

Last week Heinrich passed on some information that will be of considerable interest to you. Hitler came from the front to Berlin for two days and Ribbentrop had a long conference with General Oshima, the Japanese Ambassador. Oshima has been in communication with General Tojo, the new premier, who has advised him that Japan will soon be ready to strike southward. This means the Dutch East Indies and Singapore.

Heinrich says there is just one hitch. Oshima has asked Hitler pointblank whether Hitler will implement that part of the Tripartite Pact that calls for Germany to declare war against the United States if Japan does. The Japanese militarists take the viewpoint that any movement southward will constitute an outright gamble unless they succeed in taking the Philippines at the same time. They contend that to leave this American outpost on their flank would endanger their entire enterprise. Therefore, they want to go to war against the United States at the same time that they open hostilities against the British Empire. According to their interpretation of the agreement, it would be up to Hitler to keep considerable American naval forces occupied in the Atlantic. Hitler is not so sure whether he likes this part of it. If the Russian war had developed as he had anticipated, he would have unhesitatingly acceded, for in his calculations with regard to the United States he had counted on disposing of the Russians in one campaign. Now it has become doubtful if this can be done.

The ironic part of it all is that it was Hitler himself who had pressed the Japanese toward war with Great Britain in order to draw British forces away from Suez and the Levant to the Far East. Now it is the Japanese who are pressing for action, eager to seize their golden opportunity. Heinrich says he cannot see how Hitler could avoid his commitments to Japan without endangering the Axis structure. This means that Germany will have to go to war against the United States, while she is still heavily involved in Russia. Heinrich has heard that after the conversation with Oshima, Hitler called in Raeder and Doenitz* for a consultation. Nothing definite is known, but Heinrich believes that Doenitz was instructed to prepare his entire fleet of long-range submarines for action in American waters.

That is the way matters stand at present. The situation will probably remain in a state of flux until Hitler has definitely made up his mind. Judging from past experiences, this is apt to be any day. As soon as there are some definite indications, I shall try to let you know.

Once again, I was so glad to receive your letter.

Affectionately,
LINDA.

The second letter came from Manfred. It was one of the most interesting we had ever received. It read:

Dear Willy:

When I had myself transferred from Hitler's headquarters to Heydrich's staff it was in order to escape from a madhouse. Now it appears that I went from the frying pan straight into the fire. To be connected with Heydrich in his present work is the same as doing yeoman service in hell.

But let me start from the beginning. As I told you in Havana, we had been ordered to make a speedy journey and to return as quickly as possible. We did not make any overnight stops after leaving America and completed the flight from the Caribbean to Germany in the incredible time of five days. Immediately upon arrival in Berlin, Heydrich was appointed Acting Protector of Bohemia and Moravia, in the place held by Baron Konstantin von Neurath. The next day Heydrich and his entire staff, including myself, were installed in the Czernin Palace in Prague.

To give you a clear understanding of events, I shall attempt a brief retrospect. As you know, the Czechs were very quiet during the Polish campaign and, in fact, up to the beginning of the war with Russia. Even during the first month of this war, things were relatively calm. But when it became evident that the Russians were putting up a stiff

---

*Admiral Karl Doenitz, Naval Chief of Staff of the German U-boat fleet. In January, 1943, Admiral Doenitz was appointed Grand Admiral and in this capacity succeeded Grand Admiral Raeder as Commander-in-Chief of all German Naval forces.

resistance, the situation in the Protectorate changed. The Czechs decided that Russia was going to be Hitler's nemesis, and they determined to do their part to bring it about. They went on a rampage.

Sporadic small-scale sabotage had been noticeable in late July, but it was in August that the trouble really began. A brand new Autobahn* leads from Vienna by way of Bruenn and Silesia to the principal army supply depots in Poland. Vast quantities of ammunition and other supplies produced in the Austrian factories and in the Protectorate travel over this route in a steady flow, day and night, because of the absence of a direct waterway connection between these Reich territories and the German rear on Russia's central front. In the vicinity of Olmuetz, the Autobahn passes over a series of high bridges crossing the valleys formed by numerous branches of the Morava River. Although heavily guarded by storm troopers, the two principal spans were blown up on the night of August 14th and all traffic was suspended for sixteen days. The perpetrators were never found, but twenty-four storm troopers were executed for criminal negligence.

Likewise in August, a German motorized division fighting in the Roslavl sector of the central front in Russia discovered that fully two-thirds of its artillery shells were duds. The shells had been manufactured at a factory near Tabor in the Protectorate. The whole personnel of the factory—800 persons—was arrested and sent to a concentration camp where some of them "confessed." The result was 78 executions and three times this number of prison sentences. Italian munitions workers were sent to the factory, but the resultant production delay occasioned by the shut-down extended through three weeks. A direct result of this act of sabotage was the virtual annihilation of that motorized division by a Russian counterattack.

But this was only the beginning. Whether a concerted movement existed among Czech munitions workers directed by a central leader, or whether it was independent and spontaneous in each case, the fact remains that in late August and early September considerable quantities of artillery duds were found in various sections of the Russian front. In some cases, German offensive operations were brought almost to a halt because of this. The duds came from numerous shell-loading plants in the Protectorate, both large and small. The army command recognized that it was dealing with a dangerous situation and demanded drastic measures.

On September 7th, while I was still in America, Baron von Neurath, the comparatively easy-going Reich Protector, summoned a conference at the Czernin Palace. Among those present were the Czech President,

*Germany's new motor express highways are called Autobahnen.

Hacha, Premier General Elias and Chief Inspector Huber of the Gestapo. It was decided to cut the food rations of the Czech population in half, this reduction to last until the saboteurs were apprehended and delivered to the authorities.

What followed was not quite what the conferees had anticipated. On September 10th workers of three factories in the Prague suburbs went on strike, the first time this had occurred since Reich occupation. Two days later virtually all factories in Bruenn followed suit. On September 15th, the workers of the vast Skoda munitions plants near Pilsen stayed at home. Within one week nearly 1,500,000 workers, men and women, had refused to work. Not a wheel turned and industrial activity in the Protectorate, so vital to the Nazi war program, ceased.

The same week witnessed outbreaks of mass sabotage on a scale never before attempted. Factories staffed predominantly by German, Italian and Bulgarian workers continued operation, and it was against these that the saboteurs went to work. A large chemical factory near Lutin was wrecked by several explosions, with a loss of 116 lives, in addition to 500 injured. The blast occurred during the night while the night shift was on. A power plant at Tabanice, supplying electricity for a dozen large factories in the surrounding district, was put out of commission by strewing gravel between the moving parts of generators. Fire of incendiary origin destroyed large stocks of buna* in a tire factory at Vlasin and caused serious damage to factory buildings. During the night of September 15th several rail sections were unbolted on the roadbed south of Prague. The Budapest-Berlin express, racing past at dawn, crashed down the embankment. Among the thirty-six killed and two hundred injured, were two generals and several Gestapo officials returning from Serbia. The saboteurs must have received advance information about the passengers. These are just a few happenings in that hectic week.

The blow that really damaged most was struck in the early morning hours of September 18th. All Czech workers of the huge Skoda plant— one of the largest in Europe, as you well know—had been on strike for three days. But some specialized departments were operated by imported workers and still in production. One of them made vital parts for armored cars used in large numbers in the Russian war as armored cavalry. These particular armored cars are based on a former Czech model and some of their parts are manufactured almost exclusively at Skoda. While the department was under particularly heavy guard because of the strike, it was rocked by a tremendous explosion and a large part of it was destroyed by the resultant fire. The damage was so

*Synthetic rubber material.

extensive that operations had to be suspended for thirty days. In fact, the military damage caused by this single act of sabotage was greater than that caused by British night bombings of any German city to date.

Hitler, when told of the situation, at his eastern front headquarters near Chernigov in the occupied Ukraine, made a hurried trip to Breslau. There he was met by Goering and Himmler. The latter insisted that he could not allow Hitler to continue to Prague because, under existing conditions, he could not guarantee the Fuehrer's safety there. This was too much for Hitler, who raged and ranted and then, at Himmler's suggestion, ordered the dismissal of Reich Protector Baron von Neurath, who was instructed to retire to his estate in Wuerttemburg, there to await the Fuehrer's displeasure. Himmler suggested that Heydrich be appointed with orders to bludgeon the Czechs into "unqualified submission." That is where we entered the picture.

From the very outset Heydrich—whom the Czechs call "Reznik"*—was extraordinarily lucky. On the Protector's desk he found a report concerning the discovery of a secret Czech radio transmitter that had operated from a point in the Bohemian Forest. This station, the report asserted, had been in constant communication with the Czechoslovak government-in-exile in London, although later on it became known that instructions had actually been emanating from Russia, not London. Evidence in the report seemed to point to two men known to be old friends of the Czech Premier, General Alois Elias.

Heydrich, conforming with established Gestapo custom to start all clean-ups from the top, summoned General Elias. He was prevented from going after President Hacha because the latter was seriously ill. The fact that both Hacha and Elias had loyally co-operated with the Nazi authorities counted for nothing with Heydrich. As a matter of record, it was definitely established later on that Elias had had no connection with treasonable activities. Neither had his two friends. They had merely expressed the opinion that Nazi strength was too formidable even to think of a revolt and that any such attempt would only cause untold suffering among the Czech people. This opinion had been relayed over the secret radio transmitter, without the knowledge of the two men involved.

Heydrich demanded of General Elias the issuance of a Czech decree declaring that all food ration cards held by striking workers and their families were forfeit. Storekeepers issuing provisions against the invalidated cards would be subject to the death penalty. Elias declared that he would not participate in such an inhuman measure that struck alike at the guilty and the innocent. Heydrich had the General arrested

*In Czech, meaning, the butcher. Heydrich also was known as the Hangman.

on the spot. That same evening he was brought before a specially convoked military court, and after a routine procedure of only fifteen minutes, he was convicted of "preparing to commit high treason" and sentenced to death.

The next day, Czech Deputy Premier Jaroslav Krejci, Minister of the Interior General Jezek, and Minister of Communications Dr. Havelka, were arrested and promptly sentenced to death for "contemplated treason against the State." They, too, in a session of the Czech government, had refused to sanction the measure proposed by Heydrich. Within twenty-four hours, sixteen high Czech officials committed suicide in preference to being dragged before Nazi courts.

When Heydrich failed in his attempt to pin the responsibility of his contemplated measure on the Czech government, he resorted to a technicality in the Protectorate Statutes. He proclaimed a state of civil emergency in the nine industrial key districts affected by the strike. This placed all civil officials under the military command, and Heydrich found himself in a position to promulgate whatever measures he deemed most effective without consultation with the Czech government. He decreed a ten o'clock curfew; any person found on the streets after the affixed hour was subject to immediate arrest or, in the event of attempted flight or resistance, to being shot on the spot. All meeting halls, theaters, concert halls and other places of amusement were closed. The possession of firearms or explosives was punishable by death. Persons approaching within two hundred meters of any railroad right-of-way or main highway would be shot on sight. Damage to industrial property of any sort carried the death sentence without any right of appeal. The ration cards of all workers who did not return to their jobs, as well as their families, would be invalidated in three days.

General Elias was not executed. On the second day after his "trial," he was brought before Heydrich. With his customary suave manners, Heydrich lectured the General on the futility of opposing the Reich. The General replied with dignity that he and his associate ministers had at all times co-operated with Reich authorities. In spite of this loyal attitude he found himself condemned to death for no valid reason. Under the circumstances he would appreciate it if the sentence were carried out with no further delay.

Heydrich is a past master in the art of torture. Not torture by flogging, kicking or beating. These crude forms of violence Heydrich leaves to the small fry in the Gestapo machine. His methods are more studied and refined, therefore more effective. He specializes in torture of the soul.

While Heydrich was talking to General Elias a subordinate entered with a batch of documents that he placed on the desk for his chief's signature. Heydrich said he would attend to the matter presently and the subordinate withdrew. A few moments later Heydrich was called from the room. Of course there was a peephole watcher. He saw the General quickly glance at the topmost document, then rise and look through the papers. Four of them were pardons for Elias and the other condemned ministers. A fifth was an order for the execution of the General's family.

When Heydrich returned, the following conversation developed:

Elias: "These papers were left for me to read, of course. I did. What do you want me to do?"

Heydrich: "It was a mistake to leave the documents on my desk."

Elias: "Let's not quibble over the technical details of your methods."

Heydrich: "The Fuehrer places emphasis on the utmost leniency and generosity. Alas! there are cases where leniency reacts against the vital interests of the Reich."

Elias: "What do you want me to do?"

Heydrich: "Maintenance of order and discipline in the Protectorate are vital to Reich security. You are better informed on local problems than the authorities representing the Reich. I should like to know whom the Czech population might come to regard as potential leaders of a revolt."

Elias: "To the best of my knowledge there are no such leaders."

Heydrich: "I believe I stated distinctly, potential leaders. Even remote possibilities must enter advance calculations. I am not in the habit of taking chances."

Elias: "What would happen to such men?"

Heydrich: "I have no direct authority in the matter. It will be entirely in the hands of the courts to decide, after careful weighing of the evidence."

Elias: "The courts will be extremely handicapped because there can be no evidence."

Heydrich: "In that case you ought to be fully reassured."

The General hesitated. Heydrich pulled out the fifth document and dipped his pen into the inkstand. General Elias broke down.

On the following day, Generals Josef Svatek, Hugo Votja, Michael Dolezal, Franz Horacek and Joseph Bily were summarily executed. The last two were those who had expressed the opinion that attempted revolt would lead to great suffering among the Czechs. So far as I know, there was no court procedure.

On that very morning a fire broke out, in a warehouse in a Prague suburb, which consumed large numbers of army shoes. Heydrich had

Otokar Klapka, the Nazi-appointed mayor of Prague, arrested and executed for "criminal negligence in office." Two days later Gestapo investigators reported that the fire had originated from a short circuit in the electric wiring. Both these Gestapomen disappeared. They should have known better.

The fact is that Heydrich was none too certain that his brutal measures would be successful. He feared that the strike might develop into a general revolt, like the one in Serbia, with mass assaults on munitions factories and food depots. This fear prompted him to do away with the men who might conceivably lead such a revolt. He also brought an additional 70,000 storm troopers into the Protectorate, raising the total occupation forces—Gestapo and military—to almost 300,000 men. The vicinity of the Skoda works alone was garrisoned by some 30,000 troops. All this vividly illustrated the anxiety felt for this important industrial bastion in Central Europe.

The fears proved exaggerated. The Czechs, faced with starvation, submitted. When the three-day ultimatum expired, the vast majority returned to their jobs. Factory wheels were humming again. Railroad and trucking lines resumed their regular schedules. Production returned to normal. A few of the saboteurs were denounced and executed. The crisis passed. From the front Hitler telegraphed Heydrich his thanks for a "splendid handling of an explosive situation."

Heydrich is now firmly entrenched. Having put down a brewing revolt with strong measures, he is now more than ever convinced of the efficacy of his ruthless methods. During the first ten days of his rule in the Protectorate he ran up a record of 1,216 executions. The official register for the same period shows 425 cases of suicide. The number of those who secretly ended their lives is unknown.

This is the tragic story as I have seen it. Frankly, I feel I must get away from this sort of thing. I shall try to get back to my old position at Hitler's headquarters. Even that is preferable to this. If I succeed I may be able to write you again.

In warm friendship,
MANFRED.

Transmission of reports from Germany now became more difficult than ever. It was a long time before we again heard from our friends there. As a matter of fact, the following batch of letters did not reach us until long after the United States had been treacherously attacked by the Japanese, and Hitler had served upon our country his declaration of war. The letters came to us via a long detour over South America.

The first of these reports was from Manfred, who wrote:

Dear Willy:

I did succeed in getting away from Heydrich's staff and back to my old post at Hitler's field headquarters. In a way, the change did me some good. Again there has been a great deal of travel about the occupied areas of Russia, so that I am able to give you a fairly comprehensive picture of conditions here.

To begin with, the destruction here is not nearly so all-embracing as the Russians claim. This is especially true in the southwest. Bessarabia was taken largely undamaged. There is every reason to believe that she will produce a fairly substantial crop next summer. In Ruthenia, the larger cities suffered most of the damage. Lemberg* is half destroyed, so are Tarnopol and Stanislau. The Galician oil wells were partly dynamited by the Russians, but it was a poor job, and their restoration is well under way. It is expected that the wells will be in operation before spring.

Farther east, Odessa is fairly wrecked. The peculiar part, however, is that the Russians did the most damage to buildings. They left the port facilities in good shape, except that the main channel is blocked by wrecked vessels that must be cleared away. The reason for this is that the Russians tried until the very last to evacuate as much as possible by sea and needed these facilities. When our armies moved in there was no time to complete the destruction. Nikolayev and Kherson fell into our hands virtually intact. Some last-minute demolition was attempted in the shipyards, but it was only partly successful. Several half-finished warships were left on the ways and the chances are that these may be completed at some future time.

The mining properties in the Krivoi Rog district could be operated at once if the labor were available, but most of the miners were evacuated by the Russians. Their families remained, but these are, for the most part, women and children. Dniepropetrovsk was largely destroyed. What machinery the Russians were unable to move out has been smashed beyond repair. It is highly doubtful if any restoration here will be attempted in the near future. The big turbines and generators in the power plants are useless.

On the other hand, Kiev has virtually escaped destruction. Some buildings suffered from delayed action mines planted by the Russians, but the damage was comparatively negligible. The destruction caused by German bombings is likewise of a minor nature. Most of the ma-

*Lwow.

chines in the factories were dismantled, but the greater part of these were found on railroad cars that the Russians could not move out because the rail lines to the east had been cut. The civilian population could not be evacuated for the same reason, and about three-fourths of it remained. The haul in scrap metal throughout the Kiev area is tremendous.

About four-fifths of the agricultural areas west of the Dnieper remained unimpaired, but whether this will do Hitler any good remains to be seen. Most of this area was under collective and state farm cultivation and whatever agricultural machinery the Russians were unable to move out was badly smashed by them. About one-half of this year's crop was removed or destroyed by the Russians; the rest was seized by the Germans and hauled away.

But east of the Dnieper, one meets an entirely different picture. Here no large encircling movements had been possible and the Russians executed a rather orderly retreat, destroying whatever they could in their path as they withdrew. I was as far east as Poltava and the picture is one of utter desolation. I have not seen what happened in Kharkov, Stalino and Taganrog, but from the descriptions I have received there appears not much left except scrap metal.

The Ukrainian population has accepted its lot calmly, on the whole. Perhaps this is due to the way in which their menfolk in the Russian army were treated by the Germans. All prisoners of war of Ukrainian nationality were immediately segregated and offered the chance of working for the Germans in their homeland or of being taken away to prison camps in the Reich. The vast majority remained to work in special units under army rule, mostly in the supply services and salvage work. However, those who desire may enlist in special Ukrainian volunteer legions, and quite a few have done so. They are being carefully investigated before they are accepted for enlistment. Only those whose families are in the occupied areas are accepted. They are told that their relatives will be held as hostages for their good behavior. I doubt if all this is permissible under international law, but it is still being done. I have not been in the north, but I understand that Lithuanian, Latvian and Estonian legions are also in the process of formation.

While the Russian campaign has been marked by notable tactical successes, it has thus far failed in its principal objectives and this is generally recognized by both the army and the political leaders, including Hitler himself. The reasons for this failure lie in the unexpected strength of Russian resistance and unfavorable weather conditions. The Russians might have been overcome, but the weather was too powerful an antagonist. The autumn rains came early and were unusually heavy. They were followed by unexpected cold which almost put the Luftwaffe and the panzer divisions out of commission.

The army command recommend suspension of operations for the winter because they could not possibly fight successfully in such weather, but Hitler would have none of this. He insisted on the capture of Moscow and ordered a great November offensive. The army field command argued that the supply line could not be maintained until communications in the rear had been reorganized. Hitler refused to listen. Von Brauchitsch, who had been ill for weeks, requested that he be relieved of the responsibility. Although no official announcement has been made, he relinquished his command early in November. Hitler, with Keitel as aide, assumed the command. They drove the troops incessantly, but to no avail. Now the field commanders say that the November offensive was sheer madness and that none of the gains that it made can possibly be held.

For the first time since the beginning of the war, Hitler finds that he is the object of bitter criticism by his generals. While at Vyazma, during the November offensive, he worried himself into a physical wreck. He has lost face and he will have a great deal to explain. This, probably more than anything else, so affected him that he has become utterly impossible. On November 26th he was made to leave the front for Berchtesgaden, and it was left to Field Marshal von Bock to extricate the army from its dangerous position.

The costs of the Russian campaign were beyond expectation. Up to December 1st, a total of 1,527,835 German casualties were listed. Among these were 442,715 officers and men killed; 1,036,420 officers and men wounded; and 48,700 officers and men missing. This includes the regular army, the S.S. troops* and the Luftwaffe. I obtained these figures through the office of the Quartermaster General and you may take them as absolutely correct. I do not care what official figures Hitler may present. This does not include losses suffered by Rumanian, Hungarian, Italian and Slovak troops. I cannot give you anything on these.

I cannot tell you how thoroughly sick I am of war and everything connected with it. Just now I am in Berlin and in another day or two I shall be off for home and a month's rest. Very likely you will not hear from me for quite a long time.

In warm friendship,
MANFRED.

*Elite Guard.

The second letter came from Gottlieb, who had this to say:

Dear Willy:

Our countries are now at war with each other. This, of course, does not affect our personal relations. But just now I do not know how, and to what extent, I shall be able to keep you informed. It has been very difficult these past months. If we should withdraw our consular and diplomatic staffs from South America, communications would become practically impossible.

Hitler has been at the Berghof this past week. Just the same, little of consequence is going on now. He returned from the Russian front physically wrecked and is now under the care of Evi Braun. Complete rest has been prescribed for him and no callers are permitted, especially not for discussions of affairs of state. When he went to Berlin to read his proclamation of war against the United States before the Reichstag, he was given special injections to bolster his strength. But people recover from nervous breakdowns in a few weeks if given proper care, and Hitler is certainly receiving that. It is likely that by New Year, if not before, he will be active again.

It seems to be my lot always to be the one to send bad news. Linda was arrested for spying. I cannot give you complete details because she was taken in custody by the Military Security Police, not the Gestapo. From what I was able to learn, she secured a copy of the Military Convention between Germany and Japan that had been at Karin Hall because Goering is currently representing Hitler. She was caught with it and you can imagine what followed.

She spent forty-eight hours in confinement and then Heinrich discovered what had happened. You know, I have never thought very highly of Heinrich, but I have changed my opinion. He certainly has guts, for it is one thing to take risks, as we have done, and quite another to walk directly into the lion's den. Yet this is precisely what Heinrich did.

If this affair had been in Gestapo hands, he never would have got away with what he did. Furthermore, in forty-eight hours the Gestapo would have put Linda to the torture. But the Military Security Police, in comparison with the Gestapo, is a civilized organization, with still part of the old army tradition, and Heinrich's story was accepted. Personally, I think he put it over because it was so daringly conceived.

Heinrich told them that before departing, Hitler had asked that a copy of the convention be forwarded to him at Berchtesgaden. However, there was no copy at the Chancellery. Heinrich said that he knew that one had been sent to Karin Hall, and on his own authority he had asked Linda to get that copy immediately and forward it to him.

313

The Military Security Police would have, of course, verified this story with anyone in the Reich except Hitler. It was Heinrich's daring in connecting the Fuehrer with it that made his story stick. Even then, he had to satisfy them on two counts. First, why he gave his instructions to Linda instead of going through the regular channels. To this he replied that Linda was his fiancee (this was not true. but he had to give this explanation) and that since the Fuehrer had asked for it posthaste, he had wanted to bypass all red tape.

Second, they asked him why, when he did not receive the copy from Karin Hall immediately, he did not inquire what had happened, instead of waiting forty-eight hours before coming forth with his explanation. To this Heinrich replied that shortly after making his request he learned that a copy had already been forwarded to the Berghof without his knowledge. He was occupied with important duties, and since the Fuehrer's wishes had already been met, he did not consider it vital to advise Linda immediately. It was only on the third day, he said, that he learned what had happened. Then he came forward immediately to tell his part in the affair.

Linda was asked why she did not give the facts at the time of her apprehension. To this she replied that she did not know why Heinrich had asked for the copy and she did not want to involve her fiance. The Military Security Police still believes in gallantry. They found such devotion touching and the matter was closed.

Further details I do not know. But it appears rather obvious to me that, although danger was averted this time, neither Linda nor Heinrich will be able to send you information, at least not until this episode is completely forgotten. This may take quite a long while.

As for myself, I do not know when I shall be in a position to communicate with you again. Until then, my friendship remains the same.

Grüss Gott!
GOTTLIEB.

The third letter was from Linda, herself. She wrote:

Dear Willy:
Our world has become a twisted place. You set your sights and think you will follow them to the end. Then, before you know it, you find yourself all reversed, with the sights pointing in an opposite direction.

We here are subject to one man's will, while you over there claim that you are free. I wonder if anyone in this world is really free. If we were, it would be anarchy. Each human being is subject to the influence of others—their ideas, preferences, teachings, loyalties, even their aversions. Frequently, we do not even know that these influences touch us. Some are like the thief in the night. They sneak up on us, surprise us, and there we are.

However, first I shall give you some information that should interest you professionally. As you probably know by now, Goering and Petain have met. The meeting was requested by the Frenchman.

Hitler, of course, had made it clear long ago that he would not speak again with Petain. Nor is he in a condition at present to discuss anything with anyone. Evi Braun, I understand, is trying to "rehabilitate" him, as she always does. Therefore Goering decided to confer with Petain himself.

The meeting was held at the station of St. Florentin, south of Paris, in the Occupied Zone. Petain arrived with Admiral Darlan. Goering was accompanied by Ribbentrop and Otto Abetz. All three speak fluent French and Goering at the outset suggested that they dispense with cumbersome interpreters. Petain was flattered, of course.

The party adjourned to Goering's salon car, where luncheon was served. Over the meal they reminisced about the First World War and Goering told a number of amusing stories on himself. The atmosphere was almost friendly.

After lunch, Petain explained that he had made a great personal sacrifice in that he retired his old friend and brother-in-arms, General Weygand, in deference to German wishes. France, he complained, had met German requests in more respects than one, but the German official attitude remained cool and aloof. To this Goering said:

"Let us be practical men and deal in realities. France lost the war to Germany, and after every war it is the loser who must pay. I realize that France has paid heavily, but it was her own fault. At one time our two countries were about to become partners. Had that plan been successful, the war might have been over by this time. You preferred to follow a different path, and the results were tragic.

"You are now trying to build up something in France," Goering continued, "in accordance with your own conceptions. That is strictly a French affair, as I see it. But England and America do not see it that way. They pretend sympathy with you because that is part of their policy. Actually they desire every country in the world to do their bidding. Should the Anglo-American combination win the war, your regime will be finished and the men who wanted to build it will go down with it. I am sure that you understand that.

"On the other hand," Goering said, "look at it from our side. We are engaged in a war for the survival of Europe. Unless the periodical conflicts in Europe cease, it is doomed to economic extinction. You remember how the victors of the First World War mishandled the affairs of Europe. It was principally the fault of England. England's policy for centuries has been to pit European countries against each other, so that she can retain the balance of power. The result of this disastrous policy has been the emergence of Bolshevism as a world factor. If France had joined Germany at the outset, Bolshevism would have been swept from the face of the earth. France chose a different path. We know how tough Bolshevism is, for we have run up against it. We still expect to beat it, but we also feel that it is not our fight alone, but that of all Europe.

"This is the current situation," Goering explained. "England and America have joined Bolshevism because their fear of us is greater than their fear of Bolshevism. Under the circumstances we can take only one point of view, that those who are not with us, are against us. Those who are against us will be beaten so long as we have the power to do so. I assure you that our power is still strong. I also assure you that we shall use our power ruthlessly and relentlessly—c'est la guerre!

"I have not come here to propose a bargain," Goering told Petain. "Our mind is made up. It is for you to make up yours. If you look upon Europe as a whole, and espouse the European cause, France will share in all the benefits that will result from an European victory. The idea that we should want to destroy fifty million Frenchmen is utterly absurd. If you prefer to watch the battle and not participate, we can only conclude that you are against us. In that case we shall bear down on you with all the methods at our disposal—not because we want to, but simply because we must.

"I am sorry to say that the present government of France has shown that it cannot cope with realities," Goering went on. "It has not shown the necessary firmness. The proof is obvious, because France today is seething with unrest. The French mind is utterly confused. Admiral Darlan is a man whom I hold in high esteem. So far he has achieved excellent results in centralizing the administration. But he is not capable of the absolute ruthlessness that the present situation demands. This is not to his discredit—it simply is not in him.

"It may sound strange to you if I say that we can deal only with a government that is without heart. You understand, I am sure, that we are not attempting to choose your men for you. That is your task. When you have a government on which we can depend, we shall be ready to deal with France as an equal in the European commonwealth of nations. Until such a government is in power, we must continue the present status of France, although it is unsatisfactory both to you and to ourselves. There simply is no sense for us in striking terms with a government incapable of living up to its commitments. The times call for strong men who will not shrink from strong measures."

So much for the Goering-Petain meeting. No decisions were made.

It is quite obvious that Goering was referring to Laval as the man with whom Hitler is prepared to deal.

Now I must strike a personal note and I find it rather difficult. I am afraid that I have taken too many things for granted. I have always figured that if I got into serious difficulty I could make my escape to Switzerland, as Clara did, and that it would be relatively easy then to get to America. Perhaps the wish was father to the thought.

I understand that Gottlieb has informed you of what happened to me. I acted very foolishly, I must admit. I could have gotten the information from Heinrich without any risk on my part. I just did not think at the moment and had to pay the penalty of my thoughtlessness. It is thanks only to Heinrich's daring action and deep devotion that I am alive and free today. He took an immense risk on my account.

I am going to marry Heinrich. I shall try my best to make him a good wife. I know that you will agree with me when I say that Heinrich is a splendid man, and he has always loved me.

I shall always remember you in deep friendship, and there may come a time when we shall meet again. I sincerely hope so.

In friendship,
LINDA.

The fourth letter was a source of amazement to us. It was from Heinrich himself. He had never before written personally. That he finally did so, and the manner in which he did it, was evidence of his sterling character. He had this to say:

Dear Willy:

You are fully informed on the course of events here. I have very little to add. I had to act the way I did. I am certain that if you had been in my place you would have done the same.

Linda and I are going to be married. I shall be frank in telling you that this is what I have always hoped for. I have loved Linda for a long time and, knowing her as you do, you will understand.

I undertook to co-operate with you along certain lines, for reasons of my own, and these reasons still stand. However, we are faced today with a radical change in the situation. Our two countries are at war with each other, but this was only to be expected. Both you and I understood that it would come.

But, there is Linda and her changed relationship toward me. When people get married they assume obligations. At least I look at it that way. There are certain things that can no longer be done. Among them is the assuming of risks that may jeopardize those we love. For the present I can only say this—we must wait and see how things work out.

There is something I have wanted to tell you for quite a while, only I did not want to do it through Linda.

There can be no question that the ambitions of Hitler and the Nazis have brought about this world catastrophe. We agree on that. And I can tell you that there are many Germans who agree with us both on this. But there is also another side to the picture.

Perhaps you will remember what we discussed at the time of our last meeting, now almost two years ago. I told you that Hitler's revolution contains nothing new. It is merely a combination of ideas and methods which he has borrowed from other nations. He took the glorification of personal leadership from the Japanese. He derived the conception of the corporate state from Mussolini. He appropriated centralized autocratic leadership and the Gestapo system from the Bolsheviks, although he will never admit that. He resurrected the age-old bugaboo of anti-Semitism. All this is generally known. What people do not realize is that the very cornerstone of the Nazi doctrine, the conception of the master race, is not Hitler's either. He took it over—lock, stock and barrel—from the British!

During your personal visit to Hitler's study you have no doubt seen that "The Life of Sir Cecil Rhodes" occupies a prominent place in Hitler's library for personal use. Perhaps you have wondered why? I can tell you that in his apartment at the Reich Chancellery Hitler keeps another set of the same work. Once I saw one volume open on his desk. I saw a passage which Hitler had framed with a fat red pencil mark. It is the passage where Sir Cecil Rhodes speaks of the English, "We are the first race in the world and the more of the world we inhabit the better it is for the human race."

Take any volume of Hitler's official speeches. Go through every one of them. You will find the ever-recurrent leitmotif: "Why should forty-five million Englishmen rule the world when there are ninety million Germans who have a greater right to it!"

Of course ninety million Germans have no God-given right to rule the world. But neither, for that matter, have forty-five million Englishmen. Which brings me to what I really wanted to say.

We Germans who do not agree with Hitler and the Nazis, have always looked upon America as the champion of a free world. The American system of government has been so successful in our eyes that we would like nothing better than to see the same system applied to every people in the world, to every race—white, black, brown or yellow.

We trusted and believed in America. Then we read about the Atlantic Charter. We understand that the President of the United States has placed his signature under that document and pledged himself, and his country as well, to its principles. And then we read further that all people now under British rule are exempt from the provisions of the Charter except on such conditions and at such time that England considers good for them.

Now, my friend, we freedom-loving Germans are not stupid. When we read that all peoples of the world shall be free to decide on the kind of government that they want for themselves, except those under British rule, we ask ourselves, why has this momentous exception been made? And our next question is, has the United States been hoodwinked by one of England's old imperialist tricks?

I do not know the answer. Perhaps you do. All I can say is that I am deeply disappointed, and so are many other Germans who think like I do.

Now I have unburdened myself. As matters stand, I do not know what the future holds in store for any one of us. Perhaps, if Fate so wills, we shall be able to continue our association, and meet again under happier auspices. If not, please remember me always as,

Your devoted friend,
HEINRICH.

CHAPTER 24

AND SO THE GREAT ADVENTURE ended. When we entered it, before the outbreak of this global war, we did not know where it would lead. We could not sense the tragedies that were to become part of it.

Our principal aim was to obtain information. We believed it vital that the American public should understand the machinations of imperialist diplomacy and scheming going on behind the scenes. As we continued our work, the devastating purposes of Hitler and his Nazi clique became clearer and clearer. Marching from one easy victory to another, enlarging the scope of conflict from month to month, he began to realize his once-wild dream of world domination by his Germanic master race. When his resources were threatened, he allied himself with an Asiatic power whose philosophy, methods and ambitions were identical with his. Between them, they are contriving to carve a world where human life is cheap and where freedom is the idiot's dream.

We soon realized that in this conflict involving the fundamental freedoms of humanity, our country was destined to become the chief crusader for human rights. Preparation for this titanic clash of two radically different world conceptions demanded all knowledge of the enemy's purposes, his craftiness, his resources and his methods. We knew that it was impossible to work against such powerful forces in the dark, and we hoped to contribute our bit toward bringing some light.

It was unavoidable that we should make some errors. To use a hackneyed phrase, only the permanently idle are free from mistakes. It was necessary that we ferret exclusively in the camps of our country's potential enemies. We were not understood, nor did we expect understanding. We could not, it should be obvious now, reveal our sources of information. In Germany, those who believe in freedom are not safe.

There were many who sought to undermine our work. Whether from ignorance, or self-adulation, or mental maladjustment, or plain intolerance, we do not know. We found that there are people in our own country who profess to believe in freedom, but who refuse to put their belief into practice when it affects their professional or financial interests. Often when we were able to reveal startling information that could have emanated only from Hitler's secret councils—and actually had—we were accused of siding with the Nazis.

None of this mattered, nor does it matter now. Time and events have proved that we were correct. And it is possible to check our broadcasts with communiques that appeared in the daily papers, usually several days, or even weeks—sometimes months—after we had told about them. We are proud that at least nine times out of ten we have hit the ball squarely.

We were wrong when we refused to look at the handwriting on the wall, signifying the fall of France. While we knew all about the assembled Nazi might, we still kept hoping that daily the miracle would come. It was a case of wishful thinking pure and simple, but the overwhelming majority of our countrymen joined us in it.

We were wrong, too, when we refused to believe that Hitler would attack the Soviet Union. We simply felt that Hitler could not undertake, at that time, so vast a task. Our informants did not fail us even then. It was simply that the transmission belt had broken down temporarily and we were left to our own devices and information that was several weeks old. It pointed toward a military alliance between Hitler and Stalin, and we continued presenting it that way.

At that, our friends did their best to set us right. In that fateful code message from Liechtenstein which led the Gestapo on Wolf-gang's trail, they tried to convey the new trend of affairs to us as best they could. The radio message and its decode can be found in a national weekly.* It read, in part: "Trouble is on the way— red." The reference to red, of course, meant Soviet Russia, but we were too blind to see its proper meaning.

The editor saw it, but too late, and shared our discomfiture.

At the time of the Japanese attack on Pearl Harbor and the entry of the United States into the war, we were enjoying a vacation. Two days later we were back on the job, but with a program of an entirely different character. No longer was it our job to give "inside information," whether we had it or not. Information of any kind belonged first to our authorities in Washington, to be released as and when they deemed it best, under the rules of wartime censorship.

Our important job then was to make the best possible use of the background of our information. It was to impress upon the American people the tremendous task they had before them, combating the most powerful and ruthless group of enemies ever known.

As for our friends whose devotion to the cause of freedom had made our adventure at all possible, little can be added.

Wolfgang is gone.

*Liberty Magazine, issue of June 19, 1941. The German invasion of Russia began June 22.

Clara still is in Switzerland, wanting desperately to help us and fervently hoping that some day she and her son may come to America.

Linda and Heinrich are married. Heinrich succeeded in being transferred to the capital of a country which, at this writing at least, is still considered neutral. They have remained our friends and write from time to time.

Manfred and Gottlieb still are with the Gestapo. We occasionally hear from them, but their messages are few and they require a long time to get here. Klausmann's new whereabouts cannot be revealed.

We are grateful to this gallant band who risked their lives so that others might be aware of the growing menace in the world. We hope and pray that they have not served in vain.

EPILOGUE

Endless quantities of water have flowed over the dam of world events since we started writing this book in the days immediately after Pearl Harbor. Our country's entry into the war arena as a principal belligerent has inflicted many changes on what used to be called the American Way of Life. A good many of our national habits had to go by the board for the duration. This was as it should be. Total war cannot be won except through total effort.

The first direct impact of the new turn of events on van Narvig's life and mine was that our sons in the armed services were dispatched to distant battlefields. This, likewise, was as it should be. It was one of the sacrifices demanded of all Americans.

One advantage gained from our country's entry into the war was that it put an end to the political feuds, bickerings and compromises that had characterized American foreign policy in the days when the United States was still trying to cling to the slender thread of nonbelligerency. In the course of these feuds many a fortune suffered and many a reputation was besmirched, as always happens when public opinion is lashed by conflicting emotions.

I found myself in this latter category. Having steadfastly refused, for imperative reasons, to disclose publicly my sources of information, matters gradually reached a point where my motives were questioned in some quarters and my radio program was said to be of a "controversial nature." Some of those whose personal curiosity I declined to satisfy even went so far as to call me a "phony."

One bank manager, in an otherwise friendly conversation with van Narvig, said, "I liked to listen to the broadcasts of this fellow, Wythe Williams. But some of my friends insisted that since he knew so much about that man, Hitler, he was probably in league with him."

I used to laugh at such statements. But eventually it was brought home to me that it was no laughing matter. Commercial sponsors shy away from what they consider programs of a controversial nature, believing that they have an adverse effect on the sales of their products and go against the established principles of sound advertising. The broadcasting policy of radio stations, especially the larger networks, is naturally attuned to the wishes of their paying customers. Unless they adopted this policy they would find it difficult to operate at a profit.

Because of the transmission expenses connected with our exclusive reports from overseas, van Narvig and I had always been faced with a considerable overhead. This in turn could be met only by a commercial sponsor, as the radio stations themselves carry no provision for such expenses. Without a sponsor willing to carry the cost, I had to abandon broadcasting over a nation-wide network.

Immediately after Pearl Harbor I offered my services on a non-profit basis and they were accepted by an independent New York station. This activity I maintained for fourteen months, whereupon conditions compelled me to suspend it. These broadcasts were confined largely to the interpretation of war news, with the exception of those comparatively rare occasions when I was in a position to present exclusive information.

After Hitler's declaration of war against the United States, we did not hear from our German friends for a long time. We took it for granted that the thin link connecting them with us had been definitely broken, much to our disadvantage. However, in early summer, 1942, information commenced drifting in once more by a circuitous route. Our friends still held to their convictions and they had not forgotten us.

By the very nature of things, all such information was turned over to United States authorities and only the data made available for such a purpose were presented in my broadcasts. Other data, with approval of the censorship, were included in magazine articles.*

More than ever it became necessary to protect the sources of this information. We are in no position to reveal the contents of these later letters, with the exception of one very interesting report received late in 1942, from which we shall quote:

The term Neuordnung Europa's (New European Order), has been resorted to by Reichsfuehrer Hitler in his official speeches ever since the invasion of the Low Countries and France. All these references were more of a figure of speech. Actually, no definite plan of any sort regarding the new organization of the European Continent was evolved, either in 1940 or 1941, although all sorts of vague projects floated in the air. The men chiefly responsible for Germany's war policy took the view that it would be futile to engage in such political projects until the principal war objectives had been attained. Thus it was only in 1942 that a definite scheme bearing on the Europe of the future, as seen by German eyes, was submitted to the highest Reich authorities.

Actually, there are two separate plans, each worked out and sponsored by persons of radically different views. Each presupposes a different basis and each approaches the subject from a different angle. One may be called the Haushofer-Rosenberg Plan and the other, the Foreign Ministry Plan.

The Haushofer-Rosenberg Plan

The originator of this plan is Professor Karl Haushofer, leading German geopolitician, who assisted Rudolph Hess in writing the second part of "Mein Kampf". In dealing with the problems presented by the

*The *Reader's Digest*, issue of December, 1942, of April, 1943, and others.

Slav populations of Eastern Europe and the Balkans, Haushofer leaned heavily on Dr. Alfred Rosenberg, ex-Bolshevist of the Lenin era and later sponsor of Wotanism as a new religion that should supplant Christianity.

The Haushofer-Rosenberg Plan presupposes that the cycle of Anglo-Saxon world domination has ended and that a cycle of purely Germanic domination is taking its place. Its basis is the Germanic master race, succeeding the English master race as expressed in the writings of Sir Cecil Rhodes. Its model is the Roman Empire of republican days.

The prime factor of this plan is a strong Germanic core around which the New Order would be grouped. It entails the loss of individuality by certain peoples and the splitting up of others. The Dutch are to be merged with the Germans. The same goes for the Danes, Norwegians and Swedes, subject only to certain linguistic easements. The Flemish population of Belgium is to go the way of the Dutch, as are the German-speaking parts of Switzerland. Certain non-Germanic peoples within the geographical orbit of the Germanic race, such as the Czechs and Slovaks, are to be "Germanized" or subjected to slow racial extermination.

The second phase of the Haushofer-Rosenberg Plan deals with the so-called colonial peoples (Kolonialvoelker). These are to retain certain features of racial self-government, but their national economy is to be made part of that of the Reich. This will be achieved by the abolition of all customs barriers, the institution of a common economic plan controlled from Berlin, and the adoption of a common monetary unit —the Reichsmark. Counted among these colonial peoples are Hungary, Serbia, Bulgaria, Rumania, Poland, Lithuania, Latvia and Estonia.

The third phase of the Haushofer-Rosenberg Plan deals with the allied peoples (Bundesgenossen). These are Italy, France and Spain in the south, and Finland in the north. In the case of the southern allies the plan advocates what it calls "counterbalancing." Each is to be made of approximately equal economic strength and made dependent on the Reich for the preservation of this strength. Finland is to become the "guardian of European culture" in the north. These allied peoples are to be tied to the Reich by means of far-reaching economic and military agreements.

The fourth phase of the Haushofer-Rosenberg Plan deals with the advance protectorates (Vorpostenschutzgebiete). These include all conquered Russian territories to the east of the colonial peoples. The claim is that the population of these territories could not withstand the "barbaric pressure from the East" without the military protection of the Reich. To insure this protection for "all time," these territories are to be subject to intense Germanic colonization. The tacitly admitted aim is to place the colonial peoples between ever-tightening German pincers from both west and east.

The Foreign Ministry Plan

This plan is not the exclusive product of the Reich Ministry of Foreign Affairs. Military figures were consulted and had a large part in its framing. The plan refrains from the advocacy of a Germanic master race. Its basic thesis is the establishment of a "European Federation of Equals." It provides for individual constitutions, self-government and linguistic prerogatives. The principal union features are: A common customs tariff, common currency, common educational principles and a common defense establishment. With regard to member states separated from the Soviet Union, the plan recommends a Reich guardianship of 25 years, to "prepare the populations for self-government in accordance with European ideals."

The big joker in the Foreign Ministry Plan is that it provides for Reich domination of the proposed federation without actually saying so. This would be accomplished by the setting up of a common defense establishment dominated by the German General Staff.

Such were the ideas of Nazi leaders on the New European Order at the height of Hitler's military penetration eastward in September, 1942. Subsequent events have torn gaping holes in those plans. The Russian counteroffensive, the defeat of the Afrika Korps and the Allied occupation of French North Africa have given Hitler and his cohorts other things to worry about. Their chief concern has become to hold on grimly to their Fortress Europe. But the report illustrates vividly the probable fate of conquered Europe, had the Nazis been given sufficient elbow-room to carry their schemes to fruition.

There is no more to say. Van Narvig has gone abroad once again, but nothing can be told about it until our country's war effort has been crowned with Victory.